EUROPEAN POWER AND THE JAPANESE CHALLENGE

Also by William R. Nester

THE FOUNDATION OF JAPANESE POWER
JAPAN AND THE THIRD WORLD
JAPAN'S GROWING POWER OVER EAST ASIA AND THE WORLD ECONOMY
JAPANESE INDUSTRIAL TARGETING
AMERICAN POWER, THE NEW WORLD ORDER AND THE JAPANESE CHALLENGE

European Power and The Japanese Challenge

William R. Nester
Assistant Professor of Political Science
St. John's University of New York

150th YEAR

MACMILLAN

First published 1993 by
THE MACMILLAN PRESS LTD
Houndmills, Basingstoke, Hampshire RG21 2XS
and London
Companies and representatives
throughout the world

ISBN 0–333–57896–1 hardcover

A catalogue record for this book is available
from the British Library

Printed in Hong Kong

To Four Great and Beloved Dogs
Flame, Duchess, Cincy and Lady

Contents

List of Tables

Introduction

In the fifteenth century, the development of new ship designs and navigation devices allowed Europe's 'great powers' to globalize their conflicts. Over the next four centuries, gunpower, innovative tactics, efficient administration, an unprecedented drive and ability to accumulate wealth, and balance of power imperatives enabled Europeans to colonize the world. Power, however, ultimately proved as ephemeral for the Europeans as it has for all other conquerers; West Europe's long reign over the world ended in 1945. Since then, the United States and Soviet Union have been the unchallenged military superpowers; one by one European colonies in Africa, Asia, and elsewhere achieved independence; and Japan joined the United States as a global economic superpower. Europe's decline seemed as absolute as it was relative – during the 1970s and 1980s, words like 'Europessimism' and 'Eurosclerosis' were coined to describe Europe's socioeconomic stagnation.

International relations and the basis of power itself have experienced revolutionary changes over the past half century: nuclear (mutually assured destruction, MAD) and industrial (greenhouse effect) power enable humans to destroy the entire world; liberal democracy's triumph over communism has ended most ideological conflict; the world's 180 sovereign states are being drawn increasingly closer economically, socially, politically, culturally, and environmentally. Competition and conflict in an interdependent world remain as virulent as ever, but are increasingly shaped by economic rather than military means and ends. Few states face any threat of armed men and machines spilling over their borders; all states face the challenge of creating and distributing wealth. The contested frontiers are those of markets, science, technology, and production; a state's power is now measured largely by its manufacturing, technological, and financial prowess rather than its number of soldiers or weapons. Power once flowed largely from gunbarrels – wealth was converted into military force with which to conquer more wealth. Power today flows from bankvaults – wealth is invested in productive industries which amass yet more wealth as the nation's corporations expand around the world. National security remains based on power.

Amidst all these remarkable changes and challenges, Europe is making a comeback. European unity, that ancient, unfulfilled dream of conquerors like Charlemagne and Napoleon, is fast becoming a reality. A United States of Europe has spasmodically evolved since France, Germany, Italy, and the Benelux countries signed the 1951 Treaty of Paris which led to a common coal and steel regime. The 1957 Treaty of Rome committed those countries to creating a Common Market, and since then the original six have been joined by Britain, Ireland, Denmark, Greece, Spain, and Portugal. The 1985 Single European Act set a 31 December 1992 deadline for the complete dismantlement of the Community's internal trade barriers and erection of uniform external barriers. The creation of a common European currency and central bank in 1996 will complete Europe's economic integration. Soon thereafter, the Community may well unify politically with Brussels presiding over the nation-state of federal Europe.

The Community's membership will also steadily expand. In October 1991, after two years of tough negotiations, Brussels and the seven nation European Free Trade Association (EFTA) agreed to mesh their markets if not their organizations. The marriage of the Community's 345 million consumers with EFTA's 35 million will give European producers enormous scale economies and immense bargaining weight to negotiate access to the markets and business opportunities of other nations. Although Brussels continually asserts that the Community will be no more protectionist than before, outsiders fear the creation of a 'fortress Europe' closed to foreign goods. Other West European states, the newly liberated East European states, and even Turkey are clamoring for membership, while the Americans and Japanese are rapidly carving out their own trade blocs in North America and East Asia respectively to offset the European giant.

European unity, however, does not guarantee a renaissance of European wealth and power. Although the scale economies of common market and industrial policies will help, Europe's industries face withering foreign competition. Unification may be too little too late to spark a European comeback. In 1967, Jean Jacques Servan-Schreiber's book *Le Defi Americain* warned of an imminent American economic threat to dominate Europe.[1] The American threat, however, proved ephemeral. Since then American power in Europe and elsewhere has declined rather than grown.

Today, it is a Japanese rather than American colossus which bestrides the global economy, and poses the greatest challenge to any revival of European power. Tokyo has mastered a superior means of creating, distributing, and securing wealth, a means whereby Japan's development gains are often at the expense of other countries and are made with the conscious intention of surpassing, and economically and politically dominating those countries. Japan's manufacturing, financial, and technological power is second to none; its corporations either outright dominate or seriously contest virtually all the world's markets; its economic growth continually outstrips that of all its Western competitors. By virtually all measurements, Japan surpassed the United States in economic power and dynamism during the 1980s, and has entangled it in a growing web of financial, manufacturing, technological, and increasingly, political dependence. Japan's GNP will surpass that of the United States within twelve years if current growth rates hold, thus making the Japanese on average twice as wealthy as Americans. Vital American economic and political decisions are increasingly made with one eye and ear directed at Tokyo, thus serving Japanese as much as American national interests. Europe may well suffer the same fate. Japan's economic juggernaut is seemingly invincible; its trade surplus, investments, and political power within Europe are steadily deepening.

Japan's threat to dominate Europe is markedly different from America's earlier hegemony. For several decades following 1945, the United States eclipsed Europe by virtually all political, manufacturing, financial, technology, and military measures. Europeans may have resented their loss of global power and prestige to the upstart Americans, and frequently chafed at what they perceived as America's heavy-handed, insensitive, or outright aggressive actions throughout the world, but American hegemony over Europe was constructive rather than exploitive. The Americans and Europeans shared a common interest in rebuilding the continent, integrating it within a revitalized global economy, and containing the Soviet Union. All along, Washington encouraged European integration and tolerated a lop-sided economic playing field which was gradually leveled as Europe's economy revived.

Europeans contrast America's liberal hegemony with its open markets, easy access to technology, and military umbrella with what they fear will be Japan's neomercantilist hegemony, characterized by continued trade and investment surges that capture or destroy one European firm or industry after another; a web of nontariff barriers that continue to lock out competitive foreign products; limited, high cost access to Japan's technology and finance; and massive Japanese lobbies in Brussels and the national capitals which manipulate the Community policies to allow an even deeper penetration.

Some Europeans clearly recognize this challenge. Ironically, a European warning against the Japanese challenge predates Servan-Schreiber's against the United States. In a special supplement to the Economist in 1962, Norman MacRae presented a sweeping analysis of Japan in which he bleakly revealed that 'they could beat us competitively in a much wider field of industry than most people in Britain begin to imagine . . . The British economy has lessons to learn from Japan, not the other way around'.[2] In 1991, the former French Prime Minister Edith Cresson argued the same point more colorfully when she stated that 'There is a world economic war going on. France is not waging it . . . Japan is an adversary that doesn't play by the rules and has an absolute desire to conquer the world. You have to be naive or blind not to see that.'[3] Cresson sees a severe imbalance of power, outlook, and strategies between Europe and Japan: 'I'm against the clear imbalance that exists between the European Community, which is not protectionist at all, and the Japanese system which is hermetically sealed.'[4] Among Japanese, Cresson has inherited US Trade Representative Carla Hills' title as the 'crowbar lady' (*kanateko o motta josei*), which Hills earned during the testimony for the position before Congress in 1989 when she pledged to open Japan's markets with 'either a crowbar or a handshake'. Cresson's remarks, while certainly not diplomatic, capture growing fears about the Japanese challenge among Europe's elite and public alike.

What will be Europe's fate? Will unification allow the scale economies, strategies, and energies vital for a revival of European power? Will a United States of Europe ever truly emerge, and if so, will it prove any more effective in countering Japanese neomercantilism than the United States of America? Will Japan's economic threat of the 1990s prove to be as ephemeral as America's of the 1960s?

Or will Japan's success over the United States be repeated in Europe, with Tokyo's economic and political power within the Community expanding indefinitely? Will Europeans watch impotently as one industry after another succumbs to the Japanese onslaught, battered by dumping and finally bought out? Will Japan's lobby network in Europe be as successful in shaping European policy to its own ends as it has American policy?

These questions will be addressed in three sections. Parts I and II analyze the goals and policies of the European Community and Japan, respectively, from 1945 through today. Part III focuses on the direct struggle between Europe and Japan, with Chapter Five analyzing the balance of power, and Chapter Six the relationship's evolution and most important industrial battles. Chapter Seven analyzes how far Europe has come and how far it must go toward achieving the dream of unification, countering Japan's challenge, and reviving its global power.

Part I:
The European Community

1 European Unification: Institutions and Loyalties

'If we don't all hang together, we will most assuredly all hang separately.' (Benjamin Franklin, 1775)

Napoleon once said that he would rather fight than join a coalition. Few states, however, are powerful enough to act on their own. Britain in the nineteenth century and the United States in the mid-twentieth century did have enough power and wealth relative to their rivals to do pretty much as they pleased around the world. Geoeconomically if not geopolitically, Japan is powerful enough to expand everywhere while ignoring the pleas of other states for Tokyo to open its markets and cease its dumping offensives. But most states must follow the simple tenet that there is safety in numbers.

European integration has been driven as much from concerns about geopolitical power – both increasing Community power and balancing internal and external powers – as it has the geoeconomic benefits of larger-scale united markets and production. There is a virtuous relationship between economic wealth and political stability. As it was originally conceived, European integration was designed to: (1) allow industries larger production and market scales; (2) bind Germany and the other members in a web of economic ties so tight that those states would never again consider resolving their differences by anything other than peaceful means; and (3) offset American economic and Soviet ideological power.[1] To these ends in 1951 six nations – West Germany, France, Italy, Belgium, Holland, and Luxembourg – signed the Treaty of Paris launching the European Coal and Steel Community (ECSC). In 1957, the six signed the Treaty of Rome creating two new communities, the European Economic Community (EEC) and the European Atomic Energy Community (EAEC, Euroatom). The Merger Treaty of 1967 allowed the EEC to absorb the other two organizations into its own structure to create a genuine European Community (EC).

But despite these achievements, unification's impetus weakened as the German, Soviet, and communist threats receded. Even as the rapid growth and prosperity of the 1960s gave way to the stagflation of the 1970s and early 1980s, the Community's commitment to ever greater unification remained stalled and largely forgotten. While they acknowledged the benefits of European-wide markets for most goods, the national governments largely continued to protect sensitive products and attempted to build 'national industrial champions'. New members – Britain, Ireland, and Denmark in 1973 and Greece in 1981 – joined a Community which was dismissed as irrelevant by many. The term 'Eurosclerosis' was coined to describe a Europe characterized by economic and cultural stagnation, high unemployment, seemingly constant strikes and labor strife, poor quality goods and services, and endless political squabbling.

Then in the mid-1980s, Brussels threw off its sloth to forge a consensus on completing by 1992 a second major unification drive, thus largely fulfilling the Rome Treaty aspirations which had languished for almost three decades. The 1986 Single European Act, based on the recommendations of a 1985 White Paper, required each member to harmonize standards and markets in 270 areas by 31 December 1992. Throughout the late 1980s and into the 1990s, 'Euro-optimism' replaced 'Europessimism' as the Community leaders and most of its population were infused with new energy, enthusiasm, and initiatives for greater unification and the benefits it promised. The Community embraced Spain and Portugal as new members in 1986, negotiated a free trade agreement with EFTA in 1991, and embarked on a range of political initiatives in East Europe.

What prompted this second unification stage? During the 1980s, it was largely a new external threat – Japan – which inspired Europe's push toward integration. During this time it became clear to all that the members' 'national champion' strategies had failed abysmally. Despite a population three times larger and similar living standards, the European Community failed to muster the technological, industrial, scientific, and entrepreneurial talents necessary to compete with Japan, which had surpassed the United States by most economic indicators during the mid-1980s.

This chapter analyzes Europe's evolution toward unification. The first section examines the theories of functionalism and neofunctionalism which both inspired and were inspired by Europe's efforts. The following section will explore the interplay of leaders, ideas, external threats, and internal divisions that prompted efforts either to build or block unification. The final section will explore the meaning, dimensions, and limits of the European Community.

THE THEORETICAL BASIS OF EUROPEAN INTEGRATION

Integration or Functionalist theory was developed by the European federalists of the 1940s. As originally conceived, functionalism asserted that states would naturally integrate as they created international institutions to deal with common 'functions' or shared responsibilities in managing such technical interests as trade, investment, crime, welfare, immigration, or pollution, to name a few. Over time these new international interests, institutions, and outlooks become national interests, and politicians, bureaucrats, interest groups, and the public adjusted their loyalties accordingly. Nation-states would eventually submerge their rivalries, identities, and sovereignty into supranational states. According to Ernst Haas, functionalism is the

process whereby political actors in several distinct national settings are persuaded to shift their loyalties, expectations, and political activities toward a new and larger setting, whose institutions possess or demand jurisdiction over the preexisting national states.[2]

The theory seemed to make sense. In the 1950s and 1960s, Europe and other regions created an array of international institutions to manage common issues. But functionalism did not live up to its billing. European integration, upon which most functionalists based their theory and hopes, stalled in the 1960s and would not revive for another two decades. Integration elsewhere in the Middle East, East Asia, the Andes, and Southeast Asia rarely got seriously beyond the talking stage, and when it did the new institutions inevitably atrophied as national interests prevailed. The world's largest functionalist experiment, the United Nations, was gridlocked by East-West and North-South rivalries. According to Ginsberg,

the development of regional integration theory outstripped the development of regional communities . . . Impatience with theory and outcome was partly based on the misconception that Europe in the 1960s was a disappointing outcome rather than an ongoing process. Integration theory failed to deal with the central question of time: How long does an integration 'process' take before it reaches its completion? It has been difficult to place the process into a time framework, as there is no identical historical antecedent with which to compare it.[3]

Leadership explains the Community's awkward, stop-and-start unification process. Functionalist theory cannot account for the emergence of a Jean Monnet or Jacques Delors to promote unification, or a Charles de Gaulle or Margaret Thatcher to impede it. The Community was founded, nurtured, and expanded by a series of committed individuals like Robert Schuman, Jean Monnet, Alterio Spinelli, Paul-Henri Spaak, Konrad Adenhauer, Alcide de Gasperi, Walter Hallstein, Etienne Davignon, and

Jacques Delors. Where would the Community be today if de Gaulle had not derailed its progress in the 1960s, or a succession of leaders from its inception had not emerged continually to promote European integration? Neofunctionalist theory emerged in the late 1960s and 1970s to explain these integration setbacks.[4] Functionalism failed to explain how nationalism, sovereignty, and history could impede integration, the role of real or perceived external threats in forging alliances, and integration's limitation or collapse once that threat was contained or removed. Neofunctionalists attempted to remedy these defects by exploring these internal and external factors in depth, all the while continuing optimistically to maintain that integration would eventually occur, although they acknowledged that the process would be one of two steps forward and one backward along winding paths over a long period.

More specifically, neofunctionalists addressed the issue of economic integration. Given market imperfections and the success of neomercantilist trade policies in Japan and elsewhere, why would nations join a common market? The cost/benefit matrix for common markets is not easy to calculate. There are winners and losers when a free market is created. In the short run consumers will clearly win from lower prices and better quality goods, while unemployment will increase as weaker firms fail to adapt to the increased competition. Over the long term, the survivors will strengthen from their access to economies of scale and thus become more competitive in other markets. But will the national economy be better or worse off after union? The difficulty for governments is in weighing the advantages that some of their industries may possibly achieve in greater efficiency and profits over the long term while other industries possibly go bankrupt in the short term. Studies have repeatedly exposed the costs of fragmented markets. For example, buying national digital switches annually costs Europeans an extra $30 billion compared to American costs of $9 billion and Japanese of $6 billion. Personnel computer modem cards cost $250 in Britain and only $24 in the United States.[5] But despite these clear ongoing costs, unification's uncertain long-term effects often seem even more forbidding.

External threats rather than business costs are usually the deciding factor in the integration calculus. Like states confronted with a common military threat, states will ally to resist a common economic threat. European integration is as much a result of international as internal forces, although in its first decades geopolitical rather than geoeconomic threats were the primary impetus. The devastation of two world wars followed by the Cold War and American pressure on West Europe to unify against the Soviet threat were the most powerful incentives during the 1950s and 1960s. Japan's growing superpower status from the mid-1970s was the primary reason for the Community in the mid-1980s to agree to achieve a higher stage of economic union by 1992.

There is strength in numbers. Schmitter was one of the first to explore the power of a regional bloc. According to him:

one of the subsidiary motives facilitating the original convergence is a diffuse desire to increase the collective bargaining power of the area toward other international actors . . . Given a minimal threshold of initial commitment and joint policymaking, regional actors . . . will find themselves engaged in the elaboration of a common foreign policy where none existed previously.[6]

As a result of these integration efforts,

if performance in the attainment of original goals is satisfactory, it seems probable that since they are by definition discriminatory they will elicit a reaction from adversely affected outsiders. The latter may threaten reprisals against the regional unit as a whole or they may try to join it. Even where joint performance is weak and inconsequential, outsiders may decide to treat the embryonic regional body as if it were already a viable, authoritative policymaking unit. Regardless of the goal performance the regional actors are likely to seek to exploit their new community by joint appeals and threats to nonparticipants.[7]

The European Community has achieved considerable bargaining power and international status since its inception. But these Community foreign policy and power achievements may be a natural outgrowth of other integration efforts. Haas and Rowe explain this process:

The members of a common market . . . may not initially profess many objectives directed against nonmembers. Integration theory . . . suggests that they will very likely develop such objectives whether or not they were initially so committed. In common markets . . . the process for trade liberalization among members soon leads to pressure for a common commercial policy toward nonmembers, which in turn creates pressures for a common monetary policy . . . Certain domestic groups that have experienced distinct benefits from the organization may wish to safeguard them by preemptive acts of commercial or legal discrimination against rivals in nonmember countries. All such motives are offensive and lead to steps extending the grouping or sealing it off more completely from the rest of the world . . . Defensive motives are perhaps more common. Whenever actors in a setting of regional integration experience dependence on the outside world, they look toward regional unity as a means for obtaining more autonomy. Common external tariffs and quotas . . . serve such a purpose. Other nations in the same region begin to experience the need to join the grouping, or make special arrangements with it in order to share in its benefits, or at least not be disadvantaged by it.[8]

Ginsberg examines how the Community exemplifies this process:

enlargement generally encourages defensive EC-level policies toward nonmembers; increases EC international political and economic clout; broadens the EC foreign policy base of operations and expertise; partially demarcates the EC from the outside world in terms of food, industrial, and labor self-sufficiencies; and tightens access for nonmember imports.[9]

The integration process can assume widely different paths and degrees. Ginsberg argues that

European integration was conceived as a regional development confined to an exclusive group of states seeking common goals. Furthermore, regional integration can and does continue with or without strong central bodies. Regional integration is not necessarily institution-bound. Member governments find it convenient to seek cooperation in areas not covered by the Rome Treaty. To reiterate, although cooperation may be achieved in areas not covered by treaty mandates and outside formal bodies . . . the result is still an extension of the integration process.[10]

Are there geographical limits to integration? Ginsberg poses some provocative questions:

Where does regional integration end (if it does) and global interdependence begin? Is interdependence a looser form of integration on a global level, or integration a tighter form of interdependence on a regional level? Is the key difference between the two logics in the connotation that integration is often placed within an institutional framework and interdependence is not? Can we have one without the other, one at the expense of the other, one subsumed by the other, or both functioning commensurately or intermittently? Are both mutually exclusive or inclusive? Do the two logics differ only in their geographic and institutional context, if mutual dependence is a condition of both regional integration and global interdependence?'[11]

He concludes that 'regional integration may result in part from regional interdependence, but interdependence will not likely lead to global or regional integration. Attempts to use the two terms interchangeably will prove futile as they represent quite different levels of analysis.'[12]

On the other hand, perhaps global integration is simply a matter of time. If the same processes are at work, what took Europe decades may take the world a century or more, only because the world is more complex and diverse. Integration is an out-growth of modernization – as economies develop they naturally become more interdependent. Most people in pre-industrial societies lived in isolated villages and subsisted largely on the output of their own fields and crafts. Industrialization shattered that isolation and unified people into an increasingly complex web of economic, social, and political ties within, and to a lesser extent, between nation-states. People increasingly transferred their central loyalties and identities from their villages to the nation. Post-industrialization in turn shatters the often artificial boundaries of nation-states. Ties between states at once challenge and complement ties within states. If the modern era was, among other things, characterized by the growth of sovereignty and nationalism, the post-industrial or post-modern era may well be the era of deepening political, economic, and cultural internationalism. The individual's identity and loyalty fragments from the state to, depending on the context, his or her career, education, class, race, political party, interest group, city, region, ancestry, gender, sexual preference, and hobbies. However, at the same time there is an increasing understanding that 'we' – all human beings – are linked not just through a global economy, but by deepening global environmental crises which may eventually devastate the planet.

Are the Community's integration efforts significantly different from the nation-building of Germany or Italy in the nineteenth century, or any other nation-state before or since? A century and a half ago, Germany and Italy were geographic expressions, the gleam in the eye of a handful of fervent nationalists who dreamt of forging one nation out of a collection of sovereign states with differing dialects, traditions, animosities, and interests. Today Germany and Italy are unified politically, economically, linguistically, and culturally. Certainly, the linguistic and cultural differences within the Community far exceed those within any of its members. With nine official languages the Community appears to be a tower of Babel. Yet the time and resources devoted to interpretation, translation, and publication are more an unwieldy inconvenience than a significant obstacle to unification. Community officials are increasingly as much European as national in identity while interest groups and political parties are linked across borders. Perhaps the same process will eventually encompass the entire world.

THE EVOLUTION OF EUROPE

Although for twelve hundred years (319–1519), Europe was united spiritually by the Roman church, it remained splintered into countless political and economic shards, and even its spiritual union was destroyed by the Reformation. Charlemagne (742–814) was the first ruler since the Romans to attempt to unify the continent, and this dream has persisted ever since, illuminated by a sporadic procession of thinkers and conquerors. Although over a period of two hundred years (1096–1291), eight crusades of European knights set sail in a Quixotic quest to liberate the Holy Land from Islam, the efforts were uneasy alliances rather than any indication of attempted political unification at home. In 1304, the jurist and diplomat Pierre Dubois proposed a European assembly of kings and princes which would attempt to deal with conflict through Christian principles. His plan was ignored. In 1648, Europe's kings and princes joined to sign the Treaty of Westphalia, but they embraced sovereignty, not unification. Shortly thereafter, Maximilien Bethune, the Duc de Sully, proposed a European confederation to stave off the Turkish threat, but his pleas were unheeded, as were William Penn's arguments in 1693 for a European assembly that would negotiate the end to war. More recent Europeanists included Jean Jacques Rousseau, Jeremy Bentham, Henri Saint-Simon, and Victor Hugo. Although Napoleon failed to conquer the continent, the coalition which defeated him did attempt to bring order if not unification to Europe with the Congress of Vienna (1815), stimulating a succession of shifting alliances and agreements over the next century.

It took World War One's vast physical and psychological devastation for the great powers to consider alternatives to the nation-state system. The emphasis, however, was on global cooperation rather than European unification. At the Versailles Conference (1919), President Wilson led the cry for greater international cooperation through his Fourteen Points whose centerpiece was a League of Nations in which participants would settle conflicts through negotiation rather than force. Although the League of Nations was created, it failed to achieve its peace-keeping goals.

During the interwar era, prominent Europeans picked up the cry and urged greater European integration. The Austrian aristocrat Count Richard Coudenhove-Kalergi founded the Pan-European Union and the newspaper

Paneuropa in 1923 which both lobbied for a European federation. Other advocates included Eduard Benes, Czechoslavakia's foreign minister, and the future French prime ministers, Eduard Herriot and Aristide Briand. Briand was decisive in forging the 1925 Locarno Pact between Britain, France, Germany, Italy, and Belgium, in which the signatories agreed to renounce war between themselves and guarantee borders, and set up the Study Group on European Union within the League of Nations Secretariat. These efforts culminated in 1928 when sixteen nations, including all the great powers, signed the Kellog-Briand Pact in which governments renounced the sovereignty right to wage aggressive war.

Agreements codifying visionary attempts to renounce war proved easier to achieve than resolving economic nationalism. The first concrete step toward West Europe's economic integration occurred in 1922 when Belgium and Luxembourg established the Belux economic union. In 1930, Norway, Sweden, Denmark, the Netherlands, Belgium, and Luxembourg signed the Oslo Convention in which they agreed to coordinate tariffs, and followed this initiative up with the 1932 Ouchy Convention in which they agreed to lower tariffs. But these attempts by the smaller European states to lower trade barriers and increase cooperation were offset by the large countries which showed either indifference or outright hostility. In 1931, Britain abandoned its policy of free trade and signed the Ottawa Agreement, creating the imperial preference system which discriminated against all countries which were not members of the British Empire.

Despite the divisive or cooperative efforts of Europeans during the interwar era, it was clear that the fulcrum of global power had shifted across the Atlantic to the United States. American policies first destroyed the global trade system with the 1930 Smoot Hawley legislation which raised tariffs 50 per cent, thus sparking a world trade war, and then tried to rebuild it starting with the 1934 Reciprocal Trade Act which authorized the president to negotiate free trade agreements with other states. But the nationalist genie was out of the bottle. Just as economic prosperity, and political stability and moderation were clearly linked, so too were economic despair and political extremism. Economic collapse helped fuel Japanese, German, and Italian fascism and imperialism.

It took a world war before the White House could overcome America's entrenched political and economic isolationism and lead the rebuilding of the global economy. Washington understood that a revival of global trade was vital to winning the war and keeping the peace thereafter. To these ends, the United States negotiated the 1941 Lend Lease Agreement and the 1942 Mutual Aid Agreement with London in return for British promises to work toward free trade and a removal of imperial preferences. The 1944

Bretton Woods Agreement (signed by forty-four countries) created the International Monetary Fund (IMF) and the International Bank for Reconstruction and Development (IBRD or World Bank), which were designed to stimulate the postwar trade system through a fixed, convertible currency system anchored to the dollar and gold.

But it was not just Washington that pushed economic interdependence. During World War Two, some European leaders and virtually all the resistance groups advocated postwar European unification as the solution to the perennial tragedy of war and instability which has plagued the continent throughout its history. Prime Minister Winston Churchill became the leading advocate of European federalism. Shortly before the German blitzkieg, Paris rejected Churchill's plea that 'there shall no longer be two nations, but one Franco-British union'.[13] Undismayed, Churchill returned to the theme of a united postwar Europe in speeches and broadcasts throughout the war. The governments in exile of the Netherlands, Belgium, and Luxembourg agreed in 1944 to create a customs union and tax system.

Elsewhere, among the resistance movements, the idea of European federalism was first clearly expressed by the jailed Italian activist Altiero Spinelli in July 1941 when his Ventotene Manifesto was smuggled out of prison. Other resistance movements picked up the theme and in 1944 groups in Italy, France, Poland, Czechoslavakia, the Netherlands, and Yugoslavia issued calls for a postwar European Federation. In July 1944, federalists gathered at a conference in Geneva and called for a European constitution, a directly elected supranationalist government, and the merging of national armies into one European army.

Yet, promising as were the federalists' wartime declarations, the movement fell apart after the war. Churchill and the Conservatives were ousted in a 1945 election and the Labour Party rejected any calls for economic or political union. Meanwhile, shorn of their common enemy, the former resistance movements split into communist and noncommunist factions, and their push for federation fell apart.

Only the United States continued to champion greater European as well as global integration. Washington led in the creation of the United Nations as an improved version of the League of Nations, with the same goals of collective security and the peaceful settlement of conflicts. The UN Economic Commission for Europe (ECE) attempted to coordinate greater European cooperation. Washington followed up its Bretton Woods agreements by negotiating the General Agreement on Trade and Tariffs (GATT) in October 1947, in which the initial twenty-three signatories and subsequent members agreed to negotiate the steady reduction of trade barriers and the creation of a common external tariff.

But no serious attempts were made to integrate Europe until the Cold War's emergence. Within two years after Germany's defeat, Washington's wartime alliance with Moscow had deteriorated into mutual antagonisms and threats. Stalin tightened his grip on East Europe by imposing communist governments in each country, while elsewhere communist parties exacerbated existing political and economic chaos. The Soviet threat was primarily political. The world's largest communist parties (after those of the Soviet Union and China) were those of France and Italy, and they were prepared to take over those countries through either the ballot box or barricades. Faced with the threat of communist election victories or revolutions across Europe, the Truman administration adopted the policy of containment in which Soviet advances would be resisted through extensive American aid to beleaguered noncommunist governments while Washington tried to rebuild the global economic system. Western European governments could immunize their countries from communism through economic integration which would in turn stimulate greater economic growth and political stability.

Western Europe's first concrete step toward unification was stimulated by the Marshall Plan or European Recovery Program, announced in June 1947, by which Washington extended aid to needy European countries. The Congressional Act which authorized the appropriations for the Marshall Plan made the program dependent on the Europeans forming an organization which would distribute the aid to the needy and guide economic recovery. Washington simultaneously pressured the Europeans to create a customs union which would remove all internal tariff trade barriers and create common external tariffs.

Later that year, sixteen countries formed the Committee of European Economic Cooperation (CEEC) which drafted a study on those countries' aid needs and the best way to meet them. The following year the CEEC was reorganized into the Organization of European Economic Cooperation (OEEC) which would administer Washington's aid under a complicated formula based on each country's trade and payments deficits. The OEEC was governed by a Council of Ministers in which each member state had one representative. Decisions had to be unanimous. Agencies and committees were formed to deal with specific problems. Among the more important related institutions were the European Payments Union (EPU), created in 1950 to extend trade credits, and the European Productivity Agency (EPA), set up in 1953 to coordinate the spread of technical expertise. Although the OEEC succeeded in achieving its goal of administering Washington's aid program, it failed to act as the foundation of European integration because of its large, diverse membership, institutional weaknesses, and differences of opinion on the subject. In 1957, the OEEC was transformed into the Organization for Economic Cooperation and Development (OECD), into which non-European members were admitted starting with the United States and Canada. Today the OECD has twenty-four members of which sixteen are European.

American aid was a vital component of Europe's revitalization and integration. Between 1947 and 1951, the United States pumped over $14 billion into Western Europe, or over $177 billion in current dollars. At its height in 1948–9, American aid accounted for about 5 per cent of Italy's GNP, 6.5 per cent of France's, and 11 per cent of the Netherlands.[14] In addition, Washington created the European Payments Union which recycled dollars to overcome the dollar gap. The program was terminated in 1958. Indirectly, the United States subsequently granted an enormous and incalculable sum of aid for over four decades by maintaining relatively open markets while tolerating continued European protectionism, all in the name of reviving European and global economic prosperity and integration. Washington has also indirectly expended trillions of dollars toward Europe's defense since 1947, thus relieving the Europeans of a considerable weight of their defense burden. About 30 per cent of the Pentagon's $290 billion budget in 1991 was committed specifically to Western Europe, and the figure rises to half of the budget with allocations added for the defense of the Atlantic, Mediterranean, and Persian Gulf regions.

Independent of the OEEC, some countries achieved a certain degree of political cooperation and economic unification throughout the late 1940s. The Nordic countries created Scandinavian Airlines (SAS) in August 1946, and in February 1948 Denmark, Iceland, Norway, and Sweden formed the Joint Nordic Committee for Economic Cooperation which was intended to explore the feasibility of creating a customs union. Although the Committee failed to create greater economic union, they did coordinate their citizenship laws in 1950, communications in 1951, and form the Nordic Council in 1952. The Benelux countries achieved a common external tariff and abolition of internal customs duties in 1948, although trade remained inhibited by a variety of other means.

Surprisingly, military cooperation was a European rather than an American initiative. France and Britain signed the 1947 Dunkirk Treaty in which they pledged to aid each other in case of attack, and the following year extended the alliance to the Benelux countries through the Brussels Treaty. Both treaties were as much designed against a revival of German power as the Soviet threat. The Dunkirk Treaty explicitly stated that its aim was to prevent the possibility that 'Germany should again become a danger to peace'.[15] Signatories to the Brussels Treaty were determined to resist both the Soviet Union and 'take any and all steps which might become necessary should there be a return to a German policy of aggression'.[16] But the Brussels Pact went beyond military concerns, advocating 'cooperation in economic, social, and cultural matters'.[17] The five allies appealed to the United States and other countries to join their alliance. In April 1949, twelve states including the United States signed the Atlantic Pact which formed the North Atlantic Treaty Organization (NATO), popularly described as an alliance designed to 'keep the Russians out, the Americans in, and the Germans down'.

The creation of the OEEC and NATO were important steps toward reinforcing European security, but fell short of any significant European integration. In the late 1940s, a range of influential Europeans and groups began to advocate European federalism. The groups included both nation-based movements and such European-wide organizations as the European Union of Federalists created in 1946, the International Committee for the Study of European Questions, composed of interested European parliamentarians, and the International Committee of the Movements for European Unity in 1947. These groups and others were led by such powerful former or current prime ministers as Winston Churchill, Leon Blum (France), Alcide de Gasperi (Italy), Paul-Henri Spaak (Belgium), and Konrad Adenauer (Germany), who saw integration as largely the means for the restoration of their countries' prestige, power, and for West Germany, respectability, in the postwar world. The efforts of these groups and individuals led to the Hague Congress of May 1948 in which several hundred representatives from sixteen countries called for a European Assembly, and formed the United Europe Movement, with Churchill as president, to lobby national governments and industry to that end. An American Committee on a United Europe movement was formed the following year to lend financial and lobbying support to the movement.

These efforts were successful. During 1948, the governments of France, Belgium, Italy, Germany, and Britain approved a feasibility study under the Brussels Treaty for a European Assembly. On 29 January 1949, the Brussels Pact announced its support for a Council of Europe 'consisting of a ministerial committee meeting in private and a consultative body meeting in public'.[16] On 5 May 1949, ten states signed the Treaty of Westminster which created the Council of Europe to be located in Strasbourg. The Council first met in August 1949. It was composed of two bodies. The Committee of Ministers met twice yearly and included one representative from each member, each armed with veto power. The Assembly was composed of representatives appointed by the national governments, which were soon divided into transnational political parties. The Assembly is an advisory group for the ministers. In the negotiations for the Council, Britain successfully resisted the efforts of countries like France, Italy, and the Benelux to create a more powerful institution. The Council gradually acquired new members over the next four decades and now includes twenty countries.

The creation of the European Coal and Steel Community (ECSC) in 1950 represented a giant leap from the small steps that had been previously taken toward European unification. Two Frenchmen, Robert Schumann, the Foreign Minister, and Jean Monnet, head of the French Planning Commission, led the ECSC's conceptualization and creation. Their proposal to Bonn in 1950 was quite simple and straightforward: 'the French government proposes that Franco-German coal and steel production should be placed under a common High Authority in an organization open to the participation of the other countries of Europe'.[19] This proposal repeated recent calls by the Assembly of the Council of Europe and UN Commission for Europe for unification as a way to resolve the immediate problems of a coal shortage and steel surplus. Monnet's intentions were clear from the beginning: 'I don't give a damn about coal and steel, what I am after is European Union . . . [The High Authority] would erode the existing nation-state system, gradually replacing them with a federal regime'.[20] Schumann and Monnet intended their plan to promote several related goals:

> first to see the Plan as the first step towards an effective political integration, and second the political conviction that stability and union within Western Europe rested ultimately upon a rapprochement between France and West Germany . . . The pooling of coal and steel production will immediately provide for the establishment of common bases for economic development as a first step in the federation of Europe, and will change the destinies of those regions which have long been devoted to the munitions of war, of which they have been the constant victims.[21]

The Schuman Plan postulated a simultaneously pacified and contained Germany, enhanced prosperity, and locked out the Soviet Union; it was proposed at a time when federalists governed France, West Germany, Italy, Belgium, and Luxembourg, while Washington was in complete accord.

The scheme perfectly fitted Chancellor Adenauer's desire to remove France's International Ruhr Authority which had controlled German production in the Saarland since the war's end, to help restore West Germany to a respected place in Europe, and to bring about greater and more efficient steel production. On 9 May 1950, Paris and Bonn announced their intention to combine their coal and steel industries under a 'High Authority' and invited other nations to join them. Concerned at what it considered a surrender of some sovereignty to a 'high authority' and still retaining its traditional aloof attitude, Britain refused membership that year, but the Benelux countries and Italy soon joined. On 3 June 1950, the six began nine months of negotiations over the details of the ECSC.

The Treaty of Paris was signed on 18 April 1951, and ratified a year later. According to the Paris Treaty, the ECSC was designed to stimulate 'economic expansion, growth of employment, and a rising standard of living', and would be instituted over a five-year period in which members would dismantle tariff and other trade barriers and then establish a common market. Headquartered in Luxembourg, a nine-member High Authority ran the ECSC, whose members were generally composed with two members from France, Germany, and Italy, and one each from Belgium, the Netherlands, and Luxembourg. Decisions were reached by a qualified majority of members. A special tax on coal and steel production financed the High Authority. The High Authority was supervised by the Council of Ministers. Appropriately enough, Jean Monnet was the first High Authority president.

But the ECSC was more than an economic regime. The Paris Treaty's preamble clearly states that the ECSC's highest purpose was 'to create, by establishing an economic community, the basis for a broader and deeper community among peoples long divided by bloody conflicts; and to lay the foundations for institutions which will give direction to a destiny henceforward shared.'

Unfortunately, the ideals of a true common market were compromised from the beginning. France in particular got away with many benefits which violated the Paris Treaty: its coal industry remained largely outside the ECSC structure; its steel was sold at a lower tax rate in Germany than in France; the government continued subsidizing inefficient French coal mines; France's import licensing system was a very effective nontariff barrier. But to varying extents all the members were allowed to deviate from strict adherence to the Treaty. Overall the ECSC's symbolism was perhaps greater than its economic importance.

Whether Britain's refusal to join represented another ECSC weakness or actually a strength is impossible to determine. Britain was Europe's most powerful and independent economy, but its trade and interests were oriented toward its empire and the United States rather than to the continent. Only one-third of its 1950 trade was with Europe, and most of that was with Scandinavia. Wallace argues that

if Britain had been willing to commit itself more fully to West European cooperation in 1949–50, the pattern of cooperation in the 1950s and

1960s would have been substantially different. Britain could have provided the counterweight to a reviving Germany, in close partnership with France and the Benelux countries.[21]

Yet whether this would have impeded or accelerated European unity is unclear. Protective of its Commonwealth interests, Britain might well have been an even worse spoiler of European unity during the 1950s than de Gaulle was during the 1960s or Thatcher during the 1980s. Subsequently, the Rome Treaty might have been diluted or never signed at all. Of course, President Kennedy did pressure Britain to abandon its isolationism and try to join the Community in the early 1960s, and if Britain had already been a member it could well have countered de Gaulle's nationalism during that decade.

Britain was and to a certain extent remains torn between its 'special relationship' with the United States, the Commonwealth which emerged from its empire, and the need to forge deeper ties with the Continent. In many respects, Britain's feelings about Europe were concisely articulated by Churchill in 1930:

> We see nothing but good and hope in a richer, freer, more contented European commonality. But we have our own dream and our own task. We are with Europe, but not of it. We are linked, but not compromised. We are interested and associated, but not absorbed.[23]

By the late 1950s, the ECSC's inadequacies became increasingly apparent, while the Council of Europe's attempts to create transport, agriculture, postal services, health, and communications policies had largely failed. No more successful was the Pleven Plan, laid before the French Parliament on 24 October 1950, which advocated creating a common European Defense Community (EDC) commanding a common European army. Like the ECSC, the EDC was designed to integrate West Germany securely within Western Europe; unlike the ECSC, it included provisions for Britain's membership, the articulation of a European foreign policy, and eventual political integration. The treaty creating the EDC was signed on 25 May 1952. Paris also proposed the creation of a European Political Community (EPC) which would coordinate the range of new institutions in Europe. Yet, after lobbying the other European capitals and Washington for several years, and receiving at best lukewarm support, the French themselves lost interest in both the EDC and EPC, and their parliament rejected the ideas in 1954. Other governments failed to ratify the EDC treaty and the organization were stillborn. Following these setbacks, Prime Minister Anthony Eden proposed in 1955 a Western European Union (WEU), a vaguely conceived social and cultural as well as military organization which it was hoped would bridge Britain and the ECSC, and integrate Germany's defense within West Europe. The WEU was created and based in London, but never became more than a paper organization with no real members or responsibilities. The 'German problem' was solved in 1955 when Bonn was allowed to create its own defense forces and integrate them within Nato. By the mid-1950s, hopes for the emergence of a united powerful Europe were fast drying up.

However, vigorous leadership by Jean Monnet, who created the Action Committee for the United States of Europe in 1955, and particularly from Paul-Henri Spaak, president of both the Assembly and Council of Europe, rekindled the enthusiasm and political will for a new round of institution building which dramatically accelerated Europe's integration. In mid-1955 the Council of Ministers met at Messina and agreed to create a common market and to cooperate on the development of nuclear energy. Spaak was authorized to head a committee which would propose a blueprint for achieving these goals. The Spaak Committee Report was issued in March 1956, and adopted by the Council of Ministers at Venice in May, which then authorized the Spaak Committee to draft the appropriate treaties.

The result was the signature by the six ECSC members of the Treaty of Rome on 25 March 1957, which came into force nine months later, on 1 January 1958. Two new communities emerged from the Rome Treaty, the European Economic Community (EEC) and the European Atomic Energy Community (EAEC, Euroatom). The High Authority was transformed into a Commission, and over the next decade, the EEC absorbed the ECSC and EAEC to create a genuine European Community (EC), a process completed with the Merger Treaty of July 1967. Rome Treaty Article 13 required all members to abolish all tariffs between them in a series of 10 per cent reductions between 1 January 1959 and 31 December 1969. The Community actually eliminated all internal tariffs and created one external tariff eighteen months ahead of schedule in July 1968.[25] Other institutions were created to help manage these developments, including a European Social Fund, European Development Fund, and European Investment Bank. The purpose of these new organizations, like the ECSC, was to act as stepping stones toward full political and economic integration. Walter Halstein, who became the first president of the EEC Commission, summed up this process when he said: 'We are not just sharing furniture, we are building a new and better house.'[24]

The Community's government was reorganized. A Commission was created whose responsibility was to make and implement policy, enforce all Community draft legislation, and propose to the Council foreign, trade, agricultural, and industrial policies. The Commission's trade powers include deciding on tariffs, quotas, customs duties, transport subsidies, antidumping measures, and taking violators before the European Court of Justice. Thus the Commission combines both executive and legislative responsibilities. National governments appoint Commission members to four-year, renewable terms. Those appointed to the Commission must take a loyalty oath to the EEC. The Commission is organized into a number of directorate-generals (DGs), coordinated by the General Secretariat, which is led by a President. Decisions are reached by circulating policy proposals among the appropriate DGs, which are considered accepted if no DG imposes a veto. Proposals include noncontroversial, routine 'Point A' decisions which eventually plod through, and controversial 'Point B' decisions which are sent to the Council of Ministers meetings.

Based in Brussels, the Council of Ministers oversees and approves the Commission's work as well as making its own proposals. The Council had only six members but seventeen votes, with four each to France, Germany, and Italy, two to Belgium and the Netherlands, and one to Luxembourg. Simple majorities decided routine issues but unanimity was required for controversial issues.

There is considerable overlap of responsibility between the Commission and the Council. Both can issue regulations which are legally binding on all members, directives which are also binding but can be fulfilled by each member's discretion, and recommendations and opinions which are not binding. The Commission and Council efforts are coordinated by the Committee of Permanent Representatives (Coreper), which links the national governments and the Commission, allowing a transmission of concerns and proposals, and the resolution of differences. In addition, Coreper prepares the Council of Minister's meetings and implements its decisions. Working groups within Coreper act as go-betweens on specific proposals between the Commission and foreign ministries. The number of working groups and their subgroups vary over time but average about 150. Two other groups are responsible for smoothing troublesome issues – Coreper 1 which includes deputy ministers and deals with routine, technical problems, and Coreper 2 which meets at the ambassadorial level and deals with diplomatic issues. Despite Coreper, there continues to be a tug-of-war between the Commission and the Council over policy initiation.

Two other Community institutions were created. The Parliamentary Assembly replaced the ECSC advisory body and its appointed members were increased from seventy-eight to 142. Although its functions are largely advisory, it can censure the Commission or remove it with a no-confidence vote of two-thirds, and can reject a budget proposal (in which case the previous year's budget remains in force). The Assembly has never taken any of these drastic actions. Finally a European Court of Justice of seven justices was set up to decide any cases brought before it under the Treaty of Rome. The location of these different institutions symbolizes the Community's divided and overlapping powers. The Commission and Council are headquartered in Brussels, the Parliament in Strasbourg, and the ECSC in Luxembourg.

Although Paris was the first to ratify the EEC treaty, French nationalism complicated and ultimately stunted the organization's early development. At first de Gaulle proposed a vast expansion of the Community's powers and institutions. In 1959, French President Charles de Gaulle (1958–69) proposed regular meetings of the foreign ministers and a permanent secretariat to coordinate its efforts. The six agreed to hold foreign minister meetings four times a year. In 1961, the French Fouchet Plan proposed a 'union of states' in which there would be a council of governmental heads or ministers; unanimous agreement; a permanent secretariat based in Paris, with four permanent intergovernmental committees dealing with foreign affairs, defense, trade, and cultural affairs; and a European Assembly whose members would be appointed by the national legislatures. But, fearing the scheme was simply a smokescreen for de Gaulle's ambition to dominate Europe and that the foreign and defense policy proposals far exceeded the Rome Treaty and would complicate and possibly harm existing NATO and EEC relations, the other members rejected the Fouchet Plan.

While it continued to push for an ambitious expansion of the Community's powers, which it hoped it would dominate, Paris reversed its position on British participation by rejecting Britain's 'Grand Design' proposal of 1955, and its applications for membership in 1961 and 1967. Although Britain itself had originally rejected the chance of membership in the ECSC, it edged closer by signing an association treaty with it in 1954 and formed the WEU in May 1955 to act as a liaison. Still, it put the Commonwealth before its European relations. In 1955, it offered its 'Grand Design' which was designed to rationalize the hodge-podge of European institutions which had developed. A single European Assembly would unite Europe politically while a free trade area would create a free market with no external tariff. The ECSC members rejected the 'Grand Design', fearing that it was a retrograde move that would dilute the unity already achieved and undermine future political union. France in particular felt that Britain's plan would disrupt the close ties it was forging with Germany and allow Britain to compete with France for Community leadership.

Britain responded by creating the European Free Trade Association (EFTA), with Austria, Sweden, Portugal, Switzerland, Norway, and Denmark. Negotiations began in December 1958, resulting in the Stockholm Convention of June 1959 and the launch of EFTA in May 1960. The treaty called for free trade in industrial products and agreements on fisheries and agriculture. EFTA would have a small secretariat in Geneva, with major decisions reached by a Council of Ministers which would meet two or three times a year. London seemed to have been applying its traditional balance of power policies, in which it acted as the balancer, to trade. According to Unwin, one motive may have been to 'convince the EEC states of the virtues of EFTA's low tariffs, with the end objective of persuading them to return to the conference table to negotiate a multilateral trading agreement that would hold the two parts of Western Europe together'.[26] According to Roy Jenkins, who would become Commission President in the 1970s, 'in negotiating the EFTA we have been too much concerned with showing the Six that what they rejected is a perfectly workable arrangement. They rejected it because, whether it worked or not, it was not what they wanted'.[27]

When this strategy failed, London decided to apply for EEC membership to safeguard its interests with the member countries. On 10 August 1961, London formally applied with the stipulation that membership would allow protection for Britain's special relationship with the Commonwealth and EFTA countries, and British agriculture. Denmark, Norway, and Ireland also applied for EEC membership in 1961. The smaller EEC members favored British membership to help counterbalance French and, to a lesser extent, German power. Negotiations began in the spring of 1962. Fearing a challenge to France's leadership over the EEC and arguing that Britain was too insular and its loyalties too diverse, de Gaulle announced his veto of British membership at a news conference on 14 January 1963. The rejection caused the EFTA states to redouble their efforts at forging a genuine free trade zone. Britain, Denmark, Norway, and Ireland applied once more for membership in 1967, and repeating his same arguments, de Gaulle once more rejected them.

The growing divisions between France and the other EEC members over such issues as de Gaulle's scheme to expand the Community's powers and veto of new members climaxed in 1965 over four new issues: (1) the European Parliament clamoured for more power, particularly over the EEC budget; (2) the Commission wanted an independent source of revenue for the EEC; (3) the Commission wanted the Community to decide by majority rather than unanimous rule; (4) and all members battled over the shape of the common agricultural policy (CAP). Now arguing that the EEC already had too much power, De Gaulle opposed the first three proposals while pushing for a generous CAP in the belief that French farmers would be the major beneficiaries. The other five members favored the first three proposals and differed with de Gaulle over CAP. The result was a stand-off in which de Gaulle boycotted the Council of Ministers and threatened secession for five months in 1965. Finally, in January 1966, the governments negotiated the Luxembourg Compromise in which member states agreed to unanimous decision making, thus giving every government, and often the powerful interest groups which had put them in office, a veto over Community issues. The other issues remained deadlocked.

Meanwhile, other developments seemed to threaten the Community. European gratitude for American aid, trade, and military protection became mixed with fears of American economic domination during the 1960s. These European fears were ironic, considering that throughout his short presidency, John Kennedy had pressed Brussels to accept his scheme for a more economically and politically integrated Europe which would more equitably share the burdens of maintaining the West's common defense and the global political economy. There were equally irrational fears over German intentions. West Germany's rapidly growing economic power gave Bonn the confidence to embark on its detente with East Germany and eastern Europe (Ostpolitik) in the late 1960s and early 1970s, and some feared this represented the prelude to a German break with the West.

De Gaulle's resignation in 1969 helped break the logjam of issues and fears. Upon de Gaulle's resignation, pro-Community forces in Britain, Ireland, Denmark, and Norway immediately began organizing for membership. The December 1969 Hague Conference established a consensus on the addition of new members, as well as on CAP financing, new powers for the European Parliament (EP), and the desirability of future monetary and political union. Committees were created to explore and plan monetary and political union, and new members. France conceded on the admission of new members in return for an agreement on a more reliable method of financing the CAP. According to a Council of Ministers agreement and the Treaty of Luxembourg (signed in April 1970 as an amendment to the Rome Treaty), henceforth the EC budget would be financed by the agricultural and customs duties collected at the Community's borders plus a 1 per cent cut of the VAT tax receipts of each member. The system replaced the annual assessment of contributions from each member. In January 1972, the four applicants signed a Treaty of Accession, and on 1 January 1973 Britain, Ireland, and Denmark became full members – a referendum in Norway turned down membership. From its inception the EP had been clamouring for more power, and in early 1969 threatened to take the Commission before the Court of Justice unless budget power and direct elections were granted. Consensus was reached at the Hague Conference for eventually granting the EP more budget powers and direct elections. The Luxembourg Treaty extended the EP's budgetary powers. In 1978, the EP conducted its first direct elections. The October 1972 Paris summit of the nine produced consensus on a range of issues including accelerating economic and monetary union, establishing a Regional Development Fund by 1974; agreeing on a common commercial policy toward East Europe by 1973; and achieving common policies toward the next GATT round and Third World in 1973. But the Community's most dramatic announcement was its call for creating a European Union, although it articulated no specific timetable or blueprint.

This burst of policy, institution, and membership expansion was short-lived. The European 'miracle' came to an abrupt halt following OPEC's quadrupling of oil prices in November 1973 and the subsequent global stagflation. Brussels could do little to jumpstart Europe's stalled economy. The accession to power of Valery Giscard d'Estaing and Helmut Schmidt in 1974 did lead to Franco-German leadership on a range of Community domestic and foreign policy initiatives until their fall from power in 1984. Their most significant act was to institute the thrice- or twice-yearly summit meetings of all member government leaders in the European Council since 1974. But economic policy remained largely in the hands of the Community's capitals which continued to pursue narrow and ultimately self-defeating national strategies.

The Community's average unemployment rate of 2.5 per cent in 1973 rose to 7.9 per cent by 1979, when the global economy was bashed by a further doubling of oil prices. Not surprisingly, between 1978 and 1988, the Community's growth rate of 2.1 per cent lagged behind America's 2.9 per cent and was less than half of Japan's 4.3 per cent. After 1973, 'Europessimism' and 'Eurosclerosis' replaced the optimistic belief from the 1950s through the early 1970s that Europe's socioeconomic development would continue unhindered through higher levels of prosperity and justice. Brussels seemed impotent before these economic calamities. In 1981, Commissioner Christopher Tugendhat echoed the frustrations of many when he urged Europeans to pull themselves from the mire of 'Europessimism' and embark boldly on the path of assertive policies and greater unity.[28] But the Community lacked both the institutions and the will to escape the political economic mire. Stanley Hoffman calls the period between OPEC's quadrupling of oil prices and the Single European Act the Community's 'dark age'.[29]

The Community's travails were deepened in 1979 when Margaret Thatcher became Britain's Prime Minister. Rapidly acquiring de Gaulle's title as Community spoiler, Thatcher lodged a range of complaints against the Community, including the claim that Britain's contribution was too large, and that the CAP was unfair and should be restructured. At the European Council in Dublin in 1979, Thatcher bluntly told the other government leaders 'I want my money back!'[30] In May 1982 she vetoed the CAP budget package. Although the Council refused to accept her veto, with the argument that the CAP budget was a routine matter that was governed by simple majority, it did agree to grant Britain a limited rebate and to attempt to rein in CAP expenditures. Thatcher's antagonistic policy toward the Community mostly reflected her own nationalism, but to an extent also mirrored a growing British disenchantment. From 1979 to 1987, the Labour Party annually called for Britain's withdrawal from the EC.

Discontent with the Community was not confined to Prime Minister Thatcher or Britain. Ironically, the conservative Thatcher found more common ground with the socialist French President Mitterand than the conservative d'Estaing. Thatcher teamed up with Mitterand in 1984 to demand (and to receive) an even larger rebate from the Community. Mitterand was concerned that France would become a net donor to the Community upon the admission of Spain and Portugal. But the two leaders departed over agriculture policy; as the major recipient of CAP funds, France bulked at any significant restructuring of that program.

Amidst the gloom, there was some reason for optimism about the Community's future. The admission of Greece on 1 January 1981, and Spain and Portugal on 1 January 1986 showed that the benefits of being in the Community appeared to outweigh its costs. Still, these three poor Mediterranean countries, each with a limited history of liberal democracy, posed new challenges of assimilation. Meanwhile, in February 1985, the Danish colony of Greenland withdrew from the Community.

Given the Community's economic stagnation and growing divisiveness, why in the mid-1980s after thirty-five years of association did Brussels decide to tear down all remaining barriers and create a truly united Europe? A combination of internal and international forces have pushed every step toward greater European unity. Although many forces shaped the decision, the bottom line was a consensus that unification was Europe's last chance to arrest and possibly reverse persistent economic and political decline.[31]

Even when conditions are ripe for change, decisive leadership is vital to overcome the political and psychological inertia that favors maintaining a predictable if debilitating status quo rather than embark on the uncertainties of reform. It took a Gorbachev to confront and attempt to overcome the Soviet Union's political, economic, and social stagnation. 1992 was a Commission initiative. Acting as 'policy entrepreneur' in concert with a transnational industry coalition, the Commission forged a consensus among national leaders over the necessity for unification. And no individual was more important in pushing union than Jacques Delors, a commissioner since 1978 and Commission President since 1985. Delors has been the Community's Gorbachev.[32] In the early 1980s, the European Community seemed besieged by three powerful competitors. With the Soviet invasion of Afganistan in 1979 and the election of Ronald Reagan in 1980, detente crumbled and the Cold War seemed as virulent as ever. As always the Europeans were of two minds over their alliance with the United States. The Reagan administration's bellicose rhetoric, doubling of defense expenditures, attempted blocking of the trans-European Yamal pipeline, and embarkation on the Strategic Defense Initiative (SDI) shocked most Europeans, stimulated massive anti-nuclear demonstrations, and created a crisis atmosphere. Yet many Europeans also feared that the Reagan administration's SDI program, zero-option proposal to remove all intermediate range missiles from Europe, and astonishing announcement at the Reykjavik summit of the desire eventually to dismantle all nuclear weapons could lead to the decoupling of Europe and America, with a negative impact on European security.

But more important than the Soviet and American geopolitical threats was the geoeconomic threat posed by Tokyo. Japan's leapfrogging of the United States as the world's financial, technological, and manufacturing leader in the 1980s presented a grave challenge to Europeans accustomed to Washington's blundering but essentially even-handed treatment. Europeans feared that Japan's economic juggernaut would grind down their industries as relentlessly as it had those of the United States.

While Japan's economy continued to roar ahead, with Japanese corporations seeming to outsell their European rivals in the Community and around the world, the Community remained torn by nationalism, internal disarray, and economic stagnation. Brussels seemed to have reached its limits of unity and cooperation, and was thus impotent in the face of these vast geopolitical and geoeconomic challenges. In contrast to the neomercantilist policies that fuelled Japan's dazzling rise into an economic superpower, Europe's national strategies from the late 1940s through the early 1980s had suffered varying degrees of failure. State-protected 'national champions' failed to become international champions. Instead, state ownership of key industries exacerbated economic stagnation, inefficiency, mass unemployment, and high inflation.

By the early 1980s, the nationalization strategies and the political Left were both discredited by these development failures. Europe along with other industrial democracies experienced a conservative wave throughout the decade. Although Margaret Thatcher had been the odd leader out when she began a privatization and deregulation drive soon after taking office in

1979, by the mid-1980s, virtually all the West European countries were following similar policies, even including socialist leaders like France's Mitterand and Spain's Gonzalez. The rightward march of European politics did not embrace an American free market model. Europeans clearly understood that the White House's free market obsession had not only failed to develop America's economy, but actually undermined it. Free trade became a one-way street – the corporations of Japan and other neomercantilist states enjoyed the freedom to dump their goods in America's vast market, while American firms were denied equal opportunities abroad. American firms were becoming locked into a vicious cycle of diminishing markets, profits, and investment. America's growth rates were among the OECD's lowest, and eventually the United States was transformed from the world's banking leader to worst debtor. Europeans concluded that 'America's coatails . . . are not a safe place when the giant falters and sits down'.[33] Instead, the Europeans admired and sought to emulate Japan's development model. They compared their own clumsy, heavy-handed management of an economy where large portions were state-owned with Tokyo's deft direction of economic development by nurturing strategic industries through a range of research, technology, market, and production cartels, export incentives, and import barriers.

National strategies were clearly not enough to revitalize each country's often decrepit industries. A consensus began to jell around the imperative for a new European development strategy. Fiat Chairman Giovanni Agnelli pointed out that:

> Ironically, it was politicians who in 1957 first conceived the idea of a common market – often over objections from the business community. Now the situation is reversed; it is the entrepreneurs and corporations who are keeping the pressure on politicians to transcend considerations of local and national interest.[34]

As early as 1979, Industry Commissioner M. Davignon organized Europe's leading industrial and technological firms into the European Round Table to lobby for greater unity and rational industrial policies. The Round Table published three reports analyzing the challenges and options facing Europe, and set up over fifty European Information Centers across the Community to rally citizens around the unification banner. In 1981, the Union of Industrial and Employers' Confederations in Europe (UNIE), composed of thirty industrial associations and individual corporations, joined this lobbying effort. A 1983 pamphlet published by Philips concluded:

There is really no choice . . . the only option left for the Community is to achieve the goals laid down in the Treaty of Rome. Only in this way can industry compete globally, by exploiting economies of scale, for what will then be the biggest home market in the world today: the European Community home market.[35]

The costs of disunity were revealed by the 1988 Cecchini study which maintained that unification would bring an average 4.5 per cent rise in GDP, a 6.1 per cent drop in consumer prices, 1.8 million employment increase, 1.0 per cent increase in foreign trade, and 2.2 per cent improvement in tax collection in the medium term.[36] Unification's benefits went beyond mere statistical improvements. Failure to unify would mean Europe's continued relative decline as a percentage of the global economy.

Yet despite these business pressures and reports, throughout the 1970s up until 1985, no progress for economic union took place. During this time, those political interests which had the most to lose from Europe's unification blocked the efforts of those who had the most to gain. A 1975 committee report led by Belgium prime minister Leo Tinderman which called for sweeping political and economic union and policies was quietly shelved. It reappeared at every European Council meeting between 1975 and 1978, yet was never addressed by the participants. The 1981 Genscher-Colombo Plan was less ambitious than the Tinderman Plan, and simply called for more common policies and closer integration. Although the European Council discussed it at the 1982 and 1983 summits, it was not acted upon. In February 1984, European MP Altiero Spinelli submitted a plan in Parliament for a sweeping reorganization of the Community. The plan was overwhelmingly endorsed and forwarded to the European Council meeting at Fountainbleau. Although the Council rejected the Spinelli Plan, it did authorize the Dooge Committee to explore the feasibility of economic and political union. The Dooge report reiterated the same ideas of previous reports, and became the major issue at the European Council meeting at Milan in June 1985. The Council agreed to call an intergovernmental conference to debate the unification question and asked the Commission to draw up a blueprint for market unification.

Finally, the Community had reached a consensus over unification's vital necessity. On 14 June 1985, the Commission published the 'White Paper on Completing the Internal Market' which analyzed the Community's problems and provided a blueprint for unification. It presented over 300 proposals which had to be adopted by all members to create a single market by 31 December 1992. Underlying virtually all of these proposals was the vital need to harmonize standards. Cutting through and harmonizing the bewildering array of different technical standards was the worst unification obstacle and would be a Herculean task among such diverse countries. The White Paper advocated slicing through this seemingly impenetrable morass by asserting the concept of mutual recognition, in which governments would accept each other's standards within the framework of broad regulations to which all members must adhere. This substitution of 'Euronorms' for 'Harmonization' would allow the rapid creation and implementation of the 300 specific unification proposals. Governments would voluntarily emulate each other's standards to prevent the migration of domestic industries to less regulated economies.

At Milan in June 1986, the European Council authorized the Intergovernmental Conference to draft an amendment to the Rome Treaty that would authorize the 1992 unification. The result was the Single European Act (SEA) of 1986, which would implement the White Paper proposals, thus fulfilling the Rome Treaty goals of economic and political unification. Most of the Act's 279 specific tenets addressed the tariff, technical, administrative, and fiscal barriers dividing Europe. Others dealt with such quality of life issues as the environment, health, and welfare. The SEA inaugurated three major institutional changes. Perhaps the most important was the abandonment of the Luxembourg compromise of 1966 which based Council decisions on unanimity. Henceforth decisions would be reached by majority rule. Secondly, Brussels clarified the distribution of power and responsibilities between the Council, Commission, and Parliament. Finally, it incorporated a range of related institutions which had emerged over the previous three decades such as the European Monetary System and European Political Cooperation. The SEA came into force on 1 July 1987.

The SEA was followed up on 19 October 1988 when the Commission published *Europe 1992: Europe World Partner*, which detailed the process by which a unified market in 1992 had been agreed on, the principles which guided it, and the means for achieving it. The report attempted to allay nonmember fears by proclaiming that it would 'not be a fortress Europe but a partnership Europe' aimed at strengthening 'the concept of mutual benefits and reciprocity'.[37] At the same time, the report asserted that although its unification in 1992 would be based on free trade, the Commission

reserved the right to make access to the benefits of 1992 for nonmember countries' firms conditional upon a guarantee of similar opportunities – or at least nondiscriminatory opportunities – in those firms' own countries. In other words, the Community will offer free access to 1992 benefits for firms from countries whose markets are already open or which are prepared to open up their markets on their own volition or through bilateral or multilateral agreements.[38]

The consensus over unification did not include Margaret Thatcher, who often shrilly continued her spoiler role. Thatcher and the Conservative Party feared the erosion of sovereignty that unification would inevitably involve as well as the assertion of a powerful federal state which could mandate unwelcome socioeconomic policies. Thatcher articulated these fears clearly at the Conservative Party Conference on 14 October 1988 when she declared: 'We haven't worked for all these years to free Britain from the paralysis of socialism only to see it creep back in through the back door of central control and bureaucracy from Brussels.'[39] At the 1989 Bruges summit, Thatcher justified her 'spoiler' role with the argument that

> I am the first to say that on many great issues the countries of Europe should try to speak with a single voice. But working more closely together does not require powers to be centralized in Brussels or decisions to be taken by an appointed bureaucracy ... We have not successfully rolled back the frontiers of the state in Britain, only to see them recognized at a European level, with a European super-state exercising a new dominance from Brussels.[40]

Although Prime Minister John Major has softened Britain's rhetoric and agreed to the eventual creation of a common currency and central bank, London still rejects political unification.

Yet unification steadily proceeded, despite Britain's obstinacy. The inauguration of the Single Administrative Document (SAD) in January 1988 replaced the existing fifty-seven customs documents with one. In December 1989 at Strasbourg the European Council committed the Community to Economic Monetary Union, although it did not offer a timetable. At the same meeting eleven members signed the Social Charter which articulated a set of citizen and worker rights. Labeling the proposal 'marxist', Prime Minister Thatcher voted against it.

European economic unity became a reality on 22 October 1991 when the twelve-nation European Community (EC) and seven-nation European Free Trade Association (EFTA) concluded two years of tough negotiations and agreed to join their associations into a common market of 380 million consumers called the European Economic Area. The Treaty must be ratified by each of the nineteen parliaments, and in Switzerland by a public referendum. Compromises were reached on disputes over fishing, trucking, special payments for poor countries, and farming. In fishing, Norway agreed to accept a larger Spanish quota in its own waters when Iceland refused to open its own waters. Austrian and Swiss environmental opposition to heavy trucks was finessed when a quota was imposed on Greek trucks in those countries and Brussels agreed to reduce truck emissions by 60 per cent over twelve years. The welfare issue was resolved when EFTA agreed to chip in $1.8 billion in low interest credits and $600 million in grants to the poorer EC members. The EC and EFTA agreed to postpone liberalizing sensitive agricultural products.

The Maastricht summit of December 1991 was one of the Community's most important. The leaders agreed on a timetable for monetary union, and expanded Community efforts for industry, the environment, transportation, energy, health, education, tourism, consumer protection, and crime. As usual, Britain acted as a brake on many of these efforts. Prime Minister John Major was caught between the other eleven government leaders and the right wing of his own party. Although Major refused to sign a separate agreement committing the Community to vague social policies, succeeded in getting the words 'federal' deleted from the treaty, and was allowed to sign a protocol giving London the option of refusing to join the monetary union, his victory was symbolic at best. The treaty clearly stated that it 'marks a new stage in process creating an ever closer union among the peoples of Europe, where decisions are taken as closely as possible to the citizens', and later introduced the concept of 'European citizenship'. Britain was criticized for being on the slow train in a two-speed train to Europe's eventual union.

THE EUROPEAN COMMISSION

Although formal political union remains well behind economic union, the Community's government has evolved considerably in power and policy making. The Commission continues to be the Community's administrative center. Its responsibilities combine both executive and legislative functions, and thus it both creates and implements existing Community policies and laws. But the rise of summitry has eroded the Commission's importance as a decision making center, and it is increasingly confined to administrative duties. According to Unwin, although the Commission was 'at best a partner of national governments rather than a supranational entity . . . [although] it may still have been the motor, someone else was in the driving seat'.[41] Today the Commission is composed of twenty-three directorate-generals or ministries presided over by seventeen commissioners, with two each from the five largest members and one each from the rest. Governments appoint their commissioners who during their four year terms are supposed to act independently of their government. One-half of the commissioners are up for reappointment every four years. The Commission meets once a week and decides most policies by consensus, although majority rule is used to break deadlocks. The Commission's power has shifted with the vigor of its presidents. Walter Hallstein (1958–67), Roy Jenkins (1977–81), and Jacques Delors (1985–present) are considered to have been the most assertive in promoting policies and expanding the Commission's power and responsibilities.

COUNCIL OF MINISTERS

The Council of Ministers, composed of the twelve member foreign ministers, meets monthly to decide on policy, Commission proposals, and unresolved issues. While the Commission generally takes a European viewpoint, the Council allows members to voice national and sectoral concerns. The Council then debates and makes the final decision on the proposals and then sends them back to the Commission to implement. Before the Single European Act, Council decisions had to be unanimous; by giving every government a veto 'the most reluctant state prevailed', and its decisions were often shaped by special interests.[42] Now the Council decides by a qualified majority of fifty-four, except in matters of taxation, immigration, and workers' rights. With the Council's total number of votes set at seventy-six, voting is weighted to population, with France, Germany, Italy, and Britain allocated ten votes each, Spain eight, Belgium, Greece, the Netherlands, and Portugal five each, Denmark and Ireland three each, and Luxembourg two. Since Germany's reunification, Bonn has requested more Council votes. Three or four smaller states can block a qualified majority. The Council can then either implement the decision or issues directives to the Commission to do so. The Committee of Permanent Representatives (Coreper) includes the member ambassadors and their staff, and links the Council and Commission. The growth in Coreper's responsibilities has paralleled the Council's increase in power. A Council Secretariat administers when the ministers do not meet. The Council's presidency rotates every six months among the members in alphabetical order. In 1990, the Council met eighty-five times, mostly in Brussels.

EUROPEAN COUNCIL

The European Council is composed of all member government's leaders, and serves as the Community's highest decision-making power. The European Council first officially met in the Hague in 1969 but did not really begin sitting regularly until the 1974 European summit. The Council met three times annually up through 1985, and twice annually since then. The presidency rotates every six months. The Council includes the eleven prime ministers and the French President. It has replaced the Commission as the Community's most important decision-making center. It then issues mandates to the Commission to implement its decisions. The Commission President has the right to be in attendance. The 1986 Single European Act confirmed the Council's legitimacy as the Community's highest power.

EUROPEAN PARLIAMENT

The European Parliament is a unicameral assembly, composed of 142 seats through 1973 when the seats were raised to 198, and then increased in 410 for the first European elections in June 1979. The Parliament was further expanded to 518 members by 1986 with the admission of Greece, Spain, and Portugal. The representatives are divided among each country in proportion to their respective populations. Germany, France, Italy, and Britain have eighty-one members each, Spain sixty, the Netherlands twenty-five, Belgium, Greece, and Portugal twenty-four each, Denmark sixteen, Ireland fifteen, and Luxembourg six. With German unification, Bonn is pushing for eighteen additional seats. Each member uses its own electoral system for the Parliament, and elections thus tend to mirror national politics. Issues and policy proposals are explored through committees. Representatives sit according to party rather than nationality.

Although the 1979 election signaled the EP's emergence as a working legislature, it remains largely a debate forum which can merely propose but not legislate. Although its powers include the ability to dismiss the entire Commission, reject a Council proposal, or block the budget with a two-thirds majority, it has only exercised its budget power, and then only once. The Parliament's most assertive action occurred in 1982 when it rejected the budget in protest over the 1980 budget's implementation. This action forced the other Community institutions to work together to resolve the Parliament's grievances. The Parliament is further weakened since while it sits in Strasbourg, its committees meet in Brussels, and the 3,500-strong secretariat is in Luxembourg. Unwin writes that the 'continual movement of the EP and of documents translated into nine languages inevitably inhibits [its] . . . effectiveness. France and Luxembourg continued to resist the removal of all branches . . . to Brussels'.[43] Since 1981 the government leader hosting the European Council does give a 'state of the union' address before the Parliament.

EUROPEAN COURT OF JUSTICE

The European Court of Justice rules on disputes over Community laws, but it lacks enforcement power. It is located in Luxembourg and composed of thirteen judges and six advocates-general who are appointed for six years by the members. In 1990, the Court heard 380 cases and rendered 225 decisions.

EUROPEAN POLITICAL COOPERATION

The SEA mandated the creation and implementation of a European foreign policy, and called for greater defense and security cooperation. Formerly an informal high-level discussion group, the European Political Cooperation (EPC) now provides the primary voice for Brussels' foreign policy. EPC is designed to make quick decisions and help coordinate members' national foreign policies. Its activities are shaped by the Council of Ministers. The EPC is composed of the political directors of the foreign ministers who meet two days a month, and study groups of officials from members which deal with specific issues. Yet member states are simply required to consult the EPC before formulating and announcing their own policies. Many dismiss the EPC as a mere foreign policy 'seminar' for 'high-minded moralizing about situations in which EPC barely has an interest'.[44]

Despite its haphazard development and the flaws in its institutions, the European Community is well on its way to realizing economic and political unification.

THE FATE OF EUROPE

What then is Europe? Where does Europe begin and end? What are or should be Europe's cultural, political, economic, and geographic boundaries? These questions underlie all attempts at unification.[45] Europeans are still struggling to define what it means to be European, and how a common European identity can be forged among such a diverse collection of cultures, languages, and living standards.

Some argue that cultural boundaries define Europe. If Europe is primarily a cultural concept, born of a crucible of Judeo-Christian-Greek ideals, then the center of Europe has shifted steadily over time, from the Eastern to the Western Mediterranean in the ancient and medieval eras, to northern Europe throughout the modern era, and arguably, since 1945, to the United States. Europe's eastern reaches have been in a constant state of flux, battled over by a succession of non-Christian invaders including Mongols, Turks, and communists. If culture is vital, does Europe extend to every country of European cultural ancestry? For the past 500 years, Europeans have planted their standards and created new ones around the world, from North America to the south-west Pacific. Should Europe embrace these farflung outposts and fortresses of European culture? If Turkey or Malta can apply, why not Canada or Australia?

If liberal democracy and relatively open markets are the norm, then cannot Europe extend virtually anywhere those prerequisites are present? Liberal democracy clearly is an important European value and source of identity. Wallace reminds us that 'Greece and Turkey were suspended from participation in the Council of Europe (but not from Nato or the OECD) when they came under military rule'.[46] But clearly not every liberal democracy with relatively free markets is considered European. Israel was the first state to apply to join the original six, and its application was rejected.

How important then is geography? If geography defines Europe, and the Atlantic ocean shapes Europe's western boundaries, where lies Europe's eastern and southern boundaries? Does Europe stretch from the Atlantic to the Urals, as de Gaulle once insisted? If so what should be done about Europeanized Siberia? Does Europe actually extend from the Atlantic to the Pacific? And what of Europe's southern boundaries? The Black Sea? The Mediterranean? Europe is not one unbroken land and sea mass, but how unbroken geographically can it be? How near or far away does one of Europe's island outposts have to lie to be considered either a member or beyond the pale? If Britain or Ireland, why not Iceland or even New Zealand? And if a distant island, why not distant continents like North America?

Some argue that Europe no longer exists. Wallace points out that 'in one sense European history ended in World War II with the partition of Europe into Atlantic and Soviet systems'.[47] Contemporary Europe is in many ways an American creation. Since 1945 Washington has continually pressured the West Europeans to unite themselves and join in an expanding global political economy. In return, Washington has offered aid, open markets, and military protection against the Soviet bloc. The Atlantic system was built upon shared ideals of liberal democracy and market economies, and the willingness to defend those ideals against communism.

Washington, however, did not build Europe out of altruism. It is perhaps just as true to argue that European unification would not have occurred without a perceived Soviet military and ideological threat, and the American decision to contain it. Wallace writes of postwar politicians building Europe 'within the framework set by Russian hostility and American sponsorship'.[48] Now that the Soviet bloc has crumbled, and its newly liberated states are clamouring to join the Community, will the Atlantic system simply be stretched further eastward?

Or does Europe really exist after all? With the Cold War's end, is Atlanticism breaking up in favor of Europeanism? As early as the 1960s, de Gaulle led a growing reaction against Atlanticism, and his arguments continue to have strong adherents today. The French president's rather muddled ideas conceived of Europe as a 'third force' in the world, standing between the American and Soviet hegemonies, and extending from the Atlantic to the Urals. The idea finds favor among right-wing nationalists and social democrats, and may become more popular with the Soviet empire's breakup. To these European 'nationalists', if Europe cannot extend to the Urals without splitting Russia in two, it may well include the Baltic states and Ukraine. And if Paris is truly afraid of a post-Cold War world dominated by Washington, then Europe may well eventually include all of Russia to the Japan Sea.

But beneath the glaze of Europeanism, de Gaulle was actually just a fervent nationalist, a 'spoiler' of attempts by genuine Europeans to promote greater unity. Nationalism, rather than conflicts over Europe's cultural, political, economic, or geographic boundaries, remains the largest obstacle to unification. Europe's de Gaulles and Thatchers cite the sacred concepts of nationalism and sovereignty to argue against internationalism.

Europe's political identities and animosities are deep-rooted. The historian Frances Condick nicely captured Europe's ancient rivalries and divisions:

> The concepts of nationalism and sovereignty might seem to be recent developments, but Europe has had centuries of internal strife between those very countries now attempting to work together. Although an

international authority – the Papacy – could command obedience as the head of a universal church until the sixteenth century, its power was often wielded by factions or national political interests, and Popes were sometimes made and unmade for completely secular reasons. The knights who went on crusade against Moors in Spain and Arabs in the Middle East fought not only to drive back the heathen, but also to capture valuable lands and even to establish small kingdoms for themselves. The ruler of each European kingdom or principality decided the fate of his own people.[49]

Nationalism as a sentiment of loyalty and identity among a population sharing a common culture, language, territory, and government, is a much more recent development. The world's first modern war of national liberation broke out in Britain's American colonies in 1776. Mass nationalism did not begin to sweep Europe until after the French Revolution in 1789, a process which intensified in the nineteenth century as governments 'imposed common values, culture, historical identity, even language on their populations'.[50] The shared values of Europe's political elite during the Enlightenment were submerged into these deepening mass national identities. Yet, two centuries later, after European governments have attempted systematically to build states into nations through mass education and conscription, those same countries are being torn apart by long-suppressed or newly-emergent identities in places like Catalonia, Wales, Sicily, Corsica, and Bavaria, to name a few.

Of all the nationalisms fraying the edges of Europe's unification drive, a revival of German nationalism is most feared. The European Community was created as much for political as for economic reasons. Integration would not only allow industries larger production scales and markets, but would bind Germany in a web of economic ties so that it would never again break away to threaten the peace of Europe. The balance of power within the Community has shifted over time. The six founders tried desperately to include Britain to counterbalance West Germany. Britain's economy was greater than Germany's in the early 1950s, but was quickly surpassed by first West Germany's in 1961 and France's in 1966. With its reunification in 1989 Germany reemerged as Europe's central power, a position it had not held since 1944. Today, Germany is clearly Europe's powerhouse, accounting for over one-quarter of the Community's production. The deutschmark is second to the American dollar as Europe and the world's most important currency.

However, the difference between 1944 and 1992 for Germany and the world is extraordinary. Interdependence has completely replaced imperialism as the primary characteristic of international relations. German power is no longer to be feared, but admired, emulated, and joined. Perhaps nationalism and sovereignty are as obsolete today in a world of deepening economic, environmental, and cultural interdependence as papal power was with the rise of nation-states 400 years ago. The forces for internationalism within Europe are rapidly overwhelming most nationalist resistance.

Europe continues to evolve despite differences over its boundaries or definition. The twelve nations of Europe are clearly integrated economically (see Table 1.1), based on the free movement of goods, services, capital, and people, known as the 'four freedoms'.

TABLE 1.1   *European Community imports and exports 1977–87*

	1977	1987
As percentages of total EC exports:		
Intra-Community trade	47%	59%
Exports to EFTA	7%	10%
Exports to Japan	1%	3%
Exports to USA	8%	7%
Exports to Eastern Europe	4%	2%
Exports to other countries	33%	19%
As percentages of total EC imports:		
Intra-Community imports	45%	58%
Imports from EFTA	9%	11%
Imports from Japan	2%	4%
Imports from USA	5%	10%
Imports from Eastern Europe	3%	2%
Imports from other countries	36%	14%

Brussels is struggling to shape policies essential to promoting Europe's economic vitality. During the 1980s, the threat that the Japanese and, to a lesser extent, the Americans would leave the Europeans far behind in the high technology and information race forced Brussels to forge a consensus on economic and policy unification. The 'national champion' and nationalization policies were rejected in favor of deregulation and a gently guiding rather than a smothering government hand in the economy. Brussels helped organize a range of cooperative high technology efforts among European corporations.

Europe is bound by a growing web of organizations, with both federal and confederal characteristics. Institutions like the Common Market, the

Common Agricultural Policy, and the Court of Justice are supranational organizations in which Community law takes precedence over national law. Other institutions like the European Monetary System and European Political Cooperation are intergovernmental. Other international organizations include both Community and other members. The Western European Union, created in 1955, now has nine members. The thirty-five members of the Conference on Security and Cooperation in Europe (CSCE), include the United States and Canada. Twenty-four states participate in the Council of Europe which discusses and attempts to resolve political, social, and human rights problems. Although these international organizations frequently overlap in responsibilities and stretch the boundaries of Europe, they reinforce and reflect the steady evolution of internationalism.

The dream of European political unity received an important boost in 1985 when five countries – Belgium, France, Germany, Luxembourg, and the Netherlands – signed the Schengen Agreement in which they agreed to remove their state borders. In 1991, the European Community and European Free Trade Association agreed to join their markets into a 'Common European Space' of 380 million consumers. On 31 December 1992, the final economic obstacles to European unity were removed, creating a genuine common market. By 1999 at the latest, Europe will probably adopt a common currency and central bank.

What new members will Europe embrace? Brussels is split over whether to deepen the Community's integration after 1992 or broaden membership. Some argue that the Community can and should do both. Regardless of what path is chosen, it is clear that Europe's future will not be 'the Finlandization of Western Europe that the Americans feared, but the Brusselization of Eastern Europe'.[50] The revolutionary events of 1989 to 1991, in which Moscow renounced its empire in Eastern Europe, Berlin and the Germanies were unified, and the Soviet Union itself renounced communism and broke up into a Commonwealth of Independent States (CIS), offered Brussels extraordinary opportunities. A vision of a Europe eventually united from the Atlantic to the Black sea seems a real possibility, but has intensified the Community debate over whether to deepen integration or broaden membership. Although East Germany had already been associated with the Community since Bonn's Ostpolitik of the early 1970s, Hungary, Poland, and Czechoslavakia have applied for associate status.

What, again, is Europe? The concept of Europe is dynamic and continues to evolve. Essentially, 'Europe' is in the eyes of the beholder, whose view is shaped by their chosen cultural, geographical, political, and/or economic looking-glass. But regardless of how it is defined, Europe has clearly emerged as a cohesive, global political, economic, and cultural superpower.

2 European Unification: Policymaking and Policies

The Community's policymaking powers have evolved considerably over the past four decades. Signatories to the Paris Treaty (1951), Rome Treaty (1957), and Single European Act (1986) transferred significant national policymaking powers to Brussels.[1] A federal United States of Europe may not be far off.

Yet, despite these considerable integration efforts, power and policies within the Community are still largely determined at the national level. National governments decide most of the Community's policies, budget, and personnel. National interests clash frequently at both bilateral and Community levels. Differences continually emerge over macroeconomic, industrial, and foreign policies, reflecting the dramatically different cultures, socioeconomic levels, development policies, and histories of the members.

How are Community policies made? What are the most important Community policies? How effective have they been at achieving their objectives? This chapter will answer these questions by focusing on Europe's macroeconomic, industrial, trade, and foreign policies.

MACROECONOMIC POLICY

Liberal economists believe that the less a government interferes in an economy the better. Markets, not governments, should determine an economy's development. The only permissible government policies are macroeconomic, those designed to affect an entire economy without helping or hindering any specific sector. Most liberal economists would grudgingly allow policies which either promote growth during economic downturns or rein in growth when an economy become overheated and inflationary, although the more radical theorists would reject even these efforts as sullying market purity. Several policies can be included under the macroeconomic umbrella. Increasing government spending, and cutting tax, interest, and currency rates stimulates an economy; the converse de flates an economy. Ideally, the government coordinates these policies so that they complement rather than conflict with each other in promoting or quelling economic growth.

As always, there is a large gap between liberal theory and economic reality. Although these macroeconomic measures do affect the entire economy, they also create economic winners and losers. Government spending or fiscal policy has the greatest market distorting effect since the money goes to some sectors and not others. Although governments could theoretically cut taxes so that every business and household is equally affected, they never do. Even an across-the-board tax cut or hike will either cost or benefit some businesses or households proportionally more than others. Governments usually cut or raise taxes for specific economic sectors or classes. The same discrimination occurs when the government manipulates interest rates. Some economic activities are promoted and others hindered when a government cuts or raises the rate it charges on the funds it lends to or borrows from the private sector. Finally, the strength or weakness of a nation's currency relative to other currencies has a profound economic effect. An overvalued currency is a short-term boon to consumers and a bane to virtually every business since it encourages households and firms to buy underpriced foreign goods rather than overpriced domestic ones. In the long term, consumers are hurt as domestic industries either go bankrupt or cut wages in order to survive. An undervalued currency has the opposite effect, hurting consumers and boosting domestic producers in the short run, but helping both over the long run. An overvalued currency obviously helps import businesses over both the short and long term while an undervalued currency has the opposite effect.

The European Community has a distinct set of macroeconomic policies, including fiscal, monetary, tax, and currency measures which have an impact on Europe's overall economy, and positive and negative effects on specific sectors. Most of these efforts, however, involve Community attempts to harmonize national policies rather than assert any of its own policies. Brussels' power to conduct macroeconomic policies is severely limited. When the Community itself conducts a specific policy, the economic impact is questionable. How much are Community macroeconomic policies undercut by contradictory national policies or lost among complementary national policies? These questions are impossible to answer.

Of its macroeconomic policies, Brussels' annual budget has the most noticeable effect on specific economic sectors. Yet, since the Community budget is less than 0.1 per cent of Community GNP, and two-thirds of that budget is agricultural subsidies, the effect on Europe is insignificant. Because the Rome Treaty requires the Community to have a balanced budget, Brussels is unable to conduct a vigorous fiscal policy. Still, the budget does in fact annually run a slight deficit of about 2 per cent of the total, while some Community institutions regularly do borrow and lend money. The

ECSC and Euroatom annually borrow funds and reloan them to their respective clients. Rome Treaty articles 129 and 130 created the European Investment Bank (EIB) to assist the Community's economic convergence. Starting in 1975, Brussels began helping members with balance-of-payments problems. In 1978 it inaugurated the New Community Instrument which lent money to projects designed to promote economic unity.

Where does the Community's revenue come from? Originally Brussels relied on 'dues' from members which were assessed according to their ability to pay. More recently the Community receives revenue by taking up to 1 per cent of the national VATs (value added taxes). The budget is valued by a common currency – until 1977 the Unit of Account, from then until 1980 the European Unit of Account, since then the European Currency Unit (ECU). With such a paltry revenue source, no Community tax cut could have a discernible stimulatory effect on Europe's economy. Brussels has no ability to raise taxes beyond a ceiling granted by the national governments.

How is the Community budget made? By 30 September of each year, the Commission forwards a draft budget to the Council of Ministers based on the budget requests from the various Community institutions. Within a month a qualified Council majority must approve either the Commission budget or a Council-adjusted variation. The budget is then forwarded to the Parliament which has a month to debate and return it with suggestions to the Council which, again by qualified majority, approves the final version. The budget officially begins on New Year's Day.

The Community budget is lost in the sea of national budgets whose procurements of goods and services average 10 per cent of GNP (15 per cent if nationalized industries are included). Only 2 per cent of this procurement is obtained from foreign sources. Procurement thus acts as a massive subsidy for domestic industry. If the national governments would open up their procurements to the Community it would be a major boost for Europe's competitiveness with an annual savings of 30 billion ECU and boost in GNP of 0.6 per cent.[2]

There are countless impediments to macroeconomic unity. One is the Community's range of national and local tax systems. Direct taxes on incomes and indirect VAT and excise taxes differ wildly from one member to the next. Harmonization is impeded by the very different government spending programs and the need to finance them. All other things being equal (which of course is never the case), firms would prefer to set up shop where they pay the least taxes. Governments are thus torn between reducing taxes to help business at the cost of losing revenue and fearing that if they do not cut taxes their industries will migrate to lower tax countries.

Brussels ruled in 1987 that by 1992 it would replace the national VAT system with a two-tier system in which 'standard' and 'basic' goods could be taxed differently and governments could only value their taxes within a 5 percentage point Community norm. The Community has yet to decide specifically on how to implement this plan. Several schemes are being considered. The most likely scheme involves a two-tier VAT structure for the short run in which there would be a reduced rate system encompassing utilities, mass transportation, food, and publications at between 4 and 9 per cent, and a standard tax structure on all other products of between 14 to 20 per cent. Excise duties on such items as cigarettes, gasoline, and alcohol are even more diverse than VAT. The Commission has proposed eventually achieving, among other products, taxes of 12.71 ECU per liter of gasoline, 53 per cent on the retail price of cigarettes, and 0.31 per liter of alcohol.

The Community cannot have a currency policy until it has a common currency. There can be no genuine economic union without monetary union. For four decades federalists have advocated a Community Economic and Monetary Union (EMU) which ideally would include supranational tax, fiscal, monetary, and economic policies based upon a common currency. It was not until the late 1960s, however, that there was any serious discussion of creating an EMU. Washington's limiting of the convertibility of the dollar into gold to central banks in 1968, and Paris' devaluation and Bonn's revaluation in 1969, and America's worsening payments deficits and inflation, sparked an awareness within the EC over the need to develop a common monetary policy. Until recently, however, concrete proposals for monetary union have been repeatedly derailed by global economic crises or by those governments which fear the loss of sovereignty it would entail.

The first attempt to create an EMU began in March 1970 when the Council of Ministers convened a study group which would propose a plan for monetary union. The group was led by Luxembourg's Prime and Finance Minister, Pierre Werner, and was composed of high-ranking finance and economic officials from the Community and its members. The Werner group recommended a two-step evolution toward monetary union between 1971 and 1980. During the first phase between 1971 and 1973 the central banks were supposed to intervene in exchange markets to prevent any currency shifts greater than 0.6 per cent of the official parity. A European Exchange Stabilization Fund was created to provide short-term loans to maintain the system. During the second phase between 1974 and 1981, members would convert their currencies, remove all capital controls, and strictly fix their currencies. The stabilization fund would become a European Reserve Fund which would serve as the basis for a European central bank. In March 1971 the Council agreed on the Werner Report's proposals and authorized 7.5 billion ECU to finance the adjustments. These Community efforts to forge monetary union were vastly complicated and ultimately destroyed by the Bretton Woods collapse and OPEC's quadrupling of oil prices in the early 1970s.

For almost a quarter-century, the Bretton Woods system provided a relatively fixed, stable foreign exchange system. All major currencies were tied to the dollar which was convertible to gold at a rate of $35 an ounce. Countries experiencing payments problems could adjust their currencies to 0.75 per cent of the official parity. The system collapsed in the early 1970s. On 15 August 1971, President Nixon responded to America's deepening economic problems with the imposition of temporary 10 per cent tariffs and the nonconvertibility of the dollar into gold. In December 1971, the major industrial powers agreed to revalue their currencies about 15 per cent against the dollar and widened the band within which currencies could officially fluctuate to 2.25 per cent. By March 1973, the United States and the other major industrial democracies agreed to begin floating their currencies. In November 1973 OPEC quadrupled oil prices and sent the global economy into a tailspin.

Brussels gamely tried to forge monetary union amidst all these global economic calamities. On 24 April 1972, the Community imposed its exchange rate system, although it allowed a band of 1.125 per cent, nearly twice the 0.6 per cent recommended by the Werner Report, and established a European Monetary Cooperation Fund to assist adjustments. This 'snake', however, rapidly became dismembered as Britain, France, and Italy dropped out. By 1975 the snake was dead.

Dreams of monetary union, however, did not die with it. At the Copenhagen summit of December 1977 and the Bremen summit of July 1978, Chancellor Helmut Schmidt, acting on earlier recommendations by Commission President Roy Jenkins, pushed the other leaders for renewed efforts to work toward monetary union. In December 1978, the Council agreed to revive a version of the Werner Plan. The European Monetary System (EMS) emerged in March 1979. EMS included a European Economic Unit (ECU) which was then valued at $1.43 and would serve as the Community's accounting rather than monetary unit. All currencies were tied to the ECU and allowed a 2.25 fluctuation band. A European Monetary Fund would help members maintain these rates. Each member would contribute 20 per cent of their gold and dollar reserves to the fund which would intervene in the currency markets to maintain each member's currency within the limits.

Once again these promising steps were swept away by political and economic realities. The world experienced a deep recession in 1981 and 1982 while the dollar strengthened throughout the early 1980s, impeding Community efforts to harmonize member monetary policies. Britain refused to participate in the Exchange Rate Mechanism (ERM) and allowed its currency to fluctuate according to market forces. Although the ECUs are supposed to replace the dollar as the Community's anchor currency, the EMS has not lived up to its original goals. In different ways, each member has limited its participation, and the ECU has yet to replace the dollar in importance. But EMS is an important first step toward eventual EMU.

Yet EMS has succeeded in some ways. Although Britain remains officially outside the system and Greece, Spain, and Portugal do not use the ERM, in fact all the members are tied into the EMS and exchange rates are relatively constant. The German Bundesbank is the Community's *de facto* central bank and center of the EMS. The other members carefully follow the Bundesbank's conservative lead in interest rates. As a result Community inflation rates are low and relatively equal at the expense of slow growth and high unemployment.

Both the Commission and different governments continued to push for monetary union. Reasoning that the only way to influence the Bundesbank is to mesh it within a European bank, Paris has been the major proponent of a European central bank and currency. In April 1989, the Delors committee published the *Report on Economic and Monetary Union in the European Community*, in which they proposed a three-step evolution to a European System of Central Banks (ESCB). In the first stage Britain, Portugal, and Greece would join the EMS and each member would allow their respective central bank to become independent. During the second stage the members would adopt a treaty allowing a transfer of national monetary authority to the ESCB and fixed exchange rates. Under the final stage the national banks would transfer their responsibilities to the ESCB. The ESCB would be modeled on America's Federal Reserve system.

At the Madrid summit of June 1989, the Council, with Prime Minister Thatcher grudgingly going along, agreed to implement the first step of the Delors Report which involved a closer coordination of national monetary policies and exchange rates. On 11 December 1991, during the Maastricht summit, the Council of Europe signed a treaty which provided a strict timetable for monetary union. Britain refused to commit itself to joining a central bank or single currency, and the Council allowed it to opt out of those commitments. Having already largely achieved the first stage, the second stage begins on 1 January 1994 when the members tighten the band within which their currencies can fluctuate and create a European Monetary Institute which will eventually be transformed into a central bank.

The third and decisive stage should begin in 1996 by which date the members should have achieved sweeping monetary and fiscal reforms to be eligible for membership. To join, members must fulfill five major goals: (1)

have inflation rates no more than 1.5 per cent above the Community average of the three least inflationary members; (2) have a budget deficit less than one per cent of GNP; (3) reduce their total government debt as a percentage of GNP to below 60 per cent; (4) reduce long-term interest rates to 2 per cent or less than the average of the three countries with the lowest inflation rates; and (5) not allow their exchange rate to fall more than 2.25 per cent below the EMS average. If countries cannot meet these requirements by the deadlines they can join later. If seven of the twelve members have achieved these qualifications, the Community can then decide by a two-thirds majority whether or not to form a Central Bank and single currency on 1 January 1997. If these conditions are not met or the more immediate union is voted down, the central bank will be automatically inaugurated on 1 July 1988, and exchange rates fixed and converged into a single currency on 1 January 1999. Each nation will have representatives on the central bank board, while the national central banks will act like the regional banks of America's federal system. Although the fiscal and monetary conservatism will initially rein in Europe's economy, it should spur growth over the long term. Business costs will immediately drop as firms can discard the expensive practices of preparing invoices for each currency and adjusting to daily shifts in currency values.

INDUSTRIAL POLICY

Industrial policies target specific economic sectors, industries, technologies, products, or firms for development. Every country has industrial policies in which some industries are helped or hindered more than others.[3] The industrial policymaking process, targets, and strategies differ greatly from one country to the next. Some countries like Japan protect and nurture virtually all of their industries, and their policies are carefully planned and executed within a long-term national development strategy. Tokyo's comprehensive industrial strategy, which is shaped by five-year indicative plans and tight collaboration between the bureaucracies, business, politicians, labor, and mass media, maximizes Japan's creation of wealth and development. Industrial policies in other countries like the United States largely emerge helter skelter from the political process, without any strategic direction. Japan's economic dynamism and growing power and America's stagnation reflect the effects of their different industrial policy-making processes and philosophies.

Brussels' industrial policymaking process, philosophy, and policies are similar to those of the United States. The Rome Treaty specifically calls for an industrial policy for only two industries – agriculture and transport. Like those of the United States, the Community's other industrial policies have been shaped more by politics than careful planning. The Commission itself is split between forces which promote competition and those which promote cooperation. The directorate generals reflect the Rome Treaty's diverse goals. On one side is Directorate General IV (DGIV) which heads competition policy, and on the other is Directorate General III (DGIII) which heads industrial and technological policy, accompanied by the dozen directorate generals which nurture specific industries. The directorate generals frequently clash over their respective interpretations of their responsibilities. As in any pluralistic political system, business interests play an important role in influencing policy. The Union of Industries of the European Community (UNICE) is the most powerful business group which lobbies for effective Community trade and industrial policies. The European Roundtable was founded by Pehr Gyllenhammar, Volvo's Chairman, in the mid-1980s, to help formulate the Community's industrial and trade policies.

Brussels' first comprehensive attempt to design an industrial policy occurred in March 1970 when DGIV Commissioner Guido Colonna presented his *Memorandum on Industrial Policy in the Communities* to the Council of Ministers, which called for a single market, industrial, and technological base to be achieved by the complete elimination of all internal trade barriers and the targeting of strategic industries and technologies. Although the 'Colonna Report' received a sympathetic hearing, no concrete actions were taken for another fifteen years. Today, Europe has achieved a unified market, and there are a variety of industrial and technology promotion policies. Yet the intensity and effectiveness of Europe's array of policies vary considerably and lack a long-term comprehensive rubric.

Brussels' industrial policies have been primarily defensive, using emergency subsidy, protectionist, merger, and cartel measures to rescue beleaguered industries. Some products are considered so vital to the EC's economic dynamism that large trade and investments barriers are both imposed. For example, in February 1989, the EC reinforced its tariffs and quotas against foreign integrated circuits by imposing rules which force foreign investors to manufacture key components and the finished product within the Community in order to be allowed free movement throughout the Community. 'Buy Europe' policies are also employed. In four industries – energy, telecommunications, transport, and water supply – the Community will not accept any bid that does not meet a 50 per cent Community content requirement. During the 1980s, Brussels understood clearly that if it did nothing to aid Europe's high-technology development it would fall increasingly behind the Japanese and Americans. In response, Brussels began promoting advanced technology industries like semiconductors, computers, biotechnology, satellites, and supercomputers, to name a few. By the 1990s, the Community had a range of policies promoting different industries, technologies, and markets.

COMPETITION POLICY

Competition policy can be a form of industrial policy. It seeks to regulate two theoretically anticompetitive business or government practices: (1) the concentration of industry to the point where prices reflect not free markets but monopoly power; (2) the government use of subsidies to promote the investments or trade of specific industries which thus gives them an 'unfair' business advantage. Peter Montagnon speaks for many when he asserts that 'the development of a single market will require continued vigilance by the Commission against the formation of cartels', and cites 'mergers and acquisitions, control of subsidies, the regulation of utilities, and the link between trade policy and competition' as 'stress points' for the creation of a genuine free market.[4] This is a laudable aim as long as it promotes rather than inhibits the nation's economic development. But overzealously wielded, competition policy can actually undermine a nation's competitive abilities.

Several Rome Treaty articles arm Brussels with the power to break up anti-competitive forces. The most powerful of these is Article 87 which authorizes the Commission, or more specifically DGIV, to develop the investigative powers necessary to detect anti-competitive arrangements. In 1962 Brussels passed Regulation 17/62 which empowers the Commission to act as investigator, prosecutor, and judge of anti-competitive practices. DGIV not only acts on complaints from anyone but it can initiate its own investigations, search and seize documents from any business, and require governments to enforce any of its rulings. These powers were modified in 1982. Now a Hearings Officer who has not been involved in the investigation submits an independent ruling on the findings. In addition, the Commission must notify businesses before they enter the premises. Yet the national governments must still adhere to any ruling. Although these powers seem impressive, the Commission simply lacks the human and financial resources to supervise the Community. In 1986 alone, the Commission investigated 3,500 cases of which 80 per cent were licensing or distribution agreements. Yet of these the Commission brought only twenty-seven cases before the Court of Justice.[5] Other articles delimit the types of anti-competitive arrangements that the Commission would regulate. Article

85 prohibits production, marketing, technical, or price cartels between firms. Article 86 prohibits any firm from abusing monopoly or quasi-monopoly power.

It took the Commission almost three decades before it could translate these legal powers into actual powers. The first boost to Commission power occurred when the European Court of Justice ruled in 1972 that the Commission was justified in using Article 86 to block acquisitions by the American firm Continental Can which was trying to achieve a dominant position in Europe's canning industry. The Court reasoned that trade distortion is bad regardless of whether it is caused by cartels or mergers. Bonn began controlling mergers and acquisitions in 1973, and in July the Commission requested similar sweeping powers from the Council. Although the European Parliament approved the request in February 1974, the Council eventually shelved it because the national governments refused to grant the Commission the ability to overrule their own policies. Another landmark case occurred in 1987 when the Court ruled that the Commission was justified in use of Article 85 to block Philip Morris' acquisition of a large percentage of Rothman's Tobacco holdings in 1981, which would have allowed a merger of the two corporations. Fearing that the Commission could use Article 85 retroactively, corporations pressured Brussels to rewrite the articles in less ambiguous language.

Another anti-competitive action is government subsidies to business. This is not a serious Community problem since member state aid to industry is relatively small. In 1988, the total amount was about 85 billion ECU, or 2.5 per cent of Community GDP, which was distributed through 1,000 known aid programs. About half of this aid propped up industries with political power but relative economic unimportance like agriculture, fisheries, and coal, or with public utilities like railroads. Agriculture, of course, is also heavily subsidized through Brussels' Common Agricultural Policy. Steel and shipbuilding are the most richly subsidized of heavy industries. State aids to manufacturing vary considerably among members. In 1986–8, of the four largest members, Italy gave 6.7 per cent in value added aid to industry, France 3.5 per cent, Britain 2.5 per cent, and Germany 2.7 per cent, or an average 85 billion ECU. Aid to sunset industries far exceeds aid to sunrise industries.[6] This practice is prohibited by Article 92.

The Rome Treaty is more ambiguous on state subsidies to industry than industrial concentration. Article 92 bans any aid which 'distorts or threatens to distort competition by favoring certain undertakings or the production of certain goods', but allows aid which promotes regional development, common European interests, serious economic problems, or fosters development without conflicting with common European interests. Article 93 requires member states to give prior notification of any plans to grant new aid or alter the existing aid programs, whereupon the Commission can approve or disapprove. In practice, the Commission simply reviews each government's general aid program and only examines specific grants when they are extremely large or in sensitive sectors. The Rome and Paris treaties also allow subsidies for transportation, steel, and agriculture. Brussels has banned outright export credits and other subsidies for intra-Community trade, but allows it for trade to third countries. Brussels is split over whether or not to allow aid to ailing companies or industries.

Since the 1986 Single Europe Act, the Community's economic policies have evolved through a series of official reports and new regulation, including T. Padoa-Schioppa's *Efficiency, Stability, and Equity: A Strategy for the Evolution of the Economic System of the European Community* of 1987, Paolo Cecchini's *The European Challenge, 1992: the Benefits of a Single Market*, of 1988, and Jacques Delors' *Report on Economic and Monetary Union* of 1989. These studies share the common themes of rejecting managed in favor of free markets as the basis of economic development. Delors' report concluded that:

> Competition policy – conducted at the Community level – would have to operate in such a way that access to markets would not be impeded and market functioning not distorted by the behavior of private or public economic agents. Such priorities would not only have to address conventional forms of restrictive market practices and the abuse of dominant market positions, but would also have to deal with new aspects of antitrust laws, especially in the field of merger and takeover activities. The use of government subsidies to assist particular industries should be strictly circumscribed because they distort competition and cause inefficient use and allocation of scarce economic resources.[7]

Shortcomings in the Community antitrust policy remain despite these developments. In September 1990, Brussels ruled that the Commission could only regulate mergers and acquisitions 5 billion ECU or larger. (Aggregate annual Community turnover is 250 million ECU or larger, and less than two-thirds of that turnover is within any one Community member.) National governments would deal with anything smaller according to their own laws. Antitrust exemptions are allowed if the arrangement can be proved to improve production, distribution, and technology for consumers, and no substantial competitive loss occurs. Under these new rules, the Commission will prosecute annually only about twenty-five cases.[8] The Commission is hobbled by a lack of qualified personnel to investigate these cases and there are still no clear guidelines in determining when firms 'abuse' their 'dominant' market share. Governments can slip around the anticompetitive restrictions in several ways. One is for governments to override the Commission by citing 'national security' concerns. Another is to subsidize an industry's research and development efforts, either with direct cash infusions or indirect tax write-offs. Then there are the sheer number of industrial aid programs – over 1,000 national government and 36,000 local government programs throughout the Community.[9] The Commission simply cannot regulate more than a small percentage. Finally, the Commission has no authority to regulate public corporations which are the most notorious examples of state subsidies. Given these loopholes, the Community's competition policy will never succeed in being any more than a slight deterrent on antitrust violations of all but the biggest and most notorious government and industrial violators.

AGRICULTURE

Ironically, agriculture remains heavily protected in industrial democratic countries. The farm lobby is powerful and unyielding in its efforts to maintain high levels of subsidies and protection, and rejects all arguments that the resources it receives could be better invested elsewhere in the economy. The farm lobby counters that self-sufficiency in food is a basic requirement for national security, and thus agriculture is a special industry whose massive government aid is justified.

The Rome Treaty articles 38 through 47 committed the Community to creating and implementing a 'common agricultural policy' (CAP). Article 39 clearly states the CAP's goals: (1) increasing productivity; (2) ensuring a fair living for farmers; (3) stabilizing markets and prices; (4) assuring necessary production; (5) guaranteeing reasonable consumer prices. The Commission's first agricultural regulations were issued in 1960, and there has been a steady stream of new regulations ever since as the Community attempts to fulfill its mandate. In 1964, the Commission began negotiating common agricultural prices and within four years achieved a common cereal price. The Mansholt Plan submitted in 1968 was an attempt to regulate systematically Europe's farm production and markets. It had three objectives: (1) to encourage any technical innovations, investments, and research which could contribute to higher productivity; (2) to improve markets by building up agricultural storage, transportation, packaging, processing, and sales facilities; and (3) to alleviate regional disparities in farm productivity. By 1972, a range of new subsidies and policies had been created to implement the Mansholt Plan's objectives.

The Commission directly regulates agriculture under broad guidelines set by the Council. As in other industries, the Commission has attempted to break down domestic barriers and erect common barriers to foreign imports. Markets are controlled in several ways. Minimum prices are set for production, particularly in dairy, cheese, sugar, and cereals and to a lesser extent pork, wine, fruit, and vegetables. Excess production is bought and stored to prevent any price decline. Each year the Council debates and approves intervention prices for each product which have been proposed by the Commission after consultation with the European Parliament. Prices are uniform for the Community and set in ECU values. Thus, prices can fluctuate with exchange rates. The Monetary Compensation Amounts (MCA) are subsidies which cushion farmers from any adverse swings in currency value. The European Agricultural Fund (EAGGF) is responsible for determining the amount of farm subsidies and then issuing them. Its outlays have soared from 11,900 ECU in 1968–72 to 151,600 ECU in 1983–7, and amount to about 1 per cent of Europe's GNP.[10] About 70 per cent of all agricultural products receive price supports. Bonus subsidies are extended to producers with large-scale production.

Agriculture has steadily declined in importance to Europe's economy. In 1950, agriculture accounted for 30 per cent of Europe's employment and 10 per cent of its production. In 1985, it had declined to only 9 per cent of total employment and 3 per cent of the economy. These figures are expected to decline further. There has been a steady increase in farm size and productivity. Between 1960 and 1985, the area per farm worker doubled from six to thirteen hectares, the share of holding smaller than ten hectares declined from 70 per cent to 62 per cent, and the average farm size increased from eleven to seventeen hectares. Productivity in certain products has jumped significantly. Between 1958–60 and 1984–6, kilograms of milk production per cow rose from 2,900 to 4,400, 100 kilograms of wheat per hectare from 23 to 58, and 100 kilograms of sugar-beets per hectare from 400 to 510.[11]

The importance of agriculture to each member state's economy also varies widely, being greater in the poorer countries like Greece, Portugal, Spain, and Ireland, and less significant in the industrially advanced countries. There are also wide differences in agriculture's importance between the regions of each member. Productivity levels in the same products also varies considerably from one member to the next, with differences related to the degree of mechanization, fertilization, and farm size. For example, the average Community farm size was about ten hectares, while Italy's averaged six hectares and Greece's only three hectares.

Europe's food production in most products has outstripped population increases, so Europe has shifted from being a net importer to a net exporter of many products. In 1985, of five cereals, Europe produced more than it consumed in all but maize for an average 114 per cent self-sufficiency rating. The Community also enjoyed a 101 per cent self-sufficiency rating for meat, 108 per cent for cheese, 129 per cent for butter, 107 per cent for wine, 102 per cent for potatoes, 125 per cent for sugar, 102 per cent for eggs, and 107 per cent for vegetables.[12]

CAP has been the Community's greatest success and failure. No industry has been promoted more vigorously than agriculture. CAP has successfully achieved virtually all of its objectives except one – reasonable prices for consumers. When producer and consumer interests conflict, it is farm interests which prevail. Farmers continue to receive high subsidies and protection. Meanwhile European food prices remain considerably higher than global market prices, with the average product roughly 175 per cent higher. Although food prices are stable, consumers are hit twice, with higher prices, and higher taxes to support those prices.

It is not just consumers who are penalized by CAP. CAP also hurts foreign producers. The Community's policies of protecting domestic production, subsidizing exports (restitutions), and dumping excess production on world markets has provoked periodic protests from the United States, Canada, Australia, Argentina, New Zealand, and other more efficient agricultural producers.

As in other industrial nations, the power of Europe's farm lobby rather than European interests shapes agriculture policy. Price supports have encouraged overproduction, and 'wine lakes and butter mountains' have grown within European warehouses. Europe's economic future does not depend on continuing to produce heavily subsidized grain, beef, and wine. By favoring agriculture with three-quarters of its limited budget, the Community has less resources available to invest in industry and technology, and consumers have less money to buy manufactured products.

STEEL

Europe's steel industry has been targeted for development from the formation of the European Coal and Steel Community (ECSC) in 1952. ECSC had the power to shape private firms' investment, technology, production, price, and marketing efforts. Article 58 of the Paris Treaty grants the ECSC the power to declare a 'manifest crisis' in which it can impose production quotas and inflict huge fines for noncompliance. It used these powers to unite Europe's steel markets, production infrastructure, and producers. The abolition of customs barriers led to a 129 per cent increase in intra-European trade between 1952 and 1957. Production has been rationalized with many smaller, less efficient (or politically powerful) steel producers either being bought out or going bankrupt during the 1950s and 1960s. Mergers between large-scale producers have continued. Steel production increased from 93 million tons in 1962 to 156 million tons in 1974, or 22 per cent of world production.[13]

The energy-intensive steel industry was particularly hard hit by OPEC's quadrupling of oil prices in 1973. Steel producers attempted to dump their products on severely contracted markets. In 1977, the Commission stepped in to persuade the major producers to form a voluntary production and price cartel (Eurofer). In response to the Commission measure, steel prices rose 20–25 per cent in 1978 but dropped thereafter as domestic producers cheated on quotas and the market contracted further. Eurofer collapsed in 1980. Citing its power under ECSC Treaty articles 58 and 61, in October 1980 the Commission imposed mandatory production quotas on 80 per cent of production affecting 300 factories, while the rest was shaped by voluntary quotas. These measures were supplemented by national efforts to ease the industry's shake-up through a range of subsidies, low interest loans, and tax write-offs.[14]

Despite these efforts the steel industry continued to haemorrhage. OPEC's further doubling of oil prices threatened to wipe out the cartel's progress. In 1980, Europe's steel production dropped to half of its 200 million tons capacity. DGIII Commissioner Etienne Davignon declared a crisis and imposed compulsory capacity reductions on 80 per cent of all steel production and voluntary quotas on the rest in return for continued subsidies. In addition, he imposed compulsory capacity reductions and negotiated VERs with fifteen foreign countries which accounted for 75 per cent of the Community's imports. Production slowly improved throughout the early 1980s until it reached 120 million tons in 1985 of which 110 million tons were consumed domestically and the rest exported. In December 1985, Brussels ceased all steel subsidies and began to phase out the production quotas and minimum prices.

National steel production is dominated by one champion. In 1985, Finnsider accounted for 57 per cent of Italy's production, British Steel for 83 per cent of Britain's, Arbed for 100 per cent of Luxembourg's, Cockerill Sambre for 42 per cent of Belgium's, Hoogovens for 96 per cent of the Netherland's, and Sacilor for 57 per cent of France's. West German had a more diversified production base with Tyssen accounting for 29 per cent, Klockner for 11 per cent, and Krupp and Hoesch for 10 per cent each.[15]

There is a balance of power among Europe's steel producers for the common market, with national buying preferences still prominent. Brussels' steel policy has generally been considered a success, according to Unwin, because 'the Commission inherited more decisive powers . . . from the ECSC than were available under the Treaty of Rome'.[16] But the policy has been expensive – ECU 33 billion through 1985, while 152,000 jobs were eliminated.[17] And while the steel industry has been saved, it will remain protected as long as the world suffers from an overcapacity of steel production with the major producers unwilling to cut back their own global market shares.

TRANSPORT

Rome Treaty articles 74–84 called for a Common Transport Policy. Only agriculture also merited an explicit designation for a special treatment. The reasons for targeting transportation are obvious – a united, efficient transportation system is essential for European unification. The articles called for set prices for carrying rates, prohibited the use of discriminatory tariffs by national governments on transported goods, and forbids governments from using the transportation system to protect industries by denying rivals the same shipping advantages. A 1962 Commission Memorandum attempted to flesh out the Rome Treaty's rather vague articles on transportation by proposing a detailed system of tariffs, market controls, infrastructure improvements, and means of coordinating the system. In 1965, Brussels required states to deregulate their railway systems and cut subsidies.

Yet, despite these initial steps, agreement on a Common Transportation Policy proved difficult as the national governments split over basic principles. Some, like Britain and the Netherlands, argued that the market was the best way to regulate the transportation system, while others like Germany and France maintained that government management was superior. Another obstacle was the tendency for national governments to resist handing over authority to Brussels. The result was deadlock.

The standoff was not broken until 1983 when the Court of Justice ruled that the Council of Ministers had to implement a common transportation policy within a reasonable period of time. Since then there has been considerable progress on creating and implementing a common policy. By 1987, Brussels had achieved a liberalization of 35 per cent of the total goods transportation by forbidding a number of practices by which governments discriminated against non-national carriers, including cabotage or carrying cargo in another member state for their customers. It also regulated shipping prices and quantities. Community inspectors were deployed to ensure that these measures were fully implemented. Transportation market liberalization is scheduled for 1992.

These policies helped ease a shift in the importance of different segments of the transportation system. Road haulage is rapidly expanding while the railroads and inland waterways have declined as a percentage of total shipping. In 1970, the railroads accounted for 28 per cent of transport, waterways 14 per cent, and roads 50 per cent, with a total of 750,000,000,000 tons shipped. In 1984, railroads had declined to a 28 per cent share and waterways to 11 per cent, while road transport had increased to 65 per cent, with a total of 969,000,000,000 tons shipped.[18] Passenger traffic has also increased steadily. In 1960, the average European spent 8 per cent of his total net income on private and public transportation; in 1983 the figure rose to 14 per cent. Air transportation expanded enormously, from 21.2 billion air passenger kilometers in 1960 to 190.7 billion in 1985.[19] Yet, despite these changes in policy and transportation usage, governments continue to regulate their respective systems heavily thus keeping a European transportation system fragmented and relatively inefficient.

AUTOMOBILES

As in other countries, the Community and national governments share the responsibility for nurturing Europe's automobile industry. The Community has made considerable progress over the years in harmonizing production standards, taxes, and state aid. In 1970, the Community identified forty-four items for harmonization, and eventually the member governments agreed to accept forty-one of those standards. The biggest obstacle was over exhaust regulations. It was not until 1989 that the Community agreed to adapt US emission standards and the installation of catalytic converters. Another area targeted for harmonization was the different VAT, excise, and other taxes imposed on automobile sales. High tax countries lose sales and revenues to low tax countries, but are reluctant to cede an important revenue source. The Community has yet to achieve agreement on taxes. Government aid to the automobile industry is another area in which harmonization has proved elusive. France, Britain, and Spain have written off considerable debt and bailed out their respective automobile industries from bankruptcy. Germany's more efficient producers strongly protest against such subsidies as giving their rivals an unfair advantage.

Thus, until 1992 each country had its own set of regulations, subsidies, and taxes. The national champion strategy of Germany, France, and Italy continued to determine the fate of Europe's producers. As in other industries, the result of this hodge-podge of policies and rules was the inability of Europe's automobile-makers to establish continent-scale production. Instead, each producer had to tailor-make cars and trucks for each country, at an enormous cost in profits, time, and material. Thus there was not one but twelve automobile markets, which imposes higher costs on producers and consumers alike.

Another controversial issue is the Community policy toward foreign automobiles imports or investments in Europe. Although American-owned, the subsidiaries of the American producers, General Motors and Ford, are largely considered European firms because of their longevity on the continent and their reliance on local parts and services. Ford built its first plant in Britain in 1911 and plants in Germany and elsewhere throughout the 1920s. General Motors acquired the British producer Vauxhall in 1925 and Germany's Opel in 1929. Both American producers have dominant market shares in Britain, significant shares elsewhere in Europe, and are steadily expanding their presence. In 1989, Ford took over Jaguar and General Motors acquired a controlling position in Saab. In 1986, the European production of Ford of 1,421,000 vehicles and General Motors' of 1,363,000 vehicles compared to a total European production of 11,309,000 million.[20] Yet, despite these long-standing ties, Ford and General Motors are excluded from the Committee of Common Market Car Makers (CCMC), which advises the Community on automobile standards and policies. However, Ford and General Motors are members of the national automobile associations which are united in the Coordinating Council of European Car Manufacturers (CLCA), which lobbies Brussels and the national governments.

Of the foreign producers, Japan has become the most controversial. It was not until the 1980s that Japan's producers began setting up shop and expanding their sales in Europe. There is no sign that the Japanese producers are seriously attempting to 'go native' in procuring local parts and services. Instead, the Japanese producers are following in Europe the same strategy they pursued in the United States. A manufacturer sets up a 'greenfield' factory, inhibits any union activity, and invites in its Japanese parts and service affiliates. The result is that the Japanese squeeze out European producers and exacerbate local employment, growth, and tax receipt problems.[21]

Europe's automobile makers lag well behind their Japanese and American rivals in productivity, quality, and global market share. The automobile industry remains a vital part of Europe's economy, with four of Europe's ten largest corporations being automobile producers. Europe's automobile producers are divided between its five 'volume' producers, Volkswagon,

Peugeot, Renault, Fiat, and British Leyland, and high performance special-
ists like Daimler-Benz, BMW, Volvo, and Saab. How many of these producers will survive into the twenty-first century is an open question. Faced
with a seemingly omnipotent Japanese industry and a resurgent American
industry, the future of Europe's automobile producers could be bleak.

ENERGY

A Community energy policy dates to the 1951 Paris Treaty which created
the European Coal and Steel Community (ECSC). Coal was Europe's
primary energy source until it was surpassed by oil in the mid-1950s. Until
then the ECSC attempted to maximize coal production which by 1951 had
fallen to less than 60 per cent of its prewar level. By the mid-1950s, the
ECSC's coal production had surpassed its prewar level, but at a price 50 per
cent higher than imported oil. By the late 1950s, the ECSC was faced
with a crisis pitting coal-producing Germany, the Netherlands, and
Belgium (who wanted to continue to protect their coal industry) against
non-producing Italy and France (who wanted to buy oil and cheaper foreign
coal). Throughout the 1960s, the ECSC High Authority responded with the
bandaid measure of increased subsidies for domestic coal producers. But
domestic coal simply became more expensive as miners emptied the more
abundant and accessible veins and the ECSC lacked the resources to pay for
the price gap with foreign energy sources.

In the 1960s, Brussels attempted to promote a more comprehensive
energy policy. In 1962, the Commission issued a *Memorandum on Energy
Policy*, followed by *First Orientation to a Common Energy Policy* in 1968.
Both called for policies which would ensure a stable, diversified energy
supply at the lowest possible price, and argued that a common energy
market was the best means of achieving these goals. Industries were encouraged to switch from a dependence on diminishing supplies of domestic
expensive coal to cheaper foreign oil. It was argued that if industries failed
to use cheaper energy resources their products would become increasingly
uncompetitive in global markets.

By 1973, the Community was dependent on oil imports for 70 per cent of
its energy consumption! In two months from November 1973 to January
1974, global oil prices rose from $3 to $12 a barrel, and in so doing dragged
the world economy into deep recession and double digit inflation. Europe's
crisis was alleviated somewhat by a 1968 Community regulation that members maintain oil and coal stocks equal to 65 days' consumption, a term
which was later increased to 90 days. But, faced with the oil crisis, Commu-

nity solidarity crumbled. Brussels failed to counter OAPEC's boycott of oil exports to the Netherlands and in December 1974 France refused to join Washington's International Energy Agency (IEA) which was supposed to act like a oil buyers' cartel.

Brussels did encourage energy diversification and conservation, setting a goal of reducing the Community's percentage of imported energy to total consumption to 40 per cent by 1985. These goals were reached. In 1985, the percentage of total energy imported had indeed fallen to 40 per cent and that of imported oil in total energy consumption only 30 per cent. But Brussels' role in this remarkable achievement was that of a cheerleader urging on conservation and diversification. It was not until October 1989 that the Commission began gathering and publishing information on Community energy sources and prices to spotlight price gouging and inefficiencies. It has not ventured any more assertive measures. The real forces behind the change were a massive French nuclear energy effort which accounts for 40 per cent of France's energy needs, the fortuitous discovery of North Sea oil, which led the expansion of European oil production from 15 million tons in 1970 to 153 million in 1985, and the attempts by industry to cut costs and improve efficiency.

The European Atomic Energy Community (Euratom) played an equally insignificant role in these developments. Created in 1957 with the task of coordinating the Community nuclear energy development, Euratom has become a world leader in nuclear technology and in October 1991 achieved an important breakthrough in nuclear fission. Most of the European nuclear successes have been nationally, rather than Community-inspired. Europe's nuclear energy quadrupled between 1974 and 1981, then doubled between 1981 and 1986; almost half of the new nuclear power plants were French. Fourteen nations have contributed to the Joint European Torus (JET) which is developing nuclear fusion technology. The Superphenix-Neras project has made considerable progress in developing fast breeder reactor technology.

UTILITIES

Utility and energy policy are closely related. Utilities are natural monopolies. Traditionally, consumers of water, electricity, natural gas, or telecommunications do not really have a choice of supply. Price must, by necessity, be fixed at an amount which covers cost yet does not hurt customers. Society's only choice, it seemed, is whether the state should own utilities outright or carefully manage the private ownership of utilities.

In utility policy, as in other areas, the Rome Treaty offers contradictory perspectives on the power of Brussels and the national governments. Although Article 90 outlaws any public or private non-competitive actions and empowers the Commission to maintain competition, Article 222 explicitly allows each member to regulate its own utilities industry. Politics determines which article is ascendant, and most member states jealously guard their legal right to determine their own utilities policy.

Throughout the 1980s and into the 1990s debate has been building over how to increase the cost and environmental efficiency of utilities. A single European energy market would yield annual economic gains of at least 16 billion ECU, or 0.5 per cent of GDP, while a Community telecommunications network would annually generate savings of 10 billion ECU. These figures do not include the incalculable financial savings to both business and households from the greater efficiency, nor to the environment from the more efficient use of resources.[22] Are these long-term yields worth the short-term costs of disrupted national markets and the bankruptcy of the inevitable losers?

A dispute between Germany and France over their respective energy policies reveals the costs of continued diversity over unity. France's nuclear policy has successfully created a cheap, abundant, non-polluting energy source. Nuclear power would dominate any free energy market. The other Community members, however, do not want to become dependent on French nuclear energy. German law, for example, forces the country to pay for more expensive, heavily polluting energy from its coal-fired plants. Both France and Germany accuse the other of unfairly subsidizing its energy industries. Bonn clearly does subsidize its coal industry by a variety of direct and indirect means, including a law that German coal must be used to fuel Germany energy. France's nuclear power industry is financed from private sources, without explicit government backing. Paris' support is more subtle. Brussels has failed to assert any Community energy utility policy. Most members guard their right under the Rome Treaty to determine the shape of their own utilities, and reject any suggestion that the Community could benefit greatly from a united energy market. A common utility market is unlikely to emerge soon.

Virtually all governments either outright own or carefully regulate their post, telephone, and telegraph (PTT) industry. By controlling telecommunications, governments can potentially help control their populations. With its ever-growing dependence on state of the art microelectronics, telecommunications is a strategic economic industry as well. PTTs virtually everywhere are monopolies whose suppliers are cartelized, whose prices are fixed, and whose consumers are captive.

Characteristically, the United States was the first country to liberalize its telecommunications market. In 1984, Washington unilaterally abolished ATT's telecommunications monopoly and opened the system to competitive bidding and entrepreneurs. The result was predictable. Japanese and European producers, safe within their own protected markets, quickly captured huge chunks of America's free telecommunications market. America's telecommunications equipment trade surplus of $0.5 billion steadily dwindled into a $3.4 billion deficit in 1988.[23] Although the Reagan administration remained blinded by its liberal ideology to the devastating effects its unilateral deregulation was having on America's telecommunications industry, Congress wrote a requirement into its 1988 Omnibus Trade and Competitiveness Act that required the White House to negotiate the opening of foreign telecommunications markets.

While America's telecommunication industry has been ravished by deregulation, the Community's continues to fall behind that of Japan's because of continued national overregulation. DGXIII regulates the telecommunications industry, and has largely attempted to develop the industry through directives mandating standardization and market opening. The European Telecommunications Standards Institute (ETSI) helps coordinate the harmonization of standards. Community telecommunications policy, like Japan's, relies heavily on 'buy national' policies. Hufbauer writes that

between 1984 and 1988, the Deutsche Bundespost awarded 99.5 percent of its contracts to German firms; while France, the United Kingdom, the Netherlands, and Portugal awarded 100 percent of their communications contracts to their own national firms. Overall less than two percent of government contracts go to firms in other member states.[24]

European telecommunication champions will not emerge as long as the members continue their national policies.

The Commission's Green Paper on telecommunications in 1987 began the debate on liberalization of that industry. The telecommunications sector was 75 billion ECU or 3 per cent of Community GDP that year, a percentage that is expected to increase to 7 per cent by the year 2000. The Green Paper advocated harmonizing telecommunications standards and slowly liberalizing the market under the guidance of a proposed European Telecommunications Standards Institute. The $1.5 billion Research on Advanced Communications Systems (RACE) project is devoted to developing all aspects of Europe's telecommunications industry. In addition, Brussels plans to spend $10 billion developing a 'Community Nervous System' which will link the members through extensive value added networks and other data base systems.

How to implement this decision remains controversial. In 1988, the

Commission used Rome Treaty Article 90 which empowers Brussels to break up antitrust arrangements to begin liberalizing the market for telecommunications equipment. France, backed by Germany, Italy, Greece, and Belgium, challenged the Commission's action before the European Court of Justice. Undaunted, the Commission used Article 90 to order the liberalization of data transmissions and other services, and began to implement its Open Network Provision (ONP), which presents standards to harmonize standards and rules. In late 1989 the members began agreeing to implement the Commission directives. Liberalization of data transmission will begin in January 1993. Nine members will continue to maintain control over licensing. Portugal, Spain, and Greece are allowed until January 1996 to comply. The Court, however, ruled in 1990 that the Commission could not use Article 90 to overrule any powers granted to the members in specific areas.

The global telecommunications industries have been growing rapidly, and with unification the Community's market has skyrocketed, expanding from $20.6 billion of a $83.4 billion global market in 1986 to $30.8 billion of $112.8 billion in 1990, and is expected to reach $48.9 billion of $184.5 billion by 2000. Meanwhile, Japan's market grew much more slowly from $7.1 billion to $8.5 billion to $13.3 billion and America's from $24.0 billion to $27.2 billion to $41.8 billion.[25] Despite Brussels' efforts, the Community's telecommunications industry has failed fully to capitalize on these opportunities. It remains weak and divided, and runs continuous trade deficits with both Japan and the United States.

BANKING AND SECURITIES

A unified banking market has evolved slowly since the Community's inception. The first symbolic steps were taken with a 1960 directive, amended in 1963, which called on members to ease their capital controls. The First Banking Directive of 1977 attempted to impose Community standards for that industry while directives in 1979, 1980, and 1982 attempted similarly to regulate the securities industry. National governments, however, used safeguard clauses to resist any genuine opening of their financial markets until recently. In 1979, Britain became the first country to remove all its capital controls, but the other members did not begin to dismantle their protected markets for another decade.

A 1988 Commission directive scheduled a complete liberalization of the Community's financial markets by 1 July 1990. Britain, Germany, the Netherlands, and Denmark completely liberalized their capital markets the following year and France, Italy, Belgium, and Luxembourg made the 1 July 1990 deadline. The 'poor four' were allowed to delay liberalization. The Commission's Second Banking Directive of 1989 require uniform banking licensing and free financial markets by 1 January 1993. Reciprocity is an important tenet of the Banking Directive which asserted that it would only license third country banks within the Community if those countries extended reciprocal access to European banks. Before a foreign bank could be licensed, the Commission would carefully study that bank's domestic financial market and then report its results to the Council of Ministers which would make a final decision. Even if discrimination is found, Brussels is required to attempt to remove the foreign barriers through negotiations, and only if the barriers remain can the Community deny a license. A 'grandfather clause' allows banks from discriminatory countries to remain in the Community if they were licensed before the directive took effect. Although Brussels originally declared that it would demand a 'mirror image' reciprocity of market share as well as opportunities, it later retreated simply to requesting 'national treatment' regardless of results. However, recognizing that 'national treatment' for foreign and even some domestic entrepreneurs is impossible in Japan, Brussels has pressured Tokyo to open its still carefully managed financial markets.

Unified finance markets could be the most important Community achievement. Financial unification means greater efficiency and investment options, more powerful global competitors, and cheaper capital prices. Capital movements between eight members have been free since 1 July 1990, with the 'poor four' – Ireland, Spain, Portugal, and Greece – gradually reducing their own capital controls. Universal banking, which allows banks to offer the whole range of financial services from savings deposits to securities trading, is now available in Germany, Denmark, Luxembourg, the Netherlands, and Britain. The City of London remains the Community's most important Eurobond and Euroequities market, to which all other markets are linked. Frankfurt, Paris, and Amsterdam are important secondary markets. Europe's banking and securities markets are close to unification.

ADVANCED TECHNOLOGY POLICY

The first step in the creation of a Common Technology Policy occurred in 1967 when Brussels created DGXII which would be responsible for research, science, and education. Then, four years later in 1971, Brussels announced the need for a comprehensive technology policy in which it would oversee numerous existing and future national and industrial efforts.

Nothing happened. No government was willing to divert resources and energies from its national champion strategy.

A Community consensus on the vital need for a Common Technology Policy emerged in early 1980s, spurred by the obvious failure of the national champion strategy and Japan's massive efforts to technologically leapfrog the United States. Tokyo's 1981 announcement of its Fifth Generation Computer project in which Japan's relevant ministries and corporations would work together to create a computer that operated thousands of times faster than contemporary computers and thought like a human being stimulated fear in both the European Community and the United States.

Using MITI's government-industry research and development consortiums as a model, Brussels helped organize a range of cooperative high technology ventures between relevant European firms, and attempted to coordinate their research and development efforts through a range of programs. The first major step was in 1978 when the Community created a four-year program called the Forecasting and Assessment in Science and Technology (FAST), in which a ten-person team coordinated research on thirty-six subjects in fifty-four laboratories across the Community. Although FAST concentrated on promoting biotechnology, the information industry, and technology applications to the workplace, it proposed a wide range of high technology projects to the Council of Ministers. The program was renewed for another four-year term in 1983.

Other Community programs followed. In 1982, Commissioner for Industry Etienne Davignon established the Information Technology Industry Roundtable, which included representatives of the Community's twelve largest microelectronic firms. The Roundtable led to the 1983 creation of the European Strategic Program for Research and Development in Information Technology (ESPRIT), the European equivalent of MITI's Fifth Generation project, and the related effort, Research for Advanced Communications technologies in Europe (RACE). ESPRIT ran from 1984 to 1988, and involved a massive effort by dozens of European firms to research advanced microelectronics, software, advanced information, computer aided manufacturing, and other high tech projects. Half of ESPRIT's $1.5 billion cost came from Brussels and half by the participating firms. The $3.2 billion ESPRIT II began in 1987, ran until 1992, and targeted an even wider range of leading edge microelectronics projects. In order to qualify for an ESPRIT research grant, the applicant's proposal must include collaboration between firms or research facilities of two or more members.

A comprehensive high technology policy and range of specific projects emerged after the passage of the Single European Act in 1986. Armed with the SEA mandate to create and implement a comprehensive high technology policy, the Commission issued a four-year plan running from 1987 to 1991 which subsidized information, telecommunications, energy, biotechnology, and marine technologies with 7.7 billion ECU. Although this figure sounds impressive, the Community's annual technology subsidy accounts for only 4–5 per cent of the total budget. In 1989, Brussels paid $26 billion and the member governments a total of $98 billion in industrial subsidies, a combined amount equal to 3 per cent of Community GNP.[26]

These Community programs and all others are coordinated and funded by the European Research Cooperation Agency (EUREKA), an umbrella effort encompassing such specific projects as information and communication technology, robotics, biotechnology, lasers, marine technology, energy, environmental protection, and transportation.[27] In addition to RACE and ESPRIT which target information technologies, other EUREKA industrial and technology policies include: BRITE, EURAM, and BCR which apply new technologies to existing industries; FLAIR and ECLAIR which target biotechnology; JET, NET, and CCR which target nuclear fusion, safety, and waste management; MAST which develops seabed and marine mining; and COMETT and FAST which train and exchange scientists, researchers, academics, and engineers. To date EUREKA has distributed $6.3 billion among over 300 research high-tech projects and 1,600 participating firms.

The Joint European Submicron Silicon Initiative (JESSI) is the Community's most comprehensive effort toward mastering a range of products from high definition television to future generations of semiconductors and fiber-optics. JESSI will run from 1989 to 1997 with the goal of mastering the next generation of semiconductors, equipment, materials, and manufacturing processes. JESSI was funded with $5 billion, of which the Community and member states paid a quarter each, and the corporations chipped in the rest. This financial commitment is ten times Washington's contribution to a similar high technology program, Sematech, which inspired JESSI.

The Community's most notable success has been in aerospace. Thirteen states are members of the European Space Agency which has sponsored three major projects, Arianespace which commercializes the launch of satellites, and Eurosat which launches telecommunications satellites. To date it has launched over sixty satellites, has a better track record than NASA in getting and keeping satellites up, and is building a $4.8 billion space shuttle. Airbus is a consortium of German, French, British, and Spanish firms which develops and produces passenger aircraft. Airbus has surpassed MacDonald Douglas in global market share and is gradually creeping up to that of Boeing.

Although most EC research consortia are open to American firms, they remain largely closed to Japan's corporations. But Brussels may eventually ban American participation in Community high technology projects if Washington continues to discriminate against European firms in American projects. From January 1990, IBM was allowed to participate in JESSI, but only in return for IBM allowing European participation in its X-ray lithography project. Ironically, Japan's participation in European projects may be allowed despite the aversion towards it. Japan's corporations are so far ahead in so many technologies that European firms, like their American counterparts, increasingly may have to rely on joint ventures with their Japanese rivals in order to stay in the race. These Faustian bargains with the Japanese, however, may prove ultimately as self-defeating for the Europeans as they have for the Americans.

Unifying markets will prove relatively easy to accomplish. Unifying the efforts of specific industries or sectors will prove more difficult. The Community's high technology programs may be too little, too late. Although the Europeans agree that coordinating their research and development efforts is the only way they can possibly stay in the high technology race with the Japanese and Americans, the EC has only attempted to form a few European consortia, and those efforts fall far below Japan's hundreds of research, production, marketing, import, and export cartels. Europe ran a $40 billion deficit in electronics in 1990, and it is estimated that the Community's semiconductor makers alone will need $10 billion and the computer industry $100 billion to survive the 1990s.[28]

These problems were clearly identified in May 1989 with the publication by the European Information Technology Industry Roundtable of the *White Paper on European I.T. (Information Technology) Industry and the Single Market*, in which it outlined its goals and strategy:

> Up to now, R & D initiatives of the Commission have created confidence and strengthened European cooperation within the industry. But concentrating on R & D cooperation is no longer sufficient . . . The next step should be to set a goal-oriented strategy with the objective of gaining competitive advantage. This requires the creation of major initiatives targeted at specific markets and technologies.[29]

NATIONAL INDUSTRIAL POLICIES

Despite Brussels' attempts to promote Community industrial policies, industrial policy remains the prerogative of each nation. The Community industrial policy is the sum of its parts, and each country has its own mix of policies. There has, however, been a convergence in industrial policy-making and policies over time. Most countries have adopted a corporatist relationship between management and labor in which the government acts as the 'honest broker' in resolving differences.

But despite these cooperative arrangements, policy consensus in most countries has been lacking or fleeting. Since 1945, only Paris has consciously attempted systematically to develop its economy by targeting strategic industries. Elsewhere, industrial policies have evolved in a sporadic fashion in response to external challenges and internal difficulties. The ability to forge a consensus depends on political stability and the degree of political polarization, while the relative success of these policies in fostering development has been just as varied.

How do we account for the differences in national strategies? It is difficult if not impossible to untangle the multiple strands of culture, historic opportunities and impediments, foreign economic and military challenges, population size and quality, geographic location, access to technology, and policy choices that shape a national development strategy. The larger and more affluent a country's population, the more it can afford to be protectionist since it can produce a wider range of products within its borders. Countries with smaller populations generally are more dependent on trade for essential products and thus must be more selective in using protectionism to promote development.

Europe's economic development since 1945 must be understood within the context of its pre-1945 development. In the nineteenth century Britain, as the first industrial country, could afford to promote free market policies. Its industries enjoyed a comparative advantage and it was in Britain's interests to pressure other countries to open their markets to British products. Elsewhere however, particularly in Germany, the state played a powerful role in nurturing industrialization by extending subsidies, erecting import barriers, building infrastructure, suppressing labor, fostering mass education, encouraging cartels, and promoting exports. The result was that by the late nineteenth century, Germany had industrially surpassed Britain while France and other countries were rapidly closing the gap. Finally, in the 1930s, faced with a global trade war and the continued relative decline of its manufacturers, London itself abandoned liberal policies in favor of neomercantilism.

Between 1940 and 1945, the twelve nations which now form the Community suffered sharply varying degrees of war destruction, economic disruption, and underdevelopment. Nearly half a century later the twelve vary just as greatly in their degree of prosperity, economic dynamism, and development, and the strategies behind their achievements and shortcomings. Germany, France, Italy, and Britain together account for about 70 per cent of Europe's GNP and half its population, and this section will first concentrate on the different strategies of these four, and then give an overview of some of the smaller states.

Germany

No Community member suffered more from World War Two than Germany. With over 5 million dead, its cities and industries in ruins, its population on the brink of starvation, its territory cut in two, and what industry that survived threatened with expropriation, Germany's economic future seemed bleak indeed. Since then West Germany has rebuilt its shattered industries, cities, and infrastructure, created and distributed enormous wealth, is transforming itself from an industrial into a postindustrial society, is attempting to remake East Germany in its own image, and has emerged as the dynamic core of Europe's political economy.

Yet, like Japan since 1945, Germany experienced no economic miracle in the sense of divine intervention. There are many parallels between German and Japanese development. Germany's economic success in the postwar era, like that of Japan, was built upon nearly a century of state-led industrial development which targeted strategic industries with cartels, import barriers, subsidies, tax breaks, and export incentives. Like Japan, an industrial latecomer, Germany's state played an decisive role in the nation's development. Friedrich List provided mercantilism's theoretical rationale, while Bismarck and his successors nurtured strategic industries into global champions. Industries were allowed to form cartels until 1923 when antitrust laws were imposed, and after 1933 cartels and government coordination of investment, production, and distribution further boosted Germany's growth. Germany's bank-centered industrial groups have been as effective and powerful as Japan's.

West Germany's development since 1945 has been labelled market-oriented. In reality, although much less than Japan's, West Germany's economy is shaped as much by careful management as free trade. The government and business work closely to develop key industries and regions. Management-labor relations are cooperative and virtually strike-free. As in Japan following the war, vast infusions of American aid, a forgiving peace treaty, and integration within what became the European Community provided a very favorable development environment in which Bonn's policies succeeded in building West Germany into a dynamic economic powerhouse.

Yet, unlike Japan and France, West Germany has no systematic industrial development plan that shapes the entire economy and all its major industries. As in most other countries, West Germany's industrial policy is the sum of hundreds of separate and sometimes conflicting policies which have been conceived in response to specific opportunities or problems. Bonn's assistance to industry increased dramatically after 1973 in response to the stagflation caused by OPEC's quadrupling of oil prices that year and further doubling in 1979.

West Germany's federal structure distributes power and policy responsibility between Bonn, the states (*lander*), and local officials. Theoretically, state and local government are fiscally independent of Bonn, and, accounting for four-fifths of public investments, state and local government have considerable industrial policy power. Bonn's power is further restricted by Parliament's upper house, the *Bundesrat*, which is composed of state representatives and approves all major policies. Bonn's assistance to such regional industries as steel, shipbuilding, and coal reflects the power of state and local officials. Yet the state and local governments depend on Bonn for about half of their revenues. Using the power of the purse as a considerable bargaining chip, Bonn continually negotiates with state and local government over public investment decisions.

Like the continent's other political systems, West Germany's proportional representation system allows any party a place in Parliament if it receives over 5 per cent of the vote. The result is a broad representation of society's interests and, except for 1957, continual coalition governments which are solidly anchored in the center of the political spectrum. This political stability and moderation has allowed Bonn's industrial policies to remain consistent despite the political shifts from the Christian Democrats (1948–69), Social Democrats (1969–82), and Christian Democrats again (1982–present). Each government's power has rested on a coalition with the mainstream Free Democrats, and a consensus among all three parties over West Germany's policy goals and means.

West Germany's bank-centered industrial groups are similar to Japan's *keiretsu*, and are the economy's dynamic powerhouses. Because each industry has several powerful firms, and each of those firms is a member of a powerful industrial group, Bonn has never had to follow the strategy of France and Italy which have attempted to merge weak industrial firms lacking the protection of a group into one 'national champion'. Banks hold shares in firms and can send officials to help manage troubled firms. This close bank supervision nips many development problems in the bud, rendering state bail-outs largely unnecessary. As in Japan, the bank's ability to manage the investment decisions of the group has declined as firms have become more prosperous and obtain most of their financing from retained earnings and bond issues. Within German firms, cooperative management-labor relations have been a model for other industrial countries. Through tough but constructive bargaining, decisions are reached which maximize benefits for both the firm and workers. Since 1945, the average number of days lost to strikes in West Germany has been even lower than in Japan.

West Germany's reconstruction was swift. As early as 1948, Ludwig Erhard, the Director of the 'self administration' in the British and American zones dismantled central planning, created a convertible Deutschemark, removed price and wage restrictions, deregulated manufacturing and distribution, and created a central bank, later called the Deutsche Bundesbank. But Bonn continued to aid the market by subsidizing strategic sectors like public utilities, shipbuilding, steel, mining, agriculture, and housing through low taxes, generous depreciation allowances, and industrial 'cooperation'. In addition, in a strategy similar to the Bank of Japan's 'window guidance', the Deutsche Bundesbank rationed scarce credit to these industries to insure they had ample access to low interest capital. Finally, Marshall Plan aid reinforced these industries and helped rebuild the nation's infrastructure. Germany's coal and steel cartels were 'Europeanized' with the 1951 Paris Treaty, an economic boost to all the members. Export dynamism was considered central to West Germany's development. The Deutschemark was devalued in 1949, and export industries subsidized. West Germany has enjoyed virtually continuous trade and payments surpluses since 1951. From the mid-1950s, Bonn played a decisive role in rebuilding the aircraft industry and nurturing a nuclear energy industry.

By the late 1950s, West Germany had achieved full employment, annual average growth rates of 4 per cent, productivity advances greater than wage increases, and minimal inflation. Free markets are a by-product, not a source of economic success. Given West Germany's dazzling economic growth, Bonn felt confident enough to loosen its reins over the economy in the late 1950s. Although the 1957 antitrust law restricted cartels, West Germany's economy continued to enjoy a range of rational macroeconomic and industrial policies. Tax rebates, preferential loans, and a range of subsidies to strategic industries and technologies and backward regions remained important. The Economics Ministry published policy guidelines for strategic sectors in 1966 and backward regions in 1968 by which subsidies were to be extended to the entire industry rather than single firms, would be temporary, would assist rather than replace markets, would be undertaken only in cases of severe economic disruption, and would help firms to help themselves.

In 1972, 42 per cent of government R & D subsidies were targeted on nuclear energy, 21 per cent on data processing, 21 per cent on aerospace, and the remaining 12 per cent on other technologies.[30] Exports were strongly encouraged. The Deutschemark remained undervalued despite a 5 per cent revaluation in 1961. In two decades West Germany's share of world exports doubled, from 5.7 per cent in 1953 to 11.3 per cent in 1973. Labor shortages appeared, and Bonn encouraged the 'temporary' immigration of workers from southeast Europe and elsewhere to man the economy's least appealing jobs. By 1973 West Germany hosted over 2.3 million 'guest workers' who . made up over 10 per cent of the workforce. This influx of foreign workers and their families was a mixed blessing, providing an economic boost at a social cost.

Like the rest of the world, West Germany's economy was battered by OPEC's 1973 quadrupling of oil prices. Growth was halved, the Deutschemark, inflation, and unemployment rose, and 2 million manufacturing jobs (20 per cent of the total) disappeared after 1973.[31] These problems were exacerbated by OPEC's 1979 doubling of oil prices and the 1981–2 global recession. Unemployment reached a plateau of around 10 per cent during the early 1980s and has only slowly declined from there since.

Bonn reacted to these crises by abandoning its more market-driven strategy of the 1960s and taking a more active role in guiding the economy. Boon emulated Japan's long-standing policies by imposing nontariff barriers to protect threatened industries. In addition to continuing to funnel massive subsidies into heavy industry, the government has expanded programs for medium- and small-sized businesses. Firms were allowed to bypass the Cartel Act's restrictions on collusion by merging. Still, outright state ownership of industry remained relatively limited at about 7.5 per cent of total employment and 10 per cent of value-added throughout the 1970s.[32] Since the mid-1980s, West Germany's economy has regained its former dynamism. Like the economies of other industrial countries, West Germany's was boosted by the Reagan's administration's strong dollar policies (1981–5) which simultaneously battered America's export industries and promoted foreign export industries. West Germany's export surge of the 1980s and 1990s helped alleviate many economic problems.

Bonn continues to play a powerful and deft role in leading development through rational industrial policies. The degree and means of Bonn's industrial policies have varied considerably over the decades, flexibly shifting with society's needs and external challenges. West Germany is described as a 'social market economy' in which the country's prosperity is nurtured by the government providing conservative macroeconomic policies which generate low interest rates and inflation; rational industrial policies which aid strategic industries by building infrastructure and permitting both cartels and competition as appropriate; and refereeing conflicts between management and labor so that firms and industries can overcome problems with minimal disruption. Essentially, Bonn's policies aim at steadily expanding the economic pie while ensuring that everyone gets a relatively fair cut.

The triumphant celebrations over the Berlin Wall's fall in 1989, reunification the following year, the Cold War's end, and the transfer of the capital from Bonn to Berlin proved fleeting. Reunification unleashed a range of new challenges and problems, the central one of course being how to integrate two completely different socioeconomic systems and development levels. West Germany's 60 million people had a per capita income as much as four times greater than East Germany's 19 million. West Germany had a dynamic economy which was largely privately owned while skilfully managed by the government. In East Germany, the state owned all production and had grossly mismanaged the economy through rigid five-year plans.

Reunification also stirred concern elsewhere in the Community over the spector of German hegemony. Germany's economy was by far Europe's most dynamic,while the Bundesbank and Deutschemark were unofficially Europe's central bank and lead currency, respectively. Now, with a united German population of 80 million, Germany would have the most representatives of any country in the Community organizations.

Berlin has managed these economic and political problems with finesse. Economic integration and equality between Germany's haves and have-nots will take decades and trillions of Deutschemarks, but progress is steadily being made. Likewise, Berlin is attempting to assuage worries over German hegemony by pressing all the more vigorously for European unification. The enormous costs of financing unification will weigh heavily on West Germany's economy for the indefinite future. Yet West Germany's super-efficient dynamic economy can shoulder the burden and united Germany will emerge eventually all the stronger.

France

If German mercantilism emerged in the mid-nineteenth century, France's originated with the mid-seventeenth century policies of Louis XIV's minister, Jean-Baptiste Colbert. Although to varying extents all the Community members are striving to emulate Japan's successful targeting and nurturing of industries, France continues to pursue the most systematic industrial policies. Like Japan, France is a highly centralized state whose national government dominates policy at the provincial and local levels. France's economy is managed by an elite corp of bureaucrats who have graduated from the best universities and enter government after passing an extremely competitive exam. The government carefully formulates and implements industrial policies which target strategic sectors, industries, technologies, and firms for development. French industrial policies are designed to build competitors, not welfare recipients. Former Prime Minister Raymond Barre succinctly described the government's role as

> to say to the 'patrons': So you want to do such and such? We'll help you. But if in five years you have not succeeded, we'll drop you . . . We must not hesitate to cut out the dead wood . . . the sectors where we cannot compete. The future of France does not depend on the number of ships which we build at a loss, nor on the production of steel which we cannot sell.[33]

But there are significant differences. Unlike Japan whose economy has been dominated by massive industrial groups since the nineteenth century, France's industrial tradition is one of small family-owned firms producing a relatively narrow range of products. Where Tokyo promotes several to a half dozen powerful firms in each industry, Paris has generally tried to nurture one national champion. Although both countries have over 100 public corporations, Japan's complement, while France's are often in, the private sector. Virtually all of Japan's industrial policies have been remarkably successful in developing strategic industries and the overall economy. France's policies have failed to produce national industrial champions which can compete globally or to master old technologies or create new ones. France's industrial policies will never match those of Japan's. Yet, compared to other Community members, French industrial policies have been largely successful. French economic growth and per capita income has generally exceeded that of other European countries. France's distribution of income, however, is less equitable than the Community average.

Unfortunately, there is no French equivalent of Japan's Ministry of Finance (MOF) to lead macroeconomic policy, or Ministry of International Trade and Industry (MITI) to coordinate industrial policy. Instead, French industrial policies are administered by a range of fiercely competitive departments and agencies. The Commissariat du Plan is responsible for France's economic plans. It is composed of government, management, and labor representatives. The Interministry Committee to Manage Industrial Structure (CIASI) is France's leading industrial policy making group composed of high-ranking bureaucrats which meets weekly and determines a strategy for weak firms and industries. CIASI has acted chiefly as a marriage broker between weak and strong firms to overcome problems. The merger is sweetened with government subsidies, low interest loans, and tax breaks. If a white knight cannot be found, CIASI itself may take over and reorganize the firm, shedding unproductive units and firing excess employees. France has numerous funding institutions. More prominent are the Economic and Social Development Fund (FDES) which extends subsidies and low interest loans to industry, the Institute for Industrial Development (IDI) which provides long-term financing for loans and equity to needy sectors, and the Special Fund for Adjusting Industries (FSAI) which gives grants or soft loans to firms which create more than fifty jobs.

Despite the five year plans which guide them, France's industrial policies have experienced considerable shifts since the late 1940s up through today. A consensus on France's industrial policies did not emerge until the mid-1980s. Until then succeeding socialist and conservative governments would reverse the policies of their predecessor. Depending on their economic philosophy and prevailing problems, governments have nationalized or privatized key economic sectors, with resultant disruptions to France's economy. According to Patrick Messerlin, since 1945

> the French state oscillated between two different approaches, each equally well represented along the major political streams. These two approaches agree on one thing: the firm – and not the market – as the key issue in the economic and industrial debate. The first of these approaches – supported by people as different as Jean Monnet, President Pompidou or Pierre Mendes-France – takes a positive view of the firm and, accordingly, sees the public role as one of supporting and protecting French firms, if necessary in the face of market forces . . . The second approach takes a negative view of firms, seeing them as the focus of social exploitation. This approach is well represented . . . from . . . the Communist and Socialist parties to those who share a nostalgia for 'pre-industrial' economic organizations in the parties of the extreme rights.[34]

In 1945, Liberated France faced enormous reconstruction and hyperinflation problems, exacerbated by a socialist-communist coalition government which came to power in 1948. The answer to these problems for both socialist and conservative parties was nationalization. Paris nationalized the banking, insurance, energy, and telecommunications industries between 1945 and 1947, and in the 1950s extended government ownership to automobiles, aerospace, and data processing. Labor truces were bought with wage increases indexed to inflation. Despite this heavy government hand, there was no one national bank which coordinated the government's investment plans for public and private industries. Instead, capital was funneled into targeted industries by such special agencies as the Caisse des Depots, FDES, Credit National, Credit Agricole, and other institutions. As in Japan, large industries were funded at the expense of medium- and small-sized firms. Much of this finance came from the United States. The Marshall Plan contributed 16 per cent of total investments and 35 per cent of public investments between 1948 and 1951. The heavy state role and lack of coordination was costly. From 1950 to 1958, France's average growth rate was 3 percentage points lower than Germany's and 1 point lower than Italy's while its average 5 per cent inflation was 4 points higher than Germany's. France's growth rate, however, far exceeded that of the United States and Britain.[35]

President de Gaulle's eleven years of rule between 1958 and 1969, and subsequent conservative governments gave France political stability and sensible policies which bolstered economic growth and genuine development up through 1973 and have kept the country afloat through a gauntlet of economic crises since then. France's exports and wealth was stimulated by the franc's 17.5 per cent devaluation in 1958 and 10 per cent devaluation in 1971. Meanwhile, Paris followed rational macroeconomic policies of fiscal restraints and tax policies which promoted a virtuous savings/investments cycle. In the mid-1960s, fearing domination by America's corporations and, to a lesser extent, German and Japanese firms, the government inaugurated its 'national champion' strategy of encouraging mergers between firms within each industry through such incentives as generous tax write-offs and cheap government-backed loans. This strategy was very successful. From 1960 to 1973, France's average annual growth rate of 5.5 per cent exceeded Germany's 5.0 per cent rate, although its average 4.5 per cent inflation was well above Germany's 2.9 per cent rate. France enjoyed a 9 per cent share of global exports in 1973.

Exports suffered after the franc was revalued in 1971 and began to float upward after 1973. During the 1970s, Paris began to reevaluate the national champion strategy. The profitability of 'national champions' was lower than other firms in the same industry, while their indebtedness was greater by 30–35 per cent.[36] In 1977, in an attempt to stimulate more competition, Paris passed France's first antitrust law. Paris' subsidies to industry, however, increased steadily throughout the late 1970s into the 1980s. France's web of institutions proliferated as Paris created new institutions to manage each sector.

In June 1981, a socialist-communist-radical party coalition took power and nationalized five major corporations and all but 1 per cent of the remaining private banks. The public sector skyrocketed from 8 per cent to 23 per cent of total manufacturing, and 30 to 100 per cent in energy, steel, nonferrous metals, glass, chemicals, electronics, automobiles, aerospace, and shipbuilding.[37] The result was a disaster. Two years later, Mitterand's government reversed this policy in favor of privatization. Yet Paris remains committed to targeting and nurturing the development of strategic industries. In 1990, Paris announced the commitment of an additional $1 billion to Groupe Bull, France's largest computer maker, and $500 million into Thomson, France's largest consumer and military electronics firm to help it develop high-definition television (HDTV). Shortly after taking office in spring 1991, Prime Minister Cresson asserted that 'Safeguarding and promoting industry will be my priority'.[38] Cresson, however, realized that France cannot go it alone and attempted to forge an EC policy on promoting Europe's high technology industries. After she left office in April 1992, her successor Pierre Bere Govoy promised to continue her policies. It is unlikely, however, that simply channeling more money to strategic industries or more Community coordination of these efforts will be enough to overcome Japan's immense and widening economic lead.

Italy

If there is a miracle economy in Europe, it that of is Italy. In 1945, Italy was poverty-stricken, wracked by hyperinflation and stagnant growth, and threatened by a powerful communist party. Italian industry was mostly small scale, labor-intensive, undercapitalized, and technology-poor. Italy had a dual economy in which a few relatively modern industries and firms provided most of the wealth and exports while the rest of the economy was composed of small family firms and farms. The country was split between the relatively developed north centered around the Turin-Milan-Genoa triangle, and the Third World south (the *Mezzogiorno*).

Today, after four decades of steady high growth, Italy is prosperous, with a diversified and dynamic economy. In the mid-1980s Italy surpassed Britain in GNP and per capita income. Yet problems remain. Metternich's assertion that Italy was a geographic expression still has some validity. Despite four decades of government efforts to eliminate the gap, there remains an enormous difference between the economic dynamism and culture of the industrialized north and the still largely agrarian south. With good reason Italian bureaucracy is still derided at home and abroad as one of Europe's most inefficient, corrupt, disorganized, and bloated. Social security, health, unemployment benefits, and welfare are limited. Massive government red tape and widespread tax evasion remain serious development problems. The greater the bureaucratic inefficiency and lower the tax receipts, the lower the ability of the government to manage the economy either directly or through tax incentives. Most Italian industries are dominated by one or a few powerful private firms, and by four state holding corporations enjoying virtually monopoly power over their respective sectors. With its underdeveloped financial and stock markets, Italian corporations remain dependent on the banks for a major portion of their capital.

Italy's industrial policies were largely piecemeal collections of subsidies, tax breaks, low interest loans, and import protection for industries, sectors, firms, and regions. These policies accumulated over the decades without any overriding philosophy or direction. Pippo Ranci writes that

the Italian Parliament produces several hundred legislative Acts each year, minutely defining minor matters, and each of these requires separate approval by two chambers, often preceded by multiple examination in several parliamentary commissions. Important laws may thus languish for years before being adopted.[39]

From 1945 to the early 1960s, Rome rejected Mussolini's corporatism and industrial policies in favor of free-market oriented policies. There was no massive nationalization of industry, protectionism, or price and wage controls. However, the large existing state-owned industries were not privatized, and the government did subsidize strategic sectors like steel, mining, gas, oil, and fertilizers. Rome also heavily subsidized infrastructure in the *Mezzogiorno* and provided tax incentives for industry to locate there. Extensive land reform starting in 1950 converted disgruntled tenant-peasants into land-owning farmers with a stake in the system and growing buying power. By the late 1950s, Italy achieved full employment.

A center-left government ruled Italy for a decade from 1962 to 1972. The government increased spending for such social sectors as education, welfare, health, public transportation, and housing, and made the tax system more progressive. They also nationalized the electricity industry in 1962. A labor crisis erupted in 1969 when the three major unions cooperated in wringing large inflationary wage and benefits increases from industry and forced the Parliament to pass a Bill of Workers' Rights Act which made it difficult for employers to fire redundant or inefficient workers. Italian inflation rose and productivity fell. The lira's revaluation in December 1971 added to Italy's economic woes. Despite these problems Italy enjoyed virtually continuous trade and payments surpluses between 1958 and 1973.

The growing inflation, lower productivity, and lower growth in Italy in the early 1970s was harshly exacerbated by the lira's floating in 1973 and OPEC's oil shock later that year. Of the major industrial countries, only Japan depended on oil for a higher share of its total energy needs. Rome struggled to control stagflation throughout the 1970s into the 1980s, and began to target strategic industries with a range of subsidies, protection, and cartels.

OPEC's further doubling of oil prices in 1979 and the severe recession of 1981–3 caused inflation, unemployment, and interest rates to spiral and growth drop just as dramatically. During the early 1980s, Italy experienced the same wave of conservatism that was sweeping the other industrial countries. Rome tried a different policy path of reining in its overall spending while continuing to inject subsidies into strategic industries, pursued monetary policies that stimulated a virtuous savings/investment cycle, and cut taxes. About 30 per cent of government subsidies were targeted to the steel industry, 32 per cent to automobiles, 18 per cent to chemicals, and the remainder scattered among a dozen other industries.[40] Italy's recovery was aided by the lira's steady devaluation during the mid-1980s. The result was the steady rise in productivity, manufacturing, and exports starting in the mid-1980s.

Italy remains a curious mix of too much and too little government. Price controls affect everything from haircuts to bread yet there is no regulation of cartels, the stock market, or inside trading. Most observers agree that

> shortcomings in legislation and administrative action are evident in Italy ... Legislation must be more consistent and timely, public administration should be more competent and reliable. The state is not only weak but also unpredictable and inaccurate.[41]

Italy has developed despite rather than because of the bureaucracy. Italy's entrepreneurs are as dynamic as its bureaucrats are inept.

Britain

Britain's decline from the greatest industrial and trade power of the late nineteenth century to the 'sick man of Europe' in the 1970s was steady and seemingly irreversible. How could the leader of the industrial revolution fall so behind other countries?

Geoffrey Shepherd argues that Britain's decline reflects

> a deep-seated institutional conservatism – a resistance to change – with historical roots in the industrial and imperial successes of the nineteenth century. This conservatism was reinforced after World War Two – until the 1970s at least – by a strong political consensus favoring policies of full employment and social welfare. The macroeconomic difficulties that

resulted from the imposition of these policies on a weak economy further removed attention from the micro-economic problems of the industrial sector. Moreover the consensus helped reinforce vested interests opposed to industrial change.[42]

More specifically, until the 1980s the unions rather than managers often determined corporate policy; the government, finance industry, and education system remained aloof from manufacturing in general and troubled strategic industries in particular; entrepreneurship was inhibited by a range of cultural, institutional, and financial obstacles; and manufacturers enjoyed privileged access to the empire and more recently the Commonwealth, and thus have not had to face the full fire of global markets.

There was a relatively steady seesaw in power between the Labour and Conservative parties until 1979. With a 'first past the post' rather than proportional representation system, the Liberal party has largely languished in the political wilderness despite getting as much as 25 per cent of the vote in some elections. The Labour party remains a powerful force in British politics. Britain is one of the few democratic industrial countries in which organized labor has actually strengthened since 1945. The percentage of union workers rose from 39 per cent in 1945 to 52 per cent in 1976! The union's legacy has been 'industrial disruption and . . . a brake on technical change; in the broad they have helped concentrate the collective British mind on issues of income redistribution, while making consensus on policy towards industry very difficult'.[43] Although union power has declined steadily throughout the 1980s into the 1990s, the government is still grappling to overcome its legacy.

Britain's industrial policies have been largely defensive reactions to unforeseen problems and pressures, rather than systematic attempts to develop key industries and the overall economy. Until the 'Thatcher Revolution', there was an economic policy consensus, but it focused on cutting up an existing economic pie more equitably, rather than expanding the pie so that most would enjoy a larger though uneven share. One plus was that with consensus there were not the policy shifts which France experienced. Although the steel industry experienced nationalization and privatization, most industries have been free of such shifting policies.

The postwar Labour government (1945–51) followed full employment and redistribution policies. In the late 1940s, the government nationalized coal, electricity, transport, gas, and iron and steel. Antitrust legislation was passed in 1948. No policies addressed Britain's low productivity, backward technology, or limited entrepreneurship. After the Conservative party gained power in 1951 it reversed most price and production controls, and privatized the iron and steel industry. But it also passed the Restrictive Trade Practices Act in 1956 which reinforced the 1948 cartel law by cracking down on collusive practices.

During the 1960s and early 1970s, there were some incremental shifts in favor of rational industrial policies. In 1961, the government attempted to emulate French-style indicative planning by creating the National Economic Development Council (NEDC) and its secretariat (NEDO), which brought together representatives of government, business, and labor to set economic priorities and policies. In 1965, Parliament passed the Science and Technology, and the Development of Inventions Acts to encourage R & D expenditures and efforts. In 1966, the Industrial Reorganization Corporation (IRC) was created to assist industrial restructuring. London targeted such industries as textiles, shipbuilding, machine tools, and aerospace with a range of subsidies. In 1972, several institutions were combined into the Department of Trade and Industry. Yet despite these new institutions, the government continued to be mostly hostile to business, entangling it in a web of regulations and restrictions.

Britain entered the Community the same year that OPEC quadrupled its oil prices. London responded by reinforcing its industrial policies. Labour ruled through the mid-1970s and kept Britain afloat largely on the huge North Sea oil reserves. These reserves have been a mixed blessing. Although they temporarily freed Britain from oil dependence on unstable foreign sources, they also led to overvaluing of the pound, thus undercutting exports and subsidizing imports, to the detriment of British manufacturing.

In 1979 Margaret Thatcher led the Conservative Party to national victory. The Thatcher government sharply broke with the political consensus favoring a paternalistic, redistributive government. The Employment Acts of 1980 and 1982, and the Trade Union Act of 1984 helped break the back of union power by requiring democratic procedures and removing many of their legal immunities. The government won victories with labor in steel (1980), the civil service (1981), the national health service (1982), and coal (1984–5). It privatized British Aerospace, the National Oil Corporation, British Telecom, and the gas boards, and reduced subsidies for the steel, shipbuilding, and automobiles industries. Government economic regulatory institutions were either cut back or eliminated.

These measures were extremely successful in stimulating economic growth. Britain grew rapidly throughout the 1980s and narrowed the economic gap with more prosperous Community members. In the early 1990s, however, the expansion boom stalled, prices rose, and the market fell. Whether Prime Minister John Major can revive Britain's flaccid economy remains to be seen.

Other European Countries

In his book *Small States in World Markets*, Peter Katzenstein analyzed the industrial policies of seven European countries: Belgium, the Netherlands, Denmark, Austria, Switzerland, Norway, and Sweden.[44] Although there were significant variations, Katzenstein found that the seven share a common pattern of political and economic development. Along with West Germany, the seven have a 'corporatist' political economy in which there is: (1) an ideology of social partnership expressed at the national level; (2) a relatively centralized and concentrated system of interest groups; and (3) voluntary and informal coordination of conflicting objectives through continuous political bargaining between interest groups, state bureaucracies, and political parties. Katzenstein distinguishes this 'democratic corporatism' from the 'liberalism' of the United States and Britain or the 'statism' of Japan and France. He argues that 'political laissez faire is a luxury of large industrial countries, a luxury in which the small European states cannot indulge'.[45]

The corporatist politics and policies of these states were shaped by several important forces. Democratic corporatism emerged in these countries during the 1930s as they struggled to overcome economic depression, political polarization, and class conflict. Unlike larger countries like Germany, Italy, or Spain, the political right was as small and fragmented as the political left. Conservative landed interests were smaller and urban proletariat interests larger. The result was compromise rather than dictatorship. Each country either created or improved a system of proportional representation, which allows a wide representation of interest groups and a tendency toward centrist coalition governments which satisfy most groups along the political spectrum. In addition, the government acted as the 'honest broker' in management-labor conflicts over wages, benefits, technology, and productivity.[46]

Another influence is the small size of these countries and their subsequent vulnerability to international competition. Generally speaking, the smaller the country, the potentially stronger the corporatism, and the larger the country, the potentially weaker the corporatism. Unlike the economic superpowers like the United States and Japan, or middle-ranking economic powers like Germany, France, Britain, or Italy, the small industrial states must maintain open markets in return for access to global markets, because their domestic markets are too small within which to develop economies of scale or to threaten to close off in retaliation for foreign predatory trade tactics. Because they can only produce a relatively limited range of goods, they must import everything else. And in order to pay for their imports they must single-mindedly ensure that their export industries are competitive. Whether they are members of the EC or EFTA, these small states push for liberal trade policies with the rest of the world, and fiercely resist the more protectionist inclinations of their larger neighbors in response to global competition.

The Seven must constantly intervene in their economies to help key sectors adjust to international competition through such policy tools as subsidies, tax holidays, nationalization, concentration, collaboration, and state-assisted research and development, and regional development. Government planning, however, is indicative rather than directive. Government and business constantly search for special product niches to develop. Andrew Boyd succinctly captured this niche strategy in which planners and business leaders

> try to identify a gap which, although quite modest in size, evidently needs filling; and to fill it neatly and quickly, with a product that requires only a small amount of material . . . [and] quite a lot of imagination . . . Mass production is inappropriate; a small team of craftsmen, working under personal supervision, usually gets the best results . . . but they cannot hope to be left undisturbed in possession of their 'niches'. The trick then is to keep one jump ahead by innovation or adaptability.[47]

Corporations form strategic alliances with foreign firms for technology, production, markets, and research and development. Like Japan, these states tend to have dual economies in which there is a highly competitive export sector and a highly protected service sector which soaks up employment. The trade dependence, government expenditures as a percentage of GNP, and extent of nationalized industries in these small states far exceeds those of the larger industrial states or Japan, while their average tariffs are lower and retaliation against foreign trade predators fewer.

There are differences between these states. Katzenstein distinguishes between the relatively passive, 'liberal' industrial policies of governments like Switzerland, the Netherlands, and Belgium and the active 'social' industrial policies of governments like Austria, Denmark, and Norway. Sweden combines elements of both patterns.[48]

FOREIGN POLICY

From its inception, the Community has attempted to achieve and articulate a common policy on different international issues, but its ability to do so has varied from one issue and time to the next.[49] Nonetheless, the Community has become a major power in the global political economy. Brussels has diplomatic relations with over 130 nations and forty international organizations and conferences. Although the primary focus of its foreign policy is to enhance the Community's geoeconomic interests, the EC has also actively attempted to assert its interests in geopolitical issues like conflicts in the Middle East, Indochina, and Central America, the Soviet invasion of Afghanistan, and the Yugoslavian civil war; or in human rights issues in South Africa, the former Soviet bloc, and elsewhere.

The legal basis for the European Community's foreign relations was established by Rome Treaty articles 110–16, 228, and 238; ECSC Treaty's chapter X, and Part Two of the transitional provisions; and the Euroatom Treaty's Chapter XI. These articles largely empower Brussels to create and implement a common commercial policy. Article 229 grants the Direct Commission powers to conduct relations with such international organizations as the GATT, OECD, and UN.

Who makes foreign policy? As in other issues, foreign policy is split among several institutions. Until 1986 when it was superseded by the European Political Cooperation (EPC), the Commission was primarily responsible for foreign policy making and implementation. Within the Commission, the External Affairs Directorate General (DGI) is specifically responsible for foreign policy. Its eight directorates are divided among those responsible for a specific region, international organization, or function. Other DGs which share foreign policy responsibilities include DGVIII (development), DGIII (internal markets and industrial affairs), DGIV (competition), DGVI (agriculture), and DGVII (transport). Committee 113 assists the Commission in implementing its foreign policy responsibilities.

Other institutions have been proposed to deal specifically with foreign policy, but until recently none of the schemes got off the ground. During the 1950s and early 1960s, Brussels considered then rejected such plans as the European Defense Community and the European Political Community (both 1954), and the Fouchet foreign policy plan (1961–2). De Gaulle fiercely resisted any attempts to enlarge the Community's powers. After he left office, the Community once again took up the goal of unification, in 1969 at the Hague summit. The leaders asked the Council of Foreign Ministers (CFMs) to prepare a proposal on greater political cooperation. The CFMs presented a report at the 1970 Luxembourg summit in which they proposed, among other things, the creation of the European Political Cooperation (EPC) as a means of coordinating policy between the member states outside the Rome Treaty framework. The EPC was seen as a way to conduct foreign policy without the divisiveness of attempting to amend the

Rome Treaty. Each member's sovereign right to conduct its own foreign policy would be retained. The only obligation was to consult and attempt to coordinate over key issues.

The EPC's role evolved slowly thereafter. Although the Community agreed on the need for a permanent political secretariat, it split between the French who wanted it in Paris and the others who favored Brussels. Progress was made in forging the building blocks of a common foreign policy, with the first step occurring in May 1971 when the EC made a statement on the Middle East, and it increasingly spoke with one voice at international organizations and on regional and bilateral problems. At the 1973 Copenhagen summit, the Commission was allowed to attend all EPC meetings, required all members to consult each other before deciding on national foreign policies, and delegated coordination to the CFMs. But a second Davignon report issued at the summit backpeddled somewhat from the original report by stressing the non-binding aspects of a common policy which would 'ensure a better understanding of the major problems of international politics through regular information and consultation; . . . to promote the harmonization of views and the coordination of positions; . . . to attempt to achieve a common approach to specific problems'.[50]

According to Rothacher, the 'shock of realising its [the EC's] impotence during the fourth Middle East War and the oil crisis in 1973 signalled the "hour of birth" of coordinated European foreign policies'.[51] At the 1974 Paris summit, the European Council was created as the Community's highest authority, composed of the heads of government and/or state which would meet triannually to decide policy. The Council meetings would be attended by the CFMs, Commission, and EPC. The 1976 Tindemas Report, the Genscher-Colombo Proposal, and the London Report (both 1981), among other things, all called on the Community to have a full foreign policy, and proposed reorganizing the institution to streamline the policy making process. The foreign policy proposals of all three reports were rejected.

The 1986 Single European Act legalized the EPC and integrated it within the Community under the aegis of the Council. Although the EPC now has a secretariat, it depends on the Committee on Permanent Representatives (Coreper), Commission, Council of Foreign Ministers, and other bodies to accept and implement its policy proposals. The Council President is also the EPC President. EPC meetings immediately precede or follow the monthly CFMs meetings. There are over 100 working groups on foreign policy. All EPC meetings are secret.

How does the Community forge the different interests of twelve sovereign states into one policy? The obvious answer is that Brussels emphasizes the members' common rather than their divergent interests. States join the Community because it is in their national interest to do so. The Community is based on common interests, and the depth and breadth of these interests will expand with the Community's integration. There have been surprisingly few conflicts over foreign policy. De Gaulle, Thatcher, and Papandreou have acted as spoilers or independents on Community initiatives. Ireland's neutrality is one significant obstacle to an enlarged military role. Greece tilts to the left on many international issues.

Just what have been the primary Community foreign policies? In his excellent study, Roy Ginsberg identified 480 Community foreign policy actions between 1958 and 1985, of which 167 (35 per cent) occurred up through 1972 and 313 (65 per cent) from 1973.[52] Altogether over the twenty-seven-year period, Brussels conducted 204 bilateral (42 per cent), 178 multilateral (37 per cent), forty-two unilateral (9 per cent), thirty-three interregional (7 per cent), and twenty-three security-related (5 per cent) actions.[50] Most of these foreign policies involved integration, which accounted for 99 per cent of the actions in the earlier phase and 65–70 per cent in the second phase. Ginsberg maintains that 'the granting or denial of membership to European states under Article 237 of the Rome Treaty is perhaps the EC's most important foreign policy. Each decision entails changing the size, scope, nature, and even direction of the EC'.[53]

The Community's foreign policy watershed was OPEC's quadrupling of oil prices and OAPEC's boycott of oil to the Netherlands in November 1973, which also represented Brussels' most glaring failure. European unity dissolved as each member scrambled to cut its own oil supply deal with OPEC and OAPEC, dispatching foreign ministers to the region, promising lavish increases in aid, and distancing itself from Israel. The Council allowed a delegation of Arab foreign ministers to attend and steal the show at their December 1973 Copenhagen Summit. France refused to join other Community members in joining the Washington-sponsored International Energy Agency (IEA), which attempted to act as a buying cartel to offset OPEC.

Since then, like Tokyo, Brussels has followed explicit policies geared toward lessening the Community's dependence and vulnerability to foreign sources of energy and raw materials. Although Europe depends on foreign oil for 80 per cent of its total oil, compared to Japan's 99 per cent dependence, the Community's import dependence on raw materials is comparable to Japan's: copper (81 per cent), iron ore (79 per cent), tin (87 per cent), tungsten (99 per cent), aluminum (61 per cent), uranium (75 per cent), phosphates (99 per cent), lead (53 per cent), zinc (68 per cent), and 100 per cent for manganese, chromium, cobalt, nickel, and platinum.[54] Brussels has attempted to secure its foreign sources of energy and raw materials by taking a balanced policy toward the Arab-Israeli conflict, allowing preferential market access for the sixty-six developing Lome states, and following conservation and diversification natural resource policies. The more interdependent the Community becomes with the rest of the world, the more assertive the Community has become in safeguarding its access to global markets, raw materials, and energy.

Brussels has engaged in a range of multilateral global issues. Since the early 1960s, the Community members have coordinated their efforts in the United Nations and tried to vote and negotiate as a bloc. The Community was granted UN observer status in 1974, which enables the Council President to address the General Assembly annually. The Community participates in all the UN organizations. Brussels also participated in the six rounds of the United Nations Conference on Trade and Development (UNCTAD) which created the general system of preferences (GSP) for developing countries. In 1984, the EC signed the Law of the Sea Treaty, the first time a UN Convention was signed by an international organization.

The Community's most consistent multilateral involvement has been with GATT. It has represented its member states at GATT's Kennedy (1962–7), Tokyo (1974–9), and Uruguay (1984–90) negotiation rounds. It has also frequently found itself before a GATT panel investigating allegations of unfair trade. Between 1948 and 1985, the Community was involved in sixty-two GATT cases, of which it was the defendant in forty-two complaints.[55]

Article 30 allows the GATT agreement to be amended by a two-thirds affirmative vote of members. The Community's most controversial policy toward GATT involves its attempts to reform some of that organization's flaws. Article 1 of its Charter asserts GATT's basic principle of Most Favored Nation (MFN) whereby any bilateral lowering of trade barriers must automatically be extended to all GATT members (Contracting Parties). MFN protects small nations which lack the power to negotiate favorable bilateral trade agreements against the large states which enjoy that power. It also vastly reduces the range of trade negotiations that would have to be conducted if bilateralism prevailed.

Although the EC is solidly committed to maintaining MFN, it has attempted to reform Article 19 which actually encourages neomercantilism. Article 19 allows states to retaliate against foreign predators only if they apply sanctions against all their trade partners, most of whom are probably trading fairly. Thus Tokyo, for example, can continue to pursue its export offensives and import barriers with impunity, since it is unlikely that the victimized countries would risk jeopardizing their relations with other countries in order to retaliate against Japan. Likewise, under Article 6 states can impose countervailing duties against foreign subsidized exports only if they can prove material damage to domestic firms, an often near-impossible task.

The European Community is committed to free trade within its own borders and fair trade with everyone else. On 19 October 1988, the Commission published *Europe 1992: Europe World Partner*, which detailed the process by which a unified market in 1992 had been agreed on, the principles which guided it, and the means for achieving it. The report attempted to allay nonmember fears by proclaiming that it would 'not be a fortress Europe but a partnership Europe' aimed at strengthening 'the concept of mutual benefits and reciprocity'.[56] At the same time, the report asserted that although its unification in 1992 would be based on free trade, the Commission

> reserved the right to make access to the benefits of 1992 for nonmember countries' firms conditional upon a guarantee of similar opportunities – or at least nondiscriminatory opportunities – in those firms' own countries. This means that the Community will offer free access to 1992 benefits for firms from countries whose market is already open or which are prepared to open up their markets on their own volition or through bilateral or multilateral agreements.[57]

Perhaps the most powerful pillar of European power is market power. Brussels' ability to act as the gate-keeper for 380 million affluent consumers gives it tremendous potential power to force its foreign rivals to reciprocate. The Community is clearly based on free trade principles. Yet most Community officials are hardnosed realists on international trade issues. They reject the neoclassical notion that countries which dump their products overseas while protecting their home markets are only hurting themselves while helping others. They recognize that in reality neomercantilist countries build up their own wealth and power at the expense of others.

Brussels is armed with an array of legal powers that enable it to retaliate against foreign predatory dumping and protectionism. Rome Treaty Article 10 empowers the Commission is empowered to act independently of the member governments in fulfilling its trade responsibilities. Through Articles 113 and 116 the member states confer on Brussels the power to conduct trade policy and negotiations on their behalf, including the ability to impose antidumping and countervailing duties against foreign trade predators, and manage the customs union. Article 113 identifies five policy areas: (1) changes in tariff rates; (2) the conclusion of tariff and trade agreements; (3)

the achievement of uniformity in measures of liberalization; (4) export policy; and (5) measures to protect trade in case of foreign dumping or subsidies. Article 3 states that the EC must conclude a common commercial policy toward third countries, while articles 110–16 detail the implementation of such a policy. Article 111 maintains that member states 'shall coordinate their trade relations with third parties' during the transition period to a common commercial policy while Article 113 asserts that the policy 'shall be based on uniform principles, particularly in regard to changes in tariff rates'. Article 115 allows members to impose import restrictions in defense against foreign predatory trade. Article 164 empowers the European Court of Justice to decide any conflicts between national and Community trade policy in favor of the latter. In the EC Commission v. EC Council, Case 221/70 (1971), the Court further ruled that any new trade rules enacted by Brussels automatically precludes members from following their own policies in that area. Article 210, reinforced by a series of favorable European Court of Justice rulings in July 1964, March 1971, November 1975, and November 1978, grants the EC the 'legal personality' to conclude treaties with foreign powers and force its members' treaties to conform to its standards and policies.[58] In other words, the EC can establish diplomatic relations and exchange embassies with foreign countries or international organizations. To date the EC has over 150 diplomatic missions accredited in Brussels. Articles 228 and 229 empower the Commission to open and conduct trade negotiations with other states and international organizations. Article 234 forces all members to eliminate any existing agreements with third states which are incompatible with the Rome Treaty. Article 238 allows for extending the EC's free trade benefits to nonmember states.

Given this array of powers and the global geoeconomic stakes, Brussels has usually not hesitated to retaliate against foreign, and particularly Japanese, predatory trade practices. Martin Wolf writes that like that of any other industrial democracy,

> the trade policy of the European Community is made by compromises among strongly represented regional and industrial interests – but even more so. Given the need for compromise among members states, there is a tendency to agree on the lowest common dominator of protection. The allegedly more liberal countries then salvage their conscience by asserting that they are compromising their principles in favor of the still greater principle of European unity. The tendency to agree on protectionism is reinforced by the fact that decisions are ultimately taken in the Council of Ministers, which will consist of the industry or agricultural ministers

directly concerned . . . [B]ecause of the nature of the European Community, it is only rarely that it can agree on any far-reaching initiatives in global arrangements, where the running has been left almost entirely to the United States. Finally, once reached it is only with great difficulty that a Community position can be modified.[59]

The Community has been particularly active in retaliating against foreign dumping, which occurs when a foreign manufacturer exports its goods at below production costs. The Community's power to investigate and retaliate against foreign dumping exceeds that of the United States. America's anti-dumping process is complicated and transparent, and dumping violators more often than not escape penalty. The Commerce Department and International Trade Commission share responsibility for dumping cases, and must open their books to public inspection. Those found guilty can appeal to the courts. In contrast, the Commission investigates and decides whether dumping has occurred, and then imposes a penalty if the accused is found guilty. The Commission limits the information it provides the accused to 'nonconfidential information' to the parties, so that it has enormous power to act with discretion and decisiveness. Foreign predator traders in the Community are unlikely to get off on technicalities, as can often occur in the United States. Appeals by guilty parties to the European Court of Justice are rarely successful, because the Court's role is to rule on whether the Commission has followed the correct investigative procedures, rather than the case's substantive merits.

Local content rules have become entwined with dumping issues. Although there is no uniform EC ruling on what percentage of a product must be made locally to count as a European product, it did impose a 45 per cent local content standard on televisions in December 1970 and tape recorders in April 1971. In June 1987, the Community adopted new anti-dumping rules which addressed the problem of screwdriver assembly plants. Penalties can now be extended to foreign investors which set up screwdriver assembly plants within the Community in an attempt to evade earlier dumping penalties if the value of foreign parts exceeds domestic parts by at least 60 per cent. In effect, this ruling created a Community local-content rule of 40 per cent, even though Brussels denies there is an official standard. In July 1988, the Council amended its local content 'screwdriver assembly' law to allow the imposition of an antidumping duty if: (1) any products manufactured within Europe are subject to an antidumping duty; (2) where assembly has begun after that firm was made the subject of an antidumping investigation; and (3) where the value of the parts in the assembly originating in a country subject to an antidumping duty are more than 50 per cent of all other parts. Altogether, a 'screwdriver operation' will only be subject to an antidumping duty if the total local content is 40 per cent or less.[60] Many European industries felt even these measures were not enough. In November 1988, the French electronics industry association called for local content rules of 60 per cent rather than 40 per cent.[61]

Reciprocity has been a guiding EC principle since the mid-1980s. President de Clerq articulated this principle at GATT's Uruguay Round in September 1986 when he proclaimed that

> the Community feels that many of the present tensions affecting world trade find their origin in the fact that concessions negotiated between the various contracting parties have in reality not resulted in effective reciprocity. It is therefore essential that the Ministerial Declaration should establish the objective of achieving a genuine balance in the benefits accruing to contracting parties from the GATT.[62]

De Clerq's position was in response to Japan's continued neomercantilist policies.

Although the Community upholds reciprocity as the basis of its international economic relations, the concept remains vague and controversial. Some argue for a 'mirror image' reciprocity in which market shares as well as opportunities would balance; others just request the 'national treatment' of equal opportunity even if those markets are more restricted than the Community's. President de Clerq stated on 29 August 1988 that when 'international obligations do not exist . . . we see no reason why the benefits of our internal liberalization should be extended unilaterally to third countries. We shall be ready and willing to negotiate reciprocal concessions with third countries'.[63]

The EC is attempting to extend the reciprocity principle to specific industries. For example, Article 7 of the Community's 1989 banking directive authorizes the Commission to investigate allegations that foreign nations deny Community banks 'effective market access and competitive opportunities comparable to those accorded by the Community to credit institutions of that country'. If such discrimination is found, the Commission can then seek Council approval to conduct negotiations with the discriminatory government to remove those restrictions. Brussels could retaliate if the foreign country refuses to reciprocate by withdrawing privileges that its firms enjoy in the Community.

Brussels and other victims of predatory trade have attempted to bypass GATT's flaws by negotiating 'voluntary export restraints' (VERs) and 'orderly marketing agreements' (OMAs) with neomercantilist states. In order to comply with GATT, settlements are sealed by the exchange of letters in which the victim requests that the predator keep its exports within reasonable bounds while the predator acknowledges the request. These agreements proliferated during the 1970s, from four in 1971–3 to 100 to 1974–7.[64] The trouble with VERs and OMAs is that producers from both countries benefit temporarily from the cartel arrangement while the consumers of the targeted nation pay higher prices. These arrangements also encourage neomercantilism. Japanese firms, for example, follow a strategy whereby they subsidize the dumping of their products overseas by gouging Japanese consumers in their protected home markets. If the targeted state attempts to negotiate a VER or OMA, Tokyo will dig in its heels while its firms capture ever larger market share and bankrupt their foreign rivals. Yet, at some point the Japanese want a VER or OMA. With a trade cartel agreement, the Japanese firms enjoy windfall profits from the cartelized market within which they have carved enormous shares.

During the Tokyo Round, for quite different reasons, Washington and Japan blocked a Community effort to negotiate a reform of Article 19 so that the victim of predatory trade can retaliate only against the neomercantilist state. Washington upheld Article 19 because of its liberal ideology and policies; Tokyo because of its neomercantilist ideology and policies. Assailed by continuous Japanese dumping attacks, in 1979 the EC announced that it would unilaterally apply a more selective safeguard policy.

Most Community foreign policy involves regional rather than global issues. The reason, according to Ginsberg, is that since

> the EC is itself a regional unit, it prefers organizing its relations with other regions or regional groups, such as the states of Lome Convention, Association of Southeast Asian Nations, southern Africa, Gulf Cooperation Council, Central America, and Mediterranean Basin. A cornerstone of EC foreign policy is to promote other regional cooperation efforts through EC tariff cuts and foreign aid.[65]

Since the early 1960s, Brussels has negotiated a series of agreements with groups of developing countries which conferred preferential trade benefits to the latter. In 1963, the EEC and the eighteen members of the Association of African states and Madagascar signed the Yaounde Convention, in which the latter were designated Associated States and goods from both sides were given tariff reductions, except in the case of protected agricultural goods. The EC also extended aid and investments through the European Development Fund and European Investment Banks, respectively. The relationship was institutionalized through a Council of Associates, parliamentary conference, and Arbitration Court. Under the 1969 Arusha Agreement, Brussels negotiated a similar arrangement with the East African Community. That same year Brussels lowered tariffs on tropical agricultural products at the Yaounde Conference. In 1973, Brussels negotiated the Lome Stabilization of Export Earnings (STABEX) program with forty-six African, Caribbean, and Pacific (ACP) states, a number which has since been increased to sixty-six. That same year, however, Brussels asserted a more protectionist policy when it negotiated and signed the multifiber agreement on behalf of its members, which imposed quotas on textile imports from the developing world. The 1975 Lome Convention included the British Commonwealth within the Yaounde Convention. Altogether fifty-eight developing nations were represented in the agreement, which included a stabilization fund to support their product's export prices and allowed free access to the Community for most agricultural goods without reciprocity. Both sides granted the other Most Favored Nation status. The Mineral Export Earnings Stabilization (MINEX) is a Lome offshoot in which Europeans and representatives of mineral-rich developing countries negotiate prices, production, and investment. Under the 1979 and 1984 Lome conventions Brussels agreed to increase its aid to those countries. Other Community trade agreements include those with Uruguay (1973), Mexico, Israel, and Sri Lanka (1975), Bangladesh, Pakistan, Algeria, Morocco, and Tunisia (1976), Egypt, Syria, Jordan, and Lebannon (1977), Yugoslavia and Brazil (1980), India and the Association of Southeast Asian Nations (ASEAN) (1981), and the Andean Pact (1983). The premier focus of Community policy toward the Third World, however, has been the Mediterranean Basin in the Community's backyard. The EC has signed trade and aid agreements with every state in the region except Libya and Albania.

In contrast to the Community's comprehensive policy toward the Third World, neither Brussels nor Washington has a coherent or explicit policy toward the other. This is ironic considering that Washington was the godfather of West European unification, pressuring the Europeans to work together through the Organization of European Economic Cooperation in order to receive Marshall Plan aid and applauding each step toward unification since. But the Atlantic alliance overshadows all other bilateral relations. Although Europe's leaders and public have often criticized American military interventions elsewhere, support for NATO remains strong even in the post-Cold War world. President Kennedy's 1962 'Grand Design' and Kissinger's 1973 'Year of Europe' policies were both efforts to elicit greater burden sharing and consultation with Europe over geoeconomic and geopolitical issues. Both policies failed to elicit anything more than criticism for what was perceived as Washington meddling in European affairs. Washington, in turn, has frequently complained of Europe's soft line on issues like the Iranian takeover of the US embassy and the Soviet invasion of Afghanistan. Since 1974, the Community has occasionally provoked Washington's temper by taking independent positions on regional conflicts in the Middle East, Central America, southern Africa, and elsewhere, and on the gas pipeline to the Soviet Union.

There have been geoeconomic conflicts as well. In 1963–4, Washington and Brussels 'fought' the 'Chicken War' over Community restrictions on its poultry market. President Nixon's August 1971 suspension of the dollar's convertibility into gold and imposition of a temporary 10 per cent tariff increase, devaluation of the dollar in December 1971, and floating of the dollar from March 1973 caused resentment on the other side of the Atlantic. Since then the major geoeconomic conflict has been over the Community CAP policy. The deadlock on the farm subsidies issue was the main reason for the collapse of the GATT Uruguay Round in December 1990.

But these sporadic geopolitical and geoeconomic squabbles have proved largely ephemeral. Relations between Washington and Brussels remain strong. The United States and Europe have exchanged permanent diplomatic missions, and ranking officials meet biannually to discuss outstanding issues.

The EC has increasingly taken an active role in geopolitical and human rights issues, even when they do not directly impinge on Community interests. Its first human rights stand occurred in 1965 when it imposed economic sanctions against Rhodesia in compliance with a UN resolution. The Community's first independent imposition of sanctions, however, occurred in 1967 against the military government which came to power in Greece and lasted until 1974. In addition, it has at various times imposed economic sanctions on Turkey, Spain, Poland, Grenada, Argentina, South Africa, and Yugoslavia.

The EC has intervened in several regional conflicts since its first joint policy declaration on the Middle East in May 1971. Since 1974, it has conducted an evenhanded policy toward the Middle East. In 1980, the Community extended *de facto* recognition to the Palestinian Liberation Organization (PLO) and supports a homeland for the Palestinian people. In 1974, it conducted its first security-related action when it aided anti-Marxist forces in Portugal's civil war. But attempts to mediate conflicts in the Middle East (1980–1), Central America (1984), the Persian Gulf, and Southern Africa failed in part because the United States was opposed.

During the 1980s, the Community steadily forged a military organization and policy autonomous from NATO. Europeans revived the West European

Union (WEU), which had languished since its founding in 1955, in response to the Reagan administration's doubling of the defense budget, bellicose rhetoric, and seemingly erratic and irresponsible military adventures in Central America, Libya, Lebanon, Southern Africa, Grenada, and elsewhere. In October 1984, representatives of the nine member states met and reorganized the institution into a think tank on European security issues. Other think tanks like the Eurogroup and Independent European Program Group have acquired more prominence in debating policy options.

Paris and Bonn have had defense ties since 1955 when France first stationed troops in West Germany. The Paris-Bonn alliance allows the French to maintain the illusion of being independent of NATO while in reality forming a major component of its defense. The 50,000 man French II Crops of three tank divisions is stationed in West Germany, plus 10,000 civilian workers and 30,000 dependents. These ties expanded throughout the 1980s. Joint exercises were expanded and in 1987 Paris acknowledged that it would extend the deterrence of its nuclear forces to cover West Germany, theoretically alleviating the need for Bonn to acquire its own nuclear forces. Even after de Gaulle took France out of NATO, although not out of the defense treaty, there was no question that France would not join the defense of Europe against a Soviet attack. On 26 March 1987, Prime Minister Raymond Barre made this commitment explicit when he asserted that 'all must be made aware that for France, the battle begins the very moment West Europe, and primarily West Germany, suffers aggression'.[66] In 1989, Paris and Bonn formed the Defense and Security Council to coordinate planning and policy. The Council is composed of the German Chancellor, the French President and Prime Minister, and the foreign and defense ministers and army chief of staffs of both countries. In 1987, Chancellor Kohl proposed the creation of a Franco-German brigade as an alliance symbol, which was finally created in October 1990 with 4,200 men in two infantry battalions, one armoured battalion, and one artillery battalion. Mitterand and Kohl emphasized that the closer defense ties between their countries and the West European Union's revival was meant to supplement rather than replace NATO.[67] The WEU and the Paris-Bonn alliance are frequently criticized for not adding one soldier to defense but merely another layer of bureaucracy to an over-institutionalized Europe.

Few observers fail to see the irony in West Europe finally beginning to accept the responsibility for its own defense at a time when the Cold War is over and the Soviet empire dismembered. Yet a Soviet military threat to the West was always grossly exaggerated. George Kennan was right all along – the Soviet threat was primarily ideological. Communism breeds in economic stagnation and gross inequality. Soviet expansion via foreign communist parties is thus best contained by predominantly economic rather than military means. By rebuilding Western Europe and Japan as pillars of a revitalized global political economy, Washington could contain Moscow's ideological threat. The communist threat had in reality largely dissolved by the 1950s as Europe and Japan achieved a virtuous cycle of economic growth and distribution, and political stability. Over time, isolated and surpassed by the global economy, the Soviet Union would mellow and crumble, with its remnants eventually rejoining the civilized world.

Today, with the revolutionary transformation of East Europe and the Soviet states from quasi-totalitarian rule into market economic and political systems, Europe's military security concerns have considerably lightened. If there is any threat from the East at all, it is through the mass invasion of refugees unleashed by the economic collapse of the new regimes. The EC has launched massive aid and economic initiatives to prop up the nascent East European and Soviet democracies, and throughout 1991 and 1992 attempted to mediate the Yugoslavian civil war.

The European Community's foreign policies have been extensive. How successful have they been? Some critics assert that Brussels' foreign policy is all "'sound and fury signifying nothing", a massive diplomatic system producing verbiage but few substantive achievements'.[68] Christopher Hill provides a balanced analysis:

> European foreign policy is not a flop: it serves functions which are undramatic but nonetheless real, such as the development of a coherent Western outlook on international relations which is not simply a pale echo of the United States . . . It has helped to draw together a disparate group of states together in a broadly common cause, and is thus able to reinforce the internal movement toward cooperation . . . If it is not a complete flop, however, the Community clearly is not a true power bloc . . . Although third states may show many signs of accepting that the Community is an important actor in certain sectors of international activity, there is a qualitative gap between the perceptions held of NATO and the Warsaw Pact, and those of the EC.[69]

The Community's most successful foreign policy has been toward itself. Unification has overcome a range of traditional and contemporary political, economic, and cultural animosities that in the past frequently resulted in war, to build a prosperous, dynamic, democratic political economy embracing 380 million people.

Part II
The Japanese Challenge

3 Japan at Home: The Corporatist State

During the summer of 1991, Japan was rocked by the revelation of two immense interrelated financial scandals. In June an investigation by the Tax Office of twenty-one Japanese securities firms revealed that they had kicked back over $1.5 billion to over 600 favored clients, including organized crime bosses (*yakuza*) and a government pension fund. The Big Four securities firms – Nomura, Daiwa, Nikko, and Yamaichi – accounted for about $1 billion of the total. Then in August it was revealed that Japan's largest banks and other financial institutions had handled over $5 billion in fraudulent loans. Yet even these huge amounts of money and types of corruption were considered only the iceberg's tip.

Why did the kickbacks occur? Whether they wanted to or not, after the stock and real estate markets began to tumble in 1989, according to Japanese business imperatives, Japan's securities and banking corporations had to compensate their favored clients. The compensation accounted for only 0.4 per cent of the industry's assets, a small price to pay to retain favored clients and keep out foreign financial firms. The brokerages and banks claimed that their transactions were perfectly legal. The law states that compensation cannot be promised, but says nothing about being rewarded. Certainly, the paybacks to favored clients were promised, but Japanese style, with a wink and nod. There is no documentation.

How could the brokerages and banks afford to suffer such huge losses? And why did not the omniscient Finance Ministry intervene, stop the illicit kickbacks, and punish the perpetrators? Quite simply, like all other sectors of Japan's economy, the financial sector is protected. For over four decades, the Ministry of Finance (MOF) has used 'administrative guidance' to develop the securities and banking industries into global champions. These policies have been extremely successful. The world's six largest banks and four largest securities corporations are all Japanese. No Japanese bank has failed since 1942.

The MOF was not only perfectly aware of the extra legal securities and banking practices: it encouraged them. The Big Four and other securities firms gained windfall profits from the fixed commissions allowed by the MOF, and then used those profits to underwrite losses by their favored clients. It was only when the compensation threatened to sink the industry that MOF signaled that no more compensation need be paid, and none was after March 1990.

Despite a decade and a half of 'liberalization', Japan's financial markets remain very much an insiders' game, in which prices and shares are set by relationships rather than free markets. The MOF, the financial firms, and LDP are tightly knit. About fifty MOF officials annually 'descend from Heaven' into high-level sinecures (*amakudari*) in Japan's securities and banking industries. The security and banking firms are big contributors to the ruling political party, the LDP, by some estimates supplying as much as one-half of the LDP's finances.[1]

How did Tokyo handle the scandal? As with other scandals, Tokyo responded with several slaps on the wrist of those most prominently involved. The MOF 'encouraged' the presidents of Nomura and Nikko to resign, which they did on 24 June. Considering the forced resignation unjust, Nomura's president then blew the whistle on MOF's complicity. The MOF then admitted that it knew that the firms were improperly subsidizing their clients, but adopted the industry's argument that although promising to pay such kickbacks are illegal, actually paying back money is not illegal. Finance Minister Ryutaro Hashimoto announced he would take a 10 per cent pay cut for three months.

As the banking scandal and more embarrassing details were revealed, the pressure built on Tokyo to respond more vigorously. The MOF announced on 8 October that Nomura, Japan's largest securities corporation and perpetrator of the scandal, would have to close temporarily more than half of its domestic branches and some of its key departments. It also recommended ending the fixed commissions that contributed to the problem, but resisted a proposed bill that would dramatically revise Japan's Securities and Exchange Law that would impose penalties on any violators of the compensation rule. Taking its cue, the Tokyo Stock Exchange levied small fines on the twenty-one firms. In yet another empty gesture, Finance Minister Hashimoto resigned on 14 October 1991 two weeks before he was scheduled to step down.

The scandal proved extremely costly to Japan's financial industry. The disclosures further depressed Japan's stock markets, with daily sales averaging 300 million rather than the 1 billion at height of the bull market in 1989. European and American investors are avoiding any deals with the Japanese financial giants, while the twenty-five foreign brokerages in Japan capitalized on the scandal by managing to double their market share from 8–9 per cent in 1990 to 16–17 per cent by late 1991.

Despite these favorable outcomes for themselves, foreign reaction was one of angry criticism. The US Securities and Exchange Commission began an investigation into whether the Japanese had conducted similar compensation schemes in the United States. Washington, however, refused to press Tokyo to establish a Japanese Securities and Exchange Commission with the full power to investigate and prosecute violators. Of course, even if Tokyo created such an agency there is no guarantee that it would be any more effective than the toothless Fair Trade Commission (FTC) in preventing Japanese business collusion.

The 1991 securities scandal revealed that Japan's economy remains carefully managed by webs of cartels, favoritism, and personal relationships rather than free markets and law, despite all contrary claims. The machinations of Japan's securities firms and banks are simply Japanese business as usual. There are no free markets in Japan. All Japanese markets are carefully managed by the most powerful firms, which occasionally throw foreign firms a bone or two if their governments exert enough concerted pressure.

There is an enormous and unbridgeable chasm between the image that the Japanese so vigorously cultivate of a free market Japan, and the reality of carefully managed markets, hundreds of cartels, and widespread law breaking. In reality, close collusion rather than unbridled competition fuels the 'Japanese miracle'. Foreigners do not sell more in Japan, even when their products have a competitive advantage, because they are either outright shut out or allocated only a tiny market sliver by Japan's government and business.

How does Japan's political economy run? How are policies made and implemented? Just as there are no free markets in Japan, there is likewise no Japan Inc. in which the country is run like a giant corporation in which the government is the board of directors and each industry a corporate division. This chapter will analyze Japanese corporatism, with sections on each leg of the governing triad, policymaking, and policies.

THE GOVERNING TRIAD

Who runs Japan?

Japan is a very viable liberal democracy with a written constitution, multi-party electoral system, independent judiciary, and clearly defined and enforced civil rights for its citizens. Yet, in many ways, Japan's liberal democratic institutions are shaped by values and behavior which have evolved for over 1,500 years. Virtually all analysts agree that Japan is run by a 'governing triad' of elite bureaucrats, conservative politicians, and corporate executives, an arrangement described as 'corporatism without labor'.[2] Stockwin describes the dynamics governing ruling triad relations:

> the LDP depended upon the bureaucracy for technical expertise and legislative initiative; the bureaucracy depended upon the LDP for parliamentary majorities in favour of government legislation, and for jobs on retirement; the LDP depended upon big business for electoral funding; big business depended upon the LDP for political backing, advantageous policies, and political stability; big business depended upon bureaucracy for favours in the drawing up and implementing of legislation (and more broadly in the exercise of bureaucratic discretion); the bureaucracy depended upon big business for jobs on retirement.[3]

Of these linkages, perhaps the most important is the second careers (*amakudari*) of Japan's elite bureaucrats in private or public corporations, or the LDP. In 1990, 228 top officials received executive positions in firms that they had supposedly been 'regulating'. Of 434 positions in seventy-two public corporations, 79 per cent were held by former bureaucrats.[4] The Triad's bonds are further tempered by graduation from the same universities, particularly Tokyo University, and intermarriage.

All these bonds are reinforced by the cultural values of hierarchy, conformity, and groupism, and accented by a fierce and persistent Japanese nationalism. There is probably no industrial democracy which is more nationalistic than Japan. Although Japanese claim that *sangyo damashii* (industrial spirit) has replaced the wartime *yamato damashii* (Japanese spirit) as Japan's psychic energy source, in a sense *sangyo damashii* is simply a modern manifestation of Japan's traditional spirit. Japanese will rally around the flag on any trade dispute, no matter what the merits of the case.

Japan's tight government-business relationship is centuries old. The exchange of government protection for business finance developed through the quasi-totalitarian political system of Tokugawa rule (1600–1868), and the state-led industrialization of the early modern (1868–1945) and modern (1945–present) eras, and is cemented by both deep cultural and pragmatic bonds. Bower writes:

> Japanese companies believe that it is helpful to have organizations such as MITI that use the best intelligence possible to provide a view of the industrial situation and powerful bureaucrats to negotiate with other ministries and the Diet. The bureaucrats at MITI believe it is essential to

have strong, independent private companies to develop and implement strategic plans. These beliefs contribute to the basis for a consensus-building process in which the companies accept an interference from, or a dependence on, the government that German, United Kingdom, and United States companies would find unacceptable.[5]

While virtually all analysts agree that the 'governing triad' continues carefully to manage Japan's economy, they are divided over exactly how it is managed, and which leg of the triad, if any, is predominate. Most Japanese and foreign observers agree with Chalmers Johnson that in Japan the bureaucrats rule and politicians reign. According to Johnson, Japan's elite bureaucracy 'makes most major decisions, drafts virtually all legislation, controls the national budget, and is the source of all major policy innovations in the system'.[6] Others argue that the conservative Liberal Democratic Party (LDP) is increasingly taking the lead in policy making if not implementation.[7] Although most would agree that Japan's prime minister is weak, not many would go as far as Karel van Wolferen that Japan has no political center and no one really rules the country.[8]

Who is right? The correct answer is that it depends on the time and the policy. Elsewhere I have argued that Japan's political economy has developed from a bureaucratic-dominant corporatism in the late 1940s through the mid-1960s, into a corporatist system in which there was a relative balance of power among the elite from the late 1960s to the early 1980s, and since then into a neo-corporatist system in which other groups – labor, the opposition parties, entrepreneur firms, and foreign firms – play an increased symbolic if not substantive role.[9] Japan's growing prosperity increasingly frees the corporate world from bureaucratic control, the LDP policy groups (*zoku*) are increasingly setting the policy agenda, entrepreneurs and foreign firms are slowly enhancing their market slivers in some industries, and three decades of pressure from Washington and Brussels have pushed Tokyo to reduce some of its most blatant neomercantilist policies. Japan's political economy and policymaking system have become so complex that it is impossible to say which leg of the triad is more powerful. The mix of actors and their power balance varies sharply from one issue to the next. Generally speaking, the bureaucracy and business tend to shape most incremental policies while the LDP steps in and decides in crises. The only constant is that, except for farm policy, one or more of the triad is the dominant force shaping that particular issue.

These changes, however, have not been revolutionary. Japan's political economy largely remains corporatist in structure and neomercantilist in orientation. Policy-making power has steadily decentralized amongst thousands of mini-triads at the national, provincial, and local levels, composed of business interests, politicians, and bureaucrats, and bound by the ability to siphon off massive amounts of wealth and power from the system. Consensus building (*newmawahi*) among the related mini-triads or power clusters in any given issue is incredibly time-consuming and complex, as each seeks either to defend or enhance its own position and has a veto power over any final decision. National interests provide the parameters in which decisions or nondecisions are reached. The result is that, more often than not, protectionism has increased rather than diminished, although in much more insidious and opaque forms. Japan has been called a 'reactive state' which only changes in response to domestic or foreign crisis.[10]

Policy councils (*shingikai*) are the most important means of forging a national consensus around particular policies. There are 214 official *shingikai* attached to the ministries and agencies with the responsibility for acting as public policy forums. These councils are composed of representatives from Japan's ministries, business, LDP, mass media, universities, labor unions, and opposition parties with an interest in each particular subject. They do not make policy, but simply debate and eventually forge a consensus on policies delivered from the ministries and LDP policy groups.

Legislation is formulated and passed in a zig-zag pattern through the political system. About 100 laws are annually enacted by the Diet, of which about 85–90 per cent originate in one of the ministries. Until recently the ministries researched and wrote appropriate bills and sent them on to the LDP's Policy Affairs Research Council (PARC) for approval. Increasingly, however, the bureaucrats and the LDP policy groups (*zoku*) work together to draft bills and policy, and then submit them to the appropriate PARC division for approval. After the Cabinet approves the bill it is sent to the LDP Diet Strategy Committee which determines the bill's timing and priority, and then sends it on to the appropriate committee. The bill can be altered slightly in committee if it is controversial and there are enough opposition party members.

Although, according to the Constitution, the Diet is supposed to be Japan's highest authority and law maker, in reality the Diet simply ratifies decisions made elsewhere in the system. Despite the continual bickering, there is tremendous cooperation between the political parties. The Japan Socialist Party (JSP), Democratic Socialist Party (DSP), and Clean Government Party (CGP) vote with the LDP 90–5 per cent of the time, and the Japan Communist Party (JCP) goes along on 75–80 per cent of the votes.

Japanese policymaking often experiences gridlock during a crisis when each important interest in an issue can wield a veto over decisive action. These policy gridlocks are becoming more frequent as power within the governing triad steadily defuses to traditionally secondary ministries, industries, and corporations while Japan's growing economic power collides more frequently with foreign national interests.

Foreign governments are increasingly the ghosts at Japan's policymaking tables. Powerful and persistent foreign pressure (*gaiatsu*) may well be the only means of cutting through these iron triangles. In international negotiations, Japan's political and bureaucratic leaders have been known not only to advise their foreign counterparts to criticize Japanese neomercantilism but even to threaten retaliation. Only then can the leadership convince elements of the triad in question to concede on some point, even though the concession is almost invariably symbolic rather than substantive. The public relations cost of Japanese intransigence is high. Although some Japanese admit that foreign pressure is necessary and progressive, that the same foreign pressure will be denounced as 'Japan bashing' across Japan's political economic spectrum. Meanwhile, the foreign understanding of Japan as a thoroughly neomercantilist state will deepen.

THE BUREAUCRACY

Powerful bureaucrats have ruled Japan for almost 400 years since the country was unified in 1600. It is the bureaucratic rather than political or business elite which provides long-term direction for Japan's economic development, although since 1945 the bureaucrats have gone from the economy's steering wheel to the back seat. Vogel writes that:

> The Japanese bureaucracy provides vigorous direction on many major issues . . . and during this process they are in close touch with all relevant groups to make sure they understand the evolving decisions . . . The relevant groups are not expected to agree with all decisions made by the bureaucrats. Sometimes a group's interests are not in keeping with the emerging decision, and this group must be made to understand the necessity of the decision and the well-considered impartiality of the decision. If that group is disadvantaged by this decision, then it is understood that they will be given special consideration now or in the future. The long-term continuity in bureaucratic leadership, unimpaired by changes of politicians, ensures the reliability of bureaucrats in carrying through future commitments.[11]

Although Japan's corporatism and industrial policies have often been compared to those of France, according to Wilks and Wright, 'Japanese bureaucratic capacity for authority, control, and innovation outstrips the French'.[12]

The government bureaucracy seems to be set up on the principle that 'less is more'. Japan's 1.2 million bureaucrats account for only 4.5 per cent of the population or 9 per cent of total employment, compared to figures of 6–9 per cent and 12–15 per cent, respectively, in other industrial democracies. Of these officials, 40 per cent have entered by passing one of three examinations, but only about 18,000 have passed the Class I exam into the higher civil service. These elite officials are largely graduates of the Faculty of Law of Tokyo University (*Todai*), which has the country's highest admission standards and was founded in 1877 for the express purpose of training Japan's future officials. In 1991, twenty-two of the twenty-four new members of the Ministry of Finance, and at least half of all the other ministries were *Todai* graduates. The National Personnel Authority (NPA) is responsible for administering the three civil service exams, and selecting and training officials.[13]

Becoming an elite bureaucrat is not as popular as it once was among Japanese college graduates. In 1978 a record 60,948 students applied to become one of 1,000 top ministry or research institute officials; in 1990 the number of applicants had dropped to 30,102. A 1990 National Personnel Authority survey revealed that 84 per cent cited 'low salary' and 55 per cent 'tough work conditions' as reasons for not applying. Despite the drop in application, there are still enough top applicants for the ministries so that they need never fear losing their brain trust. Of the 1990 applicants, about half – 14,836 – applied for the 'elite track'. Of this number only 508 passed the gauntlet of exams, of which 310 accepted government posts.[14]

Yet, powerful as are Japan's officials, the bureaucracy itself is split between and within the twelve ministries, dozens of agencies and commissions, and over 100 public corporations. Each ministry is divided into six to twelve functional bureaus (*kyoku*), which are subdivided into departments (*bu*), and departments into sections (*ka*), an arrangement known as a 'slivered administration' (*tatewari gyosei*).

The Prime Minister's Office (PMO, *Sorifu*) is responsible for consensus building and policy coordination among the ministries, politicians, and business groups. Yet its powers are limited. The Cabinet is composed of the Prime Minister, twelve ministers, and several agency heads. The LDP president automatically becomes the Prime Minister, but the president is chosen only after a fierce battle among the LDP's half-dozen factions. The Prime Minister then chooses his ministers for political rather than professional reasons, and generally allocates among the leading members of each faction in proportion to that factions' numbers of Diet members. The ministers are rotated rapidly to satisfy the LDP factions' demands for status. The average length in office is little over a year. Their role is primarily to act as advocates for their ministry's policies and budget requests.

Where then is macroeconomic industrial, trade, and foreign policy power concentrated among the ministries? Among twelve ministries, the Ministry of Finance (MOF) is supposed to govern macroeconomic policy, Ministry of International Trade and Industry (MITI) industrial policy, and the others the specific industries for which they are responsible. In reality, although MOF and MITI are the two most powerful ministries, every ministry has its own client industries whose status, power, and income it fiercely protects. The lines between the 'policy ministries' (*seisaku kancho*) like MITI and MOF, and the other 'operational ministries' (*jigyo kancho*) are becoming increasingly blurred as they battle over policy turf. All have become industry-nurturing ministries (*genkyoku*). Ito notes that in March 1984 MITI was struggling with nine different bureaucracies: with the Ministry of Posts and Telecommunications (MPT) over telecommunications; with the Ministry of Education (MOE) over computer software copyrights; with MOF on financial liberalization; with the Science and Technology Agency (STA) over biotechnology; with the Ministry of Foreign Affairs (MFA) over GATT negotiations; with the Ministry of Construction (MOC) on the technopolis program; with the Ministry of Transport (MOT) over the urban traffic system; with the Ministry of Agriculture, Forestry and Fisheries (MAFF) over agricultural market liberalization; and the Environmental Agency (EP) over the conservation of lakes.[15] Nowadays, MITI is not the most protectionist ministry. Instead, the other ministries defend their special clients just as fiercely as does MITI. The power of these other ministries has been reinforced by their alliance with the LDP policy groups (*zoku*), relationships which have evolved over the past two decades and are increasingly entrenched. In return for support against MITI, the politicians extract as much public works spoils from the system as possible and carry it back to their respective districts.

In addition to struggles between the ministries, there is a constant tug of war between the ministries and the LDP and business. As if these struggles were not enough, within each ministry, the technical officials (*gikan*) are increasingly challenging the elite officials (*jimukan*) for primacy in managing high technology projects. Competition between and within the different institutions represents an incessant war of all against all over policy turf (*newabari arasoi*).

Despite this diffusion of power, MOF remains by far Japan's strongest ministry. Not only is it solely responsible for Japan's macroeconomic policies but, as we have seen, through highly rational and interventionist industrial policies it has also nurtured the banking, insurance, and securities industries into global champions.

MOF's most important power, however, is its responsibility for shaping the annual government budget. By determining who gets what, MOF has the final say over each industrial policy. Budget making consumes the entire fiscal year. In April the bureaucracies begin compiling their budget requests for the next fiscal year. In July MOF submits a draft budget to the government which allocates financial ceilings for each government bureaucracy and program. Each government bureaucracy then works with its political and business associates to fulfill specific requests and needs, which are formally submitted and reviewed by MOF between September and December. MOF then submits a preliminary budget to the ministries around 20 December which commences a final round of negotiations. MOF sends the final budget to the Budget Committee of the House of Representatives toward the end of January, which approves it and sends it on to the House floor for approval in February. The budget is then submitted to and passed by the House of Councilors during March and become law in early April.

Japan's fiscal policies have changed dramatically since 1945. From 1945 to 1949, MOF was heavily politicized and continually ran enormous budget deficits to patronize the then separate conservative parties, the Liberals and Democrats. Deeply concerned with this fiscal irresponsibility, Washington dispatched a financial expert, Joseph Dodge, to Japan in February 1949 to reform Japan's macroeconomic policies. One of Dodge's most important reforms was to force the government to balance the budget. From 1949 until 1965 Tokyo not only balanced the budget but the rapid economic growth actually stimulated enough tax receipts so that there were frequent budget surpluses, which were returned as rebates to households and businesses. Starting in 1965, Japan began running steadily larger international payments surpluses, and politicians and businessmen increasingly pressured MOF to boost its spending for public works and welfare. MOF complied and from 1965 to 1974 Japan financed its modest budget deficits with bonds rather than taxes. These budgets became enormous in the mid-1970s as Japan's economic growth was halved with OPEC's quadrupling of oil prices and the global recession and public works and welfare programs started in the early 1970s increasingly demanded more money. Japan's outstanding debt to GNP ratio rose rapidly from 9.8 per cent in 1975 to 28.8 per cent in 1980. Tokyo finally reined in its burgeoning budget deficits in the early 1980s, by reducing its budget increases from 1.8 per cent in the fiscal year 1982 to –0.1 per cent by 1984, and cutting its bond dependence ratio from 32.6 per cent in 1980 to 11.6 per cent in 1988. Japan's outstanding debt to GNP ratio, however, continued steadily to rise to 43.5 per cent in 1988.[16]

Yet another tremendous power source is MOF's access to Japan's postal savings money, which it shares with MPT. Japan's postal savings system of over 18,000 post offices is an important source of both policy and political power. The system is the world's largest bank, and its money is ultimately deposited in the MOF controlled government corporation, the Fiscal Investment and Loan Program (FILP). MOF can channel that immense ocean of funds virtually anywhere in the economy for both economic and political reasons. The postmasters themselves hold hereditary positions which are appointed by the LDP and they have enormous local political power to mobilize support during elections and funds anytime.

Compared to MOF's 17.010 trillion yen and 14,518 personnel in 1990, MITI had only 5,530 personnel and 726 billion yen ($5 billion) in funds, or about 1 per cent of the total budget. Judged by personnel or budget, MITI ranks only eighth.[17]

But size can be deceptive. Since its creation in 1949, MITI has led Japan's industrial policies. MITI's Industrial Policy Bureau, whose head is second only to MITI's vice minister in importance, is the most powerful of these institutions. Industries are nurtured through the relevant industrial bureaux: Basic (metals, petrochemicals), Machinery and Information (microelectronics, automobiles), and Consumer Goods (textiles, paper and pulp). Trade policy is administered by two bureaux: the International Trade Policy Bureau, which is divided into divisions representing different global regions and coordinates Japan's overall trade strategy; and the International Trade Administration Bureau, which deals with such tactical trade issues as trade promotion, export insurance, and emergency import programs. Working closely with MOF, EPA, and other relevant ministries and agencies, MITI has continually guided the economy to higher levels of industrial and technological development.

MITI's powers were enormous during the 1950s into the 1960s. The 1949 Foreign Exchange and Foreign Trade Control Law and 1950 Foreign Investment Law empowered MITI to control any capital, technology, and products flowing into and from Japan. These sweeping laws were reinforced by scores of industry-specific laws and thousands of other laws, regulations, and ordinances which gave MITI enormous power to direct the economy.

MITI's technology procurement and dissimination policies were probably its most important. With the power to close the gate to foreign exports and investments, MITI limited competitive foreign firms to a cruel choice. Unable to sell directly from their home countries or a factory in Japan, foreign firms could only license their technology to their Japanese rivals.

Between 1950 and 1980, MITI and other ministries negotiated over 25,000 technology or product licensing agreements with foreign firms, worth $6 billion: a tiny fraction, however, of the financial resources, manpower, and time it would have cost Japanese firms to develop that technology on their own.

MITI used these powers to lead the transformation of Japan's economy from that of a Third World country into the economic superpower it is today. Japan's most dynamic heavy and high technology industries – steel, shipbuilding, petrochemicals, automobiles, microelectronics, computers, semiconductors – owe their success largely to MITI's power to block competitive imports, extract foreign technology and seed it among the leading corporations, and manage a range of production, market, technology, and export cartels.

Over the past four decades, under foreign pressure and the obligations imposed by Japan's membership in international organizations, MITI has dropped many of its most blatant industrial policy tools. MITI's power has also diminished somewhat as industries became more powerful and less dependent on government largesse, while other ministries increasingly challenge MITI for control over specific industries. Today, MITI's power is largely the power to persuade. Of course, its persuasive abilities are not based solely on the rationality of its visions. By denying licenses, cartel memberships, research results, protection, and so on, MITI can still make life hell for even the largest of recalcitrant firms.

More recently, it is clear that whether MITI advocates protectionist or liberal policies depends on the issue. Like any other ministry, MITI is primarily concerned with enhancing its own power – the means are relatively unimportant. For example, in the 1980s MITI advocated such blatantly protectionist policies as the elimination of copyright protection for software, and such seemingly liberal policies as NTT's breakup. In the first case MITI was already responsible for nurturing the software industry and thus wanted more protectionist policies. In the second case it wanted to shape telecommunications policy and the best way was to liberalize the industry away from MPT control. Some of MITI's longest-running battles are between its Agency for Industrial Science and Technology (AIST) and the Prime Minister's Office (PMO) Science and Technology Agency (STA) for supremacy over a range of issues, industries, and technologies.

At the opposite end of the power and policy spectrum from MOF and MITI are the Ministry of Foreign Affairs (MFA) and the Fair Trade Commission (FTC). Of the ministries, MFA (*Gaimusho*) is undoubtedly the weakest. With 4,328 personnel, Japan's foreign service is the smallest of the twenty-four OECD countries, only a quarter of America's and half that of Britain.[18] Without any industries to promote and largesse to distribute, MFA simply does not have a constituency, and without a constituency it has no real power. The Foreign Minister has no significant impact on foreign policy, and the ministry's views are almost invariably set aside in favor of those of the economic ministries. Rothacher reports that 'all foreign embassies in case of commercial problems formally are supposed to report to Gaimusho only. In reality they will contact directly the respective desk officer at MITI and for politeness sake will inform Gaimusho about it'.[19] Most knowledgeable observers will echo the sentiments if not the bluntness of a Sogo Shosha manager who said: 'Gaimusho is there to make nice words to foreigners'.[20]

The FTC is supposed to ensure that Japan's tough antimonopoly laws, written during the American occupation, are strictly followed. In reality, the FTC is more industry's lapdog than watchdog. The FTC almost invariably complies with the 'advice' of MITI and the other ministries to turn a blind eye to Japan's hundreds of cartels. Foreign pressure, however, has steadily built on Tokyo to allow the FTC to fulfill its legal responsibility. On 6 November 1991, the FTC filed its first criminal charges in seventeen years against eight major chemical firms which fixed the price of plastic food wrap. For the first time, the corporate heads were charged with violating the law and could be liable, if found guilty, to prison sentences of up to three years in jail and $3.85 million in fines. Does this represent a challenge to Japanese collusion? Rather than the first strike in a war against Japan's hundreds of cartels, the FTC's recent action was simply a public relations gesture designed to allay the latest crescendo of foreign criticisms of Japanese neomercantilism.

THE LIBERAL DEMOCRATIC PARTY

Conservative parties have ruled Japan for all but nine months since 1945. From 1955 when the conservative Liberal and Democratic parties joined, Japan has been ruled by the Liberal Democratic Party (LDP). The LDP has twice as many Diet members as its nearest rival, the Japan Socialist Party (JSP).

The LDP's continued power rests on a range of interrelated factors. Perhaps the most important reason is that the LDP's neomercantilist policies have created and distributed huge amounts of wealth, which in turn makes most voters LDP supporters; reelection brings a continuation of those successful neomercantilist policies, and so on. Another reason is the LDP's tendency to coopt the best opposition ideas. Ideologically flexible, the LDP promotes whatever works to further Japan's national interests and to stay in office. During the 1960s, the opposition rallied first around such ideas as curbing pollution, revising taxes, and increasing social security, but after they had gained considerable public support the LDP developed them into bills. The LDP passed six welfare laws in the early 1960s and fourteen environmental laws in 1970; reinforced welfare and social security, and created national health insurance with a succession of laws and policies during the 1970s.

But the political system itself seems to encourage continued LDP rule. Japan's national parliament, the Diet, has two houses, the upper House of Councillors and the lower House of Representatives. Of the 252 member House of Councillors, 100 are elected in a nationwide election and 152 are distributed among the prefectures according to population. A councillor's term is six years. Fifty of the nationwide candidates and 126 of the prefectural candidates are up for election every three years. Nationwide candidates are elected according to the proportion of votes their party receives. The number of councillors from each prefecture is determined by population. Upper house elections are determined by proportional representation and, as such, provide a fairer profile of public opinion. In 1989, because of a voter backlash against the Recruit scandal in which 159 members of Japan's elite, including LDP and opposition politicians, bureaucrats, and newspaper publishers, took illicit payments from the Recruit corporation, the LDP lost its majority in the House of Councillors and now rules in unofficial alliance with the Clean Government Party (CGP).

The House of Councillors, however, has only the power to delay. The 511-member House of Representative is where the Diet's power really lies. The House's electoral districts have not been redrawn since the late 1940s when they reflected an already large rural population swelled by refugees from Japan's bombed-out cities. Today, although 80 per cent of Japan's population is now urban, the electoral districts are still biased in favor of rural and semi-rural areas. Some urban electoral districts have as many as four times the number of voters as some rural districts, making farmers vastly over-represented and urban dwellers vastly under-represented. This imbalance is a major reason for the LDP's continuous rule – over half of the 400 LDP Dietmen come from conservative rural districts. Understandably, the LDP has repeatedly blocked any attempts to have the districts redrawn to allow equal representation.

Not only are Japan's electoral districts unequal, but they are multi-member, with most districts having three to five representatives. Each voter votes once, for a name, not a party. The vote is thus often split between a dozen or more candidates, with the winners usually receiving no more than

10–15 per cent of the total. Parties must carefully decide how many candidates to run in each district. If they run too many, their party votes may be spread too thin over too many candidates. If they run only one that candidate may win with a plurality large enough to have accommodated two party candidates.

How do multi-member districts help the LDP? The system rewards the best organized and financed special interests. With more money, the support of powerful interest groups, particularly business ones, and a largely conservative electorate, only the LDP can afford to run multiple candidates in each district. Although there are strict laws limiting campaign time, activities, and contributions, Japan's political system actually runs on massive amounts of money changing hands and almost perpetual reelection campaigns. Like most parliamentary systems the campaign officially lasts only three weeks, but politicians continually make the rounds of key voting blocs exchanging promises and money. The opposition parties simply cannot compete financially or organizationally in this system. During elections the anti-LDP vote is split between the four major opposition parties.

About one quarter of LDP Dietmembers are 'second generation' (*nisei*), and that percentage is expected to rise steadily in coming decades. Why are an increasing number of Diet seats becoming hereditary? Political success depends on each politician building up a collection of 'support groups' (*koenkai*) which mobilize voters and money in return for government patronage. When a politician retires he often simply passes on his *koenkai* to his son, whom he has assiduously groomed for succession over the previous decades.

Japan's political system is severely flawed. It guarantees continued LDP rule, widespread political apathy, factionalism, and corruption. Fukui and Fukai assert that:

> LDP politicians alone exert significant influence in the policymaking, budget preparation, and leadership processes, leaving little room for the effective participation of opposition politicians. At the same time, the unique multimember constituency, single-ballot election system (medium district system) used in Diet elections, combined with the extremely detailed and cumbersome campaign and fundraising regulations, have fostered a set of informal rules and practices that undermine the constitutional principle of equality and nondiscrimination.[21]

Strict campaign contribution laws, equal representation among electoral districts, and the elimination of multi-member districts in favor of one representative per district chosen by national proportional representation would level the playing field. Prime Minister Kaifu made a valiant attempt to push through a political reform package of three separate laws in May 1991, but received no significant support within his party. Instead, his quixotic gesture resulted in Takeshita and the other party leaders pulling the plug on his leadership. Even if Kaifu's plan were implemented, the LDP would have continued to enjoy a solid Diet majority since half of the electorate would continue to vote for the LDP. And in the very unlikely event of the LDP splitting into two parties, they would undoubtedly form a coalition government with each other. The public may momentarily bristle at the periodic scandals revealing the vast extent to which Japan's politicians dip into public and private tills, but when it comes time to vote they continue sending their LDP representatives back to Tokyo.

This system not only tips the balance to the LDP, it also reinforces Japanese neomercantilism. Of all the world's liberal democracies, perhaps none produces as parochial an outlook among its politicians as does Japan's. More so than in other liberal democracies, regardless of which party they support, the most powerful district groups tend to reflect narrow local rather than national interests. The system is one huge patronage system, with the politicians primarily competing to see how much of the nation's ample funds they can divert to their home districts. Given all the quirks of Japan's political system, it is not surprising that few politicians anywhere are more in the pocket of special interests than Japanese politicians. Thus a LDP Diet member 'behaves more like a "delegate", who acts as a conduit for constituency interests and opinions, than a "trustee" who votes according to his own conscience and best judgement'.[22] To win in such a system, politicians must be 'skilful at fund-raising and behind the scenes maneuvering, but are not good at explaining complex issues to the public and [have] limited experience in foreign affairs'.[23] In this system, there is no energy or time left for carefully and objectively examining Japan's position in its economic conflicts with others. Citizens vote for personality rather than policy, and, like their politicians, are primarily concerned with what their representative can bring home rather than national, let alone international interests.

The LDP is led by its President and Secretary General. The President is limited to two two-year terms. According to its party rules, the LDP is supposed to select its presidents by party-wide elections. In practice, the faction leaders prefer to make their selection behind firmly closed doors. The reasoning for the undemocratic selection process is that an open election is too expensive and divisive, with each candidate trying to outbid the others for the support of key voting blocs. The result of the 'smoke filled room' process, though, is often a compromise candidate beholden to the party elders or, more particularly, the boss of the largest faction. Former Prime Minister Tanaka was the party 'kingmaker' from 1973 to 1985, and since then Takeshita has enjoyed the title.

The Prime Minister is particularly weak if he is a compromise candidate, but every Prime Minister, no matter how powerful his factions and any allies, is restrained by the balance of power among the factions from pursuing policies that depart boldly from the status quo. Thus, when a Prime Minister makes market-opening promises in Brussels or Washington, the audience is advised not to hold its breath. Any promises will be quietly repudiated upon his return to Tokyo.

The LDP has often been compared to a mini-party system in which factions (*habatsu*) battle constantly for wealth, status, and power. There is an imbalance of power among the factions. In 1992, the Takeshita faction had 106 Diet members; Mitsuzuka (formerly Abe) eighty-eight; Miyazawa eighty-two; Watanabe (formerly Nakasone) seventy; and Komoto thirty-one, while non-affiliated members accounted for sixteen seats. The factions, not the party, are responsible for most LDP fund-raising and recruitment, and are built around a power broker who dispenses funds and positions to his followers in return for their loyalty. There is a virtuous cycle to faction power. Faction leaders offer financial support and positions in return for loyalty. The more money a leader can offer, the more followers he attracts, which in turn encourages more contributions. Thus the factions are divided by personality and financial power, rather than by issues, and play no significant role in policy-making. Members advance up the faction hierarchy on the basis of seniority, which is determined by the number of times they have been reelected to the Diet. Politicians must generally have been reelected seven times to be a minister, and twelve times to be prime minister. The Cabinet and party positions are filled in proportion to the size of the different factions. Many analysts see the factions as strengthening rather than weakening Japanese democracy. According to Ellis Krauss, 'the real limitations on the ruling party and the most effective "opposition" in the Japanese system comes from within the LDP, rather than from other parties. Factions thus provide a check on monolithic power, partially substituting for the lack of alternation of parties in government'.[24]

One must look to the LDP policy 'tribes' (*zoku*) to find real divisions over the issues. The *zoku* are clusters of politicians who have become experts in particular areas and who increasingly shape relevant policies and at the very least continually pressure the government for redress. The *zoku* are important players in the policy triads. They cut across faction lines. Many of these *zoku* were founded by former high ranking bureaucrats who 'descended' (*amakudari*) to high-ranking positions in the party.

The LDP's formal policy-making institution is the Policy Affairs Research Council (PARC, or *Seimu Chosakai*), which is led by an Executive Committee and divided into seventeen divisions (*bukai*) which correspond to the ministries and Diet committees. PARC is playing an increasingly important role in setting the national policy agenda. The LDP is also taking an increasingly important role in managing the proliferation of turf battles between Japan's ministries.

BIG BUSINESS

Japan's big business world is structured in a three-layer pyramid with the leaders of the national business organizations and industrial groups at the top (*zaikai*), followed by those representatives of each industrial association (*gyokai*), and then the thousands of individual companies (*kigyo*). The Federation of Economic Organizations (FEO or *Keidanren*) represents the collective voice of 117 industrial associations and 839 leading corporations. It is a voice, however, whose accents are diversifying as Japan's economy continues to broaden. *Keidanren* is organized into over thirty policy committees which work closely with the appropriate ministries, LDP PARC divisions, and *zoku*. The International Economic Affairs Department, for example, deals with foreign trade, investment, and aid issues. *Keidanren* has acquired a foreign policy and diplomatic role which at times surpasses MFA's in importance. Tokyo often conducts its economic diplomacy and intelligence-gathering through *Keidanren* missions to a country, region, or international organization.[25]

Big business, not surprisingly, is the LDP's largest source of money. *Keidanren*, the industrial associations, and individual corporations officially contributed a record 184.5 billion yen in 1990 ($1.5 billion), up 6.4 per cent from the previous year. The LDP then distributed this money among the different factions, of which 620 million yen went to Takeshita, 500 million yen each to the Watanabe, Miyazawa, and Abe factions, 200 million to the Komoto faction, and 100 million to non-affiliated members. The largest industrial donors were banks (2 billion yen), followed by construction and real estate companies (1 billion yen), while the five top corporate donors were the Petroleum Association of Japan (100 million yen), the Japan Iron and Steel Federation (98 million yen), the Japan Automobile Manufacturers Association (95 million yen), Mitsubishi Bank (94.8 million yen), Fuji Bank (91.8 million yen), and Dai-Ichi Kanyo Bank (91.8 million yen).[26]

The economic workhorses of Japan's *zaikai* are its *keiretsu* or industrial

* Liberal Democratic Party.

groups. A *keiretsu* is a group of firms related through interlocking stock ownership (*kakushiki mochiai*), and an exclusive bank, trading firm, and insurance firm which supplies the group members with cheap capital. A *keiretsu* can predominately conduct production (*sangyo*), distribution (*ryutsu*), or capital (*shihon*) business, but the major *keiretsu* combine all these functions. The major groups have organized themselves into a 'one set system' (*wan setto-shugi*) in which each owns at least one company in every major industry. Thus, a typical *keiretsu* might have bank, trading, insurance, steel, automobile, electronics, petrochemical, oil, construction, non-ferrous metal, mining, glass, real estate, textile, cement, distribution, paper, food, and rubber firms. In most *keiretsu*, the company presidents meet (*sacho-kai*) monthly to map and coordinate the group's strategy.

Keiretsu tend to buy from within the group whenever possible, even if the product may be more expensive or of inferior quality. Generally 30 per cent of each *keiretsu's* transactions are within the group. The trading firms are particularly notorious for discriminatory buying practices. The Big Nine trading firms account for over half of Japan's imports and exports. These discriminatory practices have been severely criticized by foreigners as a significant nontariff barrier for foreign firms attempting to sell in Japan.

Although there are hundreds of *keiretsu*, there are sixteen major ones which together include over 1,000 firms and account for almost half of Japan's GNP. The eight biggest *keiretsu* – Mitsubishi, Mitsui, Sumitomo, Fuyo, DKB, Sanwa, IBJ, and Tokai – account for about 30 per cent of GNP and are built around financial institutions like a bank, insurance firm, and trading company which supplies cheap capital to the other group members and helps coordinate their activities. Japan's other major *keiretsu* like Nippon Steel, Hitachi, Nissan, Toyota, Matsushita, Toshiba-IHI, Tokyu, and Seibu are primarily centered around a dynamic manufacturing firm, but are in turn tied into one or more of the Big Eight. As much as 20–25 per cent of each Big Eight *keiretsu's* stock is held within that *keiretsu* by the member firms, while 65–70 per cent is owned by institutional investors from other *keiretsu* and large corporations. Less than 15 per cent of Japanese stocks are held by individual stockholders and about 5 per cent by foreigners. Banks can own up to 5 per cent and insurance firms up to 10 per cent of a firm.

The six largest *keiretsu* overshadow all these others. The 182 companies composing the Big Six *keiretsu* represent only 0.01 per cent of all Japanese firms, but 10 per cent of those listed on the Tokyo stock exchange, half of Japan's 200 largest firms, and 25 per cent of GNP. The interlocking shares among the Big Six range from Sumitomo's 63.9 per cent, Mitsubishi's 63.4 per cent, Mitsui's 51.4 per cent, Fuji's 38.1 per cent, DKB's 31.6 per cent, and Sanwa's 38.1 per cent.

Each *keiretsu* manufacturing firm in turn sits atop a pyramid of medium- and small-sized manufacturing or distribution firms in which the parent firm owns from 10–100 per cent of the equity. The parent firm extends credit, managerial expertise, technology, and business in return for being the focus of the subcontractor's or distributor's primary loyalty. The latter will, for instance, either lay off its own workers or absorb parent workers as business conditions dictate. Just as the *keiretsu* bank will impose advice and personnel on a troubled member firm, a parent firm will similarly intervene in a troubled subcontractor or distributor.

The contemporary *keiretsu*, particularly the Big Six, are the postwar incarnations of the *zaibatsu* which emerged in the late nineteenth century and flourished until 1947 when the American Occupation abolished the family-owned holding companies which held them together. The *zaibatsu* stocks were sold off to the public and their leaders were forced to resign their positions. After the Occupation ended in 1952 the *zaibatsu* simply recombined, this time around financial institutions like banks, insurance firms, and trading companies instead of the outlawed holding companies.

The advantages for Japan of the *keiretsu* system are vast. Kester writes that

> by tying themselves together in groups, yet eschewing outright owner-ship and control, Japanese corporations have been able to exploit some of the high-powered incentives of the market that derive from independent ownership of assets, while relying on selective intervention by key equity owners to adapt contracts to new circumstances as needed.[27]

Horizontal and vertical *keiretsu* members share inside business and infor-mation and cheap finance.

These collusive Japanese business arrangements are reinforced by Ja-pan's lifetime employment system, by which promising employees are hired immediately after their university graduation and slowly work their way up the administrative pyramid until they retire around the age of fifty-five. Like the feudal principalities of an earlier age, the company demands complete obedience and loyalty from the employee in return for job security and assistance in finding a second career after retirement. Although only 25–30 per cent of Japanese workers are employed in lifetime employment companies, most of the rest are employed in relatively protected occupa-tions as well like agriculture, construction, and the distribution system, which soak up excess workers who might otherwise be unemployed.

Japanese firms must continually grow or collapse from the weight of supporting the lifetime system. Thus Tokyo must maintain vast webs of trade barriers and other neomercantilist practices in order to protect the lifetime employment system. If free markets existed in Japan few firms could afford the lifetime employment system – the competition would force Japanese firms to fire countless redundant workers.

The *keiretsu* ties are steadily loosening as dynamic individual companies can increasingly rely on retained earnings, bond issues, and global financial markets for most of their capital needs. Rather than parking their earnings in their *keiretsu* bank, firms are investing their funds in a range of money-making schemes (*zaiteku*). Kester quotes a manager in one of Japan's largest city banks as ruefully pointing out the changes in the relationship between banks and firms:

> A decade ago, our relationship with our clients was very old-fashioned. The clients would visit us quarterly to explain their performance, discuss their investment plans, and plead for more loans. Today it is we [the lenders] who must do the pleading. We have to make appointments with them to learn what is happening, and we must now compete with other banks for what little borrowing the company does.[28]

The *zaikai's* power is continually expanding with its complexity and wealth.

AUXILARIES

The saying 'You're either for us or against us', does not work very well in Japan. The governing triad has managed to coopt to varying extents virtu-ally all other significant groups in Japanese society. Although the opposi-tion parties may fiercely denounce the LDP and its policies on the Diet floor, they secretly collude to an extent unthinkable in Western liberal democracies. Likewise, the governing triad has largely coopted the main-stream press, which is organized into press cartels attached to specific politicians and ministries. While the mainstream press does occasionally criticize specific LDP policies or actions, it does not investigate scandals and only reports them after they have been revealed by the vociferous fringe press.

The governing triad's most important auxilaries, however, are small businessmen and farmers, which provide the LDP with votes in return for the enormous financial benefits extended both directly from subsidies and indirectly from protection from competitive imports. Distribution (15 mil-lion) and construction (5 million) workers form about 35 per cent of Japan's labor force, and with their families represent about 40 per cent of Japan's population. They are the two most important pillars of LDP urban financial and electoral support.

Virtually all of Japan's 4.6 million farmers are members of the national farm association (*Nokyo*) whose national lobbying organization (*Zenchu*) plays a powerful role in asserting continued protectionism and larger subsidies. Together with MAAF and LDP's 200 Dietmen from predominantly rural districts, *Nokyo* and *Zenchu* annually extract huge government subsidies and protection. Farmers receive their subsidies, credit, and other aid from the Agricultural Cooperative Bank (*Norin Chukin*), the world's seventh largest bank in terms of assets.

Japan's farm lobby, however, is not invincible. Only 7 per cent of Japan's population are farmers, and only 10 per cent of them farm full time, with the remaining 90 per cent gaining most of their income from other jobs. And that number is steadily diminishing. Meanwhile, as the LDP's support diversifies, and foreign pressure builds on Tokyo to open its markets, the government has increasingly resisted calls by the farm lobby for continued protectionism. In 1987, Tokyo cut its farm subsidies for the first time, and throughout the 1980s agreed to expand its quotas for all products except rice.

The governing triad has tamed labor at both the national and company level. Japanese labor was not always as quiescent as it is now. During the 1950s, many Japanese industries were plagued by long acrimonious strikes. But prosperity, and a tough line on strikes in the steel and coal industry in the late 1950s and early 1960s knocked the union teeth out, and they have been quiet ever since. Since 1970 the Labor Ministry and representatives of Japan's largest unions have met in an advisory council (*Sanrokon*) which helps mediate problems. Passage of the Employment Insurance Law in 1975 and Basic Pension Law in 1986 further dissolved any remaining major issues.

Another reason for labor's moderation has been the steady decline in union membership as a percentage of total workers from about half in the mid-1950s to less than one-quarter at present. Until the late 1980s the two largest national unions were *Sohyo* which largely represented public workers and supported the Japan Socialist Party (JSP), and *Domei* which largely represented enterprise unions and supported the Democratic Socialist Party (DSP). By 1990, they and most other smaller national unions merged into *Rengo*, which supports both the JSP and DSP as well as its own candidates for office. *Rengo* has moderated the radical unions which have joined it.

Meanwhile corporate management has coopted the workers by setting up company unions and setting them against any workers who join the more radical union, if one exists. The annual labor 'spring offensive' (*shunto*) has become no more than a three step ritual dance. In the first and most important stage during the early months of the new year, management and labor negotiate an agreement on wages and benefits. The second stage involves a workers' 'strike' which usually lasts a half day at most, and may involve only the wearing of armbands while the participants work as diligently as ever, and is sometimes even held as a Sunday rally. The decision is then formally announced a day or two after the strike.

The LDP's advantages are conversely the opposition party's weaknesses. The opposition parties are severely fragmented, underfunded, and pose no viable alternative to continued LDP rule. All the opposition parties have drifted toward the political center as Japan's political economy continues to develop. The JSP and Japan Communist Party (JCP) continue to cling to a socialist ideology which has no relevance to Japan's prosperity, problems, and prospects, while the DSP and CGP are virtually indistinguishable ideologically from the LDP. In contrast to the 1,984.5 billion yen in LDP contributions in 1990, the opposition parties remained largely starved for funds. The JCP received 32.06 billion yen, the Social Democratic Party (SDP) 6.79 billion yen, the CGP 13.49 billion yen, the DSP 2.41 billion yen, and the tiny United Social Democratic Party (USDP) 61 million yen.[29]

Japan's most important opposition parties are foreign governments and corporations, particularly those of the United States. Foreign pressure (*gaiatsu*) will remain the most important force shaping changes in Japan's economic policies. In championing the lowering of Japan's trade barriers, foreign governments are also championing the plight of Japanese consumers. The Structural Impediments Initiative (SII), negotiated between Washington and Tokyo in 1989–91, involved each side promising to reform its political economy, with Japan committed to liberalize its distribution system, financial markets, construction industry, and consumer credit.

INDUSTRIAL POLICY

Industrial policies are those designed to affect specific economic sectors, industries or firms. All nations have industrial policies, but governments vary considerably in how systematically they create and implement them. Abegglen writes that Japan's industrial policies 'are more economically rational, more internally consistent, and more generally accepted across the economy'.[30]

Why have Japan's industrial policies been so overwhelmingly successful in developing Japan from mass poverty into the world's economic superpower? Answers vary. Johnson distinguishes Japan's orientation as 'a developmental, plan rational state whose economic orientation was keyed to industrial policy. By contrast, the United States from about the same period took the regulatory, market rational path keyed to foreign policy'.[31] He then argues that Japan's developmental rational outlook is

> rooted in Japanese political rationality and conscious institutional inno-
> vation, and not primarily or exclusively in Japanese culture, vestiges of
> feudalism, insularity, frugality, the primacy of the social group over the
> individual, or any special characteristic of Japanese society.[32]

Ellis Krauss identifies five essential elements behind Japan's success.[33] First, there is an ideological consensus on the necessity for the state to lead Japan's economic development. Second, Japan has the institutions to create and implement industrial policy. Third, the LDP has been continually reelected to office, thus allowing Japan's industrial policies to be sustained for over four decades. Fourth, Japanese business is organized in industrial groups and associations which can implement the industrial policies. Finally, MITI has continually balanced the best of cooperation and competition in promoting industrial and technological development.

Tokyo guides the economy towards long-term strategic goals and the means of achieving them through a series of five-year plans and 'visions'. These plans and visions are indicative rather than coercive, and are formulated only after a consensus has been achieved among all relevant business, political, and bureaucratic interests. Within these guidelines, Japan's ministries, corporations, and politicians struggle to assert their separate interests. The goal is the economy's continual and dynamic development into a broader, more technologically driven, and greater wealth producing range of industries. The state also identifies the most innovative and cost-effective technologies and techniques, and shares them with all relevant industries and firms.

The tools of Japan's trade and industrial policies have changed significantly over the past four decades. As Japan's economy developed and its corporations conquered markets around the world, the American and European governments pressured Tokyo to give up one industrial policy tool after another. Today, MITI no longer uses currency controls or MOF window guidance as a means of channelling low cost capital to targeted industries. Meanwhile, the reliance of Japanese firms and industries on the government for funds and technology has steadily lessened. Corporations now obtain most finance from their group financial institutions, retained earnings, and international lenders, and no longer need MITI to help them armtwist technology from foreign firms. Japan's financial liberalization has steadily raised capital costs to global market levels.

As some policy tools have lessened in importance, others have become more important. The bureaucrats rarely use their legal powers, and even when they do it is in the form of directives (*tsutatsu*) issued to the firms 'requesting' their compliance. All along Japan's officials have preferred to rule by 'administrative guidance' (*gyosei shido*) rather than 'administrative directive' (*tsutatsu ni yoru gyosei*) or 'administration by law' (*horitsu ni yoru gyosei*). Japan's laws are written by the bureaucrats in a way which gives them sweeping powers over the designated industry or technology. Administrative guidance is just as effective and leaves no paper trail that could be pursued by zealous FTC officials or foreign governments. Both officials and businessmen are free from possible litigation.

Japan's officials have myriad ways to penalize recalcitrant firms without resorting to law. Licenses, certificates, low interest government loans, or membership in a research cartel can all be refused. Bureaucrats are notorious for 'losing' or 'misplacing' the applications of maverick firms, or blandly stating for months or years that the application is still under review. Murakami points out that these powers are particularly effective in bullying newer firms because

in leading modern industries in postwar Japan, entry of a new firm was often very difficult, if not impossible. Particularly in the case of large-scale process industries relying on import technology . . . the government could effectively regulate new entries by controlling licenses to import technology as well as by exerting influence on loan financing, which aspirants to those industries often needed in large amounts.[34]

As a result, Japan's political economy has been fragmented into hundreds of administrative fiefdoms distinguished by 'an array of administrative regulations and guidance . . . [which provides] a quasi-legal framework . . . relatively free from . . . changes'.[35]

Cartels are the most usual means of achieving Japan's industrial and technology goals. Japanese market, technology, production, import, and export cartels remain vital in giving Japanese corporations a competitive edge over their foreign rivals. Legally, most Japanese cartels are outlawed. The 1953 antimonopoly law permits only recession and export cartels, which must be approved by the Fair Trade Commission (FTC). But in reality, the FTC all along has meekly approved cartels designated by MITI or the other ministries while along with the other ministries turning a blind eye to the hundreds of other cartels which do not receive official approval. In 1991, there were sixty-eight areas exempt from the application of the antimonopoly law, of which fifty-six were price and production cartels.[36] But Japan's markets are carefully managed by countless other cartels. The industrial groups continue to discriminate in favor of members and related Japanese firms, and against foreigners in purchases. Japan's markets remain protected by a bewildering web of subtle government and private nontariff trade barriers. Japan's markets remain carefully managed by collusion among Japanese firms and officials.

Only rarely has the FTC protested against particularly outrageous cartels, and even more rarely attempted to stop one. After years of pressure from Washington, Tokyo finally relented and agreed to increase its antitrust penalties. In June 1991, the FTC raised surcharges collected on illegal cartels from 1.5 per cent to 6 per cent and announced that violators would be liable for prison terms of up to three years; in March 1992, it announced that henceforth it would raise the maximum fine on firms from 5 million yen ($38,000) to 100 million yen ($752,000), although the maximum fine for individuals will remain 5 million yen. Most observers snickered at these changes. The larger fine is pocket change for the big corporations, and there is no sign that the FTC is any more eager to fulfill its legal responsibilities.

As Japan's economy roars through the 1990s toward the twenty-first century, research cartels may contribute the most to Japan's development. Research cartels are organized and presided over by a ministry or agency, and composed of companies which share the costs and research with the government for development of a designated technology or product. They allow the government and firms to share costs and risks, pool human and technological resources, and eliminate duplicated efforts, thus accelerating the pace and diffusion while decreasing the costs of innovation. There are scores of these research cartels addressing virtually every technology, product, or industry imaginable.

How are these research cartels formed and managed? The ministry or agency announces plans for developing a particular technology and invites the leading firms to submit research proposals. The bureaucracy carefully examines the proposals and then selects those with the best technological and financial abilities to participate. One or more prominent firms are designated as the coordinator or leader, and the group is legally incorporated. Although the number of participating firms varies considerably, the average number is twelve. After considerable pressure, Tokyo has allowed foreign participation in several research cartels.

The national research cartels vary in their ability to achieve their respective goals. Each firm wants to take out more than it puts in. The leading firms in particular tend to withhold their best minds and secrets from the cartel. Thus, the cartels often resemble a high stakes poker game in which the participants carefully play each hand, even though the pot is distributed after the game. The vast majority of these research projects are successful while only 10 to 20 per cent fall short of their goals.[37]

Tokyo's ability to transform its high technology corporations and industries into global leaders is well known. Japan's semiconductor, fiber optic, supercomputer, virtual reality, high definition television, superconductor, and magnetic levitation technologies, to name a few, are far ahead of their European or American rivals. Japan would not have those technologies and the tremendous wealth they generate, let alone lead the world in them, if Tokyo had not targeted them for special development.

Japan's biotechnology field provides an interesting example of an industry which Tokyo has so far failed to transform into a global leader.[38] It has been shaped by the efforts of several industrial associations and a half-dozen ministries. The industry is organized by the Japan Pharmaceutical Manufacturers Association (JPMA), the Federation of Pharmaceutical Manufacturers Asssociations (FPMA), and the Pharmaceutical Wholesalers Association (PWA). The Japan Medical Association (JMA) plays a secondary role in influencing policies. Although the Ministry of Health and Welfare (MHW) traditionally responsible for regulating the industry, the Ministry of Education (MOE), the Science and Technology Agency (STA), the Ministry of Agriculture, Forestry, and Fisheries (MAFF), and MITI began struggling over the industry's fate during the late 1970s, and continued to do so throughout the 1980s and 1990s. Each bureaucracy devised and implemented its own biotechnology policy which attempted to promote a particular aspect of the industry. During the 1980s, the United States had an impact on Japan's array of biotechnology policies. The rapid advances of over 100 small American entrepreneur firms in the early 1980s stimulated Japan's ministries to promote a Japanese effort, while during the mid-1980s, Washington pressured Tokyo to lower the barriers protecting Japan's vast biotechnology markets.

Despite concerted efforts, Japan's biotechnology industry remains fragmented, uncompetitive, and most of its firms would be swept away if they had to operate in anything resembling a free market. Because this area is so backward, Japanese firms have been allowed to form joint ventures with foreign firms to gain access to their technology. Eighteen of the 100 largest firms, and four of the top ten in the 1980s were either partly or wholly foreign-owned.[39] Japan's biotechnology policies must be considered a qualified success despite these disappointing results. The industry would not exist at all without concerted protection and subsidies of various kinds, and Japan would thus have no role in biotechnology.

In contrast to policies designed to promote Japan's technological leadership, there are those designed to transform depressed industries. After two and a half decades of an average annual growth of 10 per cent, Japan's economy skidded to a halt following OPEC's quadrupling of oil prices in 1973. For the first time, Japan was faced with managing industrial decline rather than growth. For a while, 'backward-looking' (*ushiromuki*) investments to declining industries surpassed 'forward-looking' (*maemuki*) investments to cutting-edge industries in importance. The Depressed Industry laws of 1978 and 1983 empowered the government to restructure declining industries by negotiating with those affected firms the formation of production and price cartels and proportional capacity reductions.[40] The government managed the decline of shipbuilding, petrochemicals, electric furnace steel production, chemical fibers, chemical fertilizers, paper, ferroalloys, and aluminum smelting. The ministry would commonly organize the industry into four or five groups with several large, medium, and small firms in each. Each group would organize production cutbacks while competing against the other groups. The government would assist adjustment with low-interest and deferred government and private loans, import protection, export promotion, special depreciation allowances, and government and private procurement.

The travails of Japan's shipbuilding industry were the most traumatic.[41] The Ministry of Transportation (MOT), with MITI's assistance and empowered by a series of laws elaborating the basic Shipbuilding Law of 1950, had used a range of cartels, technology infusions, low interest loans, export promotions, and import protection to build Japan's shipbuilding industry into the world's most powerful. By the early 1970s, Japan's shipbuilders had become the world's lowest cost producers and conquered half the world's market!

But orders for new Japanese ships plunged with the stagflation of the 1970s – by 1979, demand was only 10 per cent that of 1973.[42] The industry shed over 133,000 of 361,000 shipbuilding workers during the time, received government and private loans, and organized into several groups which cooperated in cutting back production facilities, production, and prices, and often shared remaining facilities. The MOT implemented these policies through the Japan Shipbuilders Association (JSA) representing the seven largest and nineteen of the medium-sized firms, the Cooperative Association of Japanese Shipbuilders (CAJS) which represented more than 100 medium and small firms, and the Association of Manufacturers Related to Shipbuilding (AMRS). Conflicts and negotiations over how much each firm would cut back and the amount of assistance were constant and bitter. This adjustment was complicated by European Community protests against Japanese dumping of ships in foreign markets, thus exacerbating the crisis for Europe's shipbuilders. In addition to MOT, MITI got involved because of the ripple effects on steel and other basic industries; the MFA because of the conflict with the EC; the MOF to provide financing; the MOL because of the labor cutbacks; the Economic Planning Agency (EPA) to provide new plans; the Small and Medium Enterprise Agency (SMEA) to protect those firms of that size; the FTC because of possible antitrust violations; and the MAFF because of the fishing boat, sugar, and liner board industries.[43] The result was the survival and transformation of Japan's shipbuilders into an even more competitive, cost-effective industry which retains about half of all world ship construction.

Japan's industrial policies are not omnipotent. There are plenty of examples of the results either exceeding or falling short of the plan. Friedman offers the example of Japan's machine tool industry and argues persuasively that it developed despite rather than because of MITI's intrusion: 'not one post-war market or production plan came close to being realized; the machinery industry grew in a pattern the reverse of what the bureaucracy sought'.[44]

Yet, when results fall short of expectations, one must ask what would have happened if the government did nothing. Of course, that is a question which can never be answered, but it is safe to say that even the most disappointing of Tokyo's programs are better than nothing. For example, the Fifth Generation Computer program did not succeed in producing a computer that can think like a human being thousands of times faster than present computers. But it did succeed in achieving some important technological innovations which probably would not have occurred if market conditions had prevailed. While the means have changed, the industrial policies of MITI and the other ministries are as important as ever in developing Japan's economy into ever higher technology and value-added industries. And Japan's governing triad will continue to rule Japan and develop the economy to ever higher levels of wealth and power in the world.

4 Japan Abroad: The Neomercantilist State

In two generations Japan was transformed from a war-devastated, poverty-stricken country into the world's most dynamic economic superpower. Tokyo's single-minded drive for global power has been harshly criticized. Recently, the former French Prime Minister Edith Cresson asserted that there 'is a world economic war going on. France is not waging it . . . Japan is an adversary that doesn't play by the rules and has an absolute desire to conquer the world. You have to be naive or blind not to see that'.[1] Cresson wanted to reverse a severe imbalance of power, outlook, and strategies between Europe and Japan: 'I'm against the clear imbalance that exists between the European Community, which is not protectionist at all, and the Japanese system which is hermetically sealed'.[2]

Cresson's views were severely criticized by the Japanese and their foreign spokespeople, who claim constantly that Japan's markets are the world's most open and that foreigners sell little because they do not try hard enough and their goods are poorly made. As evidence, Japanese point to average tariffs lower than America's and Europe's, and to a series of 'market opening packages', ten alone in the 1980s. No markets in the world are more competitive than ours, the Japanese constantly argue. We work harder, save more, and invest more – that is the secret of our success!

Are Cresson's fears justified? Does Japan somehow threaten an unsuspecting Europe? Or are Japanese claims true? Does Japan epitomize the 'magic of the marketplace'? Is Japan's success simply attributable to corporate hard work and constant attention to improving quality and cutting costs? Just what are Japan's foreign policy goals and the means to obtain them? This chapter will analyze those and related questions by first examining Japan's traditional relations with the outside world, and then exploring the range of policies it has pursued since 1945 which fall under the rubric, foreign policy.

TRADITIONAL FOREIGN POLICY

For over 1,500 hundred years until the modern era, Japan's foreign relations were limited by a combination of geographic isolation and disinterest. Japanese tribute missions would occasionally set sail for China while the trickle of trade with the continent expanded and contracted with Japan's political struggles. Limited as they were, these contacts were vital to Japan's development. Japan borrowed and assimilated much of its high culture from the continent, including Buddhism, Confucianism, Chinese imperial institutions, and the fine arts.

Japan's foreign relations were overwhelmingly peaceful. In the prehistoric era, the Japanese enclave of Mimana in southern Korea existed for several hundred years but was finally overrun by Korean armies in 562. Whether it was established by force or peaceful migration is unknown. Japan's only historic example of imperialism occurred a millenium later in 1592 when Hideyoshi, dreaming of conquering East Asia, sent a Japanese army to Korea. The Japanese overran the peninsula but were defeated by Chinese and Korean armies at the Yalu River, and were withdrawn. A second invasion by 140,000 Japanese troops in 1597 was likewise recalled after Hideyoshi's death the following year. Likewise, Japan only twice in its premodern history faced the specter of foreign invasion – the failed Mongol attacks of 1274 and 1281. The latter invasion was defeated by a typhoon which destroyed the Mongol fleet, a salvation attributed by the Japanese to a 'divine wind' (*kamikaze*).

There is a dynamic relationship in Japanese history between foreign influences and shifts in domestic power.[3] Over a millenium and a half of Japanese history, there have been a half-dozen cycles in which new regimes displaced old decadent ones during periods of extensive foreign contact. The ambitious power seekers use foreign technologies and ideas to strengthen their position and undermine those in power. Having taken power, the new regime then engages in wholesale cultural borrowing to consolidate and legitimize its power. But eventually this orgy of cultural borrowing reaches a saturation point and a reaction occurs in which the Japanese elite severs its foreign relations. The regime then matures and slowly decays. Foreign relations are renewed. The loosened control over the country enables ambitious opponents to utilize a new wave of foreign technologies and ideas to undermine the regime, and the cycle repeats itself.

The last three great cycles of Japan's regime change and foreign relations have been with the West. Japan relations with the West have always been ambivalent and often downright acrimonious. The first Westerners – three Portugese priests on a Chinese junk – arrived in 1542. For the next 100 years, Japanese lords absorbed a range of European technologies and ideas into Japan's culture, the most significant of which was firearms. The skilled use of artillery and muskets helped bring an end to feudalism in Japan, just as it had earlier destroyed European feudalism. But like previous regimes, the Tokugawa clan which unified Japan in 1600 eventually reached its saturation point with European culture. In 1637 the Tokugawa closed off the country to virtually all foreign relations (*sakoku*) and attempted to wipe out Christianity.

In 1853, a mere decade after China's defeat by the Western powers, the American Commodore Perry commanding a half-dozen gunboats – the infamous 'black ships' – sailed into Tokyo Bay and requested that the 'emperor' receive a letter from President Fillmore calling for open ports and humane treatment of shipwrecked sailors. Perry left promising to return the next year for an answer. In 1854, the Tokugawa agreed grudgingly to abandon Japan's isolation and allow limited foreign relations.

But, as with previous regimes, the wave of new foreign ideas and technologies were most successfully utilized by opponents of the existing regime to undermine its rule. A *coup d'etat* in January 1868 by the two leading rebellious provinces, Satsuma and Choshu, and their allies swept the decrepit Tokugawa from power. Under the slogans that 'knowledge shall be sought for all over the world' of the Charter Oath of April 1868, and 'Western ideas, Japanese spirit' (*wakon yosai*), the new Meiji regime embarked on a systematic attempt to build Japan into a modern power by the wholesale adoption of western technological, political, economic, and social institutions and ideas. This modernization drive included, among other things,

> the posts, the telegraphs, the railways, the trigonometrical survey, improved mining methods, prison reform, sanitary reform, cotton and paper mills, chemical laboratories, water-works, and harbor works – all are creations of the foreign employees of the Japanese government. By foreigners the first men-of-war were built, the first large public edifices erected, the first lessons given in rational finance.[4]

During the early modern period (1853–1945), Japan's view of the West shifted between the two extremes of an uncritical adulation and unbridled contempt. The great Japanese educator Yukichi Fukuzawa argued in 1885 that Japan 'should escape from Asia and cast our lot in with the civilized countries of the West . . . We should sever all relations with our bad Asian friends'.[5] Others believed Japan should build up its military strength, defeat the Western powers, and embark on a step-by-step conquest of east and southeast Asia. In 1854 Yoshida Shoin articulated a strategy that Japan actually followed, with some variation, over the next ninety years:

> If we dispose of sufficient naval vessels . . . it should be possible for us to bring the [Western] barbarians under control . . . seize Kamchatka and

the [Sea of] Okhotsk, absorb the Ryukyus, teach the Koreas a lesson, extract tribute from them . . . divide the territory of Manchuria to the north, absorb Taiwan and the Philippines in the South. In fact it will be possible for Japan to establish itself as a power with a gradually expanding sphere of influence.[6]

The object of Japan's systematic modernization program was eventually to transform Japan into a great power which would be accepted as an equal by the Western powers. But the Meiji leaders realized that industrialization and political, economic, and social reforms were not enough. Great powers were imperial powers, and Japan embarked on a step-by-step conquest of north-east Asia, first by cracking Korea's isolation with gunboat diplomacy in 1876, seizing the Ryukyu Islands (1877), fighting wars with first China (1894–1905) to gain Taiwan and the Pescadore Islands, then Russia (1904–5) eventually to gain control of the Korean peninsula and influence in Manchuria, and finally joining the Allies against Germany in World War One to acquire the western Pacific islands and increase Japanese influence in China. Japan's modernization and imperial efforts were rewarded by an alliance with Britain in 1902, the abandonment of their unequal treaties by all foreign powers during the early 1900s, and a seat as one of the Big Five powers at the Versailles Conference ending World War One.

But despite these enormous successes, Japanese did not forget the humiliations of the forced opening of Japan in the mid-nineteenth century, the 'Triple Intervention' by Russia, France, and Germany in 1895 which forced Tokyo to surrender Port Arthur and the Liaotung Peninsula which it had captured during its war against China, or the refusal of the other Big Five powers to allow an 'equality of the races' clause written into the Versailles Treaty. Tokyo had been patient in the face of these reversals, never losing sight of its long-term goal of expelling the Western powers from Asia and dominating the region itself. For example, after the humiliating Triple Intervention which forced Japan to give up the Liaotung Peninsula and Port Arthur that it had seized during the Sino-Japanese War, Japan's Foreign Vice Minister, Tadasu Hayashi, wrote:

At present Japan must keep calm and sit tight, so as to lull suspicions nurtured against her; during this time the foundations of her national power must be consolidated; and we must watch and wait for the opportunity in the Orient that will surely come one day. When that day arrives Japan will decide its own fate; and she will be able not only to put into their place the powers who seek to meddle in her affairs, she will even be able, should this be necessary, to meddle in their affairs.[7]

Japan's rise into a great power and the devastation of the Europeans during World War One gave Tokyo the opportunity it had longed for. Starting with the invasion of Manchuria in 1931, the Japanese embarked on a fourteen year step-by-step conquest of east and south Asia which cost the lives of 20 million Asians as well as those of thousands of Britons, Americans, Australians, and other Allied soldiers and civilians. Japan's quest for an East and Southeast Asian empire ended only with Tokyo's unconditional surrender on 15 August 1945 after the atomic bombing of Hiroshima and Nagasaki.

POSTWAR FOREIGN POLICY

Japan was dramatically transformed by defeat in war and the resulting revolutionary changes imposed by the American-led occupation, which destroyed Japan's military and totalitarian political institutions and imposed on its ruins a liberal democracy. Yet, despite this transformation from totalitarianism to liberal democracy, the Japanese have never lost sight of their goal of global hegemony even during the bleakest of setbacks and defeats. And nationalism, not internationalism, remains the solid basis of Japan's foreign policies.

Prime Minister Cresson's blunt assertion that Japan intended to dominate the world may have been undiplomatic but it was not inaccurate. Tokyo has single-mindedly attempted to obtain four major goals since Japan was forced into the global economy in 1854: (1) territorial integrity and sovereignty; (2) rapid and balanced political economic development; (3) global political economic power; and (4) international recognition of these accomplishments.[8]

The means to achieve these ends have varied little since 1853 when Commodore Perry first sailed into Tokyo Bay. Throughout its modern era, Japan has followed a policy of 'moving with the most powerful' (*nagai mono ni makareyo*) to allow Japan quietly and single-mindedly to strengthen itself to the point where it can overwhelm its rivals and assert its dominance. Masayoshi Hotta, the Shogun's prime minister, offered the ominous advice in 1857 that

> our policy should be to . . . conclude friendly alliances, to send ships to foreign countries everywhere and conduct trade, to copy the foreigners where they are at their best and so repair our own shortcomings, to foster our national strength and complete our armaments, and so gradually subject the foreigners to our influence until in the end all the countries of the world . . . acknowledge our hegemony.[9]

Prime Minister Shigeru Yoshida (1946–7, 1948–54) restated this strategy succinctly a century later when he said in 1952 that Japan's destiny

> was to be a global power, and the expansion as well as the security of the
> state was best guaranteed by close alliance with the dominant Western
> power in Asia and the Pacific . . . just as the United States was once a
> colony of Great Britain but is now the stronger of the two, if Japan
> becomes a colony of the United States it will eventually become the
> stronger.[10]

Yoshida firmly established Japan's foreign policy on the track of global economic expansion while avoiding any significant defense expenditure, genuine aid to others, or any other political entanglements in regional or global issues (*seikei bunri*). The essence of Japanese neomercantilism is the targeting of strategic industries for development by protecting them from competitive imports and assisting their eventual conquest of global markets. But Yoshida and subsequent Japanese leaders could not have succeeded without massive American help. General Douglas MacArthur, the Supreme Commander for Allied Powers (SCAP) which ruled Japan, pushed through massive land, labor, industrial, bureaucratic and policy reforms which transformed Japan's economy, while demilitarizing and democratizing Japan by abolishing the military and imposing a liberal constitution whose Article 9 literally forbad Japan's rearmament.

American and Japanese goals closely coincided. Having 'lost China', Washington sought to make Japan the cornerstone of containment in the Far East. Japan would be the 'workshop' or 'engine of growth' for Asia. George Kennan even talked of creating for Japan an 'empire to the South . . . we've got to get Japan back into the . . . old Co-prosperity sphere'.[11] To these ends, Washington developed 'triangular trade' between the United States, Japan, and southeast Asia in which Japanese manufactured goods were exchanged for southeast Asian raw materials and energy. Washington even went so far as to assign officials in its embassies to promote Japan's trade with those countries and tied some American aid to purchase of Japanese products. Of course, Washington's unabashed promotion of Japanese economic power in southeast Asia strained its relations with the region's European colonial powers.

After North Korea's attack on South Korea in June 1950, Washington promoted Japan as a military as well as political economic ally. The White House ordered MacArthur to create a 75,000-man 'national police force' and soon thereafter began negotiations with Tokyo for a mutual security treaty. Although most Japanese leaders favored an American guarantee for Japan's security, they rejected any continued American bases in Japan or significant Japanese rearmament. But Washington made it clear that a peace treaty restoring Japan's sovereignty would only be granted with an alliance. Yoshida finally forged a consensus on the need for compromise, and on 31 September 1951 in San Francisco, Japan signed a peace treaty with most of its former enemies and a mutual security treaty with Washington. Tokyo succeeded in reducing the number of troops requested by Washington as its contribution to the alliance from 350,000 to 180,000.

Having regained its sovereignty, and building on the triangular trade and economic reforms pushed through by Washington, Tokyo embarked single-mindedly on the neomercantilist policies which transformed Japan from mass poverty to mass affluence and global power. Yet even though Japan's economic power extends worldwide, the cornerstone of Japan's foreign policy remains the United States. Former Foreign Minister Saburo Okita (1978–9) wrote in 1989 that 'Japan's relations with the entire world have been shaped by being under America's economic, social, and political wing for more than forty years'.[12]

Japan's corporations achieve enormous economies of scale by combining their own protected market of 120 million consumers with America's largely wide-open market, now 250 million. Japan first achieved a trade surplus with the United States in 1965, and has steadily widened its surplus through the late 1960s and into the 1970s. It was the Reagan administration's inept policies of overvaluing the dollar and tripling America's national debt which increased Japan's trade surplus with the United States to crisis proportions. Japan's surplus soared from $15 billion in 1981 to $59 billion in 1987, and remained $50 billion in 1992, despite the yen's doubling in value after 1985. About one-third of Japan's trade is with the United States, and Japan still huddles under America's nuclear and conventional shield.

As Japan's economic superpower grows, trade conflicts become more frequent. Washington complained of Japanese dumping as early as 1955, and as Japan's corporations became more internationally competitive, Washington's complaints against Japan's neomercantilism grew more frequent. Relations remained largely untroubled, however, until the Nixon administration, when the White House negotiated a textile OMA with Tokyo; took the United States off the gold standard and devalued the dollar against the yen and other currencies in 1971; recognized China in 1972; threatened to boycott soybean exports; and allowed the dollar to float in 1973. Although only the textile agreement was specifically directed against Japan, the Japanese saw all these as 'shocks' administered by an anti-Japanese White House. Nor was it only the Americans who complained. During the 1970s and through the 1980s and 1990s a growing chorus of countries criticized Japanese neomercantilism.

The Japanese claim repeatedly that there are no serious barriers impeding foreign products in Japan. Tokyo has been making these claims since the late 1950s after it agreed to liberalize its markets as the price for entering GATT. It has been 'opening' its markets ever since. During the 1980s alone, Tokyo announced with great drama ten separate market opening steps, each of which was supposed to make Japan the world's most open economy. In 1986 Tokyo claimed that Japan's External Trade Organization (JETRO) would henceforth devote itself to stimulating imports while it created the Manufactured Import Promotion Organization (MIPRO) to push manufactured imports!

Although no knowledgeable foreign observers take these promises seriously, what proof is there that Japan's markets are still closed?

JAPANESE MARKETS – A CLOSED SHOP?

There are no free markets in Japan. All of Japan's markets are managed to varying extents by business cartels and government guidance which attempt to minimize foreign imports. Smoking guns of Japanese protectionism can be found. A series of American government and private studies have attempted to identify specific Japanese trade barriers and determine how different the trade balance would be if Japan's markets were genuinely open. A 1985 Commerce Department report reveals that American exports to Japan would have increased $16.9 billion in 1982, essentially wiping out that year's trade deficit.[13] In 1987, Robert Lawrence estimates that Japanese manufactured imports would rise 40 per cent if free markets prevailed.[14] The Office of the US Trade Representatives annually submits estimates on substantial foreign trade barriers. The 1989 report on Japan listed twenty-nine serious specific product barriers to imports. Products barred included semiconductors, supercomputers, satellites, aerospace, optical fibers, auto parts, telecommunications equipment, insurance, soda ash, high cube containers, construction and engineering, food additives, medical equipment, pharmaceuticals, feedgrains, wood and paper products, aluminum, leather, cigarettes, legal services, and TRON (real-time operating system) while general barriers included patents, trademarks, copyrights, distribution system, marketing practices, and the large-scale retail store law. European and American producers hold a comparative advantage in virtually all the specific product areas. This list is not comprehensive – it just addresses the most obvious and egregious products and barriers.[15]

Of course, the total costs of Japan's neomercantilism to the United States and other industrial countries is incalculable. The trade deficits reveal only the partial impact, and do not include such factors as the negative multiplier effects of a devastated foreign industry.

Most Japanese protectionism occurs behind closed doors, and the evidence for it is thus circumstantial. One clear indicator of continued Japanese neomercantilism is the fact that Japan's percentage of manufactured imports to GDP has remained constant over the last two decades, while those of other leading industrial countries have all increased enormously (see Table 4.1).[16] Most of these manufactured imports come from Japan's overseas investments and not foreign firms. Those few manufactured imports are sold at outrageously high prices. A MITI-Commerce Department study in 1989 revealed that Japanese pay 42 per cent more for the same package of goods and services as Americans.[17]

TABLE 4.1   *Percentage of manufactured imports to GNP*

	1970	1987
Japan	6.5%	8.3%
USA	10.1%	37.0%
France	28.4%	59.2%
W. Germany	23.1%	44.7%
Italy	22.3%	43.1%
Britain	27.4%	78.0%

Another damning sign of Japan's persistent import barriers is the lack of intra-industry trade.[18] Intra-industry trade involves the exchange of similar products between countries. For example, Germany imports Renaults while France imports Volkswagons. The more developed a nation's economy, the greater the intra-industry trade with countries of similar development level and market size and openness. Lincoln writes that Japan's low level of intra-industry 'trade implies that its behavior is inefficient or "unfair"'. In 1980, Japan's intra-industry trade index measured only 25 compared to America's 60, France's 82, Britain's 78, Germany's 66, Italy's 61, or even South Korea's 48.[19] In 1985, Japan's index was only 23, two points lower than in 1980, compared to America's 61 which rose to 82, Germany's, which rose to 67, and South Korea's 49.[20]

Most imports continue to be natural resources, and even those are raw rather than refined minerals and energy. For example, a comparison of the copper industries of France, the United States, and Japan reveals that France and the United States import large quantities of worked copper even though they have huge domestic deposits, while Japan imports mostly copper ore and refines it at home. In 1985, only 2.1 per cent of Japan's copper imports were worked, compared with 52.5 per cent of America's and 44.1 per cent of France's. In contrast, 67.2 per cent of Japan's copper imports were ore, compared to only 0.3 per cent of America's and 0.0 per cent of France's.[21] In complete defiance of liberal theory, similar results are true for Japan's other mineral and energy imports.

Why? Japan continues to import raw materials and refine them for neomercantilist, not liberal reasons. Refined products have more value-added than raw materials. Even if it costs more, it is in Japan's interests to try to manufacture as much as possible within Japan, because wealth is retained within the country that would have flowed elsewhere with free trade.

Another reality that Japan's spokespeople cannot dismiss is the effects of the yen's strengthening since 1985. In September 1985, the finance ministers of Japan, the United States, Germany, Britain, and France agreed to intervene jointly in world capital markets to devalue the dollar. National banks essentially dumped dollars and bought other currencies. This action was successful. The yen doubled in value against the dollar over the next two years from about 245 in September 1985 to 125 by Spring 1987.

What was the result of the dollar's massive devaluation against both the yen and the European currencies? America's trade with Europe responded according to classic economic principles – a $27 billion American deficit in 1987 became a $4 billion surplus in 1990. However, America's trade deficit with Japan dropped only from $59 billion to $41 billion during the same period even though the yen doubled in value. Why the anomaly? The answer: Europe's markets largely subscribe to free market principles, while Japan's are still governed by managed market principles.

Even more curious is a comparison of European and American exports to Japan. According to classical economic theory, since the dollar was devalued against both the European currencies and yen, the Europeans should have experienced a far worse trade performance against Japan than the Americans. After all, the currency alignment between the Europeans and Japan was relatively unchanged, while Europe's increased imports of American goods presumably reflected a greater American competitive advantage. Even if Japanese trade barriers prevented any significant American penetration of its markets, surely the Americans, enjoying a devalued currency, would outperform the Europeans. In reality, the opposite took place. While Europe's exports to Japan should have lagged far behind America's, they actually expanded much faster than America's.

By what means are Japan's markets protected?

Japan's markets are protected by a series of concentric walls of which the outermost are tariffs and quotas, while the dozen or so inner walls are a succession of increasingly subtle nontariff barriers. While the outermost walls have been reduced steadily since the mid-1960s and are in significant, Japan's inner walls remain largely unbreached. The nontariff barriers can be divided into direct and indirect government policies.

Nontariff barriers directly controlled by the government remain numerous and formidable, despite continuous contrary Japanese claims. Bureaucrats implement direct government nontariff barriers through both 'administrative guidance' (*gyosei shido*) and official regulations. Japan's officials prefer informal to formal exercise of their power. 'Guidance' is more subtle and just as effective as pointing to an official regulation, and leaves no paper trail that foreign critics can point to as an example of Japanese neomercantilism.

Few Japanese corporations, large or small, ever defy an assertion of bureaucratic power, and none can long resist the enormous pressure that the ministries can wield against recalcitrant businesses. In 1987, for example, the Japanese firm Lion Petroleum, which owned a half-dozen gas stations in Tokyo, tried to import gasoline from Singapore, which was cheaper than Japanese refined gasoline. Theoretically there was a 'free' gasoline market. In reality, Lion broke the unspoken but understood rule that the officially free gasoline market was simply a public relations gesture to the foreigners; in reality, Japanese would continue to buy Japanese, even if it was more expensive. MITI banned Lion's imports and warned other Japanese gasoline producers not to sell to Lion until it gave up its foreign source. Lion soon meekly complied.

Japanese officials are also notorious for entangling competitive imports in red tape that delays, limits, and thus raises the price, of any products eventually allowed in. For example, Tokyo devises testing and certification procedures to shut off competitive foreign goods. Until recently it required all drugs sold in Japan to be tested on Japanese, thus rejecting foreign drug tests. Even the most powerful foreign pharmaceutical firms would hesitate before committing the enormous expense of duplicating their tests in Japan. Even then, there would be no guarantee that their products would be approved.

And even if the product is approved for entry, the officials will insist on inspecting each product individually rather than the entire type of product. This of course adds considerable time and expense to the import. Foreign automobile producers have been particularly vociferous at denouncing the certification process for each automobile shipped to Japan. Despite this obvious asymmetry in certification procedures, Paris has been the only government that has played hard ball with the Japanese on this blatant nontariff barrier. Other governments simply let off barrages of futile protests and demands that the Japanese abandon this neomercantilist policy. But Tokyo will only bow to concrete retaliation, not protests.

Japan's patent system is designed to allow Japanese corporations free access to foreign technology. When a foreign firm applies for a patent it must wait an average seven years for approval during which time its Japanese rivals can adapt the technology to their own products. Texas Instruments had to wait over thirty years for approval of its integrated circuit technology! During the meantime, Japanese corporations freely exploit the technology, devise products which compete directly against the foreign firm which invented the technology, and more often than not eventually bankrupt or buy out their foreign rival.

The government's indirect trade barriers are more effective than the direct barriers, because they are so subtle. Japanese still overwhelmingly buy Japanese, even when a cheaper foreign equivalent is available. Like most governments, Tokyo follows 'buy Japanese' procurement policies, and forces private firms to do the same. In 1988, MITI fiercely criticized All Nippon Airways (ANA) for buying American rather than Japanese jet engines for its aircraft. Japan's industrial groups (*keiretsu*) buy products or components first from within the group, and then, if the group does not make that product, it buys from another Japanese industrial group. They only buy from foreign sources if no Japanese sources are available. The screwdriver assembly plants that Japanese set up overseas are perfect examples of this prevailing 'buy Japanese' practice. Rather than buy from easily-available foreign sources they will either ship over components from Japan or buy from a related Japanese firm which has set up shop in that country. Mordechai Kreinin analyzed the procurement policies of Japanese, European, and American firms and found that the Japanese all bought from other Japanese sources with no bidding while the European and American firms allowed open bids and bought from the cheapest source.[22]

Japan's labyrinthine distribution system is primarily designed to serve as a welfare system to mop up Japanese who would be otherwise unemployed, but also serves as an excellent nontariff trade barrier. Sole distributor laws force foreign exporters to choose just one distributor. The foreign exporter is faced with a terrible dilemma. If the distributor has a nationwide network, it is probably already tied to a major *keiretsu* and would thus have little incentive to market a competitor's products. If the distributor is untied, it is unlikely to have any significant sales network. Either way, the sales are likely to be minimum. The distributor meanwhile will sell the product at 'luxury' good prices and reap windfall profits. About 75 per cent of Japan's imports and 45 per cent of its exports are handled by the Big Nine trading companies (*Sogo Shosha*) which are tied to one or more of the Big Six industrial groups. The conflict of interest is clear.

The xenophobia of Japanese consumer attitudes is carefully nurtured by official and private public relations alike. Japanese children are 'educated' to believe that they are from a 'small, resource-poor country', and the mass media continually drives home the same theme to all Japanese. Japanese consider those few manufactured goods that can run the gauntlet of Japan's import barriers as 'luxury' goods.

Japan's antitrust laws are among the world's toughest. Yet these antitrust laws imposed on Japan during the American occupation are meaningless. Japan's Fair Trade Commission (FTC) rarely enforces Japanese antitrust law and when it does only imposes tiny fines on the guilty. Tokyo not only turns a blind eye to their enforcement but actively encourages the creation and collusion of hundreds of market, production, or trade cartels.

Buying a manufacturing company is theoretically the fastest way for a foreign firm to build a market position in Japan. At the stroke of a pen, an acquisition can provide a trained workforce, business and political connections, distribution system, land, and factories. In the 1980s, there were over 2,000 annual mergers and acquisitions in Japan, compared to about 3,000 in the United States. Between 1980 and 1988, Japan had 8.8 and the United States 8.2 combinations per 10,000 incorporated businesses, or roughly the same percentage.[23]

It would appear that Japan's merger and acquisition market is as open as America's. The reality is that there are significant differences between the two countries, and most Japanese firms are unavailable for foreign buyouts. One difference is one of scale. Generally most Japanese mergers and acquisitions involve small or medium sized firms: during the 1980s about 80 per cent were valued at $20 million or less and 60 per cent at less than $8 million. While the United States recorded over 200 transactions valued at over $1 billion since 1981, Japan had only two – the 1989 merger of the Mitsui and Taiyo Kobe Banks, and the 1990 merger of Mitsubishi Mining and Cement Company and the Mitsubishi Metal Corporation.[24]

Japanese mergers and acquisitions largely occur within the horizontal or vertical *keiretsu*. In the 1980s, 58 per cent of all acquisitions were within the bidding firm's same business, 29 per cent were in a related field, and only 13 per cent were in unrelated businesses.[25] The usual scenario is that a parent firm will buy out a weak member of its vertical *keiretsu* in which it already owns stock. Less common is for a group bank and related major stockholders and lenders to manage the merger of two related firms within the horizontal *keiretsu*. In the 1950s and 1960s, MITI pressured dozens of related firms to merge in an attempt to rationalize Japan's economy. MITI's most famous mergers were Japan's second and fourth largest automobile corporations, Nissan and Prince, into Nissan in 1965; the merger of the three major paper manufacturers, Oji, Jujo, and Honshu in 1968; and the merger of Yawata Iron and Steel, and Fuji Iron and Steel into Nippon Steel in 1968.[26]

Unfortunately, it is virtually impossible for a foreign firm to buy out a Japanese company. Between 1955 and 1984, there were only thirty-two foreign acquisitions of Japanese firms, of which seventeen occurred from 1980 to 1984.[27] From 1984 to 1989, American firms bought controlling interests in twenty-four Japanese firms, of which eleven were simply buyouts of Japanese partners in joint ventures, and two involved the sale of one American-owned Japanese subsidiary to another American company.[28] Those acquisitions which do occur are mostly foreign firms buying out the Japanese share of a joint venture.

Official restrictions on foreign acquisitions of Japanese firms have recently been considerably reduced. Before 1980, the Foreign Trade and Exchange Law (1949) and the Foreign Investment Law (1950) empowered MOF to screen and block all acquisitions. After several decades of foreign pressure, Tokyo finally agreed to combine the two laws into the one Foreign Exchange and Foreign Trade Control Law of 1980 in which all foreign direct investment in Japan would henceforth be 'free-in-principle'. Although prior notification was required for any investment involving 25 per cent or more of a Japanese firm, MOF could only block the purchase for national security reasons. In 1984, Tokyo dropped the prior notification requirement and removed protection from eleven 'national security' firms in defense, oil, and microelectronics.

Restrictions continued. Prior to March 1991, a bidder had to register its intention with MOF and then, if it received MOF's approval to proceed, wait ten days before it could make a tender which would then be open for at least twenty days and had to be closed within thirty days. In addition, the bidder must use commissioned agents rather than its own expertise to conduct the deal. The waiting period gave the targeted firm plenty of time to either buy up its own stock or find a white samurai, while the thirty-day limit restricted the bidder's ability to try new strategies for the takeover. Now, there is no waiting period, the bidding period is extended to sixty days, and bidders no longer have to rely on commissioned agents whose loyalty and discretion was often questionable.

As Trafalger-Glen's 1985 attempt to takeover Minebea, and T. Boone Pickens' 1990–1 pass at Koito clearly revealed, there is no free market for companies in Japan, nor is one likely ever to emerge. Tokyo will never open up its merger and acquisition market. Despite the more liberal M and A law, Japan's unofficial restrictions make foreign acquisitions of Japanese firms as difficult as ever. The administrative guidance of MITI and other ministries continues to stake the deck against foreign firms, without leaving any paper trail as evidence. Japan's stock market will remain manipulated by pervasive insider-trading which in part accounts for the average fifty times earning ratio of Japanese equities, compared to an average fifteen times for American firms. Even more formidable is the continuing cultural taboo against hostile takeovers, in which an acquisition is equated with a 'high-jacking' (*nottori*), 'bribery' (*baishu*), and 'greenmail' largely conducted by Japanese gangsters (*yakuza*). To Japanese selling a company is like selling a family, an inherently immoral transaction. The combination of two different firms in the name of efficiency means that duplicates of personal, operations, and equipment will be eliminated – a direct assault on Japan's lifetime employment system. The *keiretsu* system will continue to loosen but will never break up while the taboo against hostile takeover will remain powerful. The only firms available to foreign acquisition will be small, underfinanced, entrepreneur firms. According to Kester, the *keiretsu* will simply use hostile domestic and foreign takeover efforts to discipline laggard members, while retaining tight control over the outcome. Kester writes:

> bidders will begin and end their roles in the drama only as catalytic agents of change, rarely ever becoming victors in open, competitive bidding for the target company. Though appearing nominally independent, the bidders will in fact be used by major stable stockholders as their cat's-paws in the disciplining of target-company management. In short, the threat of takeover will gradually substitute for direct stockholder intervention as the latter safeguard weakens in the face of corporate restructuring and financial liberalization . . . [F]inal outcomes will be carefully and deliberately orchestrated by, and to the advantage of, pre-existing stable corporate stakeholders.[29]

Meanwhile, an undervalued yen continues to block competitive imports and promote Japanese exports. How does Tokyo get away with it?

According to economic theory, a free currency market among industrial countries would allow those states to achieve a general trade balance. If a currency's value is determined by the demand for that currency, then, all other things being equal, demand is determined by that country's interest rates. If a country raise its interest rates (to dampen an overheated economy, finance its debts, etc.) above those of other industrial countries, then domestic and foreign investors will buy into that country's public and private interest bearing accounts. This surge in demand for the high interest country simultaneously forces up the value of that currency and depresses the currencies of the other countries. In the short run the high interest country will export less and import more while the other countries enjoy more exports and less imports. But if the interest rates remain high, other countries will eventually have to raise their interest rates to attract investments, while the original high interest country will have to cut its own interest rates in order to stimulate its now depressed economy. Money then flows from the original high interest rate country to others, thus weakening that country's currency and strengthening the other currencies. The original country's trade account balances or becomes a surplus while the other countries' trade accounts worsen. Of course, this theory assumes perfect competition.

The real world bears no resemblance to the airtight, two-dimensional graphs and equations of neoclassical theory. There is a huge asymmetry between Japan and the United States, the European Community, and other democratic industrial countries. Japan's capital and product markets remain tightly controlled and the yen finances only a small percentage of Japanese trade, while America's capital and product markets remain relatively open and the dollar finances most global trade. Thus there will always be inordinate demand for dollars and weak demand for yen. The overvalued dollar also adversely affects the currency values of other industrial countries which are tied to the dollar. As a result, Japan continues to enjoy an undervalued currency while its trade rival's currencies are overvalued, with correspondingly positive effects on Japan's trade balance and adverse effects on the trade balances of the other industrial countries.

The yen will remain undervalued for the indefinite future, continuing pushing Japanese products and harming foreign products in Japan and around the world. Tokyo continues to manipulate the currency supply and demand so that demand for the yen and thus its value remains weak and demand for the dollar thus its strength remains high. By refusing to liberalize its financial markets completely, foreign investors are inhibited from investing in Japan. Meanwhile, Japan continues to limit the yen's role as an international currency for trade or lending. In 1990, half of all international lending was in dollars while only 11.5 per cent was in yen.[30]

REASONS FOR THE CLOSED SHOP

Why do Japan's markets remain virulently protected even thirty years after Tokyo first announced its first 'liberalization' package? Why does neomercantilism persist after Japan has become the world's greatest economic superpower, enjoying immense annual trade surpluses larger than the economies of most countries?

There are many reasons why Japanese protectionism continues. The most important is economic – neomercantilism creates far more wealth, power, and security for Japan than liberalism ever would. The Japanese simply do not believe in free trade. Japan would never have conducted even its very limited liberalization without massive foreign pressure backed by the threat of retaliation. Tokyo's market opening packages are usually delivered after months and sometimes years of acrimony with its foreign partners in which they have eventually threatened retaliation, and on the eve of an important bilateral or multilateral summit. Lincoln writes that

> when Japan began liberalizing its trade barriers in the early 1960s, it did so, not because of a new-found recognition of the benefits from free trade, but because of foreign pressure. The predominant domestic intellectual rationale for liberalization from the early 1960s to the mid-1980s has been the need to meet international obligations with an implicit belief that liberalization held no direct benefits for the Japanese economy.[31]

Yet, despite Tokyo's intransigence, Japan's political economy has changed remarkably over the past five decades. During the late 1940s and 1950s, Japan's political economy was characterized by a tight bureaucracy-led corporatism in which cash-starved corporations and politicians followed ministry-created and implemented industrial policies. Ministry power, however, diminished during the 1960s and early 1970s as corporations became wealthier and politicians more knowledgeable about specific issues. The result was a Japanese 'corporatism without labor' in which there was a relative power balance among the bureaucrats, businessmen, and politicians. During the mid-1970s, Japan's political economy underwent enormous changes. Social security, universal health care, anti-pollution regulations, and welfare programs enacted in the late 1960s began to impose increasingly high costs. Although OPEC's quadrupling of oil prices halved Japan's growth rate, the economy continued to diversify. Waves of pressure from Washington and, to a much lesser extent, from Brussels, forced Tokyo to deregulate if not liberalize large chunks of its economy. With the resulting defusion of power, Japan's strict corporatism broke down into a looser neocorporatism. Entrepreneurial firms like Recruit can buy their way into privileges formerly reserved for Japan's old-guard *keiretsu*. Now the corporate world is in the economy's driving seat while the government makes suggestions rather than others from the backseat. Business follows those suggestions which it deems in its interest.

Genuine market liberalization, however, has not accompanied this decentralization of power. Ironically, the erosion of Japan's corporatist policy making and implementation regime has simply defused the power to protect to smaller groups of public and private groups. Lincoln asks

> why has Japan failed to participate in the extensive two-way flows of manufactured goods that characterize the trade of most other industrialized nations? The patterns . . . are quite extraordinary, have changed little in the past 15 to 20 years, and are a key element in the trade disputes that have become increasingly frequent and tense. The answer involves a complex set of attitudes, institutions, and policies in Japan that have created a bias against manufactured imports – a bias that many Japanese do not understand or refuse to admit.[32]

Among the reasons Lincoln cites for Japanese protection is a 'sense of superiority' which 'Japan has mobilized . . . to fuel its economic development process'.[33]

Collusion is an integral part of Japan's political economic culture. Japan's corporations are tied together in webs of financial and moral ties in which free markets do not and cannot exist. Economic transactions are not based on the price or quality of goods: they are based on relationships. The Japanese will always put concrete relationships before abstract free trade notions. Lincoln writes that

> Western economists . . . assume far too much economic rationality on the part of Japanese individuals and corporations. Economic necessity will bring changes in behavior, but these responses are always modified by norms of Japanese social behavior. As far as possible, corporations will make decisions within the context of the groups within which they operate – the web of supplier-buyer network, other firms in their industry, and the industry-government connection. This context and the group dynamic that it implies mean that economic rationality will be modified as it is bent to conform to social reality. In the case of imports, yen appreciation will lead to more imports, but pressure from import-competing manufacturers and established distributors of domestic products must be listened to, accommodated, and compensated. These social necessities mean that the inroads of imports into the Japanese economy will be blunted.[34]

Foreign governments and businesses often complain bitterly about Japanese stonewalling during negotiations and their failure to live up to subsequent agreements. Michael Blaker has extensively studied Japanese negotiating strategies, attributing most Japanese intransigence on issues to the extreme difficulty of shaping a consensus.[35] Japan's preparations for an upcoming negotiation are mostly concerned with hammering out a consensus among the myriad interests in that issue – little if any time is devoted to understanding the foreign position and its relative validity: 'Japanese leaders and negotiators were so preoccupied with their own demands that they hardly comprehended or appreciated opposing positions'.[36]

During talks, Japan's negotiators are given little if any leeway to make concessions and instead just repeatedly mouth the official policy. Their strategy is simply to hunker down and stonewall until the foreigners either give concessions or surrender on the issue itself. This hedgehog defense at the table is accompanied by intensive public relations campaigns at home to rally the public around the flag and abroad to undermine the foreign position. Japanese will only make a concession – almost always minor and symbolic – after the foreigner has made major concessions. Then Tokyo will often repackage old concessions from previous negotiations in new forms and hope no one notices.

Also common is for negotiators to agree in principle and then say they need to study the question further. If a Japanese negotiating team should make an unplanned concession under pressure, Tokyo will quickly and quietly repudiate it. Caught in the middle, Japanese diplomats frequently find themselves making promises to foreigners that they realize will probably never be approved by the government. Thus, Japanese diplomats frequently find themselves making one promise to a foreign audience and the opposite promise to their constituents.

Considering all the anti-liberalization forces inside and outside Tokyo, it is not surprising that Tokyo's 'concessions' to foreign demands for market opening are cosmetic at best. Rothacher states bluntly that: 'official declarations on the goals and priorities of Japan's foreign policies appear usually as pretty empty and well-sounding statements'.[37]

CREATING IMAGES AND NEW REALITIES

How do the Japanese counter foreign criticism of Tokyo's neomercantilism?[38]

A concerted global public relations campaign is yet another strategy designed to reinforce Japan's foreign economic penetration and counter any criticism of Japanese neomercantilism. Tokyo solidifies and expands its economic gains by penetrating and manipulating foreign governments and publics. The Japan lobby in the United States alone spends an estimated $400 million annually at the national, state, and local levels attempting to influence policies and legislation in Japan's favor.[39] Although Japan's lobby in Brussels and the national capitals of Europe is relatively small, it will undoubtedly grow to equal in clout the lobby in the United States.

What are the central messages of Japan's global public relations campaign? Japanese spokespeople are quick to dismiss any criticism of or retaliation against Japanese neomercantilism. According to the standard Tokyo line, Japan has become the world's most dynamic economy solely because Japanese work harder and enjoy the world's most free market – foreigners do not sell more in Japan because they do not try hard enough and their goods are of inferior quality. Thus, any criticism of alleged Japanese import barriers or dumping is simply racist 'Japan-bashing' by those who are jealous of Japan's dazzling success. Kenjiro Ishikawa captures the essence of this stance when he claims that recent 'criticism and unfair treatment of Japan and Japanese success have not been unrelated . . . Criticism in Western Europe of Japanese trade behavior seemed to be based mainly on memories of the 1930s'.[40] As a last resort Japanese simply dismiss foreign criticism of Tokyo's neomercantilism as 'racism'.

Foreign complaints about Japanese trade and investment barriers are similarly handled. Although Japan's trading partners have complained about Japanese trade barriers since the beginning of their relationships, no concerted effort was made to open Japan's markets until Tokyo applied for membership in the OECD during the early 1960s. Tokyo never fulfilled its promise to open its markets in return for OECD membership. From then through today, Tokyo has staved off pressure from Washington or Brussels to liberalize Japan's markets by offering packages of mostly symbolic market opening steps. During the 1980s alone, Tokyo presented ten such packages, each of which was supposed to make Japan the world's most open economy. The reality was that more subtle nontariff barriers like cartels and administrative guidance were strengthened as more formal tariffs and quotas were lowered. The result was that Japan's markets remained carefully managed to minimize any competitive foreign products.

Omiyage or gift-bearing diplomacy is an important means by which Tokyo finesses trade disputes. A high-level official will travel to a country or countries with which Japan is experiencing economic tensions with a small symbolic gift such as an aid loan or tariff reduction to reduce the conflict's intensity. These gifts generally represent no real concession since a reduction of one trade barrier is simply matched by the reinforcement of another more subtle trade barrier, while aid is usually tied to purchases of

Japanese goods and services and thus will inevitably exacerbate Japan's penetration.

Another favorite tactic to offset foreign criticism is for Tokyo to send forth a 'buying mission' to that country. In 1991, for example, in response to mounting complaints from Europe, the United States, and East Asia, MITI developed its 'Business Global Partnership Initiative', a three-year program in which it would encourage imports by Japan's firms and 'cooperation' with foreign firms, and sweetened the deal by offering certain tax reductions. Forty firms eventually signed the pledge to import more manufactured goods and expand local procurement for their foreign investments. It remains to be seen whether this much publicized action will have the slightest effect on Japan's trade surpluses.

'Concessions' are well timed. For example, on 19 March 1992 Tokyo announced that it would reduce its voluntary automobile export quota to the United States from 2.3 million units to 1.65 units, a seemingly considerable cut to those unfamiliar with the nuances of Japanese neomercantilism. Tokyo made the gesture as a 'gift' to President Bush amidst a tough reelection campaign. Bush could point to the figures and claim a great victory for the United States, even though his administration never called for the cuts and claimed it did not believe in 'managed trade'. The quotas themselves were nothing more than a blatant public relations gesture that had no effect on Japan's 31 per cent share of America's automobile market. In 1991, Japan only exported 1.76 million cars to the United States, well below the official quota, and with America in recession, MITI projected 1992 sales to dip slightly to 1.73 million. The lower quota applied only to direct exports; it did not apply to transplants sold in the United States, nor to the tens of billions of dollars worth of parts exported to the transplant factories. Japan's current one-third market share will rise steadily throughout the 1990s.

When asked why Japan does not import more manufactured goods, Japanese spokespeople will usually reply that it is because Japan already manufactures virtually all the goods it needs. When asked why, the spokesperson will reply that Japan's corporation have 'economies of scope' which allows them to expand the types of goods they produce to satisfy shifts in demand. Of course, any large industrial country could make the same claim for protectionism, that it does not need other countries' manufactured goods because it has the capability to manufacture everything it needs. But as has been seen, the other leading industrial nations operate on free-trade principles in which there will inevitably be considerable intra-industry trade.

Another Japanese justification for the much lower percentage of manufactured exports is that foreign goods are not adapted to Japanese tastes. Kazuo Sato writes that 'products made at home by small local firms fit Japanese tastes much better than foreign-made goods. We conjecture that it is for this reason that imports are low'.[41] Yet every country has taste differences which can be used as an excuse for protectionism.

Tokyo argues continually that in the case of its bilateral trade surplus with the United States Washington's huge fiscal deficits are the major cause. Budgets must be financed. Since politicians refuse to raise enough taxes to finance the deficit, the money is borrowed. Interest rates are raised to attract lenders. Foreign as well as domestic investors buy treasury bills. The foreign demand for dollars raises the dollar's value and thus the price of American exports while it lowers the prices of imports. The result is America's worsening trade deficit. America's trade deficit will diminish if Washington reduces its budget deficit. In other words, the trade deficit is all America's fault.

In reality, things are a bit more complicated than this. During the 1980s, Reagan administration policies tripled America's national debt. The dollar did rise from about 200 yen in 1981 to 265 yen in 1985, but then fell to 140–145 by 1989, despite the fact that the Reagan budget deficits were as high as ever. In 1991, Japan's interest rate actually surpassed that of the United States, yet the yen did not strengthen or the dollar fall.

How do classical economists explain these anamolies? They cannot. Liberal economists assume that Japan and the United States enjoy equally free markets. The reality is that Tokyo still carefully manages Japan's capital markets to maintain an undervalued yen. Tokyo did agree to go along with Washington, Bonn, London, and Paris to intervene in global capital markets, starting in September 1985 to devalue the dollar. But Tokyo has since decided that the dollar fell and the yen has risen far enough and intervenes to prevent any currency value shifts.

Even if it were correct, the Japanese argument that Washington's budget deficits are the major cause of the bilateral trade deficit does not, of course, explain the Community's severe and growing trade deficit with Japan. After all, the dollar strengthened against both the yen and European currencies, but Japan's trade surplus mounted with both the United States and Community.

After claiming that Japanese hard work, foreign sloth, and the American budget deficit explain Japan's trade surpluses, Japanese spokesmen often go on to claim that because Japan is a resource-poor country it must run trade surpluses of manufactured goods to pay for foreign resources. Foreign Ministry official Masamichi Hanabusa captures this excuse: 'With an extremely meagre endowment of natural resources, Japan had to pursue a policy of promoting the export of manufactures to provide jobs for its abundant labor force. The Japanese experience was unique.'[42]

The reality, of course, is that there is nothing unique about Japan's relative natural resource scarceness. Every Community member has a comparable dependence on foreign natural resources in virtually every category.[43] Of fourteen mineral and energy imports, Japan and Germany are equally dependent except for coal. Although Germany has an abundance of domestic coal, it is much more expensive than global market sources and thus an economic and political liability rather than an asset. Despite their similar resource import profiles, Germany's percentage of manufactured imports to GDP in 1987 was 14.4, while Japan's was 2.4 per cent. Japan's pleas for 'understanding' about its lack of manufactured imports because it is resource-poor can be dismissed as blatant propaganda.[44]

And Japan does not have to refine those foreign resources on which it is dependent. It could simply import products like petrochemicals or lumber which are produced elsewhere at cheaper costs. Yet it chooses to buy the rawest of materials in order to enjoy the wealth created from refining those products in Japan. In the largely zero-sum game of international trade, Tokyo's decision to refine those products, even if it will be at a higher cost, gathers wealth in Japan that would otherwise be created in the resource producing countries if the world economy operated according to free market principles.

Japanese like to point to a few success stories like Coca Cola, IBM, or Schick razors to show that Japan's market is completely open and that foreigners do not sell more because they do not try hard enough. Unfortunately, the 'success stories' are the exception that helps prove that Japan's markets remain very carefully protected. Those companies that have made inroads into Japan's markets were either able to enter Japan during the 1950s and slowly build up a position, like Coca Cola and IBM, or captured a small market niche like Schick razors.

The Japanese belief that they are members of a 'pure unique race' is of course absurd enough, but is frequently extended to other Japanese conditions. During the 1980s, foreign ski equipment was banned because Japanese snow is different, baseball bats because Japanese baseball is different, beef because Japanese intestines are different, and so on. Needless to say, even the most well-paid foreign spokespeople for Japan have trouble justifying these assertions.

Another aspect of the 'Japan is unique' argument is that foreigners can never understand Japan and thus can never truly break into Japan's markets.

Japan's web of trade barriers and collusive business activity are created by government policy, and only reinforced by Japanese culture. The limited market openings through today cannot reverse three decades of sustained and systematic protectionism and collusion. Lincoln writes that the 'reasoning becomes circular: the relationships developed when foreigners were kept out, and now their absence is taken to imply that they cannot adequately understand or participate'.[45] Japanese spokespeople seem nonplussed when it is pointed out that the 'Japan is unique' and 'Japan is the world's most open' assertions seem to contradict each other. The more powerful Japan becomes, the more it angrily rejects any foreign criticism of Tokyo's neomercantilism as mere 'Japan bashing'.

In addition to its elaborate walls of trade barriers, Japan's neomercantilism is promoted by a range of other highly sophisticated strategies. As if Japan's trade barriers and dumping offensive were not enough, the strategy behind Japan's direct foreign investments have also been severely criticized. Japanese direct foreign investments are becoming increasingly important in promoting Japan's economic superpower.

JAPANESE FOREIGN INVESTMENTS AND DEVELOPMENT AID

Japanese investments have flowed overseas in a series of distinct stages. During the 1950s and through the late 1960s, Tokyo restricted Japan's foreign investments to keep jobs and wealth in Japan, to prevent a persistent payments deficit from worsening. Several factors shaped the first wave of Japanese investments from the late 1960s through the mid-1970s. In return for joining the OECD in 1964 Tokyo promised to liberalize its economy, and between 1969 and 1972 Japan gradually loosened the harsh restrictions on both capital inflows and outflows. Meanwhile, Japan's rapid economic growth at once raised wages and increased the need for more natural resources, while many developing countries began raising trade barriers and offering incentives for foreign investors. In response to these developments, Japanese firms began investing overseas to capture foreign resources, markets, and cheap labor. Finally, Japan's unbridled industrialization caused an increasingly severe pollution problem, accompanied by increasingly powerful public demands that the government clean up the environment. In 1970, the Diet passed fourteen laws which imposed extremely stringent pollution regulations on industry. Heavily polluting firms now had an extra incentive to invest overseas to escape expensive regulations and 'houseclean' Japan. Japanese foreign investments during this first wave were largely in developing countries to take advantage of cheap labor, rich natural resource, large and more affluent markets, and largely nonexistent pollution regulations.

The second wave started in the mid-1970s and extended through the mid-1980s. OPEC's quadrupling of oil prices in 1973 which brought an era of global stagflation, combined with Japan's export offensives, caused the United States and Europe to become increasingly protective. Meanwhile, the yen revaluation and continued wage and land price hikes undermined the competitiveness of Japanese firms. Japan's industrial corporations began setting up factories within the United States and Europe to jump growing trade barriers and take advantage of official investment incentives and cheaper land, energy, and living costs.

Japan's third investment wave dates from the mid-1980s as financial and service corporations and small- and medium-sized components firms joined the large manufacturers in the United States and Europe. New Japanese direct foreign investments rose from $20 billion in 1987 to $54 billion in 1990. Japan's investments have been criticized as being little more than 'screwdriver assembly plants' in which all the value-added components are shipped from Japan, thus exacerbating rather than alleviating Japan's trade surplus. Japanese investments will continue to solidify and expand control over foreign markets and thus cement Japan's trade surplus. Meanwhile, only a trickle of foreign investments battle their way into Japan.

Tokyo has also enormously expanded its global political economic power by tying its 'aid' to Japanese goods, services, and investments. Japan's official development aid overtook the United States in 1989 when Tokyo committed $8.9 billion compared to Washington's $7.7 billion, while as a percentage of GNP Japan's 0.35 per cent far exceeds America's niggardly 0.15 per cent.[46] Most of Japan's 'increase' actually resulted from the yen's doubling in value between 1985 to 1989, which in turn more than doubled Japan's ODA from $3.9 billion to $8.9 billion. Japan's aid volume has leveled off since then with the yen's stabilization at around 130 to the dollar. In the fiscal year ending in March 1992, Japan allocated only $9.2 billion compared to $10 billion from the United States.

Where does Japanese aid go? In 1989, Asia accounted for 63 per cent of Japan's total ODA, of which 14 per cent went to northeast Asia, 33 per cent to southeast Asia, and 16 per cent to southwest Asia. 5 per cent went to the Middle East, 15 per cent to Africa, and 8 per cent to Latin America. 1 per cent went to Oceania, and 0.2 per cent to Europe, while 7 per cent was not disbursed. Of this aid, loans accounted for 55 per cent to be repaid at a 2.5 per cent interest rate, a figure far greater than America's loan component of 4.3 per cent or the Europeans' average 30 per cent.

Japan's aid program is shaped and implemented by a tug-of-war among MOF, MITI, EPA, and MFA. Most of Japan's ODA is directly administered by the Overseas Economic Cooperation Fund (OECF) and the Japan International Cooperation Agency (JICA), but a dozen other ministries and agencies have their own 'aid' programs, most of which are unashamedly export and investment subsidies for Japan's corporations.

What interests does Japan's aid serve? Japanese describe aid as 'economic cooperation' (*keizai kyoryoku*), an apt label since there is nothing altruistic or sacrificial about Japanese 'aid'. Critics dismiss the huge loan percentage as 'mercantile'. Tokyo justifies its large loan component by arguing that it encourages the recipient to use the money wisely for development rather than conspicious consumption. Officially, Japan's untied component was 78 per cent of its total ODA in 1989, the highest among the OECD. In reality, Japan's 'aid' remains overwhelmingly tied to the purchases of Japanese goods, services, and investments.

What explains the discrepancy between Japan's official statistics and actual disbursement? Japan's aid is targeted to specific projects, and only after Japan's relevant ministry and business leaders have thoroughly investigated the project's viability, with the major criteria being how far it advances Japanese exports, investments, and political power in the recipient. Having passed that requirement, Tokyo will then allocate aid to that project with the stipulation that only Japanese and indigenous firms are qualified to apply. Armed with inside information, Japan's firms or their foreign subsidiaries almost invariably outbid the local firms. Most Japanese 'aid' thus serves as a huge subsidy for Japanese exports and investments.

Will Japan's ODA increase in the future? Tokyo is committed to the OECD goal of each member donating 0.7 per cent of GNP to ODA. Tokyo has no plans, however, to implement its promise. In fact, Tokyo has fallen far short of Prime Minister Takeshita's 1988 promise to spend $50 billion on ODA in the five years to 1992, having actually budgeted only about $40 billion for the period. Most Japanese 'aid' will remain thoroughly tied to Japanese exports and investments.

Another important strategy, vigorously denied by Japanese spokespeople, is to form a yen bloc in East Asia which can eventually offset the economic blocks of Europe and North America. Questions about Japan's construction of a new 'East Asian Coprosperity Sphere' continually embarrass the Japanese. During Prime Minister Kaifu's tour of Southeast Asia in May 1991, Malaysian Prime Minister Mahathir publicly advocated Japanese leadership over a proposed East Asian Economic Grouping (EAEG). This was only the latest call by Mahathir and other southeast leaders for a more explicit Japanese hegemony over the region. Tokyo politely turns down such offers, claiming that it has no interest in leading or even constructing a regional bloc.

The reality is that, with Washington's compliance, for almost four decades Tokyo has been systematically constructing an east and southeast Asian economic bloc. These efforts have been very successful. All the Western Pacific's shipping lanes lead to Tokyo. Japan's trade, investment, and aid dominate the foreign economic relations of virtually every country in the region. In 1990, Japan's trade with China, Taiwan, Hong Kong, and the two Koreas accounted for 16.5 per cent (18.2 per cent of its exports and 14.8 per cent of its imports), while trade with Indonesia, Malaysia, the Philippines, Singapore, and Thailand was 11.5 per cent. Japan's 1990 trade surplus with South Korea was $6.9 billion, with Hong Kong $12 billion, with Taiwan $7.3 billion, with Singapore $7.8 billion, and with Thailand $5.3 billion. Almost half of foreign investment with the region and 70 per cent of aid is Japanese.

And increasingly Tokyo bolsters its economic ties with subtle but very powerful behind-the-scenes political pressure on the various governments to ensure that Japan's corporations enjoy every possible advantage over domestic as well as foreign firms. MITI and other Japanese officials are working closely with many of the governments to accord their economic planning with that of Japan. Since the 1978 economic summit Tokyo has acted as spokescountry for East Asia, thus simultaneously diverting East Asian criticism of Japanese neomercantilism by giving the impression that the region's interests will be advanced, and countering Western criticism of Japanese neomercantilism by waving the flag of an East Asian economic bloc. Yet, for public relations reasons Tokyo has no desire to formalize its hegemony over the region.

Tokyo's disavowal of its most important foreign policy goal is simply part of the strategy for deepening its hegemony over the region. Tokyo has dreamed of carving out a 'Greater East Asian Co-prosperity Sphere' since the mid-nineteenth century. The need for a Japanese bloc becomes all the more imperative as the European Community and North America trade blocs steadily deepen their inner ties and expand their criticism of Japanese neomercantilism. But a public acknowledgement of a century-old Japanese policy would cause alarm in the region as well as Brussels and Washington, and undercut Japan's advances. Instead, Tokyo remains deaf to calls by Mahathir and others while steadily deepening its ties with the region behind the scenes.

Why do the southeast Asian governments seem so willing either to outright invite or to acquiesce in Japan's hegemony? One reason is that

World War Two is rapidly becoming ancient history for most southeast Asians. Japan's imperialism in east Asia was far more brutal and prolonged than that in southeast Asia. Although millions of southeast Asians were murdered or plundered between 1941 and 1945, Japan's short-lived colonialism did stimulate powerful nationalist movements which eventually overthrew Western colonial rule which was reestablished after 1945, much as Napoleon's conquests stimulated nationalism across Europe. Another reason is that the region's exports are still largely raw materials, oil, and labor-intensive manufactured goods, which complement Japan's capital-intensive consumer and intermediate goods. Another reason is that the governments of the region are more susceptible to setting aside national interests for large Japanese political 'donations'. But most importantly, Tokyo has mastered a virtuous cycle of economic and political power throughout both east and southeast Asia. Even outspoken critics like China or South Korea find their economies forever being knitted more tightly to Japan.

Yet Japan wants not just to dominate east and southeast Asia, but eventually to assert global hegemony. As Europe and North America slowly rally against Tokyo's neomercantilism, the Japanese perceive the rapidly developing Third World, particularly in Latin America and the Middle East, as significant battlefields in the world trade war.[47] Tokyo has recognized the Third World's importance since OPEC's quadrupling of oil prices and OAPEC's boycott of oil to Japan in November 1973. Japan responded by dispatching its foreign minister to the key oil producing states of the Middle East and key resource states of Africa with promises of more aid, trade, and investments. The boycott was lifted in December after Tokyo called on Israel to withdraw to its pre-1967 borders and espoused Palestinian autonomy.

Thus was born Japan's 'comprehensive security policy' (*sogo anzen hosho*) in which Tokyo attempts to diversify as much as possible Japan's dependence on foreign resources, markets, and energy while making those sources as dependent as possible on Japanese trade, investments, aid, capital, technology, and political contributions. Meanwhile through strict conservation and efficiency measures, and the development of nuclear energy, Japan has dramatically lessened its overall dependence on foreign energy sources. Another means of increasing its economic power is for Tokyo to act as diplomatic go-between in regional conflicts. Tokyo's diplomacy in the Korean peninsula, Indochina, and different conflicts in the Middle East – efforts that many critics dismiss as mere 'message carrying' – are actually a very successful means of allowing Japan to continue trading with both sides under the guise of diplomacy.

JAPAN AND THE GULF WAR

Tokyo's comprehensive security policy was exemplified by its reaction to Iraq's takeover of Kuwait in August 1990. Many foreign observers were puzzled by Tokyo's nonchalant reaction to Iraq's invasion of Kuwait. Given Japan's dependence on oil for half its energy needs, and virtually complete dependence on foreign oil sources, why was not Japan more concerned that the Iraqi invasion gave Baghdad control of over 45 per cent of the world's proven oil reserves? By making Kuwait the 'nineteenth province' and massing a huge army on Saudi Arabia's borders, Baghdad could dictate global oil prices. The result would be a repeat of the price hikes and production cutbacks that condemned the global economy to stagflation after 1973. Iraq's position would strengthen steadily over the decades as other high cost, low reserve producers ran dry while the global economy became increasingly dependent on Iraq's ample reserves. Through war or subversion, Baghdad could eventually overthrow the Saudi regime and impose a pro-Iraqi government.

Not to worry, Japanese officials replied. Baghdad needs to sell the oil to pay off its debts and build its power as much as the global economy needs to buy that oil. True, prices would rise but probably not beyond $25 a barrel, the optimum selling price. Any higher price and producers elsewhere would attempt to undercut Iraq's prices while consumers would embark on drastic conservation measures. And anyway, Japan was only dependent on Iraq and Kuwait for about 12 per cent of its total oil.

And what about the long term? No industrial country has been more successful than Japan in diversifying and lessening its dependence on foreign energy sources while making its own industries and households super efficient consumers. Sure, Japan would be damaged by Iraqi hegemony over world oil markets, but much less than its industrial rivals. Over the short and long term, Japan would emerge all the stronger.

So not surprisingly, Tokyo rejected Washington's hardline policy toward Iraq's imperialism and instead advocated a diplomatic solution. Washington rejected Tokyo's position and pressed it to make a significant contribution to the alliance and regional development. Tokyo's subsequent offer in mid-August to contribute $1 billion in aid to the region was dismissed as wholly inadequate by the allied forces. Congress passed a resolution in early September warning that it would annually withdraw 5,000 American troops from Japan if Tokyo did not pay more for both their billeting and the Persian Gulf Alliance. Although many Japanese severely criticized the Congressional resolution, in mid-September Tokyo upped its contribution to $4 billion, of which half would go to the UN forces and half to Arab frontline states. In addition, the Kaifu government wrote a bill which would allow 1,000 unarmed members of Japan's Self-Defense Force (SDF) to join the alliance, but the bill was tabled after severe opposition and party criticism.

Tokyo's actions did not appease the allies who continued to criticize Tokyo for its footdragging and small contributions, with the epithet of 'the Scrooge of Asia' being typical.[48] Foreigners called on Japan to go beyond its 'checkbook diplomacy', and contribute at least some token military forces to the region where it receives most of its oil. Tokyo's position weakened steadily as the White House built an alliance that eventually included troops from thirty-seven countries and contributions of $54 billion, and received UN economic sanctions and approval for the use of force if Iraq did not withdraw by 15 January 1991. Although by citing Article 9 Tokyo did succeed in resisting any pressure to supply troops, as the war began in mid-January, Tokyo agreed to toss another $9 billion into the kitty, making Japan the single largest contributor and alleviating most of the pressure. Tokyo did eventually dispatch a flotilla of six minesweepers to the Persian Gulf on 26 April 1991, but only after the war ended, thus allowing Tokyo to stay behind the Article 9 figleaf.

JAPAN'S DEFENSE POLICY

Tokyo's claim that Article 9 prevented Japan from making any military contribution to the Alliance, even if it were unarmed and behind the lines, was legitimate. Literally interpreted, Article 9 of the Japanese constitution forbids any Japanese military at all:

> Aspiring sincerely to an international peace based on justice and order, the Japanese people forever renounce war as a sovereign right of the nation and the threat of force as a means of settling international disputes.
>
> In order to accomplish the aim of the preceding paragraph, land, sea, and air forces, as well as other war potential, will never be maintained. The right of belligerency of the state will not be recognized.

The reality is that Japan not only has a military, but that its $30 billion budget in 1990 was the world's third largest. How does Japan justify having a military outlawed by its own constitution? For the Japanese, relationships always take precedence over law. Japan's limited rearmament was a small price to pay for all the benefits of America's open market, nuclear umbrella, and sponsorship in international organizations like the UN, GATT, IMF, or the OECD.

Japan has never enjoyed a truly free defense ride, but it has certainly been extremely cheap. From 1950 through today, Tokyo has continually pointed to Article 9 and pervasive public opinion against a larger military to counter periodic calls by Washington to increase its contributions to the alliance. Thus over the past four decades, while the Americans and Europeans diverted an annual average 6 and 3 per cent of GNP, respectively, the Japanese have spent little more than 1 per cent. Although Japan's defense spending averaged 2–3 per cent of GNP during the 1950s, as Japan's economy continued to expand vigorously throughout the 1960s, it gradually subsided to less than 1 per cent of GNP, a rate which has been maintained through today. It was not until 1976, that the 1 per cent level was officially enshrined as Japan's defense policy. Although Tokyo breached the 1 per cent policy in 1986 by spending 1.004 per cent of GNP on defense, the 1991–6 five-year Defense Plan will annually increase spending by only 3 per cent of GNP, compared to a 5.4 per cent annual growth during 1986–90. Japan defense expenditures remain fixed at about 1 per cent of GNP. With such a light defense burden for forty years, Japan thus had about 5 percentage points of GNP than the United States, and 2 percentage points more than the Europeans to invest in its economic development.

How does the Soviet empire's collapse and the Cold War's end affect Japan's defense spending and the US-Japan security arrangement? Without a Soviet threat, the US-Japanese military alliance is superfluous. Pressures will mount in both countries for the alliance's dismantlement, as Japanese and American nationalists argue that Japan can and should defend itself.

Yet, for different reasons, both Tokyo and Washington will attempt to maintain the alliance as a bandaid to obscure the steady haemorrhaging of American power, resulting from Japan's successful neomercantilist policies employed in their geoeconomic rivalry. Conciliators on both sides will publicly insist that the alliance remains important for containing any revival of Russian power, and privately admit that the alliance is important as a restraint on any revival of Japanese militarism. The Departments of State and Defense, and the National Security Council, still retain the old mentality that a massive American commitment to the security treaty is still essential and that any tough stand on geoeconomic issues might jeopardize the alliance. Economic and military issues must be kept strictly separate, thus preventing Washington from using Japan's geopolitical dependence to resolve geoeconomic conflicts. Tokyo, of course, does all it can to nurture these irrational policies. Its steady infiltration of and growing power to manipulate America's political system may prevent any shift to a more rational policy even as public officials privately agree that Washington is increasingly serving Japanese rather than American interests. Japan will continue to benefit from its largely free defense ride. Given Tokyo's growing power over America's political economy, Washington has no choice but to comply with such take it or leave it token efforts.

CONCLUSION

Some criticize Japan's foreign policy for being 'value free' (*issai no kachi handan no shinai gaiko*) and advocate Tokyo adopting a 'principle based foreign policy' (*rinen gaiko*). The reality is that Tokyo's policies, both domestic and foreign, have been based consistently on one central value – Japan's national interests. Japan's policies will remain thoroughly neomercantilist for the indefinite future.

There are many strange anomalies which undermine Japanese claims that Tokyo does not pursue systematic neomercantilist policies or that Japan's markets are not carefully managed by powerful cartels. While Japan's 'smoking guns' – the low rate of manufactured imports, the comparative performances of America vis-a-vis Europe and Japan, and of Europe and America vis-a-vis Japan – all point to continued massive, systematic management of Japanese markets, it does not reveal the 'trigger men'. Circumstantial evidence points to Japan's countless cartels as being either outright managed or encouraged by Tokyo. But Japan's lack of transparency in such neomercantilist policies usually prevents any nailing-down of just who is responsible. Meanwhile, Japanese spokespeople, pointing to low tariffs and quotas, can continue to chant the mantra that Japan's markets are the world's most open.

While asserting this free market claim, they also dismiss criticism of any Japanese cartel, distribution, or other trade barriers as simply reflecting customs which are 'unique' to Japanese culture and are thus inviolable. There is a chicken-and-egg relationship between political economics, culture, and policy. Japanese frequently defend their range of nontariff barriers by claiming they are cultural, and thus presumably beyond reproach. There is no doubt that Japanese *keiretsu*, insider trading, the distribution system, 'buy Japanese' attitudes, cartels, and business based on relations rather than price or quality; the tendency for customs officials to examine each item of a huge shipment which imposes huge costs in time and money on the foreign producer; government and business collusion to devise industry standards that discriminate against foreigners; the way local shops are allowed to veto any plans for the building of a large retail store in their midst, to name a few discriminatory practices, are all manifestations of Japan's political economic culture. The question is, however, what role official policy had in shaping those practices. All the aforementioned collusive practices are not only sanctioned but often coordinated by Japan's government. The bottom line of these practices is that they allow Japan to create and retain wealth that might otherwise flow overseas had free markets prevailed.

Among many other foreign analysts, Scalapino rejects Japan's cultural uniqueness excuse for its neomercantilist policies. He argues that in 'an interdependent age, "uniqueness" is not an acceptable excuse [for neomercantilism]. One nation's domestic structure and policies impinge upon those with whom it is intertwined'.[49] From a foreign perspective, Japan does not keep its trade promises. After wearing down their foreign opponents by stonewalling on an issue, sometimes for years, the Japanese will endorse some general principles and promise changes that they have no intention of keeping (*soron sansei, kakuron hantai*). Tokyo has been promising 'genuine market liberalization' for over three decades. Each announcement ends with the promise that once implemented Japan's markets will be the world's most open. During the 1980s, Tokyo announced ten separate market opening packages. 'Concessions' continued to appear through the 1990s. Hence, if Tokyo suddenly waved a magic wand and genuinely removed Japan's tangled web of trade barriers, most foreign observers would merely shrug their shoulders in disbelief.

But that, of course, is not going to happen. Japan's trade barriers are deeply entrenched in Japan's political economic culture. Protectionism is an addiction in which some leads to more. When a government props up one inefficient industry through subsidies and protection it means other industries must work even harder to nourish the protected. Japanese policies protect efficient and inefficient industries alike. The inefficient are protected for political reasons and the relatively efficient industries are protected so that they can produce enough excess wealth to support the inefficient industries. If Japan's markets were genuinely thrown open, there would be widespread bankruptcies, mass unemployment, and a deep, intractable depression. The agricultural, construction, and distribution industries, which employ about half of Japan's work force, would be all but wiped out, toppling the rest of the economy like so many dominoes.

Can the world live with any more sustained Japanese neomercantilism? International trade is largely a zero-sum conflict in which one side's gains are all the others' losses. Japanese neomercantilism continues unabated, and virtually all of its policies can be considered neomercantilist. Washington and, to a lesser extent, Brussels, have negotiated respite from Japanese dumping and trade barriers in select areas, but there has been no systematic attempt to contain Japanese neomercantilism. And given the liberal orientation and decentralized political economy of both the United States and European Community, such an effort is unlikely to emerge. Japan's power over the global political economy will continue to expand steadily for the indefinite future.

Part III
Japan Versus Europe

5 The Imbalance of Power

What is power? Power is the ability to get others to do things they otherwise would not do. Power is thus a means to an end, although that end may be to acquire more means of asserting power. The means can range from rational or subliminal persuasion to the threat or application of force. All individuals and groups of individuals on the planet are involved in power relationships in which they struggle to assert their interests, often at the expense of others. At a global level, the most important group is the state. States wield power in pursuit of their interests.

What is the essence of state power? How do we measure the balance or imbalance of power among states? Does power flow from gunbarrels, from uniformed soldiers massed for review, columns of tanks charging across a desert, jets roaring off the flight decks of aircraft carriers, nuclear missiles waiting malevolently in their silos? Or is money power's bottom line? Has not power always rested in the hands of paymasters and moneymakers? After all, soldiers and armaments must somehow be paid for. And anyway, while most clashes of state interests involve something other than military power, some use of wealth is always present. But what determines a state's wealth and how that wealth is used?

In a conflict among two or more states, we can weigh the relative size and quality of their respective militaries, populations, wealth, diplomatic corps, natural resources, geographic location, national cohesion, ideologies, and so on. And obviously, different types of conflicts would require different types of power resources. A trade conflict would be resolved with a different matrix of power than the military invasion of one country by another.

But until the battle begins the participants have only potential power. Ultimately, we can only truly measure a nation's power by the results of the conflict in which it was wielded. Underdogs can score upsets. The victories of favored nations can be pyrrhic. Power is relative. Even the smallest of states in territory, population, wealth, natural resources, or military forces can be considered powerful if it achieves its goals.

How is power manifested in an increasingly interdependent post-cold war world? Kenneth Twitchell coined the concept of 'civilian actor' to designate those governments which shape international relations through the skilful application of diplomatic, economic, and legal rather than military power.[1] The concept is not as startling as it first appears. Virtually every national government can bear that label. Although military crises and war continue to dominate the popular image of international relations and power, most states are at peace most of the time. International wars or even brinksmanship are extremely rare in international relations, relative to the number of states and the possible combinations of armed conflict. Military power will become increasingly anachronistic as the world becomes ever more interdependent. In an increasingly interdependent post-Cold War world virtually all states will be civilian actors, although many of them will continue to maintain large military establishments.

And to what ends will those states wield power? More than ever, national security is centered on maximizing the creation and distribution of wealth. The wealth of nations is shaped by many factors: how a state mobilizes its natural, technological, and human resources, the ideology upon which it is based, its geography, and the presence or absence of neighboring aggressors, to name only some of the more prominent. With interdependence the creation of wealth in one country depends on its creation elsewhere. That is not to say that all economic transactions are positive – that everyone benefits equally from economic growth. As will be seen, some states in an interdependent world can still enhance their own wealth by pursuing policies that simultaneously economically weaken others. And the global economy's future is threatened by a range of interrelated international environmental crises like the greenhouse effect, depletion of the ozone layer, overpopulation, deforestation, species depletion, pollution, and so on. In an interdependent world teetering on the brink of environmental disaster, cooperation is essential for the viability of all.

Japan and the European Community have led the world in the transition of their policies from the traditional emphasis on military power to a focus on the creation of wealth as the ultimate source of national security. Unfortunately, there is a significant imbalance of material power between Europe and Japan. By virtually any manufacturing, financial, technological, trade, or growth measure, Japan is more powerful than Europe. And, more importantly, Japan pursues its national goals by singlemindedly mobilizing all relevant power sources in any issue. The Europeans are materially and organizationally inferior to the Japanese. Thus Japan has been able to prevail in most bilateral issues.

What accounts for this power imbalance? Ideology is perhaps the ultimate source of power. The power and fate of a nation or alliance rests ultimately on its ideological foundations. It is ideology which determines how and to what ends a state is organized. Material and ideological power are deeply entwined. History has proven repeatedly that a state inferior in population, natural resources, or territory can militarily or economically defeat a state superior in those attributes if its ideals enable it to organize itself more vigorously, and to struggle more determinedly than its rival.

There is an imbalance of ideological power between Japan and Europe. The ideals which organize and motivate Japan are simply more powerful than those which organize and motivate the Community. According to John Pinder,

> the Japanese challenge is not just competition from what economists rather misleadingly call comparative advantage in a few selected sectors of industry. The sectors in which Japan is now pressing Europe so hard should be seen, rather, as the vanguard from a better organized economic system which will increasingly mount a general challenge so long as the organization of Europe's system remains inferior.[2]

Japan's political economy is organized around the principles and strategy of neomercantilism, whereby the state actively leads economic development through rational industrial and trade policies which attempt constantly to maximize exports, minimize competitive imports, and target strategic industries and technologies for development. Although Tokyo claims that it is committed to free market principles and now has the world's most open markets, in reality its policies remain solidly neomercantilist.

The European Community is committed and organized around the liberal principles of open markets and minimal government interference in the economy. Largely in response to Japan's neomercantilist challenge, Brussels has recently tried to push its own industrial policies which target strategic industries for development. But these policies may be too little too late in their ability to promote European industries. Industrial and trade policy initiatives rest largely in the hands of Europe's national governments and vary considerably from France's heavy to Britain's light state roles.

The imbalance of power between Japan and Europe will be analyzed through three sections. The first section compares liberal and neomercantilist theory, revealing the strengths and weaknesses of each in promoting national power. The second will examine how liberalism and neomercantilism have shaped the respective policies and power of Europe and Japan. The final section will compare the material balance of power.

THE IMBALANCE OF IDEOLOGICAL POWER: LIBERALISM VERSUS NEOMERCANTILISM

Trade, of course, has existed ever since the first human exchanged one item for that of another. And ever since they were first created, governments have interfered with the exchange of goods and services through taxes, the support of some industries or repression of others, and their own demands for goods and services. Some philosophical traditions either outright condemned some aspects of trade or treated it as a necessary evil. During the Middle Ages, the Catholic Church ruled that usury – requiring borrowers to pay interest on their loans – was a sin. Confucianism cast merchants to society's bottom rank since they simply exchanged rather than actually produced goods. Yet, despite the hundreds of thousands of years of trade and government interference, systematic economic theories are relatively recent in the history of thought.

It was not until the publication of Adam Smith's *Wealth of Nations* in 1776, espousing free trade, that anyone systematically attempted to develop an economic theory. Liberalism is based on several simple assumptions. Economic and social development can best be achieved if governments minimize their involvement in the economy and remove all market restrictions. Governments cannot pick the winners and losers of the economy; only the market can. The market is shaped by the forces of supply and demand, the 'invisible hand' which provides everyone's wants. If people demand something, then entrepreneurs will eventually produce it. Competition keeps prices low, quality high, and provides only enough production to supply demand. Free markets reward enterprise and initiative, but everyone is ultimately cared for.

What determines the production of individuals and countries? Countries, like individuals, cannot and should not attempt to produce everything. Every country, like every individual, is assumed to have a unique set of natural strengths and weaknesses. Free trade allows every state to specialize in the production of those resources with which it is best endowed and then trade those products for everything else. This concept of 'comparative advantage' was developed by the British economist David Ricardo in his *Principles of Political Economy and Taxation*, published in 1817, in which he compared British textile and Portuguese wine production. Britain had a comparative advantage for raising sheep and thus producing wool textiles, while Portugal had a comparative advantage for producing wine. Of course, Portugal could try to raise sheep and Britain produce wine, but it would be cheaper for each country to specialize in the product for which they have a comparative advantage and then trade for the other products.

Free trade theory is deeply flawed. It is based on numerous ideal assumptions never duplicated in the real world, including perfect competition and the absence of scale economies. Liberalism is also discredited by several theoretical contradictions, the most blatant of which is that neoclassical economists acknowledge that governments can sometimes temporarily set aside free trade and target an industry for development, but only if that industry is an 'infant'. The neoclassicists fail to explain why the government may nurture an infant but not a more mature industry. If such nurturing allows the nation to achieve jobs, wealth, and technology that it might not otherwise have, then why differentiate between infant and mature industries?

In reality, there is no such thing as a free market. Realists argue that 'the invisible hand is conspicuous chiefly by its absence and that the state is needed to supplement market forces'.[3] Or, as Commission President Delors succinctly put it: 'The invisible hand is itself in need of guidance'.[4] 'Level playing fields' do not exist anywhere. Every government consciously or unwittingly shapes markets through a variety of means. They vary only in the degree and means by which they do so. At a minimum, government spending, regulations, taxes, and debt profoundly affect the decisions, opportunities, and costs of firms and investors in markets. But every government picks winners and losers as well, whether it admits it or not, by providing incentives to some sectors, industries, and firms and obstacles to others. Governments differ only in whether their industrial policies are largely shaped by politics, planning, or, rarely these days, by outright ownership of production. Firms or investors do not act alone. Governments,

> along with associations of employers, banks, labor unions, think tanks, laboratories in business or the universities and even other lesser institutions . . . are all part of the normal decision-making complex behind industry. They are strands in the fabric, not foreign bodies crawling over it from outside. Therefore, industrial policies are best understood as all forms of activity by which the establishment in the widest sense tries to influence industrial management in directions collectively seen as desirable.[5]

The choice is not between either total freedom or total government control of the economy. The real question is what is the best mix of government-business relations and business cooperation and competition that produces the most national wealth and power. Most governments recognize that markets are myopic. Markets cause investors and firms to focus on immediate profits and opportunities, while remaining largely blind to long-term possibilities. Governments can overcome market imperfections. They can provide a strategic direction to the economy by providing incentives to firms and investors to channel their resources into the dynamic growth industries of the future, thereby providing a country with far more wealth and power than would have occurred with a purely market approach.

In contrast to liberalism's abstract ideals, neomercantilist theory and policies are solidly rooted in the real world. Neomercantilism is a twentieth-century variation of mercantilism, a government policy prevalent during the early modern era. Both mercantilism and neomercantilism attempt to maximize exports and minimize imports to enrich the country. Under mercantilism, the state channels excess wealth either into the economy or a powerful military with which to defend or expand the realm. Neomercantilism and mercantilism differ chiefly over the military's importance. Mercantilism existed in a Hobbesian balance-of-power world, in which wars were frequent and each state tried to carve out its own autonomous realm to exploit economically. Neomercantilism exists in an interdependent world in which military power is largely superfluous to international relations and an outright drain on the nation's wealth. Security is based on economic rather than military power. Under neomercantilism, wealth is used to create yet more wealth.

But how is wealth created? Liberals asserts that trade is a positive-sum game in which everyone benefits from free trade. Nations with open markets will be more prosperous than nations with closed markets. Neomercantilists argue the opposite. Trade is a zero-sum game in which there are clear winners and losers at the consumer, producer, and national levels. In such an environment, entrepreneurs are inhibited rather than encouraged. According to Alexander Hamilton, 'Capital is wayward and timid in lending itself to new undertakings, and the State ought to excite the confidence of capitalists, who are ever cautious and sagacious, by aiding them overcome the obstacles that lie in the way of all experiments'.[6] By protecting one's own markets and encouraging its industries to dump their products in foreign markets, governments can systematically develop their own economy and destroy foreign rival industries. In the long term, the neomercantilists country's industries can conquer global markets and thus reap global profits, which can in turn be reinvested for similar efforts in other strategic industries.

A neomercantilist state will always create wealth faster than a liberal state. In the short run, the liberal state's consumers will benefit from lower prices while the neomercantilist state's consumers will be penalized with higher prices. But in the short and long term the neomercantilist state's producers will profit from their protected home markets and access to open foreign markets as they enjoy a virtuous cycle of ever greater scale economies, profits, investments, and market share, and ever lower costs. Meanwhile the liberal state's producers will steadily lose ground in a vicious cycle of smaller scale economies, profits, investments, and market shares, and ever higher costs. In the long term, with greater wealth and higher value-added industries, the neomercantilist state's consumers will enjoy greater buying power, even as they continue to pay higher prices. The gap in wealth and power between the neomercantilist and liberal states will continue to widen. The liberal state's development will be increasingly shaped and stunted by the neomercantilist state's policies.

Liberals and neomercantilists also war over who is best able to pick industrial winners and losers – the market or the state. Liberal economists argue that only the market and not objective experts can and should pick industrial winners and losers. Neomercantilists counter that reality, as always, is far more complicated than the two-dimensional world of neoclassical theory. Purely free markets do not exist anywhere on a national level. Even in the freest of markets, say in the United States or Hong Kong, government policies will, often unwittingly, either assist or hinder firms and industries. Paradoxically, the more liberal a nation's political economy, the more politicized its industrial policies. The United States Congress is a brawling market place in which representatives sell out to the best organized and well-funded special interests. As a result, scarce resources continue to boost politically entrenched textile and agribusiness interests while political neophytes like cutting-edge high technology firms lose out.

Likewise, neomercantilists reject the liberal notion that all industries are of equal value to the economy – that paper clips are as important as computer chips if their market value is the same. Industries vary considerably in how they stimulate related industries, technology advances, the size of wages, market demand, and economies of scale, and profits. Thus, neomercantilist governments target 'strategic' industries for development as the locomotives of the nation's economy.

There are many types of industrial policies, each tailored to the needs of that targeted industry. Industrial policies can help 'sunset' (mature) industries adjust to tougher foreign competition, or nurture 'sunrise' (infant) industries into maturity. The policy tools of import protection, subsidies, cartels, tax credits, low interest loans, and export incentives are available to mature and infant industries alike. There is often a reduction in government aid between an industry's infant and mature development levels when the industry becomes strong enough to compete largely unassisted in world markets. Protectionist measures have changed over time. Tariffs used to be the most important instrument of industrial policy as industries grew behind tariff walls. But more recently a range of nontariff trade barriers and industrial promotion have become significant as nations have negotiated away their tariffs under GATT.

As Japan's development has proven, neomercantilism is the only means for industrial laggards to catch up with and surpass the industrial leaders. If Japan or Germany had adopted free trade policies in the mid-nineteenth century they would have never experienced any significant degree of industrialization because Britain's manufactured goods enjoyed such a profound comparative advantage. Conversely, industrial leaders have an incentive to promote free trade in order to maintain their own lead. Friedrich List understood this well:

> free competition between two nations which are highly civilized can only be mutually beneficial in case both of them are in a nearly equal position of industrial development, and that any nation which owing to misfortunes is behind others in industry, commerce, navigation . . . must first of all strengthen her own individual powers, in order to fit herself to enter into free competition with more advanced nations.[7]

During the 1980s and into the 1990s, neomercantilist theory has been boosted by the development of the 'strategic trade paradigm'.[8] The paradigm systematically refutes the ideal world of classical economic theory and constructs a very sophisticated model which explains the contemporary global political economy. Governments can overcome market imperfections through the economic triad of strategic industrial, technology, and trade policies. As the time frame for product cycles continues to diminish, a government's role in targeting and promoting a strategic industry, product, or technology can be the decisive factor in which country masters it. Even the most powerful corporation cannot shoulder the research costs of the more arcane aspects of genetics, nuclear physics, or microelectronics, or the development costs of such industries as aerospace, nuclear energy, or highway construction, to name a few from each. Governments must bear most of the financial burden in such industries. Paradoxically, as the world becomes more interdependent, trade and development are increasingly zero-sum. A country with neomercantilist policies can simultaneously accelerate its economy development while dampening the development of other countries.

Is neomercantilism a flawless panacea for creating national wealth and power? Although it is rooted in the real world, neomercantilism is no development cure-all. It is much easier to select strategic industries for development than actually to nurture them into global champions. Most policies from most states fail to develop global champions. Scarce financial, technological, manufacturing, and human resources are often squandered through inefficiency and misdirection. Another problem with neomercantilism is that protectionism breeds protectionism. If one industry is protected, thus allowing those firms to raise prices, then governments will usually have to protect related industries so that their competitive advantage is not hurt by the higher priced components of the original industry. In a zero-sum competitive global political economy, however, the alternative is often not to have had those industries at all, with the result that the nation would have enjoyed even less economic growth and wealth.

What makes for a successful industrial policy? According to Katzenstein, 'one political ingredient is essential for an active industrial policy intent on structural transformation: a left that is weak and politically excluded from policy making at the national level'.[9] Since the late 1940s, only Japan has been fortunate enough to keep socialists continuously out of government. Also vital are harmonious management-labor relations. Japan's managers and workers not only cooperate in developing their company but will conform to government directives in developing the national economy. In contrast, European worker-management relations vary considerably from one country and industry to the next, but are generally adversarial. Workers will often continue to strike and refuse to compromise even when the result is the company's competitive loss and even destruction. And finally, industrial policies must be made by independent analysts rather than by politicians. If, as is so common in the United States, the most systematic industrial policies are targeted on industries important for their political clout rather than their strategic value, the nation's development will suffer accordingly.

How can one evaluate the effectiveness of an industrial policy? The 'what ifs' of history provide interesting if unanswerable questions. We have only the historic record of a targeted industry's performance, and no concrete means of comparing it to alternative policies and results. Yet we can surmise that, for example, if Tokyo had not targeted the automobile industry then Japan's historic growth rate and accumulation of wealth would have been much lower. Three-quarters of America's $41 billion deficit with Japan in 1990 was in automobiles or automobile parts. Without its own automobile industry, Japan would have had to import automobiles from the United States and Europe, allowing the Americans and possibly the Europeans a trade surplus rather than deficit with Japan. Since the automobile industry is a strategic industry with profound multiplier effects on the rest of the economy, without a Japanese automobile industry, the United States and Europe would today be much wealthier and Japan much less so. How much, though, is impossible to say.

Neomercantilism can be a risky policy. If every state adopted rigid neomercantilist policies world trade could collapse as it did during the 1930s. Yet global or even bilateral trade wars are extremely rare. No country can produce all the products it needs for successful development. Although governments can accelerate and shape their nation's development by targeting strategic industries, they cannot produce oil or crops from their land if there is no oil or fertile soil, cannot lead in every product or technology race, or enjoy the same consumer market sizes within which to develop economies of scale production. Thus trade is essential for all states, and world trade will continue to expand as governments skilfully bargain with each other for market shares and needed products and technology.

THE IMBALANCE OF INSTITUTIONAL POWER: SOCIAL CORPORATISM VERSUS INDUSTRIAL CORPORATISM

Ideology is a vital determinant of a nation's degree of economic dynamism and development. Liberalism and social democracy permeate contemporary Western Europe. Pinder sees a danger in this: 'European politics are still imprisoned by nineteenth-century ideologies that suppress our economic development'.[10] He argues that Europeans are divided between championing either liberalism or socialism as the 'true' development model. Socialism posits that development can occur only if the state owns and directs everything; liberalism that the state should not direct or own anything. In the real world, both models inhibit rather than enhance development. The choice is not between the state owning and directing everything or nothing, but in whether the state can organize the political economy so that it is driven by the best aspects of competition and cooperation. According to Pinder:

> Liberal individualism, which realized the forces of technological progress in the industrial revolution, ignores the interdependence in the modern economy and society. The specialization and scale of production have linked the different parts of the economy in a complex machine that will not function properly if some of the parts are defective or missing; and the society that has to run this complex machine reliably is not likely to do so if equality and fraternity are eclipsed by liberty. Thus the interdependence of the economy needs to be reflected in an integration of the economic and of the social system; and this requires, among other things, industrial, manpower, and social policies and a relationship between the social partners which go against the grain of the liberal individualist philosophy.[11]

The Community lacks a consensus on the means and ends of development. Does development mean simply cutting up the existing pie more equitably?

Many Europeans believe so. Can genuine development only occur through free markets and a government *laissez-faire* outlook? Many other Europeans believe so.

Japan is not burdened by these ideological deadends. Japan's development strategy is neither liberal nor socialist but combines the most progressive aspects of market-led and state-led capitalism. Japan's cultural values, of the group over the individual and cooperation over competition, obviously give the Japanese an important advantage in organizing and running a complex modern economy. Japan is the quintessential neomercantilist state. According to Chalmers Johnson 'the study of Japanese-type economies holds the potentiality of overturning large bodies of received Western theory . . .'.[12] In Japan elite bureaucrats carefully analyze which industries provide the nation with the most wealth, technology, and power, both now and into the future, and then target those industries for development. National enterprises are protected by import barriers while they master the production of goods and services which reap wealth for the economy and taxes for the government. Japanese firms then dump their excess production in foreign markets to destroy their foreign rivals.

Europe's polarization between liberalism and socialism and Japan's neomercantilism both demand large powerful states. Politics and policy-making in Japan and most European countries follow very different patterns from American-style federalism and the balance of power among the three branches of government. The hyperpluralism of American politics in which policies are shaped by free-for-alls of seemingly countless interest groups is absent in Japan and most European countries.

Instead, to varying degrees, politics in Japan and the European nations are shaped by corporatism, which is:

a pattern of interest group-state bureaucracy relations of interdependence; formal inclusion in government administration for purposes of assistance in policy implementation, in exchange for guaranteed access to government officials, legitimation of interest groups in ministerial advisory and consultation processes . . . and bureaucratic protection and patronage. The end product of corporatized relations between the state and interest groups is cooperation between the various parts of the public and private sectors in the pursuit of commonly agreed policy goals. Corporatism can also result in diminished levels of organizational autonomy . . . Interest groups become the instrument of mobilization where the state, in determining the economic and social priorities, sees a need to intervene in the operation of the free market and countenance various forms of assistance and control over sectors of the economy.[13]

How do corporatist political and policy-making systems evolve in states? Michael Shalev explains that corporatism 'is after all only a description of certain institutional arrangements which can themselves hardly be understood without reference to class structure, power, and conflicts'.[12] Alexander Gerschenkron argues that the timing of a nation's industrialization and corporatism are interrelated.[13] To these factors, one must add culture, history, and international forces as major forces shaping a state's political economy. Early industrializing states like Britain and the United States had liberal political economies, while in late industrializing states like Germany and Japan the government played a very powerful role in shaping development.

While many of its members have corporatist political economies, the European Community itself is evolving from an economic confederation into a very decentralized federal system in which most power continues to lie in the national capitals. Community policies, when they emerge at all, are more often than not watered-down versions of original proposals. Far-reaching policies that address important issues are often shelved for lack of consensus. The Community will continue to be hobbled by this hyperpluralism even after it creates a central bank and common currency in the late 1990s.

Meanwhile, Japan's system will remain largely one of centralized power and policy making. That is not to say that Japan's political economy is not rapidly changing. I have explored Japanese corporatism in depth in *The Foundation of Japanese Power*, in which I argue that Japan has passed through three distinct types of corporatism – 'bureaucratic-dominant corporatism', 'corporatism', and 'neocorporatism', and may be developing into a 'neopluralist' political and policy model.[16] But even if Japan does evolve into a neopluralist system, it will continue to outstrip the Community in the ability to devise and implement rational industrial, trade, and technology policies.

THE GLOBAL POLITICAL ECONOMY: LIBERALISM VERSUS NEOMERCANTILISM

How does the global political economy reflect the philosophies of liberalism and neomercantilism? During the 1940s, Washington organized the global political economy along such classic liberal principles as 'most favored nation' (MFN) and cajoled other nations into joining the International Monetary Fund (IMF) and General Agreement on Trade and Tariffs

(GATT) which were international organizations designed to promote free trade.

These policies were very successful. Global trade and development have risen steadily over the past five decades. There are currently over 110 members of both organizations with other nations clamouring to join. Until today Washington has continuously supported free trade and the organizations which promote it, in word if not always in deed.

Yet, ironically, the world appears to be becoming more rather than less protectionist with states increasingly managing their trade. The global political economy is coalescing around three increasingly distinct trade blocs: the European Community, United States-centered North America, and Japan-centered East Asia. Trade expansion within each bloc exceeds trade between the blocs. The efforts of both the Europeans and Americans to accelerate integration during the late 1980s was a direct response to Japan's rapid rise into a global manufacturing, financial, and technological superpower.

GATT has become increasingly obsolete as the global political economy grows more complex. Conceived during an era when tariffs and quotas comprised most trade barriers, GATT simply cannot adapt to the webs of very subtle nontariff barriers maintained by the Japanese and others. The Uruguay Round (1986–93) clearly revealed GATT's inability to deal with issues like intellectual property protection, service industry trade, direct foreign investment restrictions, or agricultural subsidies.

The cost of compliance with GATT is high. Existing GATT rules reward neomercantilists. Article 19 allows a state victimized by foreign dumping and subsequent trade deficits to erect temporary trade barriers, but only if they are across the board, thus hitting fair and foul traders alike. Faced with the dilemma of either adapting harsh measures or none at all, governments instead negotiate 'voluntary export restraints' (VERs) or 'orderly marketing agreements' (OMAs) with the predatory state, in both of which exports are restrained with quotas rather than by tariffs. The predators are rewarded because they are guaranteed a market share within which they can boost prices to recoup losses earlier sustained by dumping. Domestic and foreign producers enjoy windfall profits, while consumers are gouged and the domestic government's treasury is largely unaffected. The Japanese have mastered the game of launching sustained dumping attacks in strategic industries like automobiles, semiconductors, or microelectronics, capturing a large market share and battering their foreign rivals, then eventually, after the foreign government threatens to retaliate, negotiating a VER in which the Japanese firms enjoy a huge market share and profits. In such cases trade is clearly a zero sum game in which the winners are those whose domestic markets are protected, financial pockets are seemingly endless and ultimately backed by the government, and export offensives are ruthlessly conducted until the opposition is either destroyed or rescued by its government.

Nations negotiate VERs because they are allowed to under GATT. The biggest problem with VERs is that the quotas allow the foreign as well as domestic firms to enjoy windfall profits at the expense of domestic consumers. Tariffs would eliminate this inadvertent subsidy to the foreign producers. Governments which impose tariffs high enough to remove the foreign firms' comparative advantage would not only protect threatened domestic strategic industries, but would enjoy the revenues that under quotas go to foreign firms.

Liberal economists warn ominously that the increasing neomercantilism will escalate into a trade war which could destroy the global political economy and impoverish everyone. Yet the world political economy continues to expand steadily despite increased protectionism and managed trade. What can explain this seeming paradox? Why have the liberal economists failed once again to explain reality?

Trade and protectionism seem to expand together for several reasons. First, governments have become more adept at managing trade disputes so that they do not escalate into full-fledged trade war. The Japanese have become masters of 'trade brinksmanship' in which they launch continual dumping campaigns to destroy foreign rivals while maintaining webs of outrageous trade barriers, stonewalling any foreign protests against such practices, then offering some purely symbolic concession when faced with retaliation. A related reason has been the success of Tokyo's brilliant strategy of entangling other countries in networks of trade, investment, financial, technological, and political dependence so that those governments would hurt themselves as much as Japan if they chose to retaliate. In addition, trade disputes are generally confined to one product or import barrier. Although there may be escalation within that sector, there is rarely horizontal escalation to unrelated sectors. A proliferation of vigorous trading also helps prevent any global trade war. Competition expands and stiffens daily as more and more countries are developing dynamic export industries. Two or more countries involved in a trade dispute realize that other exporters will simply take their place if a full-fledged bilateral trade war ensues. Thus they have an incentive to limit rather than escalate their conflict.

Just as governments are inhibited from launching a full-scale trade war against their rivals, they have likewise lost the power to engage in competitive currency devaluations. Everyone, that is, except the Japanese. The creation of a unified global financial network has undercut the ability of most governments to manipulate currency markets. The amount of private money sloshing through global currency markets dwarfed even the efforts of the Group of Five countries to devalue the dollar after September 1985. With its wide-open financial markets and the dollar's role as the global currency, Washington has lost the ability to shape the dollar's value unilaterally. Meanwhile, Tokyo's financial markets continue to be an insider's game while the yen's use as a trade currency is carefully restrained. The result is a perennially overvalued dollar and undervalued yen, and thus devastatingly absymal trade performances for the United States and most other countries whose currencies are tied to the dollar, while the Japanese continue to enjoy vast trade and account surpluses.

How is the Community responding to an increasingly neomercantilist global political economy? It continues to claim its commitment to liberal economic values, stating repeatedly that there will be no 'Fortress Europe'. But the larger and more affluent the Community's market becomes, the greater becomes Brussels' potential ability to offer Japan access to that market in exchange for European access to Japan's closed markets. Increasing numbers of European business and political leaders are demanding that Brussels acknowledge that Tokyo will never voluntarily open its markets and should instead simply demand that Tokyo allocate market shares to European producers until an overall balance is achieved. So far, however, Europe's liberals have held the neomercantilists at bay.

THE IMBALANCE OF POLITICAL ECONOMIC POWER

By virtually all measures, Japan is the world's most dynamic economic, outgunning and outmanoeuvering the Europeans on virtually all fronts.[17] In bulk consumption power, the Community's 345 million population far surpasses America's 250 million or Japan's 120 million, while the Community's combined GNPs account for about 22 per cent of global GNP, slightly larger than America's 20 per cent and much larger than Japan's 13 per cent. In 1990, Europe's GNP was $6.01 trillion and per capita income $18,324, compared to Japan's $2.94 trillion and $23,810, and America's $5.13 trillion and $20,414.[18] The Big Four – Germany, France, Italy, and Britain – account for about 75 per cent of the Community's population and 85 per cent of its GNP. With 80 million people, Germany is the largest by far, followed by about 60 million in each of the other three. The other members vary in size from Spain with 39 million to tiny Luxembourg with 370,000.

But Japan's GNP is far larger than that of any one European country. It surpassed Italy in economic size in 1966, Britain in 1967, France in 1968, and West Germany in 1969. Japan's economic growth has annually averaged 10 per cent between 1950 and 1973 and 4.5 per cent since, about one and a half times the average Community rate during the same periods. In 1990, Japan's economy grew 6.1 per cent compared to Germany's 4.2 per cent, France's 2.5 per cent, Britain's 1.6 per cent, or Italy's 2.6 per cent. The distribution of wealth is as important as per capita income in revealing potential market power. While 90 per cent of Japanese consider themselves middle class, Europe's per capita income varied considerably from Denmark's $24,000 to Portugal's $4,000. Japan is also superior in suppressing inflation and government debt (see Table 5.1).

TABLE 5.1   *Inflation rates and government budget deficits, 1991*

	Inflation rates	Budget deficits*
Japan	2.1%	2.3%
West Germany	3.5%	4.6%
France	2.5%	1.6%
Italy	6.1%	10.1%
Britain	3.7%	2.2%
Greece	17.6%	15.3%

*as a percentage of GNP

There is a dynamic relationship between savings and investment – generally the more a nation saves the higher its investment rate. Nations can augment their savings and investments by borrowing foreign capital, or contribute to foreign savings and investments by investing overseas. Europe's saving rates are comparable to Japan's. In 1990, Germany's household savings rate was 13.9 per cent, France's 12.0 per cent, Britain's 9.1 per cent, and Italy's 15.6 per cent, while Japan's was 14.3 per cent and the United States a minuscule 4.7 per cent.[20]

What is important, however, is not the savings but the investment rate. By virtually any measurement, Community investments have lagged far behind those of Japan and even the United States. Japan's growth in gross capital formation has continually outstripped that of both the Community and the United States (see Table 5.2). Japan's net government investment in infrastructure as a percentage of GDP from 1980–9 also outstripped its rivals, as shown in Table 5.3.[21] Another major reason for Japan's extraordinarily high investment rate has been its extremely low prime lending rate which in 1988 was 4.88 per cent compared to America's 10 per cent, Germany's 10.50 per cent, France's 11 per cent, Britain's 16 per cent, and Italy's 14 per cent.[22]

TABLE 5.2   *Gross capital formation: Japan, the Community and the USA*

	Japan	USA	Community
1969–79	4.9%	2.7%	1.9% annual average
1979–87	3.8%	2.4%	0.5% annual average
1985–88	23.7%	11.3%	11.0% annual average

TABLE 5.3   *Government investment in infrastructure as a percentage of GNP 1980–9*

	Annual averages
Japan	5.7%
West Germany	3.7%
France	2.7%
Britain	2.0%
Italy	4.8%
USA	0.3%

Productivity and investment rates are closely linked. Generally the more money a firm invests, the greater its productivity. Unfortunately, absenteeism, low productivity, inefficiency, and poor workmanship remain characteristic of most European industries. A 1989 Commission study revealed that average American and Japanese productivity in eleven industries were tied at 100, while Germany and France's productivity ranked only 65 and Britain's 42. With America's twelve industries valued at 100, Japanese productivity far surpassed that of Germany, Britain, and France in eight of the eleven industries, as shown in Table 5.4.

TABLE 5.4   *Productivity in twelve industries: Japan and the Community*

	Japan	W. Germany	France	Britain
Consumer electronics	236	43	47	28
Office/data equipment	94	45	43	37
Chemicals and pharmaceuticals	119	75	79	54
Transport equipment	95	60	54	23
Paper and printing	89	76	67	43
Industrial and agricultural machinery	103	46	49	20
Metal products	143	54	60	38
Ferrous/nonferrous ores and metals	149	92	72	66
Food, beverages and tobacco	37	47	73	56
Textiles, leather clothing	53	71	62	59
Nonmetallic minerals	43	71	64	40

NOTE: USA productivity is taken as 100 in each case.

In an interdependent world, a nation's corporate strength may be as important a pillar of national security as military strength is in a Hobbesian world. The Community's corporate strength is far surpassed by both Japan and the United States. In 1991, only three European firms were placed in the world's twenty-five largest firms in market value, compared to eleven each for the Americans and Japanese; and only seven EC firms ranked among the top fifty while nineteen Japanese and twenty-three American firms jousted within that ranking. The top 1,000 firms ranked by market value included only 239 EC firms with a combined market value of $1.334 trillion (19.8 per cent of total assets) compared to 309 Japanese firms with a combined market value of $2.246 trillion (33.4 per cent of total assets) and 359 American firms with a combined market value of $2.559 trillion (38.0 per cent of total assets).[24] Among the world's 'Fortune 500' firms over the last decade there has been a steady decline in the number of American corporations and an equally steady rise in the number of Japanese corporations, while the number of European firms has remained virtually unchanged. Between 1978 and 1989, the number of 'Fortune 500' Japanese corporations rose from 67 to 111 while Europe's rose slightly from 139 to 143 and America's plummeted from 229 to 167.[25]

The world economy runs on money. National and corporate success in the global economy depends on those nations or firms which have the greatest financial power. Over the past two decades, the shift in the global balance of banking power has been extraordinary, as demonstrated in Table 5.5.[26] In 1989, of the world's top fifty banks in deposits, the six largest, eight of the top ten, and twenty-two of the top fifty were Japanese. The seventh and ninth largest banks, and twenty-two of the top fifty were Community banks. In stark contrast only two American banks were in the top fifty.[27] Japan's banking industry is incredibly concentrated. In 1988, there were only eighty-seven Japanese commercial banks, of which thirteen held 55 per cent of the total assets! In contrast, there were 2,112 European commercial banks, 1,435 savings banks, 4,730 cooperative banks, and 1,819 other credit firms. America's financial system was even more decentralized and weak. In 1987, there were 14,207 American banks, 3,147 savings and loans, and 14,335 credit unions.[28]

TABLE 5.5   *The global balance of banking power 1970–88: the world's fifty largest banks*

1970			
	Number of banks owned in top 50	*Total assets*	*% of assets*
Japan	11	$ 89 billion	18%
Community	16	$156 billion	31%
USA	15	$188 billion	38%
1988			
	Number of banks owned in top 50	*Total assets*	*% of assets*
Japan	24	$4.662 trillion	59%
Community	17	$2.258 trillion	29%
USA	4	$484 billion	6%

The Japanese have surpassed the American in high technology by most indicators, and both countries are far ahead of the Europeans. A 1991 Commerce Department study revealed that of twelve emerging technology sectors, Japan was leading in ten and running neck-and-neck with the

United States in the other two.[29] A 1987 National Academy of Engineering study showed that Japan has surpassed the United States in twenty-five of thirty-four key areas of high technology including artificial intelligence, optoelectronics, and systems engineering and control, while of twenty-five key semiconductor technologies, Japanese producers lead in twelve, were equal in eight, and were rapidly closing the gap in five.[30] One important indicator of a nation's technological potential is the number of new patents it issues. Japan's 76,984 new patents in 1990 far surpassed Germany's 17,643, Britain's 8,795, France's 7,672, the Netherland's 5,737, Italy's 1,106, or Belgium's 330. The United States still led in patents with 104,541 registered.[31]

Of course, simply inventing new technologies is not enough. Nations must be able to adopt those technologies to new products – a process at which the Japanese excel. An important pillar of Tokyo's industrial policies has been extracting the most vital foreign technologies while limiting the access of foreigners to Japanese technology. Between 1950 and 1980, Japanese firms signed about 30,000 licensing agreements for foreign technology worth about $10 billion, which originally cost between $500 billion and $1 trillion to develop.[32] In 1988, Japan bought $2.263 billion and sold $1.785 billion worth of technology. A related indicator of the technology gap is the large difference between European scientists working in Japan and Japanese scientists in Europe. In 1988, there were 4,773 Japanese scientists in France, 4,526 in Germany, and 1,487 in Britain, while there were only 694 French, 542 German, and 1,458 British scientists in Japan. Yet, Europe's scientific gap is nothing compared to America's – there were 52,224 Japanese scientists in the United States while only 4,468 American scientists studied in Japan.[33] The Japanese continue systematically to vacuum the world's laboratories for all potentially profitable technology despite the fact that they are already the world's leaders.

Trade prowess is yet another indicator of a nation's global political economic power. Over the long term there has been a profound shift in the balance of trade power (see Table 5.6). On the eve of World War One in 1913, Britain was the world's largest exporter of manufactured products, followed by Germany. On the eve of World War Two in 1937, Britain and Germany still shared the number one position, followed by the United States. Following World War Two, the USA was the only great power to emerge with its industrial base not only intact, but enhanced by the conflict. By the early 1950s, however, the other great powers had rebuilt their industries and many other countries had developed export industries. In 1973, Germany was the world's leading exporter of manufactured products, followed by the United States. A decade later in 1984, Japan had

TABLE 5.6   *The changing balance of global trade power*
Percentages of world manufactured products exports

	1913	*1937*	*1973*	*1984*
Britain	29.9	22.4	7.4	5.5
Germany	26.5	22.4	17.4	12.9
France	12.9	6.4	7.5	6.1
USA	12.6	19.6	12.9	12.5
Japan	2.4	7.2	10.0	14.4
Others	15.7	28.4	39.4	43.1

captured the number one position, followed by Germany and the United States.

Another measure of national power is the percentage of exports and imports to GNP. For the economic great powers, the smaller the percentage of trade to GNP, the less vulnerable that country is to cutoffs and the more potential power it has to trade access to its own markets for foreign concessions from more vulnerable countries. There is a clear relationship between the population size of an industrial country and its trade dependence. The larger the population, the lower its dependence on trade as a percentage of GNP while the smaller the population, the greater the trade dependence. The economic nationalism of the 1930s forced all countries to try and reduce their trade vulnerability. In 1937, Japan's exports were still a high 40 per cent of GNP but it succeeded in reducing its imports to only 11 per cent. The three European powers increased their trade dependence again following World War Two, while America's remained low and Japan reduced its trade dependence as its huge population became more affluent and productive. In 1983, America's exports were only 8 per cent and its imports 10 per cent of GNP, and Japan's 14 per cent and 5 per cent, compared to the larger figures for the European nations (see Table 5.7).

TABLE 5.7   *The changing percentage of exports and imports in GNP*

	1913 Imports/Exports		*1937* Imports/Exports	*1983*	Imports/Exports	
Britain	17	42	21	10	29	26
Germany	21	10	15	3	35	43
France	26	13	12	7	26	27
Japan	40	34	11	40	5	14
USA	3	5	2	5	10	8

Perhaps the most important indicator of industrial power is a nation's share of technology-intensive trade. The pattern is clear from Table 5.8: Japan has nearly tripled its trade although the US remains in the lead.

TABLE 5.8 *Percentage share in international technology-intensive trade*

	1965	1984
USA	27.5	25.2
Germany	16.9	14.5
Britain	12.0	8.5
Japan	7.3	20.2
France	7.3	7.7
Italy	–	3.6

A bilateral trade account reveals much about the relative strength of the two partners. Like the United States, the European Community suffers perennial trade and investment deficits with Japan. Europe has suffered continuous trade deficits with Japan every year since 1968. Europe's trade deficit with Japan rose steadily to $7 billion in 1979 then doubled to $15 billion in 1981. Since then Europe's trade deficit with Japan rose throughout the 1980s from $13.0 billion ($19.7 billion imports in 1980 and $6.7 billion exports) to $14.6 billion in 1985 ($22.7 imports and $8.0 billion exports) to $32.076 billion in 1990. ($60.805 billion imports and $28.729 billion exports.) Imports remain three times greater than exports. Japan's balance of payments in 1990 of $28.9 billion with Europe was slightly lower than its trade surplus. Japan's exports to Europe were 18.3 per cent of its total exports and imports from Europe 12.6 per cent of its total imports.

The bilateral foreign investment balance is yet another important power indicator and relative openness. There is almost an exact balance of direct foreign investments (DFI) between the United States and the Community. In 1988, accumulated American direct investments in Europe were $326.9 billion with sales of $620.0 billion, while the Community's in the United States were $328.8 billion with sales of $606 billion. However, with 59.0 per cent of its total DFI in the United States compared to only 38.7 per cent of American DFI in Europe, the Community was much more dependent on the United States as an investment outlet.[36] Although one would think that American firms would be making major direct investments in Europe to take advantage of 1992's aftermath, it is actually European firms who are investing in the United States. In 1989, European firms spent $34 billion acquiring American firms, while American firms bought only $5.2 billion worth of European firms.[37]

In contrast to the balance of investments and economic opportunities between the Community and United States, there is a severe imbalance of investments between the EC and Japan. As elsewhere, Japanese investments reinforce gains made through exports. From 1951 to 1988, Japan invested $30.164 or 16.2 per cent of its total in the EC while EC members invested only $3.013 billion or 23.6 per cent of its total in Japan. Two years later, in March 1990, Japanese investments in the Community had jumped to $42 billion. In the first half of 1990, Japanese corporations made 25.7 per cent of their direct buyouts of firms in the European Community.[38] Of Japan's direct foreign investments, 37.6 per cent were in Britain, 24.0 per cent in Holland, 12.8 per cent in Luxembourg, a surprisingly low 8.2 per cent in Germany, 6.9 per cent in France, 3.7 per cent in Spain, 3.2 per cent in Belgium, and 3.6 per cent in the other members. In 1991, Britain and France were hosts to the two largest concentrations of Japanese factories in Europe, 187 and 122 respectively.[39] About half of Japan's EC investments are in wholly-owned, greenfield sites; in Britain about 70 per cent. Rapid as are Japan's growing direct investments in Europe, they still remain only one quarter of the $164 billion in American investments.[40]

Britain has been the investment target of choice for several reasons, including cheap labor, the English language, the infrastructure, transparency of government regulations, generally favorable investment climate, government free-trade policies, and friendly social climate. Yet Japan's investment targets are shifting. France's Poitiers defense against VTRs in 1982 is said to have prompted Japan's corporations to consider investing in countries which have been most critical of Japan, in order to leapfrog existing barriers and build up political clout in those capitals to undercut retaliatory measures. Recently, Japanese corporations have tried to spread their bets across Europe to allay criticism that the Japanese were simply using Britain as a springboard or Trojan Horse for the entire Community.

Tokyo is as adept at playing each of the twelve EC members against each other as it is playing off the fifty American states, while the Europeans are just as bad at falling into bidding wars as the Americans. The Europeans recognize the difficulty of maintaining a common defense against Japanese neomercantilism while depressed cities and regions engage in destructive bidding wars to attract Japanese investments. In March 1986, the Commission admitted that

in order to attract as much investment as possible in manufacturing, national and regional authorities have often been led into competition with each other, each offering bigger or more advantageous subsidies and other incentives. An exchange of views between the member states at Community level would thus seem necessary to counteract the tendency of Japanese investors to exploit these attempts at outbidding.[41]

Later that year, in September, President de Clerq again warned against allowing Japan to play one locality off against the others: 'We must improve coordination between member states so that we can limit this beggar-thy-neighbor policy to attract new investments.'[42]

Corporate leaders are to economic conflict what generals are to military conflict. There is an imbalance in managerial training in Europe and Japan. While the Community's annual graduation of 3,000 MBAs is minuscule compared to America's 70,000, it is much larger than the 100 or so Japanese graduates. Europe's best and largest business school is the Institut Europeen d'Administration des Affairs (INSEAD), which annually graduates 420 MBAs. However, given the widespread adulation of Japanese management techniques and the relentless expansion of Japan's economy, perhaps MBAs are superfluous at best and a business impediment at worst because of the emphasis on financial tinkering to improve the bottom line rather than on long-term increases in productivity and the creation of new consumer products. Japan relies instead on in-house company management training. Only about 10 per cent of Europe's firms provide in-company education compared to 20 per cent of American firms and 80 per cent of Japanese firms, in which about 30 per cent of all employees are always engaged in some form of training.

Aside from the sheer bulk of its economy, Europe's only advantage over Japan is the enjoyment of a much higher quality of life. The average European enjoys four to six weeks of annual vacation and thirty-five hour work weeks, while the average Japanese takes only one vacation week and endures a forty-eight hour work week. Statistically, Japan's gruelling pace is an improvement. Japanese are now in fact working less than a generation ago. Between 1960 and 1990, Japan's average yearly work hours dropped from 2,432 to 2,009, while the Labor Ministry has targeted a reduction to 1,800 hours by 1993. But Japan is unlikely to achieve that goal any time soon and these statistics vastly underestimate the amount of time Japanese actually work. White collar workers frequently put in twelve-hour days six days a week without receiving any overtime. A recent survey found that 55 per cent of Japanese employees worked unpaid overtime.[43]

Given this disparity in work hours and vacations, Japanese will inevitably reply, when asked the reasons for Japan's economic success, that it boils down to their working harder than everyone else. The reality, as usual, is far different. As measured by work hours the Japanese do work longer than their counterparts in other industrialized countries, but as measured by productivity, they do not work harder than others.

Despite their longer work hours, Japanese do not necessarily enjoy more wealth than Europeans. Per capita income, which is GNP divided by population, is not considered an accurate guide to living standards because it does not account for living costs. The purchasing power parity (PPP) is a more accurate measure of relative living standards because it compares the costs of a collection of goods. The difference between per capita income and purchasing power parity can be significant. In 1989, Japan's per capita income of $22,889 far outstripped Germany's $19,463, France's $16,884, Italy's $15,056, Britain's $14,485, or America's $20,768. According to comparative PPP, however, Japan's dropped to $15,555 compared to Germany's $15,310, France's $14,577, Italy's $13,968, and Britain's $14,272.

CONCLUSION

Despite a lower quality of life and smaller GNP, the overall balance of economic power appears to be tipped decisively in Japan's favor. Although the Community market is almost three times larger and its GNP over one and a half times the size of Japan's, the Japanese are more powerful by virtually all other economic indicators. Japan's growth rate has consistently been far higher than that of the Community average or the United States. Between 1969 and 1979, Japan's economy annually grew 4.7 per cent compared to the Community's 3.1 per cent and America's 2.8 per cent. Between 1979 and 1988, Japan's rate was 3.9 per cent compared to the Community's 1.9 per cent and America's 2.9 per cent.[44] Between 1970 and 1985, Japan's manufacturing productivity rose 206 per cent, followed by France's 190 per cent, Italy's 174 per cent, Germany's 173 per cent, America's 168 per cent, and Britain's 156 per cent.[45] After declining from $86 billion in 1986, Japan's trade surplus shot back up to $135 billion in 1992, and will steadily increase throughout the 1990s! In 1990, Japan's net overseas investments were $328 billion, the world's largest. In 1990 alone, Japan's corporations directly invested $54 billion overseas while its banks lent $36 billion.[46]

The costs for Japan of its growing hegemony over the global political economy are exceedingly light, which of course is a major reason why Japan's rise to power has been so successful. While Washington spends 5.5 per cent of its GNP on defense and official development aid (5.4 per cent on defense and 0.22 per cent ODA), and the EC 3.4 per cent (an average national budget of 3.0 per cent on defense and 0.40 per cent on ODA), Tokyo spends a mere 1.0 per cent on defense and 0.30 per cent on aid.

How does Japan use its immense power? One example is in technology. The growing dependence of European, American, and other foreign manufacturing firms on Japanese components gives the Japanese enormous power over the foreigner's fate. Japan's semiconductor manufacturers, for example, have been particularly notorious for deliberately withholding shipments for months to foreign firms in order to give Japanese electronics firms an advantage over their foreign rivals.

These economic power imbalances simply reflect ideological and institutional imbalances. In the zero-sum international trade war, neomercantilists like Japan will continually gain at the expense of those following largely liberal policies like the European Community. Tokyo's persistent neomercantilist industrial, trade, and investment policies will exacerbate these and other European weaknesses over time, spinning the Community into an ever-increasing vicious cycle of lower growth and dynamism while allowing Japan an ever more virtuous cycle of higher growth and dynamism.

Will the power balance remain decisively tipped in Japan's favor? Shackled by the deadweight of liberal and socialist ideologies and divided by ancient rivalries, until recently Europe seemed a community in name only. Europe and foreign visionaries, however, have always beheld the promise of a united, prosperous, and powerful continent. President Kennedy foresaw Europe's renaissance as the great power of the future as early as 1962 when he said

> There is arising across the Atlantic a single economic community which may soon have a population half again as big as our own, working and competing together with no more barriers to commerce and investment than exist among our fifty states, in an economy that has been growing roughly twice as fast as our own, representing a purchasing power which will some day equal our own, and a living standard growing faster than our own.[47]

After 1992, Europe will have the potential to catch up and surpass the Japanese and Americans by any political economic indicator. Whether it fulfills its tremendous potential, of course, remains to be seen.

6 European Community-Japan Relations

Until the mid-nineteenth century, contact between Europe and Japan was sporadic and mutual perceptions were shaped largely by myths. Marco Polo was the first European to hear about the distant archipelago of Japan (Cipangu), and the publication of his *Travels* popularized the image of a mythical, gold-rich island kingdom in the northwest Pacific. In 1492, Columbus set sail for the Orient, hoping to make contact with China and also to find the rich island of Cipangu. Although Columbus fell about half a world short of his goal, Jesuit missionaries managed to reach Japan in 1542, unleashing a century of feverish Japanese borrowing of Western military technology, fashions, and ideas. As in Europe's kingdoms, cannon and muskets enabled ambitious lords to smash down thin castle walls and transform Japan from decentralized to centralized feudalism.[1]

Having mastered Western weapons and tactics, and fearing that the regions it had just conquered could empower themselves with European coins, cannons, and crucifixes, the newly founded Tokugawa regime embarked on a step-by-step elimination of Western influence. In 1616 foreign trade was restricted to Nagasaki and Hirado; in 1624 the Spanish were expelled from Japan; in 1629 the regime began the forced conversion of Japanese Christians by ordering them publicly to tread on Christian images; in 1635, upon pain of death, all Japanese were forbidden either to return from or to travel overseas; in 1639 the Portuguese were expelled; in 1641 Dutch trade was confined to tiny Deshima Island near Nagasaki.

For the next 200 years, in the European imagination, Japan receded into a distant exotic kingdom ruled by fanatical samurai. Meanwhile, buried within itself, Japan shunned virtually all outside contact. But no people could remain an island in face of the second wave of Western imperialism in the mid-nineteenth century. Through Nagasaki, the Tokugawa learned with horror of how a handful of British troops and gunboats had defeated the vast Chinese empire in the Opium War (1839–42). A decade later the American Commodore Matthew Perry sailed into Tokyo Bay in 1853, demanding that the government receive a letter from President Fillmore requesting open ports, coaling stations, and fair treatment of shipwrecked sailors, and promising to return the following year for a reply. The Tokugawa were impotent in the face of these 'black ships' which could reduce Edo

(Tokyo) to starvation through blockade or to ashes through bombardment. As if this foreign threat were not enough, the Tokugawa simultaneously faced a growing challenge from the vanquished western fiefs (Han) whose lords (the Daimyo) had never lost a fierce desire for revenge. Lead by Satsuma and Choshu, the dissident Han attempted to undermine the Tokugawa with the rallying cry, 'Expel the barbarian, revere the emperor!' (*Sonno Joi!*).

Faced with external and internal threats, the Tokugawa bowed toward the more powerful of these. In 1854, the Japanese and Americans signed the Treaty of Kanagawa in which the Tokugawa accepted all three American demands. The other Western powers soon followed by dictating their own treaties, and through the concept of 'most favored nation' (MFN) the access to Japanese markets and immunity from Japanese laws granted by Edo to one power was automatically shared by all.

Although the Tokugawa bought off the external threat with these concession, it did so at the cost of its legitimacy. In 1868, the Tokugawa were overthrown by a coalition of rebellious Han, and a new regime, nominally headed by the Emperor Meiji, took power. Impotent in the face of Western military power, the Meiji regime sublimated its xenophobia and embarked on creating a 'rich country, strong military' (*fukoku kyohei*) on Western models, with the goal of eventually militarily and economically surpassing the West, and of reversing the unequal treaties imposed on Japan. By the early twentieth century, Japan had accomplished these goals. Tokyo founded a range of modern industries and forged the close government-business ties that continue today. In 1889, Japan adopted a Prussian-style constitution which contained a contradictory and ultimately fatal mix of democratic and authoritarian elements. Japan's modern army and navy embarked on a step-by-step conquest of northeast Asia with the takeover of the Kuriles and half of Sakhalin through a treaty with Russia (1875), the forced opening of Korea (1876), the annexation of the Ryukyu Islands (1879), takeover of Taiwan, the Pescadores, and the creation of special privileges in Korea following victory in the Sino-Japanese War (1894–5). This was followed by the outright takeover of Korea and the creation of special privileges in Manchuria following victory in the Russo-Japanese War, and the takeover of Germany's Pacific islands and Shantung concession in China during World War One. There were some setbacks. In 1985, Russia, France, and Germany combined to force Japan to disgorge the Kwantang peninsula. In 1916, in response to a Chinese plea, the Western allies pressured Japan to back off from its '21 demands' which would effectively have made China its colony.

But overall, Japan's imperialism paid enormous dividends, not just with colonial revenues but Western respect. In 1900, Japanese troops marched with the Western powers to smash China's Boxer Rebellion. In 1902, London and Tokyo formed an alliance. By 1911 all the Western countries had given up their tariff and extraterritorial privileges with Japan. And in 1919, Japan was seated at the Versailles Conference as one of the Big Five powers.

Unfortunately, Japan failed to understand the enormous international changes represented by the Versailles Treaty and creation of the League of Nations. World War One had materially and psychologically drained the Western powers of most of their imperial energies and antagonisms. Henceforth, the power politics and secret treaties that had characterized international relations previously were to be replaced with the Wilsonian ideals of open covenants and peaceful settlement of disputes. The naval arms race, which had so greatly contributed to the tensions leading to World War One, was halted by the Washington (1921–2) and London (1930) treaties, while fourteen countries (including Japan) signed the Kellogg-Briand Treaty (1928) which outlawed aggressive war. The League agreed to contain any aggressor nation through economic and, if need be, military sanctions.

Rather than view the Versailles system as a guarantee of Japanese security, Japan's leaders instead saw it, and the Great Power fatigue that it masked, as an ideal opportunity for further expansion into a chaotic China and the poorly-defended Western colonies in Asia. Perversely, in seeking an autonomous, self-sufficient, secure empire in East Asia, Japan's leaders ended up provoking the West into eventually destroying that empire.[2] Japan was overwhelmingly reliant on the United States for 60 per cent of its machine tools, 90 per cent of its copper, 75 per cent of its scrap iron, and 80 per cent of its oil.[3] These supplies were secure and Japan prospered as long as Tokyo did not directly threaten the United States.

Blinded to these realities, starting with the invasion of Manchuria, Tokyo embarked on a step-by-step conquest of east and southeast Asia that would not end until the atomic bombings of Hiroshima and Nagasaki fourteen years later. Japan responded to the League of Nation's condemnation of its Manchurian takeover and request for withdrawal by withdrawing from the League in 1933. The failure of the League and of the United States to mount any economic or military sanctions only whetted the appetite of Japan's expansionists. Between 1931 and 1937, the Japanese consolidated their control over Manchuria and infiltrated north China. In 1937, Japan used an unexpected shooting incident between Japanese and Chinese troops as the excuse to launch a total war against China. Japanese armies overran most of eastern China before getting bogged down in a guerrilla struggle. Again, consumed with the Depression and other domestic ills, the West did no more than feebly protest. It was not until Japan's takeover of northern Indochina in 1940 that the United States first cut back on the export of scrap iron and aviation fuel to Japan, but justified this not as a response to Japanese aggression but because of the needs of America's own defense. The freezing of Japan's assets in the United States and cutoff of oil exports to Japan in July 1941 amidst bilateral negotiations for an East Asian settlement forced Tokyo to choose between a retreat from all its conquests or a direct attack on the American, British, and Dutch territories in Asia and the Pacific. The Japanese, of course, fatalistically choose the latter. Three and a half years after Pearl Harbor, most of Japan's armies, navies, and cities had been destroyed.

Japan's relationship with the West from 1853 through 1945 had swung from conflict to peaceful coexistence to outright war. The Europeans and Americans were impressed by Japan's seeming Westernization and cooperation, and failed to understand the fierce nationalism that fueled Japan's modernization. The result, ultimately, was war. As in its first contact with the West, Japan's feelings toward the 'hairy barbarians' (*keito*) were cordial as long as Japan still had more to learn. But once Japan had surpassed the Europeans it severed its ties. The only difference between the 1930s and the early 1600s was that Japan expanded outward rather than withdrew inward.

Is Japan going through a similar cycle today?[4] Japan has been accused of an economic aggression as vigorous and certainly far more successful than its military aggression of the 1930s. Will the inevitable result be a global trade war? Or do the Japanese now understand that in an interdependent world that everyone would lose in such a war, and perhaps no one as badly as themselves? Do the Europeans misunderstand the dynamics and consequences of Japanese neomercantilism today as badly as they did Tokyo's military aggression of half a century ago? Or have both sides reached a more realistic understanding of the other so that conflicts are managed and a balance of power maintained?

This chapter will analyze European Community-Japan relations since 1945. It will first examine the mutual perceptions which both shape and are shaped by the economic relationship, and will then detail the relationship's evolution over almost five decades.

MUTUAL PERCEPTIONS

Individuals and societies deal with complex, paradoxical realities by reducing them to simple sets of images, and then acting on those images. If they have any image at all of a particular country, most people's perceptions rarely get beyond pretty tourist poster images. Or, if the country in mind has a history of bloody repression or aggression, the central popular images may be heaps of machine-gunned or decapitated prisoners of war, uniformed leaders angrily shouting and shaking their fists before adoring masses, or soldiers fighting to the death on tiny coral islands or frozen wastelands. Sometimes a country can be viewed with a mixture of positive and negative images. The greater a country's impact on the world, the more likely it will be perceived by others with two sets of lens, one good and the other bad. For example, people around the world can simultaneously view the United States as a land of opportunity and freedom and a land of poverty, corruption, and drift. Although these dual images are always present, one of them is sometimes dominant and the other dormant. Like a revolving stage with dramatically different scenes on either side, the popular foreign image of a country can shift sharply when that country, and particularly its government, does something especially positive or negative.

Popular images of foreign countries can have an important effect on international relations.[5] Mutual elite and mass perceptions form the context within which relations take place, and are at once shaped by and shape the relationship. The more positive an elite and mass image of another country, the greater the chance that any issues will be resolved rationally and amiably; the more negative the image, the greater the chance that issues will be dealt with in an atmosphere of suspicion and intransigence, if at all.

These images of the 'real world' vary considerably in their accuracy. Of course, most images are based on reality, and are shaped by that country's policies and culture. Often, however, popular images about a country continue even when that country in mind has changed dramatically. But whether positive or negative, these images rarely get beyond caricatures. Unfortunately most policymakers, let alone ordinary citizens, have neither the time nor capability to conduct an extensive enough study of another country to replace shallow images with a deep understanding.[6]

European Images

What forces have shaped Europe's views of Japan? History is certainly the most important influence. Europe's images of Japan have been shaped by their very mixed views of Asia and Asians. Periodic invasions by a succession of nomadic 'hordes' from Central Asia from the Roman Empire's fall to the Turkish siege of Vienna in the seventeenth century seems to have burned deeply into the European psyche to create a 'yellow peril' phobia. Yet, various political philosophers from Voltaire to Marx, and adventurers from Polo to Burton have extolled the exotic, sensual, and sometimes superior virtues of 'Oriental' civilization.[7]

Japan's rapid modernization and rise into a great power by the late nineteenth century reawakened the 'yellow peril' fear in many European minds and challenged their notions of Caucasian superiority. Although these fears were mollified by Japan's constructive actions at the Versailles Conference and the signing of the Washington (1921–2) and London naval treaties (1930), they were enflamed again by the brutality and speed with which Japan conquered east and southeast Asia during the 1930s and early 1940s, the humiliating defeats the Japanese inflicted on the Americans, Dutch, French, and British, and their barbaric treatment of war prisoners and civilian internees alike.

Lehmann writes that

> in the modern era, Japan is the only non-Western country to have successfully challenged Europe both militarily and economically. On the military front, Japan was, of course, defeated; but she was beaten by the United States and not by European powers. The humiliations endured at the hands of the Japanese during World War II, and the consequent loss of the European empires in Asia, will remain, for the time being at least, a feature of the image of Japan in France, the Netherlands, and Britain. In economic terms . . . Japan has challenged Europe on Europe's own terms; in other words, Japan competes with Europe precisely in those areas in which Europe excelled. The pupil has, to a considerable extent, become the master.[8]

Paradoxically, Westerners continued to harbor feelings of superiority alongside fears of a 'yellow peril'. The devastating defeat which the United States and Britain suffered from Japan in 1941 and 1942 was deepened by the racist disdain which they, along with most other Westerners, felt toward the Japanese. Although startling, Japan's defeat of China and Russia at the turn of the century were somehow seen as flukes. Despite all evidence to the contrary, the Western powers continued to see the Japanese as inferior and incapable of fighting a modern war. Thus the British, like the Americans, were taken completely by surprise in 1941. Churchill admitted to Parliament in April 1942 that 'the violence, fury, skill, and might of Japan have far exceeded anything that we had been led to expect'.[9]

European fears of Japanese economic aggression were not new. Europeans and others have complained about unfair Japanese competition ever since the country was 'opened' in 1854. Japan's protectionism has changed little since this was written over a century ago in 1890: 'European bankers and merchants in Japan . . . complain it is true, not so much of actual wilful dishonesty – though of that too, they affirm there is plenty, but of pettiness, constant shilly-shallying, unbusinesslikeness almost passing belief. Japan, the globetrotter's paradise, is also the grave of the merchant's hopes'.[10]

Europeans and others still echo this 1892 complaint of Japanese property theft: 'There is hardly a well-known European trademark that you do not find fraudulently imitated in Japan.'[11]

Europeans began to see Japan as an economic and military threat around the same time. As early as 1901, a Nobel Prize winner, Estournelles de Constant, warned of Japan's economic threat to the West, that Tokyo 'would choose the field of action which suits them best, and they will lead the pack and stimulate the organization of the industrial victory of the Far East over the West using our capital, our machines, and our methods'.[12] Constant's prediction has proven to be chillingly accurate.

The first postwar wave of alarm about a Japanese economic threat occurred during the late 1960s when Japan's economy rapidly roared past those of Italy, Britain, France, and Germany, and Japanese products began outselling those of their European rivals everywhere. Such books as R. Guillain's *The Japanese Challenge*, M. Scharnagl's *Japan: the Planned Aggression*, S. Hedberg's *The Japanese Threat*, C. Jecquier's *The Japanese Industrial Challenge*, L. Delassus' *Japan: Monster or Model*, V. Price's *The Japanese Miracle and Peril*, and J. Efimov's *Stop the Japanese Now*, captured popular fears through elite analysis.[13] These attitudes toward Japan – part disdain, part fear, mostly indecision – were summed up by President de Gaulle in October 1962 when he described a meeting with Prime Minister Ikeda as being like 'a visit from a transitor salesman'.

Although the image of Japanese as 'economic animals' was coined in Thailand in the early 1970s, it was rapidly seized and increasingly held by Europeans and others around the world as Japan's economic superpower grew and its neomercantilist and corporate policies became more widely understood. The image of Japan's ant-hill (*fourmiliere*) society was expressed in the 1979 European Commission report which described Japanese as 'workaholics living in rabbit hutches'. The view of Japanese as fanatics willing to die for their emperor in *kamikaze*-style human wave attacks has been replaced by that of Japanese salarymen mindlessly working themselves to death for the company's prosperity.

Spyros Makridakis conducted extensive interviews with European business and Community leaders about, among other things, the Japanese challenge.[14] The European respondents uniformly expressed fear and resentment of Japanese 'economic imperialism' and questioned whether European industries could survive the continued onslaught. Makridakis found that 'European government and business leaders are afraid of a repetition in Europe of what happened in the United States where the Japanese wiped out whole segments of American industry. With few exceptions they advocate tough action to defend European industry'. These actions include

import restrictions on Japanese goods coupled with guaranteed market
shares in Japan . . . [R]eciprocity must extend to highly protected Japanese sectors such as banking, construction, insurance, and even agriculture. . . . The only way to get equal access is by pushing the Japanese hard
at the negotiating table and achieving perfect reciprocity, to the point
where an equilibrium in the trade balance . . . is accomplished.

One clear shift in European perception is the 'Made in Japan' label. What
was once an image of derision, implying cheap shoddy products, now has
an image of outstanding workmanship, quality, and innovation.

How much are these views shaped by scholarship? There are very few
European scholars of Japan's civilization, particularly its modern political
economy. Nations generally study those things which are most important to
them. Europe's great scholars often studied those foreign countries which
their nations had conquered. Japan was conquered by the United States, not
a European power, and only then a century after it was first forced into the
global political economy. After 7 December 1941, the United States had to
produce a cadre of scholars with a deep understanding of the nation they
would fight and later occupy.

And scholarship is no panacea for misperceptions. The experts are often
wrong. The indepth study of a country does not necessarily bring with it
greater understanding. Knowing too much can cause as much misunderstanding as knowing too little if the scholar sees his subject too narrowly or
sentimentally. There is no evidence that America's greater reservoir of
scholarship about Japan has helped Washington identify and assert its
interests with Tokyo. In fact, it could be argued that America's wartime
generation of scholars may have helped hobble Washington's ability truly
to understand and rationally respond to Japan's challenge. America's first
generation of scholars generally tends to hold a sentimental, paternal view
of Japan as a 'unique' country that still deserves special treatment in the
global political economy. What Europe and the United States both need is
a phalanx of scholars who study Japan and recommend policies based on
objective detachment rather than sentimental symbiosis.

Japanese Images

What shapes Japan's views of itself and the outside world? Considering
themselves neither fully Asian nor Western, but a strange hybrid of some of
the better features of the two, most Japanese do not feel they fit in with
anyone. Many forces shape the Japanese self-image of superiority, uniqueness, and isolation. One major reason is Japan's hierarchical view of their

own society and international relations. In Japan, everyone and every group is either superior or inferior to all others. In the pre-modern era, individuals and groups in society were fixed in a rigid Confucian class system. In the modern era, individuals and groups can rise or fall within the socioeconomic hierarchy by their own efforts. Japanese similarly view international relations as based on a constant Darwinian struggle for power, wealth, and status in which the superior 'races' emerge by dint of their own unique attributes over 'inferior races'.

These views of 'superiority' and 'inferiority' were shaped by Japan's long isolation. For over 1,500 years, Japan's foreign relations were tenuous. Periods of intense cultural borrowing were inevitably followed by longer periods of self-imposed isolation. During the periods of cultural borrowing, Japanese largely saw themselves and their culture as 'inferior' to the foreign model on which they were dependent. But after having assimilated all they needed from abroad, Japan's innate sense of cultural 'uniqueness' and 'superiority' reemerged. Japan would then reject the foreign model and turn in on itself, or, during the 1930s, carved out its own an autonomous East Asian empire.

The same pattern occurred after 1945. Defeated, and forced by the Americans to revolutionize their failed system, Japanese first saw their conquerers and the West in largely idealistic terms. But as Japan successfully transformed itself from mass poverty into mass affluence, it increasingly grew proud of its accomplishments and disdainful of a West that it perceived as lazy, inefficient, and complacent. The 'inferior' feelings of the 1950s steadily gave way to Japan's present self-image as 'superior' economically and culturally to all others. Despite almost a half century of steady integration into the global political economy, Japan's world view is an increasingly virulent nationalism rather than internationalism.

Lehman writes that Japan's more than 200 years of isolation (1637–1854)

> was not only a historical phenomena, it remains a psychological condition. One does not emerge from more than two centuries of solitary confinement without experiencing difficulties in readjusting to the outside world. The very protracted period of incubation along with the nature of the sense of national identity and uniqueness have resulted in an extremely marked degree of clannishness. This makes communication with other members of the international community difficult. If a European image of Japan is that hers is an impenetrable society, the Japanese would tend to concur in that a *gaijin* (foreigner) cannot really understand Japan.[15]

Despite the assumption that they can never be understood, Japanese are extremely sensitive to what foreigners think about them. Lehmann writes that 'there is almost a national obsession about the national image – hence the furore caused by the "workaholics in rabbit hutches", or indeed the vexation when a decade-and-a-half earlier it was reported that de Gaulle had referred to Prime Minister Ikeda, whom he was about to meet, as "*un marchard de transistor*" (a transistor salesman)'.[16]

And what of the Japanese view of Europeans? Japan's perceptions are greatly shaped by its very ambivalent view of foreigners. There remains a diminishing reservoir of respect for Europe's cultural achievements and a feeling of obligation for borrowed modern institutions and ideas. Superficially, 'in political thought, economics, philosophy, literature, language, the cinema and television, painting, sculpture, sport, music, architecture, food, [and] dress', Japan is a very Western country.[17] Yet, the Japanese see Europe as a decadent civilization in decline, and most Japanese look down upon Europeans as economic has-beens. MITI Minister Naohiro Amaya succinctly summed up Japanese feelings about Europe when he said: 'Japan's competitive power is overwhelmingly great. If we compare it to a golf match, Japan's handicap is one while that of Europe's is 25 or 26.'[18] Japanese do distinguish between different Europeans, contrasting say their image of the lazy, inefficient, strike-prone British with harder-working Germans. But Japanese believe that eventually all Europeans will catch the 'English disease' (*eikoku byo*). Fritz Stern summarizes this view:

> The Japanese have a nostalgia for European Culture; they would like to reknit cultural ties that once were so close. But they are also exasperated by what they regard as Europe's decline into a museum of culture, into 'an old men's home,' whose inhabitants are content to live out their remaining days with whatever comfort they can find. They believe that the Europeans are morose, 'dying spiritually and economically,' unwilling to work, unwilling to compete or collaborate. Underneath the strictures remains the desire for good relations with Europe, for a better understanding with partners once considered inspiriting models.[19]

Changing Images and Realities

These mutual perception have changed greatly over the past century. According to Wilkinson, 'in the nineteenth century, Europeans regarded Japan as an exotic playground, the ultimate in sophisticated tourism, while the Japanese regarded Europe as a disciplined group-orientated society possessing the secrets of efficient industrial production. Today it is the Japanese who flock to Europe for exotic tourism and it is the Europeans who increasingly regard Japan as a disciplined society with amazingly efficient industries'.[20]

How accurate are these mutual images? Despite this reversal of images, both may well 'see the other in terms which owe more to past perceptions than present realities'.[21] The reason for this, according to Lehmann, is that Eurocentrism and Japanese isolationism (*sakoku*) and the sense of superiority continue to distort mutual perceptions.[22] Wilkinson notes the 'well-known pattern of Europe only waking up to Japan when Japan has become impossible to ignore, and Japan only waking up to an external situation when it has reached a boiling point'.[23] He goes on to argue that the 'long-run shifts in economic and political roles have not been accompanied by a corresponding adjustment of either Europe's or Japan's view of each other. Old images have persisted, thereby impeding communications and excerbating trade frictions'.[24]

Wilkinson comes perilously close to echoing the central message of Tokyo's public relations campaign that there are no real conflicts between Japan and the rest of the world, only misperceptions. Foreigners do not sell more in Japan, not because of webs of trade barriers, but because they do not try hard enough in the world's most open market and their goods are inferior. Likewise, Japanese goods sell more overseas, not because of industrial targeting and dumping, but because Japanese goods are superior. Once foreigners understand these simple realities, the conflicts will disappear.

The central European view of Japan cannot be refuted: Japan's success results from neomercantilist policies. There is a danger that Europe's industries could be devastated as thoroughly as America's if the Europeans do not mobilize, nurture, and protect their own economic resources.

EUROPEAN-JAPANESE RELATIONS (1945–80)

Japanese-Community relations have unfolded through five phases and appear to be entering a sixth. The first (1951–5) and second (1955–65) phases focused on Japan's attempts to secure first membership in GATT, and then MFN status with all the major economic powers. Japan's actual trade with Europe during these first two phases was relatively low in volume and as a percentage of its total trade, while its investments were miniscule, and Europe actually enjoyed an overall trade surplus with Japan.

Having achieved its first two objectives, Tokyo concentrated on significantly increasing its trade and investment penetration and achieving a trade surplus with Europe during the third phase (1965–73), and overwhelmingly succeeded in accomplishing all three goals. Relations were largely untroubled between the Community and Japan during this phase. Japan's neomercantilist priorities were to penetrate American and East Asian markets deeply – Europe's markets were a secondary target. They were far away, protectionist, fragmented, and of varying degrees of development and prosperity. Nonetheless, Japan's corporations made steady inroads into Europe during this time. This did not create any major difficulties because they expanded from a small base and were absorbed within the Community's rapidly growing economy while internal issues of integration and the absorption of new members overshadowed all others.

The fourth phase (1974–85) of Japan's relations with the Community was characterized by increased conflict and sporadic European retaliation against Japanese neomercantilism. The catalyst in this shift from a largely conflict-free into a conflict-ridden relationship was OPEC's quadrupling of oil prices in 1973. The result was a decade of slow growth and high inflation and unemployment in Europe and virtually everywhere else. Japan was the exception. Through the implementation of a new set of industrial, trade, and technology policies, Tokyo was able to guide Japan's economy through global stagflation with growth rates twice that of most other industrial countries. Japan's trade and investment surpluses have grown steadily while its industries leapfrog their European counterparts in manufacturing, technological, financial, and global market prowess. Japan's market share in a range of industrial products increased steadily during this phase and was reinforced by an increased number of investments despite the increased tension.

The fifth phase (1986–92) represented the Community's attempts to unify in response to Japan's emergence as the world's most dynamic financial, manufacturing, and technological power. Despite universal acknowledgement of the 'Japanese challenge', Brussels failed to forge unified policies either towards Japan or in its own troubled industries. Tokyo meanwhile accelerated its trade and investment penetration of Europe, and reinforced its conquests by building Japan lobbies in Brussels and the national capitals which it hoped would eventually become as powerful in shaping European policies in Japan's favor as its lobbies in Washington and across the United States had been in twisting American economic policies to support Japan's national interests. The character of the sixth phase (1993–future) will be shaped by Brussels' ability to capitalize on its unity by forging and implementing policies that simultaneously counter Japan's penetration of Europe, expand Europe's penetration of Japan's web of trade and investment barriers, and target strategic European industries and technologies for development.

European-Japanese relations during the early postwar years were largely antagonistic. Europeans well remembered Japan's prewar dumping offensives of low-wage products, its pirating of intellectual property, the misleading information given about the origins, contents, or quality of its goods, its pirating of other countries' intellectual property, and its export subsidies. During the 1930s, Japan deepened Europe's depression by dumping 'watches by the kilogram', textiles, and other industrial goods. Thus Europeans were united in the late 1940s and 1950s in defending their economies against the expected renewal of Japanese neomercantilism. Industrial associations, particularly textiles, in all the European states rallied against any concessions for Japan. Governments feared losing their colonial or commonwealth markets to Japan.

Championing Japan's full integration into the global economy, Washington exerted tremendous pressure on the European capitals to extend MFN and GATT membership to Japan. American motives were mixed between Cold War concerns about building up Japan as the 'workshop' and economic anchor of East Asia and the Pacific, and spreading the burden of tolerating Japanese neomercantilism with its Western allies. Tokyo submitted its application for GATT membership in 1952. Washington offered tariff concessions to the Europeans in exchange for their granting Tokyo MFN status.

For the next three years, the European Coal and Steel Community, and individual European states tried to block Japan's GATT membership and most-favored-nation (MFN) status. An April 1955 British White Paper argued that Japan's GATT membership would result in a bilateral trade war.[25] London and Paris were particularly concerned that any trade agreement with Tokyo should not disrupt their preferential access to the British Commonwealth and French Community countries respectively. Britain, France, Australia, and South Africa rejected any tariff negotiations with Tokyo before it became a GATT member while continually blocking its membership. An agreement was finally signed in June 1955 after four years of tough negotiations, which would become official when Washington persuaded two-thirds of GATT's members to sign it. By August, thirty countries had signed the treaty and Japan was officially accepted as a GATT member. But the GATT members were split over whether to grant Japan MFN. The United States, Canada, Germany, Italy, and the

Scandinavian countries granted Japan MFN, while fourteen countries including Britain, Belgium, the Netherlands, South Africa, Australia, and later France, invoked GATT Article 35 entitled 'Nonapplication of the Agreement between Particular Contracting Parties', which allows members to withhold MFN status from a member. When Tokyo hosted GATT's fifteenth plenary session in 1959, it unsuccessfully tried to have Article 35 abolished.

As a GATT member, Tokyo was required to open its trade, investment, and financial markets. In 1959, Tokyo announced its commitment to trade liberalization, the remittance of profits by foreign investors, and the removal of foreign travel restrictions, and in June 1960 promised to achieve 90 per cent liberalization within two years. Tokyo threaten to withhold its 'liberalization' from countries which continued to discriminate against Japan.

But these statements were largely for foreign public consumption in order to counter complaints about systematic Japanese protectionism. In reality, Tokyo erected even more elaborate and subtle trade barriers and weakened its antimonopoly laws so that firms could collude at home and abroad. Japan's official trade barriers during this time included a licensing scheme in which all imports were designated one of three categories: automatic approval for products considered essential for Japan's economy, automatic fund allocation if it could be funded with the existing foreign exchange holdings, and a fund allocation system in which there was a list of restricted goods. Japanese 'liberalization' partly involved shifting goods from the fund allocation system to the automatic fund allocation.

Tokyo originally protested against the signing of the Rome Treaty in April 1957, and with India called for a special GATT general conference to determine if it violated the Charter's clauses on discrimination and colonial preferences. However, following the EEC's official debut on 1 January 1959, Tokyo abandoned its ineffectual obstructionist policy and officially accepted the Community. At GATT meetings it did continue to complain about those fourteen countries which invoked Article 35 toward Japan. Meanwhile, Tokyo stepped up its divide-and-conquer strategy of exploiting Community cleavages and playing off one member against another.

Tokyo's policies toward the Community and Europe were motivated by both realistic and emotional concerns. Realistically, Tokyo was simply trying to expand its trade everywhere while concentrating its efforts on large free markets like West Germany and Britain by minimizing foreign trade barriers and maintaining extensive trade and investment barriers. But fuelling these neomercantilist policies was Japan's traditional fear of becoming isolated and discriminated against by a hostile world.

Tokyo targeted Bonn for its first free trade agreement with a European government, reasoning that it had to secure openings for Japanese corporations in West Germany's rapidly growing and prosperous economy, and that if it could not succeed in expanding its market access with a government that largely followed liberal economic policies, it would probably not succeed with other more protectionist European governments.[26] West Germany had granted MFN status to Japan in 1955 but continued to impose restrictions on 20 per cent of Japanese imports which threatened German industries. For the next five years, Tokyo and Bonn engaged in a series of negotiations over German restrictions on such products as textiles, ceramics, porcelain, sewing machines, and buttons, Japanese pirating of Germany patents and trademarks, and Japanese restrictions on chemicals, optics, and steel. Prime Minister Kishi's trip to Bonn in August 1959 to push through an agreement failed, as did the next round of talks in January and February, in part because Paris exerted pressure on Bonn to maintain restrictions to prevent Japanese imports pouring into France through the back door of Germany. In April 1960, however, Chancellor Adenauer travelled to Tokyo to negotiate an agreement which was signed on 1 July 1960. Bonn agreed to grant Tokyo full MFN with a gradual liberalization of its quotas on Japanese products to be completed in January 1965.

Over the next few years, Tokyo succeeded in signing similar agreements with the other Community and European governments. Japan's trade with the Benelux countries was the second highest after West Germany's. Tokyo began negotiations with Belgium in October 1959 and soon involved the Netherlands and Luxembourg. A three-year trade agreement between Tokyo and the Benelux was signed on 16 July 1960 in which the latter agreed to disinvoke Article 35 in return for a limited safeguard clause that required consultations in case Japanese imports caused market disruptions.

Meanwhile, the Europeans struggled to form a common policy toward Japan. The first step toward a Community policy toward Japan came in April 1959 when Bonn called for a common textile quota. The next month the Commission established Working Group 115 to investigate the Community's relations with Japan and recommend policies. But neither Bonn's call for common textile quotas or the Commission's working group on Japan achieved their goals. In October 1961 the Council attempted to empower the Commission by requiring members to consult with the Commission before they made deals with third parties. In September 1962 Brussels announced that negotiating a trade agreement with Japan was a top priority.

But the most important step the Community took occurred in November 1962 when it was decided that a safeguard clause should be included in all member trade agreements with Japan. An escape clause would theoretically allow the Europeans unilaterally to impose restrictions on Japanese imports if the imports were dumped or caused a major disruption to the economy. The members quickly incorporated the policy in their treaties. The Benelux countries revised their trade agreement with Japan to include a safeguard clause on 30 April 1963. For the next decade, Japanese and Europeans expended considerable time, energies, and frustration wrangling over the safeguard clause, whose symbolism proved far more important that its practical importance. One by one Tokyo succeeded in wringing MFN status from the holdouts and a reduction of quotas on Japanese goods from every European state.

France, predictably, proved Japan's toughest trade negotiator. Tokyo wanted access to France's domestic and colonial markets and wanted to import Alsatian potash, Moroccan phosphates, and New Caledonia nickel. In January 1962, Paris and Tokyo signed a trade agreement in which France reduced its quotas to 125 products but retained Article 35, while Japan maintained quotas on 172 French products. Specific figures were decided on the volume, type, qualities, and prices of Japan's cotton textiles, which would be handled only by officially designated French importers. The two countries signed an even more comprehensive agreement in May 1963 which was to last for six years, in which Paris agreed to reduce its quotas from 140 to eighty-four. In April 1965, Paris offered an industrial and technological cooperation agreement with Tokyo and agreed to cut its quotas from sixty-eight to thirty-eight in return for Japanese concessions on automobiles and perfume. But when Tokyo rejected the technological cooperation plan, Paris withdrew all of its concessions.

Italy also proved to be a tough negotiator. Although Tokyo successfully negotiated several agreements with Rome in which Italian quotas were reduced from 600 items to 117 in July 1961, a Japanese demand in November 1961 that Rome remove all its quotas led to a collapse in the negotiations. Negotiations continued sporadically over the next two years. In May 1963, Rome announced that it would reduce quotas from 117 to ninety.

But, except for its agreement with Germany, Tokyo viewed the other Community agreements as of secondary importance to a British agreement. Britain's application with the Community was pending and Tokyo reasoned that Japanese corporations could benefit from London's traditional liberal policies and Commonwealth links. As with the other countries, Tokyo's efforts were concentrated on persuading London to abandon a safeguard clause in any agreement. On 14 November 1962, the two governments signed a Treaty of Commerce and Navigation, in which London rescinded its use of Article 35 in return for a safeguard clause and list of products on which Tokyo promised to restrain its exports. But it would be another decade before Britain joined the Community. During this time Tokyo's closest relations within Europe were with Britain. The two countries resolved several nagging problems and forged closer ties. In January 1968, Tokyo agreed to rein in Japanese corporations which were circumventing restrictions on trade with Rhodesia. In March 1968, the two countries extended an existing ten-year agreement on jointly developing nuclear energy for thirty years.

Meanwhile, Brussels was fruitlessly attempting to forge a common policy toward Japan. In June 1963, the Commission proposed a policy which would include mutual liberalization on a MFN basis, equal Japanese treatment of European exports, a common safeguard clause, a common list of sensitive products, and measures to safeguard unfair trade tactics.[27] But the Council failed to give an official mandate to the Commission to conduct such talks. Tokyo thus got away with flatly refusing Commission requests to conduct preliminary negotiations in August 1963 and February 1964. In April 1964, the Council finally approved the Commission's common trade policy plan, including a safeguard clause and common quota involving 200 Japanese products, but then rescinded it in July 1964, probably because of an Italian veto over what was seen as an inadequate number and type of quotas.[28]

Having struck a deal with each country, Tokyo brushed off a 1964 attempt by the Commission to conclude a comprehensive trade agreement. Tokyo feared that the EEC would base any quotas on the country with the largest quotas, which at that time was Italy. In 1967, however, Tokyo requested negotiations with Brussels but the members refused to give a mandate to the Commission. Fearing their tougher policies would be abandoned, Italy and France opposed any Community agreement although the other states were in favor.

Even after receiving GATT membership, Tokyo continued to rely on Washington to help it negotiate trade agreements with the Europeans. Washington was glad to assist since more open European markets could relieve some of the pressure on the United States to absorb most of Japan's exports, while helping to expand and strengthen the global political economy. Washington was also instrumental in gaining Japan membership in the Organization for Economic Cooperation and Development (OECD). On 1 January 1961, the OEEC had become the OECD with the addition of the United States and Canada. Tokyo immediately voiced an interest in membership. Prime Minister Ikeda travelled to the European capitals in November 1962 to lobby support for Japan's membership. In April 1963, the OECD gave Tokyo's application preliminary approval pending the successful conclusion of negotiations over Japanese liberalization. Tokyo made the requisite promises to liberalize its trade and investment policies. In July 1963, Norway, joined by Britain, Greece, and the Netherlands, threatened to veto Japan's membership unless it abandoned its discriminatory policies toward chartering foreign vessels. Tokyo eventually promised to do so. In 26 July 1963, the OECD unanimously granted Tokyo membership.

How successful were these bilateral and multilateral negotiations in expanding trade between Japan and Europe? Japan's exports to Europe expanded rapidly throughout the period, while Japan ran a continual trade deficit with the Community.[29] In 1956, Japan exported $103.2 million and imported $111.3 million with the Community nations, of which it exported $34.1 million and imported $56.2 million with Germany, $38.2 million and $23.7 million with Benelux, $14.2 million and $21.6 million with France, and $16.7 million and $9.8 million with Italy. Japan's trade with Britain far surpassed its trade with any one Community member: $63.2 million in exports and $66.6 million in imports. Yet this Community trade remained a small fraction of Japan's total exports of $2.501 billion and imports of $3.230 billion, or 3.2 per cent.

Trade more than tripled over the next eight years. By 1964, Japan exported $365.3 million and imported $444.1 million with the Community, of which it exported $149.0 million and imported $249.5 million from Germany, $115.1 million and $82.1 million with Benelux, $41.6 million and $70.4 million with France, and $59.6 million and $42.1 million with Italy. Japan's trade with Britain continued to exceed any one Community member: $197.8 million in exports and $185.3 million in imports. Again, its Community trade was a small percentage of its total exports of $6.674 billion and imports of $7.938 billion, or 2.0 per cent. All of the Community nations ran large trade deficits with Japan except West Germany, which may be the major reason that Bonn continued to champion free trade.

Japan's trade with the Community almost doubled between 1964 and 1968 from $365.3 million to $692.3 million in exports and from $444.1 to $736 million in imports. Of this amount, Japan exported $287.4 million and imported $400.6 million from Germany, $233.7 million and $133.9 million with Benelux, $94.1 million and $127.4 million with France, and $77.1 million and $75.0 million with Italy. Japan exported $364.6 million and imported $257.4 million with Britain. Japan's trade with the Community represented a small but growing percentage of its total exports of $12.973 billion and imports of $12.988 billion, or 5.9 per cent.

How successful was Europe's policy, such as it was, toward Japan, and Japan's policy toward Europe? During the late 1950s and throughout the 1960s, the Community failed completely to unite and create a common trade policy or to systematically campaign for the dismantlement of Japan's trade barriers. According to Rothacher, 'national officials muddled along with their restrictive lists – never apparently thinking beyond their annual trade protocols, never considering Japan's growth potential unrolling before their eyes, hardly ever looking at the political chances which this potential was ready to offer'.[30] Relations with Japan were generally relegated to the back burner during this time. If a Japanese threat existed, it was viewed as more a geopolitical one than geoeconomic. Although some Europeans warned ominously of a growing Japanese economic challenge, most were more concerned about Japanese neutrality or an alignment with China which could tip the balance of power in the Cold War. Japan's steadily rising economic power did not become obvious until the late 1960s.

The Commission continued trying to obtain a Council mandate for conducting a common trade policy with Japan – and it kept getting turned down. The French and Italian ministers vetoed these proposals because they might dilute their countries' more protectionist policies toward Japan and the Community. In 1968, however, members agreed to allow the Commission to coordinate the various national negotiations which had been taking place with Tokyo and to approve changes in quotas and other agreements with each member. For example, in February 1970 Brussels approved Italy's reduction of quotas to forty-nine and its limit on 1,000 Japanese automobile imports. In 1968, the Commission and Tokyo began negotiating cotton textile imports and signed the first joint agreement between then and October 1969 in which the Community agreed to double its quota from 6,500 tons to 11,450 tons. Although meetings between Japanese and Commission officials became more frequent they were little more significant.

In the zero-sum game of economic competition, Europe's shortcomings were Japan's successes. Tokyo negotiated agreements with all the Community members and other European countries including Britain, which steadily reduced its quotas against Japanese imports. By April 1965, Germany had only twenty quotas, Benelux twenty-eight, France sixty-eight, and Italy 116. Although the Europeans continued to maintain the safeguard clause which allowed them to invoke barriers against Japanese imports should they be dumped or damaging to the economy, to date no European government has ever used the safeguard clause. What had enormous symbolic importance at the time has had no substantive importance, aside from the fact that it distracted the Europeans from pursuing more profitable objectives. During the late 1960s, Tokyo negotiated further reductions in each of the member's quotas while stonewalling negotiations with Brussels over a common trade policy.

The EC has run a continuous trade deficit with Japan since 1969. Starting that year, Germany surpassed Britain to become Japan's leading trade partner and for the first time Japan's exports to Germany edged its imports. In 1972, Japan exported $2.052 billion and imported $990 from the Community. Of this amount, Japan exported $986 million and imported $611 with Germany, $368 million and $229 million with France, $450 million and $199 million with Benelux, and $248 million and $151 million with Italy. In addition it exported $777 million and imported $415 million with Britain.

The quality of trade also tipped decisively toward Japan during this time and has steadily increased since. Japanese sold Europeans high-value automobiles, ships, consumer electronics, and machinery, while it bought lower-value agricultural products, chemicals, and raw materials. During the late 1960s and throughout the 1970s, Europe began to suffer recurrent Japanese dumping assaults in sensitive products like textiles, televisions, steel, ships, automobiles, tape recorders, radios, and motorcycles. During this same period, Japan's export machine blasted European and other foreign firms worldwide. In east and southeast Asia, European sales were twice those of Japan in 1960. A decade later Japan had surpassed Europe in exporting and investing to every country in east and southeast Asia, and by 1980 Japanese trade was twice that of Europe throughout the region. Japanese dismissed European claims that this dramatic shift in the region's economic power balance stemmed from Japanese dumping and tied aid. MITI Minister Naohiro Amaya said in 1977 that 'Europe woke up in the morning to find that the Rising Sun flag had been raised overnight in the area which it regards as its own traditional sphere of influence'.[31]

During this time, growing numbers of European political and economic leaders began viewing Japan as a rising trade, manufacturing, and technological challenge.[32] Many were alarmed at Japan's steadily rising trade surplus with Europe and the rest of the world, and feared that Japan would divert and dump even more products on the continent as Washington retaliated for Tokyo's neomercantilism. In November 1969, the Commission asked the Council to give it a mandate to negotiate a Community trade agreement with Tokyo aimed at achieving reciprocal and progressive trade liberalization, the elimination of nontariff trade barriers, a common safeguard clause which would prevent any sudden deluges of Japanese dumping, elimination of Japanese capital controls, and a bilateral consultation procedure. The European Parliament first clearly broached the issue of Japan's economic challenge on 2 February 1970 when it unanimously adopted a resolution supporting the Commission's mandate and the goals it was hoping to achieve through the trade agreement. The Council granted this mandate, and in February 1970, the Commission dispatched a nine-man delegation to Tokyo to open preliminary talks. This was the Commission's first major international negotiation since the Kennedy Round.

Tokyo rejected the Commission request for a safeguard clause, arguing that GATT's Article 19 would cover any dumping attacks. The Japanese then countered by demanding the removal of Community trade barriers and also that the security clause should not be extended to Italy and West Germany. The Japanese would only accept a security clause on products freed from the quotas and even then only for a limited amount of time. A second round of negotiations took place from 17 to 24 September 1970 but achieved no progress. Tokyo's stonewalling on the security clause issue was reinforced when Washington informed them that it would also demand a security clause if one was granted to Brussels. The talks eventually collapsed because of EC differences over how to manage the economic relationship, and Tokyo's divide-and-conquer strategy. France and the Benelux countries preferred to maintain the safeguard clauses they had signed with Japan following the Council's 1962 recommendations.

Tokyo then launched a diplomatic offensive in the autumn of 1970 which had mixed success. A two-week goodwill visit in September by Emperor Hirohito to Denmark, Belgium, France, Britain, the Netherlands, Switzerland, and Germany at times turned ugly as the media revived questions of the war and the emperor's guilt, and former detainees staged violent demonstrations, burning Japanese flags, attacking the emperor's car, and smashing Japanese embassy windows. The Emperor's visit was followed up by a forty-man *Keidanren* delegation in October to the Community, which promised a seven-point program including measures to boost fiscal demand, export controls by MITI in excessive cases, voluntary restraints on steel, advance warnings from JETRO when export surges would occur, support for a security clause, increased industrial cooperation, and the upgrade of Japan's economy to high technology industries.[33]

Japan's trade surplus with Europe steadily deepened, while President Nixon's New Economic Policy of 15 August 1971 which imposed, among other things, a devalued dollar no longer convertible to gold and a temporary 10 per cent tariff increases, threatened to divert yet more Japanese products to Europe. The Community's pressure on Tokyo to make a deal increased. On 25 October 1971, *Keidanren* agreed to orderly market arrangements (OMA) in various products with the Commission. The following year the agreement was extended to cover a variety of consumer electronic products, ball bearings, iron and steel, and automobiles. The joint communique announcing the agreement justified 'orderly marketing [to promote] the harmonious development of trade', a concept that would baffle doctrinaire free-trade economists but is a fact of life to trade realists.[34]

But these VERs were temporary and Tokyo failed to reduce its nontariff trade, investment, and capital controls. In May 1972, Commissioner Dahrendorf travelled to Tokyo to negotiate a breakthrough in the stalled talks, but Japan ignored his threat that a failure to meet the Community's requests could lead members to adopt Italy's stricter quotas. Tokyo countered by insisting that all issues be resolved on a strictly case-by-case basis. The result was continued deadlock. Having defeated European unity, Tokyo then made a series of restraint agreements with the members on consumer electronics throughout 1972. The Commission could only meekly approve these agreements, but tried to seize the initiative again in September when it published a paper calling for Japanese restraints on ship exports, and warned of retaliation if it was not forthcoming. Tokyo again stonewalled on an agreement with the Community.

Meanwhile London waited impatiently on the sidelines for the results of EC diplomacy. Britain too was suffering the effects of Japanese dumping in a range of products, but delayed opening its own negotiations in the hope that Brussels would forge an agreement that would include Britain once it had formally joined the EC in January 1973. According to Rothacher, London played the 'EC card', promising to act as a moderate influence within the Community in return for Japanese VERs on a dozen products including ball bearings, color televisions, and textiles.[35] In late May 1970, Tokyo agreed to a 15 per cent cut in ball bearing exports and 10 per cent rise in price in 1972 followed by a 10 per cent increase in exports in 1973, but refused to act over the other products for which London requested relief.

Free trade forces within the Community launched a counterattack on the Commission and members' tough reciprocity agreements. In December the Community's Fair Trade Commission declared illegal a secret Brussels-Tokyo textile cartel which had divided global markets between Asia for Japan, the United States for free competition, and the rest of the world for the Community.[36] Pressure was building on Brussels to rescind the range of restraint agreements which violated both the Rome Treaty and member state antitrust laws. Acting under pressure from Bonn, and fearing that the proliferation of OMAs and VERs would get out of the control, the Commission agreed in late 1973 to crack down on them. In November 1973, the Commission rejected a VER agreement between French and Japanese ball bearing producers on antitrust grounds, yet approved a range of others. The Commission was just as torn as Community members between managed traders and free traders.

Having succeeded in playing off one member against the others, and imposing temporary restraint agreements which allowed Japanese producers to raise prices and recoup losses incurred from their earlier dumping attacks to gain a dominant market share, Tokyo had no incentive to conclude a sweeping trade agreement with Brussels, something that became painfully obvious to the Europeans in 1972 and 1973. Instead, Tokyo proposed conducting regular high level consultations (HLCs) with Brussels to deal with accumulating disputes. The Community agreed and the first of these was held in Brussels in June 1973. The Japanese used the HLC as a forum to denounce the escape clause once again and to divert the Community's attention with discussions of the upcoming GATT Tokyo Round. As always, Tokyo continued adeptly to sidestep any discussion of Japan's nontariff trade, investment, and capital barriers.

Brussels still did not give up, although its position on a trade agreement with Japan remained the sum of its member's positions. In December 1973 the Council issued a statement which attempted to incorporate all the Community positions on Japan, agreeing to both soft and hardline stances on Japan's neomercantilism, pro- and anti-restraint positions, and national agreements with Tokyo as the essence of a Community agreement. It acknowledged that:

> Right now . . . confusion reigns because of the total breakdown of negotiations for an EEC-Japan trade treaty. Without such a treaty, each country is free to handle its own trade relations with Japan. The result is that, at one and the same time, the Japanese may be negotiating with industry groups, governments, national anti-trust groups, and the EEC's external trade and anti-trust departments – multiplicity of bodies that do not . . . see eye to eye.[37]

In other words, Tokyo was systematically playing its divide-and-conquer strategy against Europe and there was absolutely nothing that Brussels could do about it. The Community was divided between the free-trade oriented Germany and Britain, protectionist France and Italy, and the fence-sitters Benelux, Denmark, and Ireland, but each country could switch positions depending on whether powerful domestic economic forces were beseiged or not.

In November 1973, OPEC used the excuse of the Yom Kippur War between the Arab states and Israel to quadruple oil prices and cut back production. The Organization of Arab Petroleum Exporting Countries (OAPEC) imposed oil export boycotts on the United States and the Netherlands, and designated Japan an 'unfair country', for the support these three countries had given to Israel. These actions and the further doubling of oil prices in 1979 plunged the world economy into a decade of slow growth, high inflation and unemployment, and exacerbated the deepening economic problems among European industries and the growing competitiveness gap with their Japanese rivals. Japan's trade surplus with Europe expanded rapidly throughout the 1970s and into the 1980s.

No country was more dependent on foreign oil sources than Japan; no country responded more systematically and successfully to OPEC's quadrupling of oil prices.[38] This is clear from the comparison made in Table 6.1. In the short term from 1973 to 1975, Japan's inflations and unemployment rates were 20.3 per cent and 0.6 per cent, respectively, compared to France's 10.3 per cent and 1.4 per cent, Germany's 7.5 per cent and 3.3 per cent, Italy's 14.3 per cent and 0.2 per cent, Britain's 12.8 per cent and 1.0 per cent, and America's 3.7 per cent.

TABLE 6.1   *Growth of Japan's economy and balance of payments compared 1973–5*
Annual percentage changes

	Economy	Balance of Payments
Japan	−0.6	−7.7
France	0.8	−3.6
Germany	−1.8	4.3
Italy	−2.0	−5.4
Britain	−0.8	−3.7
USA	−3.2	6.3

After this period of initial adjustment, Japan's economy and balance of payments annually grew 5.7 per cent and 2.0 per cent, respectively compared to France's 2.7 per cent and −1.4 per cent, Germany's 3.1 per cent and −2.0 per cent, Britain's 1.1 per cent and 0.8 per cent, Italy's 3.4 per cent and 1.1 per cent, or America's 2.9 per cent and −7.3 per cent. Japan's inflation and unemployment rates were 5.8 per cent and 2.1 per cent, respectively, compared to France's 10.7 per cent and 5.5 per cent, Germany's 4.0 per cent and 3.4 per cent, Italy's 16.6 per cent and 7.3 per cent, Britain's 13.8 per cent and 6.4 per cent, and America's 9.7 per cent and 6.4 per cent.

Tokyo's trade and investment offensive following OPEC's price hikes led directly to Japan's trade conflicts with the United States and Europe. In 1975, Japan enjoyed a $3.142 billion surplus with the Community, in which its exports of $5.889 billion were more than twice its imports of $2.747 billion. Of its trade with the Big Four, Japan exported $1.744 billion and imported $952 million with Germany, $1.480 billion and $674 billion with Britain, $1.000 billion and $378 million with France, and $455 million and $298 million with Italy.

Japan's trade surplus grew with the Community steadily throughout the 1970s to reach $7,226 billion in 1979, of which Japan exported $13.709 billion, or more than twice its $6.483 billion. Of its trade with the Big Four, Japan exported $4.298 billion and imported $2.314 billion with Germany, $3.406 billion and $1.310 billion with Britain, $2.101 billion and $949 million with France, and $904 million and $799 million with Italy. Japan's exports increasingly reflected the success of its industrial policies in promoting such high value-added industries as machine tools, automobiles, steel, and microelectronics,while the Europeans continued to sell mostly raw materials, agricultural products, and chemicals. Japan's shipping industry had achieved a 55 per cent global market share. This imbalance of trade was reflected by the different numbers of citizens working in each others' markets – in 1979 there were over 10,000 Japanese working in Europe and only 1,500 Europeans in Japan.

Tokyo continued to reject all Brussels pleas for relief, and for the negotiation of a sweeping trade agreement with the Community, and intensified its negotiations with each capital over specific issues. Even though Brussels set aside its former insistence on a Community safeguard clause, Tokyo refused to negotiate a common policy in February 1974. As the Commission receded even further in importance, each national government, including traditionally free-trade West Germany, adopted increasingly hard-line positions on Japanese neomercantilism, but had little power to extract concessions from Tokyo on their own.

Brussels was not completely impotent. Japan allowed the Community to open an office in Tokyo in November 1974. A year later in October 1975, the Commission and MITI began negotiating steel restraints. At the December HLC, Tokyo agreed to restraints on steel, textiles, and ships, also to accept European safety tests on products when they were stricter or equivalent to its own.

European complaints against Japanese neomercantilism built up steadily throughout 1976. Throughout the year, Tokyo kept sidestepping a Commission request that it temporarily exempt European automobiles from Japan's exhaust standards for three years. By the autumn other issues were on the agenda, including accusations that Japanese firms were dumping ball bearings, steel, ships, and consumer electronics, while Tokyo was engaged in a 'dirty float' of the yen to suppress its true value. Tokyo rejected a Commission request to split world ship markets evenly, and instead insisted that its shipbuilders should retain at least a 50 per cent market share of 13 million gross registered tons, and would only accept a 2.5 million ton European share. Japan's ball bearing manufacturers had increased their market shares from 17 per cent in 1974 to 40 per cent in 1976. In October, the European Ball-bearing Association filed an anti-dumping complaint, claiming that sixteen Japanese makers had dumped their products at 26 to 52 per cent below production costs. Meanwhile, perennial issues like Japanese nontariff barriers continued to frustrate European diplomats and businessmen alike.

In October 1976, a *Keidanren* delegation led by its President, Doko, toured the Community to study Europe's social problems and shift to post-industrialism. Each government handed Doko a separate list of complaints and demands for action. Doko dutifully acknowledged the validity of many of these accusations, proclaimed that the trade imbalance was 'a very serious issue to which solutions must be found as quickly as possible', and promised to work to rectify these problems through Japan's systematic imposition of voluntary restraint agreements.[39] Upon his return to Tokyo, Doko in fact did attempt to urge the government's resolution of these problems, but he was renounced and disowned throughout Japan's political economy. Doko then backpeddled his proposals to a classic Japanese promise for *Keidanren* to study the situation.

Given this bewildering array of diplomatic setbacks and industrial crises, the Commission decided to be assertive at the HLC meeting on 15 November 1976. The Commission issued an 'ultimatum' which demanded that Japan either concede on ships, keep automobiles sales to Britain below a 10 per cent market share, and nontariff trade barriers before the Council of Ministers meeting of 29 November, or else the Community would respond with sanctions. Foreign Minister Yoshino sent a platitude-filled reply to Brussels on 25 November in which the only concrete concession was that Japan would import 36,000 tons of milk powder. On 30 November, the Council dismissed the letter and replied that it expected substantial progress on ships, automobiles, electronics, and steel before its next meeting. Tokyo, however, continued to reject any compromise on any of these issues while Brussels refused to back off from its demands. On 5 February 1977, Brussels announced a 20 per cent dumping duty on Japanese ball bearings. Tokyo denounced the duties and threatened to take Brussels to GATT and the European Court of Justice if it was not rescinded.

Brussels' tough stance worked, however. Tokyo only yields over its neomercantilist policies to toughness, although the concessions it makes are still more symbolic than substantive. Three days later, Tokyo offered a concession on shipbuilding in which both sides would reduce excess capacity and Japan would restrain any growth in market share while raising its ship prices. Brussels accepted. Throughout the spring Tokyo agreed to a series of other concessions, including the exemption of EC vehicles from Japan's strict emission standards for three years, cutting several tariffs, and restraining the dumping of ball bearings. The Commission imposed a price floor on all imported steel, then negotiated VERs the following year.

These 'victories' proved a fleeting respite in the trade war. Other issues such as Japanese nontariff barriers became deadlocked. Then the conflict flared again on a dozen fronts in the spring of 1978 as Japan's trade surplus steadily grew. In March 1978, Prime Minister Fukuda promised that Japan's growth rate would reach 7 per cent, its international payments steadily decline by one-third in the next fiscal year, and that the continual upgrading of Japan's economy would eventually reduce those industries in conflict with Europe's. None of these promises were kept. That same month bilateral steel talks were concluded, with Tokyo promising that its producers would not sell at margins more than 4 per cent below European special steel and 6 per cent below ordinary steel. Despite protests from France and Britain that the margins were too great and well beyond the 3 per cent margins for EFTA, the Council approved the agreement in June 1978. In April 1978, Tokyo's Ministry of Transportation agreed that the three Japanese airlines would buy the European Airbus if the government approved the credits for their purchase. Meanwhile, Britain and Italy balked at enacting their share of the 40 per cent reductions in Community shipyard capacity promised by the Commission the previous year. Tokyo had been raising prices and cutting capacity steadily since the agreement.

New conflicts emerged. In May 1978, a Commission delegation to Tokyo requested that Japan's financial system be liberalized and that European banks should be allowed the same opportunities in Japan that Japanese banks were allowed in the Community. While claiming repeatedly that there was no discrimination against foreign banks, Tokyo merely promised it would study Brussels' requests that European banks should have equal access to Japanese capital and shares of Japanese financial institutions, be allowed to float yen bonds or certificates of deposit, open new branches, and participate more in foreign exchange markets.

Then in June 1978, the two sides became deadlocked over the interpretation of GATT Article 19 allowing safeguard clauses. Brussels continued to insist on its unconditional right to impose restrictions against foreign trade predators, while Tokyo said it would accept a selective safeguard clause that would allow retaliatory restrictions only if the exporting nation or the GATT agreed. Tokyo, however, said it would accept Brussels' position if the Community abolished its seventy remaining quotas on Japanese products.

In October 1978, Prime Minister Fukuda visited Brussels and repeated earlier promises that Tokyo would stimulate domestic demand and that the trade balance would improve. He backed up these promises by pledging $3.5 billion for one-time purchases of European food, oil, Airbuses, and enriched uranium; said foreign banks would be allowed to issue bonds in Japan; and announced a doubling of Japan's official development aid (ODA) over the next three years. Yet he was quite critical of the Community, and professed his regret that in contrast to a 'very deep and broad relationship between Japan and the United States . . . Europe has not quite treated us as a true friend or a real partner, but rather as something alien to them. The days are past when Japan and Europe could be content with an indirect relationship through the United States as an intermediary'.[40] Fukuda's performance was a classic example of Japanese diplomatic *jujitsu*. After making some minor concessions, Fukuda then argued that it was Europe's animosity and not Japanese neomercantilism which was to blame for the increased conflicts.

The trade conflicts continued. Brussels retaliated against Japanese neomercantilism by imposing antidumping duties: on Japanese ball bearings in 1978; on acrylic fibers, saccharin, and stereo cassette tape heads in 1979; on automobiles, numerically controlled machine tools, and color televisions in 1981; on cathode ray tubes, light commercial vehicles, quartz watches, hi-fi equipment, fork-lift trucks, and video tape recorders in 1982–3; and on electronic typewriters in 1985. But this band-aid approach to Japanese dumping failed completely to confront Japan's systematic neomercantilist policies, or Europe's deep underlying competitive and development problems.

Japan's dumping offensives and web of import barriers remained formidable, despite foreign criticism. Japanese officials issued streams of platitudes about Japan already having an open economy, while Japan's growing surplus with the Community reflected the Europeans' inability to compete effectively. Meanwhile other officials continually promised to 'study' Community requests for Japan to buy more European goods. 'Concessions' often assumed surreal proportions – either reinterpretations of 'concessions' previously made though usually not implemented, or made on products which would have no impact on the trade balance. For example, with much fanfare, in 1978 Tokyo granted tariff reductions on European biscuits, chewing gum, and chocolate. Meanwhile, Japan's trade surplus that year rose to $6.5 billion.

The psychological if not economic low-point in relations came with the leak in 1979 of an internal Commission working paper on Japan dated

19 March 1979 which, among other things, attributed Japan's economic success as based on a

> people only recently emerged from a feudal past, a country of workaholics who live in what Westerners would regard as little better than rabbit-hutches . . . [and whose businessmen operate] like soldiers venturing out from a fortress, create havoc in concentrated areas of industry in the Community with major regional employment problems.[41]

The report dissected Japanese neomercantilist strategies, and identified Japan's export led-growth, the sectoral concentration of Japanese exports, and Japan's web of import barriers as its major components. The negative impact of Tokyo's neomercantilism was exacerbated by European disunity and the ability of the Japanese to play off different interests, and the tendency of Tokyo to shift exports from the United States to Europe in response to American retaliation, largely because Japan's exports are twice as dependent on American than European markets and thus twice as vulnerable to trade restrictions. The paper went on to call on Brussels to stimulate domestic demand and enact a much tougher, retaliatory policy to blunt Japanese neomercantilism, including import controls.

The leaked report created an uproar in Japan, with the Japanese severely criticizing what they felt was an affront to their nation. Rejecting any possibility that Tokyo's neomercantilist policies might be the central reason for the trade conflict, Japanese accused the Community of racism based on jealousy of Japan's success. Tokyo was successful once again in flexing its *jujitsu* diplomatic skills by hurling back these systematic and largely valid Brussels criticisms of Japanese neomercantilism against the Community. Red-faced Community officials apologized for the report's tone, sheepishly claiming that it was written in a polemical style in order to gain the Council's attention. Brussels covered this diplomatic gaffe by backing off from its confrontational policies and instead inaugurating a period of *detente*. In June, the Commission submitted to the European Council an extensively revised version of the report which censored the controversial statements, downplayed retaliation, and instead advocated increased industrial cooperation between European and Japanese corporations. The paper ended by noting Europe's steadily deepening trade deficit with Japan and meekly 'expressed the wish that the Japanese government . . . would help by means of appropriate measures to redress the situation'.[42]

The *detente* was short-lived. With the Community now on the defensive, Tokyo went on the offensive, repeatedly demanding the removal of European quotas and an end to dumping duties on several Japanese products. In January 1980, MITI announced that Japan's automobile producers would increase their production by 10 per cent. Britain and France responded by reiterating their respective 10 per cent and 3 per cent quotas on Japanese automobiles. An intensified Japanese automobile and consumer electronics offensive led to sales increases of 46 per cent and 113 per cent respectively, from January to August 1980, and caused even free-trade oriented Bonn to request Tokyo in vain to enact export restraints on color televisions, stereo equipment, VCRs, and car radios for two or three years. Japan's export offensives exacerbated the Community's stagnant growth and rising inflation and unemployment. Pressure grew on Brussels to negotiate sweeping trade restrictions on Japanese products. In November the Commission officially asked the Council to issue a mandate for a policy which aimed at Japan's Community-wide restraints on automobiles and consumer electronics, a stronger yen that reflected Japan's economic superpower, a liberalization of Japan's manufacturing and financial trade barriers, and equal treatment by Tokyo of Community and American requests. The Council approved the mandate.

Tokyo tried to deal with the Commission's get-tough policy by dispatching Foreign Minister Masayoshi Ito on a tour of the Community in December 1980 during which he swore he would discuss only geopolitical issues such as increased Soviet militarism, the American hostage crisis in Iran, the recent doubling of oil prices, possible policies of the newly-elected Reagan administration, and links between European and Japanese security. The Europeans, however, emphasized their desire for Japanese trade concessions. No progress was made on achieving consensus on either geopolitical or geoeconomic issues.

Ito issued a typically ambiguous statement designed to mollify both sides of the conflict. He admitted that 'developments within the European Communities which threaten the principle of free trade may possibly be intensified due to the trade imbalance with Japan and the rapid increase of imports from Japan in some sectors'.[43] But Ito undercut this by maintaining that 'the allegation attributing the present economic difficulties facing the European Communities to an increase in Japan's exports . . . is not well founded'. He then reversed himself once more by promising that

> the government . . . with due attention to the establishment of harmonious external economic relations . . . will continue . . . pursuing a growth pattern centering upon domestic demand. Furthermore the Government of Japan will continue to advise private enterprises not to export specific goods to the market of any region in a torrential manner.

JAPAN-EUROPEAN COMMUNITY RELATIONS: 1980S AND 1990S

Despite the previous decades of conflict, Tokyo has only recently turned its big guns toward Europe. Until the late 1980s, Tokyo focused much of its efforts on 'overtaking the United States' (*Beikoku ni okose*). America, with its rich united market of 250 million people, and its financial, manufacturing, and technological prowess was Japan's toughest competitor and prize. To overtake the United States meant eventually dominating virtually everywhere. In contrast, Tokyo viewed Europe as inefficient and stagnating. Japanese spoke derisively of the 'British disease', characterized by shoddy workmanship, strikes, missed deadlines, bumbling inefficiency, and an inability to compete, then extended the stereotype to most Europeans. Tokusaburo Kosaka, the Director General of Japan's Economic Planning Agency (EPA), clearly revealed Japan's priorities and strategy in a 1979 interview:

> For Japan, the relationship with the United States is much more important. The Community is one large organization with which we have a relationship. But basically that amounts to a series of bilateral relationships between Japan and West Germany, France, etc. We feel, therefore, that we should address problems in a bilateral manner.[44]

But having surpassed and heavily penetrated the United States, and with Europe's unification pending in 1992, Tokyo targeted the Community.

Thus Japan's trade strategy still involves dumping and capturing as much market share as possible, while stonewalling European protests as long as possible until threatened with retaliation, then agreeing to an export restraint in that product which allows the Japanese manufacturers to reap windfall profits and thus recoup their original losses incurred through dumping. Rothacher describes Tokyo's strategy as one of

> avoidance, though dutifully they continued to send occasional high-level missions to Europe for energy and trade talks. On sectoral trade problems they preferred unilateral Japanese producer-exporter decisions for eventual restraints . . . In the case of Japanese producers being too diverse and their exports not organized by an effective association, then a unilateral government export control measure was preferred. Most disliked were bilateral governmental agreements to limit Japanese exports, which were not only inflexible to changing market conditions, but also smelled of the discrimination of the post-war years.[45]

One highly effective method of deflating European criticism of Japanese neomercantilism is to claim continually that it is the Europeans and not the Japanese who are at fault. Deputy Foreign Affairs Minister Kenji Kikuchi captured this attitude succinctly when he claimed on 8 January 1981 that 'A few years ago it was the Americans, now it is the Europeans who seem to be trying to make a scapegoat of Japan for their economic woes'.[46] Foreign Ministry official Masamichi Hanabusa expanded this argument very clearly, and introduced the charge of racism against the Europeans, when he declared that

> certain mass-produced Japanese durable consumer products have been finding ready buyers for their qualitative excellence in Europe's market place. This is a simple economic phenomena, but the way in which it has given rise to a trade dispute between Japan and Western Europe is not so simple. European reactions to this new phenomena not only mirrors contemporary European inadequacies but also betrays an emotional tinge underlying the European perception of this emergent industrial giant of non-European cultural background . . . Japanese export successes in ships, automobiles, electronics, office equipment, numerically controlled machines, etc. are not infrequently contrasted with the plight of the corresponding European industries, almost always making Japan a kind of scapegoat for European economic ills . . . Japan is probably less protectionist than the Community in terms of tariff rates and quotas, and exchange rates are floating, what more can Japan do? After all, are not Europeans buying Japanese products because their quality is good and price competitive? The best response for Europeans would be to produce equally attractive products and make more efforts to sell to the Japanese market.[47]

In other words, European accusations of Japanese neomercantilism including trade barriers and dumping are completely unfounded and are simply attempts to mask European racism and refusal to work hard.

How have the Europeans responded?

On 26 November 1980, the Council made its most sweeping and unambiguous statement yet of Community demands on Japan:

(1)   In the sectors where a continued increase in Japanese exports would lead to difficulties, there needs to be effective moderation designed to produce early and tangible results that are applicable to the Community as a whole;

(2)   The yen should reflect the fundamental strength of the Japanese economy;

(3)   There should be no new measures on the part of the Japanese authorities to restrict imports;

(4)   There should be a clear commitment on the part of the Japanese government to a substantial and early increase in the imports of Community products;

(5)   The Japanese authorities should avoid import measures or policies which would give other major trading partners more favorable treatment than is given to the Community;

(6)   European industries should develop positive strategies to deal with Japanese competition, including not only restructuring in Europe but also greater involvement in the Japanese market;

(7)   The Japanese authorities should facilitate opportunities for European investment and banking in Japan.[48]

Clear as these goals are, Brussels has had a very mixed success in the almost a decade and a half since then in achieving them. Despite a general consensus over the seriousness of Japan's challenge, Brussels still has no common commercial policy with Japan. Instead, relations are shaped by a hodgepodge of both EC and bilateral quotas, tariffs, nontariff barriers, and OMAs. Although the Charter empowers the Commission with a range of means to manage trade, and Article 115 allows members to impose import restrictions in defense against foreign predatory trade, the Community has only sporadically flexed its trade powers.

Using a range of highly effective means, Tokyo has skilfully managed to undercut any European retaliation for Japanese neomercantilism. Although Japan's primary objectives have shifted throughout this period, its tactics have remained the same. A central strategy is for Japanese firms to conquer a vast market share and destroy their foreign rivals through concerted dumping campaigns. As early as 1952, Tokyo was skilfully staving off European complaints about Japan's 'unfair trade competition . . ., unethical use of . . . industrial designs and trademarks, and excessive Japanese government aid to shipping, shipbuilding and other industries connected with exports'.[49] Sometimes the foreign government attempts to defend its firms by negotiating an Orderly Marketing Agreement (OMA) or Voluntary Export Restraint (VER) with Tokyo, sometimes it simply abandons them to their fate. Having already conquered huge market shares, Tokyo is usually quite willing to go along. Speaking of Japan's agreements with Europe, Prime Minister Yoshida captured the essence of Japan's managed trade policies of dividing markets and fixing prices: 'where competition between them might seem unavoidable, [foreign] and Japanese manufacturers should cooperate in developing markets through a judicious arrangement of the outlets and types of goods to be reserved for each country'.[50]

Like all great strategists, Japan follows a strategy of divide and conquer. In its foreign relations, Tokyo always tries to avoid dealing with international organizations like the EC or ASEAN, instead playing off one member against the others to strike the best deal possible. Japanese corporations could always overcome French or Italian protection by sneaking in additional imports via the backdoors of more open Germany or Britain. Tokyo will continue this strategy although success will obviously become more difficult as Europe's unification solidifies.

Despite years of numerous protests by affected European firms and governments against Japanese and other foreign dumping assaults, Brussels did not first investigate such allegations until its 1979 cases against Japanese acrylic fibers, saccharin, and stereo cassette tape heads. Between 1983 and 1989, the EC investigated twenty-two cases of Japanese dumping, of which duties were imposed in seventeen, including outboard motors (1983), miniature ball bearings (1984), typewriters, hydraulic excavators (1985), photocopiers (1987), video taperecorders, dot matrix printers (1988), and audiocassette players (1989). Despite these investigations, Brussels did not first impose an antidumping duty until its July 1987 action against Japanese ball bearings. Since then additional actions have been imposed against ball electronic typewriters, photocopiers, and printers.[51]

Japan's dumping continues despite the Community's defensive actions. The variety of products that Japanese firms dump in Europe is astonishing. During the first six months of 1991 alone, Brussels commenced investigations on charges of Japanese dumping in thermal paper, electronic scales, capacitors, and floppy discs; reviewed the need to impose additional duties on compact disc players; and imposed duties on halogen lamps, audio cassettes, low calorie sweeteners, and disposable lighters. On 29 September 1991, Brussels imposed a duty of up to 54.9 per cent on Japanese fax paper producers after a finding that they had dumped their products at up to 24.8 per cent of what they charged in Japan, and undercut Community products by 22.8 per cent.[52] These products, of course, are only those which European firms have accumulated enough evidence against to make it possible to file for a Brussels investigation. The Japanese dump countless other products in concerted efforts to destroy their European counterparts.

Some products are considered so vital to the EC's economic dynamism that Brussels has imposed trade barriers. Although the EC and its members have gradually reduced their quotas on Japanese imports, in 1989, of 131 EC import quotas, 113 applied solely to Japan while the remaining eighteen applied to Japan and other countries. On 17 March 1989, the Commission declared that it would eliminate forty-two of the quotas levied solely on Japan, but virtually all these products were ones which European firms no longer produced.[53] Some quotas were strengthened. For example, in February 1989, the EC reinforced its tariffs and quotas against foreign integrated circuits by imposing rules which force foreign investors to manufacture key components and the finished product within the Community in order to be allowed free movement throughout the Community.

In the summer of 1991, a trade row broke out between Brussels and Tokyo over Taiwanese pork exports to Japan. The Community claim was that Taiwan was bribing Japanese customs officials in Nagoya to allow in Taiwanese pork priced at 30 per cent less than Community pork. Tokyo maintains a 482 yen a kilogram minimum import price to protect domestic producers, but Taiwan exporters were allowed to dump their meat in Japan's markets to the disadvantage of European rather than Japanese producers. In 1990, Taiwan's pork exports rose 40 per cent to account for a 49 per cent share of Japan's market, while Europe's fell 22 per cent to a 33 per cent market share.[54]

Although the issue may seem frivolous to observers, pork accounts for 25 per cent of Europe's food and drink exports to Japan, and is particularly important to Denmark which is the Community's biggest pork producer and has Japan as its second largest foreign market. Europe's economic future clearly does not rest on pork, but in the zero-sum global trade game every foreign market lost means the exporting country loses that much income. Brussels argues that if Japan enforces its pork import rules, Europe's pork exports could annually increase from $500–600 million to $700–900 million.

Reciprocity

Reciprocity has been a guiding EC principle since the mid-1980s. President de Clerq articulated this principle at GATT's Uruguay Round in September 1986 when he proclaimed that

> the Community feels that many of the present tensions affecting world trade find their origin in the fact that concessions negotiated between the various contracting parties have in reality not resulted in effective reciprocity. It is therefore essential that the Ministerial Declaration should establish the objective of achieving a genuine balance in the benefits accruing to contracting parties from the GATT.[55]

This 'balance of benefits' concept was inspired by the inability of European firms to penetrate Japanese markets, despite all Tokyo's claims that they were the world's most open, while most Japanese industries enjoyed a free run in Europe. The Japanese representatives at the Uruguay Round bitterly protested against the EC's call for genuine reciprocity, describing it as 'Japan-bashing'.[56] Intimidated, Brussels failed to back up its reciprocity principle with specific actions.

The bilateral economic imbalance in favor of Japan continued steadily to widen, increasing the pressure on Brussels to do something. In 1988, Brussels recommitted the Community to 'reciprocity' which it defined as 'a balance of mutual advantage' or 'a guarantee of similar – or at least non-discriminatory – opportunities for firms from the Community to operate in foreign markets on the same basis as local firms'.[57] In July 1988, President de Clerq elaborated the principle when he addressed two problems which Japan's neomercantilist tactics caused European firms and states – lack of reciprocity and playing one off against the others. De Clerq warned that in order to guarantee reciprocity,

> the Commission will check on a case-by-case basis whether similar institutions from all member states are given the same treatment in the non-member country concerned . . . in many cases we will pursue a symmetry not so much in the legal equivalence of conditions of access to markets, but rather an equivalence in their economic effects. We want to open our benefits, but on the basis of a mutual balance of advantages.[58]

Bold as were these words, once again the Community backed off from action in response to intensive Japanese criticism. Horst Kenzler, Director General for External Relations of the Commission, diluted de Clerq's remarks in October 1988 by saying that the EC did not seek 'mirror image' reciprocity.[59]

Applying the principle of reciprocity has continually proven more difficult than articulating it. On 24 June 1988, the Council approved the Second Banking Coordination Directive which directed that the Community should remove all internal barriers on capital movements, and linked nonmember firm access to the reciprocity of its country's financial regulations. The directive split the Community, with some arguing that reciprocity should be mandatory and others that it should not be mandatory for European firms in nonmember countries. In October 1988, the Commission ruled that reciprocity would not be applied to firms which had already set up shop but might be applied against newcomers. In April 1989, the Commission adopted a revised version of the directive which allowed it to authorize negotiations with countries which do not reciprocate and could limit or suspend new authorizations and acquisitions by firms of that country. Several points remain vague including just how reciprocity or its lack is measured, even though it seems to call for 'mirror-image' reciprocity. To date there have been no negotiations based on the reciprocity principle.

In the autumn of 1988, the issue of reciprocity was raised in regards to the finance industry, with similar results. Britain used the concept in its wrangle with Japan over the granting of Tokyo Stock Exchange seats to two British firms, Barclays and James Capel, which were not among the sixteen foreign securities seats granted by Tokyo in 1989. London threatened to retaliate by denying licenses to Nomura and Daiwa to sell government bonds. Barclays was eventually granted a license and the conflict subsided.

Japanese Investments

Japan and Europe, of course, have exchanged products and investments for over forty-five years, and relations have changed significantly during that time. Japanese investments in Europe remained limited until the 1970s, because Europe had neither the abundant resources or cheap labor for which most early Japanese investors were searching. There have not been any distinct waves of Japanese investments in Europe, but instead a steady growth from virtually nothing in the 1950s. Japanese investments in Europe, which rose from only $3 million in 1955 to $56 million in 1968, were mostly made by trading companies in offices, service, and distribution networks. Japan's investments rose rapidly from the late 1960s to 1980 when they reached $3.893 billion, fueled by financial and manufacturing corporations. Then, during the 1980s, direct investments soared to $42 billion by March 1990. Europe accounted for 17 per cent of Japan's global direct foreign investments, representing a steady increase from a 6.0 per cent share in 1973. Of Japan's direct investments, about 20 per cent are wholly owned greenfield sites while half a per cent were buyouts of European firms. The importance of Europe to Japanese investors has doubled. In contrast, European firms have directly invested only $2 billion in Japan. Although Japan's rise in direct investments was rapid and seems large, it is only a quarter the $164 billion of American direct investments in Europe.[60]

Despite Japanese contempt for the so-called 'English disease' (*Eikoku byo*), most of the initial investments were targeted on Britain, first in finance and services and later in production, attracted by the English language, British foreign investment incentives, and a large, almost free domestic market with access to the Community. Japan's direct investments in Britain rose from $3.9 billion in 1988 to $6.8 billion in 1990, of which less than a quarter was in manufacturing. In 1990, of Japan's total direct investments, 37.6 per cent were in Britain, 24.0 per cent in the Netherlands, 12.8 per cent in Luxembourg, 8.2 per cent in Germany, 6.9 per cent in France,

7.3 per cent in Italy, 3.7 per cent in Spain, 3.2 per cent in Belgium, and the remaining 3.6 per cent scattered throughout the rest of the Community. Although lagging in fifth place as a host to Japanese direct investments, France did have the second largest amount of Japanese factories (122) after those in Britain (187).[61]

Japanese investments were encouraged by Brussels, the national, and even local governments, which offered a range of tax holidays, subsidized loans, and depreciation allowances to attract foreign investment into depressed regions. During the 1970s and 1980s, these carrots were reinforced by the threatened and actual use by the Community and member governments of the stick of trade retaliation for Japan's continued neomercantilist export and import policies. Brussels and the national governments negotiated VERs in steel, automobiles, consumer electronics, and other goods, and imposed dumping duties on a range of Japanese products.

Japanese corporations have been particularly effective in using the divide and conquer strategy against Europe's investment-starved regions and cities by provoking them into bidding wars against each other for Japanese investments. Victory in these wars can be pyrrhic. For example, Britain paid £78,000 for each of the 3,500 jobs created in Wales.[62] And Japanese factories and other direct investments are notorious for negotiating 'no strike' and single union deals with local authorities.

The Europeans recognize this dilemma. In March 1986, the Commission admitted that

> in order to attract as much investment as possible in manufacturing, national and regional authorities have often been led into competition with each other, each offering bigger or more advantageous subsidies and other incentives. An exchange of views between the member states at Community level would thus seem necessary to counteract the tendency of Japanese investors to exploit these attempts at outbidding.[63]

Later that year in September, de Clerq again warned against allowing Japan to play one locality off against the others: 'We must improve coordination between member states so that we can limit this beggar-thy-neighbor policy to attract new investments.'[64]

Despite Japan's growing investments in Europe, the EC is still struggling to form a uniform local content rule. The first EC ruling on local content occurred in 1970 when the Commission ruled that there must be a 45 per cent local content standard on televisions in December 1970 and tape recorders in April 1971. That benchmark remained until the mid-1980s when a massive wave of Japanese corporations began to set up shop within the Community to hurdle trade barriers and antidumping duties. On 22 June 1987, the Council ruled that 40 per cent of the parts used in Japanese ball bearing assembly plants in the EC should be non-Japanese or else be subject to the same anti-dumping action then levied on Japanese imports. In July 1988, the Council amended its local content 'screwdriver assembly' law to allow the imposition of an antidumping duty if: (1) any products manufactured within Europe are subject to an antidumping duty; (2) where assembly has begun after that firm was made the subject of an antidumping investigation; and (3) where the value of the parts in the assembly originating in a country subject to an antidumping duty are more than 50 per cent of all other parts. Altogether, a 'screwdriver operation' will only be subject to an antidumping duty if the total local content is 40 per cent or less. The Commission tried to follow up these guidelines on 6 February 1989 when it ruled that all semiconductors produced within the EC by foreign manufacturers would be considered non-EEC if the etching of the microcircuit takes place outside Europe. The Commission is also counting Japanese products made in the United States as Japanese and not American in origin, and thus subject to 20 per cent duty when exported to Europe.

The Japanese exerted tremendous pressure on Brussels to withdraw its local content rule. In May and October 1988, Tokyo protested to GATT against the EC inclusion of antidumping duties against the same products by guilty Japanese firms which are made in Europe. They argued that this local content requirement gave European producers which also used foreign parts an unfair advantage over Japanese producers. For example, in May 1988, the EC imposed antidumping duties against Japanese SIDM printers but did not act against Japanese printers imported by European firms and sold under their own name. Furthermore, the Japanese warned that because of their difficulty in finding local suppliers they would not invest in the Community.

Brussels was greatly angered at being accused of discriminatory behavior by a nation which it considers the personification of neomercantilism. The Community defended its rules, arguing that they prevented Japan from dumping its products in the Community through its screwdriver assembly plants. It further argued that it had imposed sanctions as authorized by GATT Articles 6 and 20, and that investigations found an average 30 per cent Japanese dumping margin. The European Court of Justice (ECJ) at Luxembourg in 1989 upheld the EC's method of calculating Japan's dumping and amount of injury caused European producers.[65]

Another Japanese argument against the local content rule is that it is designed not so much against Japanese dumping but to encourage more Japanese investment in Europe. There may be some truth in this argument.

In March 1988, Commission President De Clerq defended the local content rules by arguing that

> direct investment from Japan into Europe increased by about 90 percent in the year following the introduction of the provisions . . . assemblers have been able to switch the source of their components with comparative ease and once this happened the Community readily accepted undertakings from the assemblers and removed the duty on the assembled product.[66]

The trouble, of course, is that the Japanese can outflank these regulations in Europe just as they have in the United States by setting up their own part-makers in Europe and buying from them. Thus, on paper it appears that a Japanese assembly plant is buying from European sources when in reality it is other Japanese firms which benefit. Not surprisedly, many European business and political leaders feel even these measures were not enough. In November 1988, the French electronics industry association called for local content rules of 60 rather than 40 per cent.[67] Karl-Heinz Narjes, a former Commissioner, maintains that even with 80 per cent local content rules for automobiles Japan can keep its key engine and transmission technology and value-added production at home.[68]

The EC's more restricted markets – tough dumping, local content, quotas, tariffs, and origin rules – have forced the Japanese to set up a much larger portion of their production in the EC as a percentage of their trade than in the United States with its largely free markets. France's Poitiers defense against VTRs in 1982 in particular is said to have prompted Japan's corporations to consider investing in countries which have been most critical of Japan, in order to leapfrog existing barriers and build up political clout in those capitals to undermine retaliatory measures. Recently, Japanese corporations have tried to spread their bets across Europe, to ally criticism that the Japanese were simply using Britain as a springboard or Trojan Horse for the entire Community.

In 1987, the EC retaliated against the Japanese screwdriver assembly plants which often worsened rather than alleviated the trade deficit. From now antidumping duties would include the screwdriver assembly plants unless they included at least 40 per cent from non-Japanese local firms. Some Europeans argue that these restrictions are not tough enough.[69] On 6 February 1989, the Commission ruled that all semiconductors produced within the EC by foreign manufacturers would be considered non-EEC if the etching of the microcircuit takes place outside Europe. The Commission is also counting Japanese products made in the United States as Japanese and not American in origin, and thus subject to 20 per cent duty when exported to Europe.

The EC and its members have gradually reduced their quotas on Japanese imports. In March 1989, the Commission informed Tokyo that it would drop forty-two quotas, but these were mostly products unimportant to Europe's economic future. As of 1989, of 131 EC import quotas, 113 were applied solely to Japan while the remaining eighteen applied to Japan and other countries. On 17 March 1989, the Commission declared that it would eliminate forty-two of the quotas levied solely on Japan, but virtually all these products were ones which European firms no longer produced.[70]

Meanwhile, like all Japan's other trade partners, the Europeans have complained bitterly about Japanese import barriers. For example, in April 1982, the Commission protested against Tokyo's continued widespread use of a range of nontariff barriers, and threatened invoking GATT Article 23 if the discriminatory practices continued. A key element of the Commission's argument were that the 'social factors' in Japanese neomercantilism – the groupism, long work weeks, meek consumers and workers, high savings, low consumption, etc. – justified the Community's 'selective retaliation'. In 1983, the Commission finally brought the charges to GATT, detailing Tokyo's systematic use of cartels, administrative guidance, testing procedures, regulations, government procurement, and specifications to discriminate against foreign products.[71]

And what became of these charges? Has Tokyo sincerely reformed its political economy along free market lines? Brussels has annually voiced these same complaints into the 1990s to largely deaf Japanese ears. And even when Brussels did directly confront Tokyo on one of these issues, the Japanese invariably were able to 'settle' the issue with cosmetic 'concessions'. The reason is that Brussels has failed to back up its demands for open Japanese markets with the threat of sanctions.

It is Washington rather than Brussels which has had the most success in battering Japan's concentric walls of nontariff barriers against specific American products. Strangely, both Washington and Brussels have rejected the idea of 'strength in numbers' and working together to carve out footholds in Japan's carefully managed markets. Japan's 'divide-and-conquer' strategy has never been more successful than in keeping the US and the EC from forging an alliance against their common trade adversary. Tokyo has played upon the fears of Americans and Europeans alike to avoid any action that can be labeled racist, even if racism has absolutely nothing to do with the conflict. When asked, American and European officials shrug off their failure to forge an alliance to neutralize Japanese neomercantilism with the fear of appearing to 'gang up on Japan'.

Automobiles

The global automobile market has expanded enormously over the past three decades. In 1960, 6.998 million vehicles were sold in the United States, 5.198 in the Community and Spain 5.198 million, a miniscule 165,000 in Japan, and 638,000 in other markets. In 1986, America's share of a global market over three times larger had risen only to 8.890 million vehicles, the Community's expanded to 11.377, others to 4.746 million, and Japan's had zoomed to 7.810 million.[72] Europe's automobile market is the world's largest, and will undoubtedly grow steadily larger as the Community and East European states become more prosperous and unified.

Whose automobiles will be sold in these vast marketplaces, particularly those of Europe? It may well be Japanese automobile makers which benefit the most from 1992. Although the first Japanese automobiles entered Europe in the late 1950s, there were no significant sales until the early 1970s and those were mostly targeted on peripheral nonproducing nations like Switzerland, Portugal, Norway, Austria, and Finland. By 1975, Japan sold about 500,000 automobiles in the Community for a market share of 5 per cent. Japan's vehicle sales stayed around 500,000 throughout the late 1970s. Then from 1979 to 1980, Japan's vehicle sales leaped 29 per cent from 585,824 to 765,000, and its market share from 7.9 per cent to 11.1 per cent, at a time when the European producers were suffering from vast overcapacity and losses caused by the global recession. Even German automobile makers were severely damaged, with production falling 9 per cent in those two years. Japanese automobile sales grew steadily throughout the 1980s.[73] In 1989, Japanese captured 1.2 million of the 12.3 million automobiles sold in Europe. The country-by-country breakdown of these figures is shown in Table 6.2.

The European market is divided into a rough balance of power among a dozen producers with Fiat and Volkswagen first with 15 per cent each, followed by Peugeot's 13 per cent, Ford and General Motor's 11 per cent each, Renault's 10 per cent, Mercedes' and BMW's 3 per cent each, and the combined Japanese 10 per cent share. Among the Japanese producers, Toyota's share was the largest with 316,000, followed by Nissan with 280,000, and Honda with 215,000, while the other six Japanese producers exporting much lower amounts.[74]

TABLE 6.2   *Japanese percentage of total automobile sales in the EC*

	1975	1989
All EC	5	10
To Italy	0.05	1.6
To France	1.6	2.9
To Germany	1.7	14.8
To Britain	10.6	11.3
To Netherlands	14.7	–
To Denmark	17.4	31.8
To Belgium	19.1	–
To Ireland	51.5	39.4

Meanwhile, foreign sales in Japan remained at miniscule levels. Although foreign sales quadrupled during the 1980s from 45,000 in 1981 to 214,435 in 1990, they still represents less than 3 per cent of Japan's automobile market. Of the foreign penetration, Germany has a 60.1 per cent share, the United States 13.9 per cent, Britain 6.5 per cent, and France, Italy, and Sweden less than 5 per cent each.[75]

How have the Europeans responded to Japan's automobile challenge? As in other industries, it was the national capitals rather than Brussels which set the policy. Country by country import restrictions, difficulty in acquiring dealerships, domestic content rule, and 'buy European' consumer preferences have limited Japan's penetration of Europe's automobile market to only 10 per cent. There is a wide discrepancy in the national quotas on Japanese and imports. Italy, Spain, and Portugal have permitted only a small quota of Japanese cars since the 1950s. London imposed its 'unofficial' quota of 11 per cent in 1976, while Paris announced the following year that it would not tolerate a Japanese market share above 3 per cent. Citing a free market commitment, Bonn watched Japan's automobile sales soar to a 11 per cent share, then negotiated a temporary VER with Tokyo. The Benelux countries have negotiated similar deals with the Japanese. Although Germany's automobile market is free in principle, Japan's market share has remained about 15 per cent since 1986, leading observers to question whether the Japanese automakers have not unofficially agreed to limit their sales to prevent any German backlash.[76] Meanwhile, Japanese have captured a 30–40 per cent market share of the open markets of Denmark, Ireland, and Greece.

The French have been the most vociferous opponents of Japan's automobile onslaught. Since 1977, Paris used 'administrative guidance' to hold imports at no more than 3 per cent of France's market. From 1979 to 1980, Japanese car registration in France jumped from 2.2 per cent to 2.9 per cent of the market. In 1980, Paris decided to get tough by adopting some of Japan's more notorious means of restricting imports. Japanese cars were held up on French ports until they could get special sales licenses. Tokyo protested with the highly ironic statement that:

> The French government has withheld type certificates for new Japanese cars since July 1980, making it impossible to sell them in France. If this move is aimed at keeping Japanese cars' share of the French market within 3 per cent, it constitutes undue discrimination against Japan, which runs counter to the spirit of GATT.[76]

Italy's tit-for-tat retaliation against Japanese neomercantilism, however, makes it Tokyo's toughest European opponent. During the 1950s, when Italian cars had an immense comparative advantage over Japanese cars, Tokyo limited imports of Italian cars to about 2,000. Rome then argued that if Japan wanted to protect its industry, fine, but it would then grant no more than an equal number of Japanese cars entry into Italy. Since then, of course, Japan's automobile industry has become the world's most dynamic while Italy's has lagged further behind. Tokyo has repeatedly demanded that Rome abandon its quota, and Rome has just as repeatedly refused, arguing that if Italian cars could not be sold freely in Japan when the Italians enjoyed a comparative advantage, why should Japanese cars be freely sold in Italy now that the Japanese enjoy a comparative advantage? Today, Rome allows the direct importation of only 2,550 cars and 750 off-road vehicles, while a further 20,000 Japanese cars arrive in Italy via third markets. Altogether Japan has less than a 1 per cent market share.

Brussels policy toward Europe's automobile makers has been at times contradictory. It has vigorously sought to limit government subsidies for the beleaguered European manufacturers. In the 1980s, the Commission rejected debt write-offs for Renault and Rover, and since 1989 required its approval for any state aid valued at over 12 million ECU. At the same time Brussels has attempted to harmonize its VAT, emissions controls, and other standards, and state aid for automobiles.

At times, however, the Community departed from its common market approach by helping negotiate several VERs with Tokyo to limit Japanese automobile exports to the Community. The first VER was in May 1976 when *Keidanren* cut a deal in which Tokyo would reduce some of its barriers against European automobiles while limiting its exports to Europe for one year. Despite this agreement, Japan's vehicle sales in Europe continued to increase steadily, while Europe's industry continued to decline. Over the next decade, although Japan's exports to the Community steadily grew, Brussels did not conclude another agreement until 1986, when it convinced MITI to promise to 'monitor' Japan's exports to Europe. Since 1986, Japan's total share of the Community has hovered around 10 per cent.

In the 1980s, the problem of Japanese exports was complicated by the problem of Japanese investments. As in other industries, Japan's automobile makers have tried to hurdle quotas and other trade barriers by building plants within Europe, and as in the United States, transplants will comprise an increased percentage of Japanese sales. Nissan has been the most active Japanese investor in Europe. In January 1980, Nissan bought a 36.8 per cent interest in Motor Iberica, Spain's largest farm equipment producer, and later that year cut a deal with Alfa Romeo to produce 50–60,000 cars annually. Nissan later increased its Motor Iberica shares to 70.4 per cent, whereupon it converted Motor Iberica to a commercial vehicle producer. In 1984, Nissan announced its decision to begin producing automobiles in Sunderland, an action which allows the Japanese to exceed Britain's 11 per cent quota. In 1990, Nissan produced 77,000 cars at its British factory and 80,000 at its Spanish factory. Nissan exports half of its Sunderland plant's annual 100,000 production.

Japan's other automobile makers have followed suit. Honda has a joint venture with Rover annually to produce 40,000 Honda Concertos and has also built an engine plant in southern England, and owns its own plant in Britain, producing 100,000 cars annually. Suzuki has a 17.3 per cent stake in Land Rover Santana in Spain, which is producing 24,000 Suzuki Escoods. Toyota has a joint venture with Volkswagen to produced one ton pickups and has opened its own plant in Britain with an annual capacity of 100,000 cars.[77] Toyota and Honda are currently building plants in Britain while Mitsubishi is forming a joint venture with Volvo. Other plants recently opened include Toyota's 27 per cent share of the Salvador Caetano plant in Portugal; Mitsubishi's 49.75 per cent share of Mitsubishi motors in Portugal; and Isuzu's 40 per cent share of IBC Vehicles in Britain. These Japanese plants are far more productive than their European counterparts. For example, in the first half of 1991, the Toyota and Nissan plants in Britain produced a respective average of 30.0 and 21.7 automobiles per worker compared to only 4.5 for Ford workers, 6.4 for Rover, and 13 for Vauxhall. In 1992, Japan's European factories will annually produce 400,000 automobiles, and by the year 2000, 1.5 million.[79]

These automobile investments allow the Japanese not only to leap national import barriers but to play off one country against the others. One major Community conflict concerns local content. Although the general EC rule of 40 per cent seemed to take precedence, a growing number of voices called for raising the local content rule to much higher levels as Japan's automobile investments increased throughout the 1980s. The French government and Ford have called for at least an 80 per cent local content rule while others, including Renault President Jacques Calvet, have even advocated that local content for automobiles should be 100 per cent.[79]

Paris, as usual, backed up its words with action. In 1988, Nissan began exporting cars from its British plant to the continent. Paris immediately barred these imports, claiming that the Nissans should be classified as Japanese cars since the local content was only 60 per cent, and protested against the large British subsidies to the Japanese corporation. London and Nissan disputed the French figures, claiming that the local content was actually 70 per cent and they were thus European cars. Nissan promised to boost the local content to 80 per cent by 1990. London and Nissan further accused France of violating Community free trade rules by barring those cars. In October 1988, Paris backed off from its position, but, in a classic Japanese-style tactic, simply counted the British-assembled Bluebirds against its 3 per cent quota. In November 1988, Italy belatedly protested against the Nissan imports by using the same arguments France had made earlier, and imposed similar restrictions. All along Spain had quietly limited Nissan imports. But, in April 1989, France, Italy, and Spain bowed to a Commission ruling and agreed not to count the Nissans against their quotas.

The controversy revealed the need for a comprehensive Community policy toward Japan's automobile challenge. MITI has monitored Japan's exports to Europe since 1986, with Japan's total share hovering around 10 per cent. On 31 May 1989, the Commission proposed that national quotas against Japanese imports be eliminated by 1992, to be replaced by EC-wide restrictions. On 6 December 1989, Peugeot-Citroen President Jacques Calvet argued that Japan's automobile sales in Europe should not be allowed to exceed twice that of European sales in Japan.[80] In September 1990, the Commission began debating a proposal to liberalize the Community's market by 1998. MITI, meanwhile, urged Japan's automakers to restrain their exports to Europe to below their 1990 levels while the Commission was debating its restrictions.

Once again, the lines were drawn between Britain and Denmark which favored less restrictions, France and Italy which proposed tougher restrictions, and West Germany which could afford a middle position. Of Europe's automobile makers, only Daimler Benz, which has an alliance with Mitsubishi, advocated a European free market. All other European automobile makers protested that the five-year breathing space does not allow them enough time to retool and produce automobiles that can compete in price and quality with the Japanese. Peugeot and Fiat led the charge to impose a ten-year limit on Japan's automobiles and include the production of Japan's European factories in the quota. They pointed to America's automobile makers which continue steadily to decline despite similar restrictions imposed in the 1980s. Prime Minister Cresson had no illusions about the means Japan used to build its automobile industry into the world's most powerful, and the danger it poses to Europe's industry: 'Japan had several decades to acquire the strength that today is wiping out the American auto industry. I don't want Europe's auto industry to be wiped out. I don't want thousands of jobs to disappear.'[81] Peugeot Chairman Jacques Clavet maintained that ideally the restrictions would continue until European exports to Japan are one-half Japan's car sales in Europe.[82]

Community quotas on Japanese vehicles took over two years to negotiate. On 30 April 1991, the Commission proposed European-wide restrictions on Japanese cars from 1993 to 1999, to sales of not more than 2.5 million vehicles or 16 per cent of the market. The Japanese would be prevented from dumping cars in the traditionally restricted markets of France and Italy. There would be a virtual freeze on Japanese imports with most of the new sales coming from transplants. In 1998 or 1999, the restrictions would be lifted. The Commission shelved proposals by France and Italy for guaranteed access to Japan and a minimum local content rule for the Japanese transplants. Predictably, the Japanese protested against including the transplants in the quota and pushed for no restrictions after five years. The members debated these proposals for another three months. On 26 July 1991, the Commission agreed to limit Japanese vehicle sales in Europe to 1.23 million annually until 2000, after which all restrictions would be completely removed. Brussels would allow Japan's automobile makers to expand their European production from the 260,000 produced in 1990 to about 1.2 million cars by 1999, well below the 1.8 million the Japanese had planned to produce by that time. Japan's car imports during that time would be frozen at 1.2 million units. Altogether Japan's transplants and imports would take up to a 16.1 per cent share, up from its current 10 per cent share. In France, Japan's imports will be allowed to climb to 150,000 or 5.2 per cent, up from their current 3 per cent, and in Italy from their 138,000 to 5.3 per cent, up from their current 2 per cent. Among the other restricted markets, Spain would take no more than 79,000, Portugal 23,000, and Britain 190,000.[83] The accord is an unsigned 'gentleman's agreement'.

Will the European producers capitalize on the breathing space created by the agreement? Brussels' VER with Japan is far more restrictive than Washington's. America's 1982 VER with Japan's producers allowed them a 21 per cent market share and did not include Japanese factories in the United States against the quota. In contrast, Brussels' VER allows the European producers a longer time and more space to enjoy a breathing space from Japan's imports and transplants. Whether or not the European producers will be able to take advantage of that time and bring their costs down and quality up remains to be seen. Renault's chairman, Raymond Levy, predicts that at least 200,000 European automobile workers will have to be laid off. Like the American producers, the Europeans are hobbled by their existing production and union arrangements, while the Japanese are free to invest anywhere on any terms while remaining protected in the vast Japanese market. Levy captured this dilemma: 'We also could build a modern plant that uses 3,000 employees to build 200,000 cars a year but to do that we would have to close one of our plants that employs 10,000 people.'[84]

Once those quotas are removed, Japan's market share may well sky-rocket. Europe's automobile producers are less competitive than their American counterparts, and have survived only because they have been more effectively protected. The half-dozen-year breathing space may not be enough to allow Europe to catch up with Japan's automobile producers who are constantly expanding and deepening their global markets, and improving their economies of scale, productivity, investments, research and development, and profits. In the zero sum war of international trade, Europe's producers could only reverse their steady losses by requiring a reciprocal market share in Japan. Until then the Europeans, like the Americans, will continue to be locked into a vicious cycle of declining production, investment, market share, and profits.

Once again, rather than work together to counter a common Japanese threat, the Europeans and Americans find themselves at loggerheads. Tokyo has very skilfully used Japan's investments in the United States as a wedge between Washington and Brussels. The Japanese have made massive political as well as economic investments in the United States, and those investments are paying off. Japan's automakers claim that they will export their American transplants to Europe and elsewhere and have extensively lobbied Washington to force Brussels to allow those exports entry. Washington knows that any European restrictions will result in the Japanese dumping even more automobiles in the United States. In May 1989, Trade Representative Carla Hills warned that Washington would 'challenge any new barriers in the GATT should they be introduced by the Community'.[86]

In September 1991, Honda became the first Japanese corporation to export Japanese transplants made in the United States to France. The exports followed several months of delays by French officials who protested that the Japanese transplants violated existing quota agreements. American officials joined Honda and Japanese officials in pressuring the French government into accepting the exports. At stake were only 175 Aerodeck station wagons, but the agreement was an important symbolic victory for Japan. The other Japanese automobile makers have followed suit in using Japanese transplants in the United States to bypass the Community's quotas. The transplant issue is a classic example of Japan's 'divide and conquer strategy'. Although the United States and Europe share an interest in containing Japan's automobile industry, Tokyo was able to enlist Washington in its attack on Paris.

Meanwhile as in Japan's other 'market opening' steps, Tokyo's 'concessions' on automobile imports were largely cosmetic public relations stunts. For example, for decades Toyota, like the other Japanese automobile makers, refused to sell foreign automobiles through its Japanese dealerships. In April 1991, Toyota announced that it would begin selling Volkswagens and Audis through its dealers, as part of a broad collaboration policy with the European makers to widen its market share in Europe.

Japan is the world's largest automobile producer and exporter – in 1990, the Japanese produced 13.487 million vehicles of which they exported 5.832 million. The European producers have tiny market shares elsewhere and may see even their dominant share in their own market diminish after 1999. Europe's automobile market is the world's largest, and will undoubtedly grow steadily larger as the Community and East European states become more prosperous and unified. Few Community automakers, however, are likely to prosper in the united market. The balance of automobile industrial power has shifted as decisively in Japan's favor against Europe as it has against the Americans. And Brussels appears as impotent as Washington in reversing the power shift. As in other industries, the national and Commission requests to Japan that it remove its trade barriers and allow reciprocal access go unheeded. The temporary quotas on Japanese automobiles may be too little too late to save Europe's automakers. As in other fields, Japanese rather than European firms may be the chief beneficiaries of a united Europe.

Microelectronics

It is often remarked that we are in the midst of a 'postindustrial information age' in which information of all kinds is the most important commodity; and microelectronics is the modern means of conveying it. The microelectronics field encompasses a wide range of related industries, including everything from the most simple Walkman to sixth generation computers.

Such seemingly arcane concepts like fiber optics, virtual reality, or superconductors are already household words and will soon be household products.

In order to maintain a viable microelectronics industry in an increasingly frenzied global market, nations must remain competitive in virtually all segments of the market, in software and hardware, in consumer and intermediate products, in research and development, and in manufacturing. To lose important segments of the vast microelectronics foodchain means eventually losing all, a blow which could be fatal to a postindustrial economy.

It is becoming increasingly difficult to compete in microelectronics. Capital costs for chip production factories alone have risen steadily from $30 million in the 1970s to $300 million in the 1990s. No European corporations can afford the amount of money and time which such investments demand. Without Community and national financial support as well as R & D and trade support, even a coalition of Europeans cannot muster the resources with which to compete in cutting-edge microelectronics.

The Japanese understand this. Japan's strategy has been to concentrate its efforts on mastering strategic links in the microelectronics foodchain, and having conquered that segment, march upmarket to gobble up, pac man style, other strategic segments. Tokyo started with relatively simple industries like transistor radios and televisions and marched steadily into more sophisticated technologies and markets like VCRs, semiconductors, computers, and supercomputers.

The Community's JESSI Planning Group understands Japanese neomercantilism and what must be done to counter it:

> The Japanese aim to become world leaders in micro-electronics. Government and firms again and again focus great efforts directly on a particular segment of the world market. For video recorders, cameras, and hi-fi systems, they have already achieved their goals. What's more, for years Nippon Telegraph and Telephone has been involved in chip research programmes of billions of US dollars per annum, the results being made available to their industry. Thus within the JESSI initiative exceptional R & D efforts and extremely high investment is necessary. The microelectronics industry cannot afford these investments alone.[86]

It was only in the 1980s that Japan's strategy clearly began to devastate Europe's microelectronics firms. Until then the Japanese had concentrated on conquering the vast open American market. Washington's response to Japan's waves of microelectronics offensives varied from indifference (as in televisions) to protection (as in semiconductors). Eventually, after taking over a huge market share in the United States and establishing enormous scale economies, the Japanese could divert their excess production to Europe.

Like the United States, the Community has offered little aid to its microelectronics industry. Europe's microelectronics industries are generally considered to be in overall third place behind those of Japan and the United States. Like their American counterparts, Europe's companies are increasingly becoming dependent on key Japanese components and, unable to compete, sell out to their Japanese rivals. It was not until the 1980s that Brussels achieved a consensus on systematically resisting Japan's assault on Europe's microelectronics through VERs or duties on Japanese dumping, and programs for boosting key technologies by cooperation among European firms. But these efforts may be too little too late.

Televisions

As in the United States, the first significant wave of Japan's microelectronics exports was televisions. Japanese black and white televisions first trickled into Europe in the early 1960s, but Japan's full-scale assault on Europe's television industry did not begin until the mid-1970s, about a half-dozen years after a similar sustained offensive had devastated America's television industry. Fortunately for Europe, because of tougher protection the Japanese failed to destroy the Community's television industry as they had America's. Those European countries which produced televisions did not want their industry to suffer the same fate as America's. Britain negotiated a VER with Japan as early as 1973, while France and Italy simply continued long-standing quotas. In 1981, Paris struck an agreement with Tokyo to restrain its television exports from third countries to France. Meanwhile, Paris has attempted to nurture Thomson Brandt into the 'national champion' via Japanese-style subsidies, protection, export promotion, and import subsidies. Brussels played no role in saving Europe's television industry – the policies were all national.

Europe's most effective television protection, according to Shepard,

has come from transmission/reception technologies (SECAM in France, PAL in the rest of West Europe) that are different from the technology systems of the United States and Japan. The PAL systems were first used, in the 1960s, in order to restrict manufacture to West European firms; in the 1970s, Japanese were gradually allowed to acquire licenses, but only for sets with smaller screens. The major PAL patents began to expire from 1980.[87]

Unfortunately, the Japanese breached even this defense. During the 1970s, the Japanese were able to acquire licensing for PAL by playing off one government against the others. Britain sold out its PAL technology to the Japanese as early as 1977 and the others followed suit. During the 1980s, the PAL patents expired so the Japanese have been free to set up production and attack markets.

How successful were these policies in saving Europe's television industry? Japan's market penetration rose from about 1 per cent in 1975 to 6 per cent in 1979 to 15 per cent in 1990. With a market of 320 million consumers, an 85 per cent market share allows Europe's television producers large-scale production and profits. Unfortunately, the Europeans have failed to take advantage of this huge protected market to bring down costs and raise quality necessary to achieve a global comparative advantage. Elsewhere, Europe's television market shares are miniscule to nonexistent. However, the mixture of national policies have kept jobs and profits in the Community that would have otherwise flowed to Japan.

The Community has been just as inactive in encouraging the development of High Definition Television (HDTV) as it was in protecting Europe's television industry. With the Americans out of the race due to Washington's refusal to nurture the industry, the Japanese and Europeans are the only real contenders in the race to develop HDTV. Because of HDTV's importance in a range of technology food chains, whoever perfects the industry will be in a position to take over dozens of related industries. Although Tokyo has been nurturing the industry since the late 1960s, the Europeans claim to have achieved a 20 per cent better picture resolution. As in television, the HDTV balance of power is drawn over the transmission systems adopted. While Japan's MUSE system transmits pictures of 1,125 line at 60 hertz, Thomson, Philips, and Bosch have developed a system called MAC which transmits 1,250 lines at 50 hertz.[88] The balance of HDTV power, however, may go to the country whose transmission system the United States adopts.

Video tape recorders

Although the Europeans succeeded in containing Japan's systematic attempt to wipe out Europe's television industry, the Japanese simply shifted their attacks to related industries. During the early 1980s the Japanese began dumping video tape recorders (VTRs) in the Community to destroy their European rivals and take over the market. Like their American counterparts, Europe's microelectronics firms, which produced VTRs, like Philips and Grundig, lobbied both the EC and its member states to level the playing ground between themselves and their Japanese rivals. Unlike the American producers, the European producers convinced a government to champion their cause. The French, as usual, have been the least inhibited about retaliating against Japanese neomercantilism. In October 1982, Paris announced that until further notice it would require all Japanese VTRs to pass through the customs office at Poitiers, and would further require all documentation to be in French, with clear identification of the country of origin. The action was rich in symbolism. Not only did the action tit-for-tat mirror one of many Japanese restrictive practices, but the Poitiers-Tours region (the exact location is unknown) was where in 732 Frankish forces decisively defeated and turned back the Arab invasion. The French officials responsible for devising and implementing the defense may well have hoped that their battle of Poitiers would prove the turning point in the war against France's latest invader, the Japanese. The hope was misplaced. Although in the two months following the new regulations, only 16,000 were cleared of the 150,000 to 200,000 VTRs which would have sailed through normally, the Japanese eventually outflanked the French.[89] Thus the Maginot Line is a more appropriate historic analogy.

Tokyo responded to the Poitiers defense by filing a complaint to GATT under Article 23 which protects GATT members whose exports are impaired by another member, and filed a similar complaint with the Commission which represents all the EC members at GATT proceedings. Tokyo had two reasons to go to GATT. One was to raise the pressure on Paris to withdraw its restrictions, but the other was to retaliate against the EC for taking Tokyo to GATT the preceding year over Japan's web of nontariff trade barriers.

After sitting on the sidelines during the television battles of the 1970s, the Commission actually initially sided with Tokyo on this issue because France's action blocked European as well as Japanese VTRs. Although the Commission argued that it was not responsible for any member's actions, Brussels strongly criticized the 'Poitiers defense', and went so far as to warn that France's continued violation of Rome Treaty Article 30 could result in prosecution in the European Court of Justice. After protesting against Brussels' position, Paris eventually withdrew its restriction in return for a Commission promise to cut an OMA deal with Tokyo on VTRs and other products. Brussels agreed and the result was a VER with Tokyo, concluded in February 1983, in which the Japanese agreed to restrain a number of products. The agreement included quotas and minimum sales prices for Japanese VTRs, which guaranteed market sales of 1.2 million units in 1983 for Europe's VTR manufacturers, Philips and Grundig, while limiting Japanese VTR sales to the Community for three years to 4.55 million sets, compared to Japan's 1982 exports of 5.5 million sets. If the European producers' sales dropped, then Japan's quota was correspondingly reduced. The Japanese held their prices level with European factory prices. VTR prices, of course, did vary according to whether the model was top quality, medium quality, or standard. VCR retail prices rose an average 15 per cent in 1983.[90]

The VER accomplished three European objectives – to reduce the total number of imported Japanese VTRs, encourage more Japanese VTRs to be built in Europe, and save Europe's VTR industry. Although the total number of Japanese VTRs sold in Europe rose from 4.55 million in 1983 to 5.05 million in 1984, it then fell to 3.95 million in 1985. The VER encouraged the Japanese to manufacture an increasingly large proportion of their VCRs in Europe. Japan exported 3.95 million complete sets and 0.6 million sets in 1983, 3.95 million sets and 1.1 million kits in 1984, and 2.25 million sets and 1.7 million kits in 1985. European production failed to achieve the 1.2 million unit target. In 1983, only 0.8 million European sets were sold in 1982 before the VER took place, 0.6 million in 1983, and 0.7 million in 1984. Despite a failure to reach its target, the quota for European production was raised to 1.5 million in 1985, and Japanese quotas were correspondingly reduced. MITI administered a 10 per cent cutback among Japanese producers in 1984.[91] Europe's VTRs continued to lose their market share despite the quotas. In 1985, Brussels almost doubled its tariff on VCRs from 8 per cent to 14 per cent while MITI announced that it would continue its export restraints on VTRs. The VER rescued Philips and Grundig from the brink of destruction.

How effective was the Commission's response to Japan's dumping of VCRs? Should Brussels have done anything about Europe's VRT industry? Neoclassical economists view failed industries with delight not sorrow; they fervently believe that a bankrupt industry will simply lead to a more efficient utilization of European labor and capital. VTRs are low-value added products and accounted for only several thousand European workers.[92] Protecting Europe's VTR industry diverted scarce resources from more important sectors.

But in reality, there is no guarantee that Japan's destruction of Europe's VTR industry would have contributed to an upgrade of Europe's economy. Those unemployed workers and managers might well have either ended up in lower skilled jobs or even on the street. Europe's economy over time may have been worse off. Others argue that Brussels was correct to protect the VTR industry, but wrong to use quotas. VERs, of course, reward the predatory traders with windfall profits. The Commission never acted on the dumping petition of Philips and Grundig. If dumping was found then the

Commission could have collected duties. A stiff tariff hike would have accomplished the same ends without granting the Japanese producers windfall profits.

Semiconductors

Semiconductors are the brains of microelectronics. Any country which can dominate global semiconductor production is strategically placed eventually to take over virtually any other segment of microelectronics. In April 1989, Philips' Managing Director C.W.M. Koots clearly identified the vital strategic importance of the semiconductor industry when he argued that integrated circuits

are the enabling technology for the continued advancement of industrial societies. As such, each region needs a viable IC industry to further its culture. Each region, therefore, needs to be substantially self-supporting. Being self-supporting means that all the elements of the so-called 'industrial foodchain' must be available domestically: everything from manufacturing equipment, and chip design and fabrication, to making the end product for the consumer.[93]

Since the early 1970s, Tokyo has aimed at achieving global domination of the semiconductor industry. The government created and developed Japan's semiconductor industry into a global leader through the classic means of organizing research, development, production, and market cartels among Japan's leading microelectronics corporations. As in other Japanese industries, Japan's semiconductor producers targeted their American rivals with sustained dumping attacks while their own heavily protected markets remained invulnerable to foreign assault. Then, having all but destroyed America's semiconductor industry, Japan targeted the Community.

Japan now dominates global semiconductor production. Of the world's nine largest semiconductor makers in 1990, the first three and sixth of the top ten were Japanese, three were American, and the only European firm, Philips, was ninth. While most of its foreign rivals stand alone, Japan's semiconductor giants are in turn integrated within horizontal and vertical industrial groups with seemingly bottomless financial pockets and protection. In 1990, Philips produced 1.932 billion chips compared to top-ranking NEC's 4.952. Meanwhile SGS-Thomson was twelfth and Siemens fifteenth.[94] The Community's semiconductor producers cling to a 12 per cent global market share, with almost all of their sales in Europe. In 1988, Philips and SGS-Thomson held the first and second largest market shares in

Europe while Siemens held fifth place. American producers were in third, fourth, sixth, seventh, and tenth place and Japanese in eighth and ninth place.[95] The Americans continued to hold steady in the Community despite losing their market share virtually everywhere else because they had set up shop in Europe during the 1960s and 1970s while the Japanese were still newcomers. This pecking order will undoubtedly change rapidly as the Japanese corporations establish production facilities within Europe. NEC and Fujitsu already have semiconductor plants in Europe, and the other key Japanese chipmakers have plans to establish others. Japan's ascent, America's demise, and Europe's steady market share in semiconductors parallel countless other industries.

As in other microelectronics industries, a viable Community policy evolved from the initiatives of individual members. From 1983 to 1989, Philips and Siemens chipped in $1 billion each to a $1 billion grant by the Dutch and German governments to the Megaproject in which Philips focused on developing a 1 megabit static RAM chip and Siemens a 4 megabit dynamic RAM. Megaproject was not a complete success. Siemens is producing its own chip while Philips shelved its project.

It was not until the mid-1980s that Brussels achieved a consensus on the need to promote a healthy European semiconductor industry, and that was only in reaction to an American initiative to save the remnants of its own industry. In September 1986, after a half-dozen years of idly watching American semiconductor firms being destroyed one by one by sustained Japanese dumping attacks, Washington finally forced Tokyo to agree to a VER on its exports to the United States and third markets while allowing foreign producers to take a 20 per cent market share by 1991. This managed trade agreement marked a sharp break with Washington's traditional free trade at any cost policies. Japan's producers immediately began expanding the volume of chips they were already dumping in Europe.

Brussels responded to the US-Japan cartel arrangement by taking it before a GATT panel in February 1987, which in March 1988 ruled that the cartel had indeed violated international trade law. Meanwhile, the European Electronic Component Association (EECA) pressured Brussels for relief and in December filed dumping charges against Japanese chipmakers. Brussels responded by pressuring Tokyo to rein in its dumping and in February 1987 MITI began allocating export quotas to Japan's chipmakers in Europe. Even with this breathing space the European chipmakers could not recover from the losses sustained from Japan's earlier dumping campaign. In 1988, Brussels tried to protect Europe's chipmakers by imposing the standard that the value-added diffusion or etching of electronic circuits on the wafer rather than simply testing and assembly was necessary for a chip to qualify as 'European'. This ruling undercut Japan's dumping campaign. In 1988, of all the chips sold in Europe, 98 per cent from European chipmakers were actually diffused in Europe, as compared to 50 per cent of American chips, and only 12 per cent of Japanese chips.[96] Even this was not enough to restore vitality to Europe's chipmakers. Japan's dumping offensive succeeded in expanding Japanese market share from 24.6 per cent in 1983 to 70.5 per cent in 1987, while devastating European producers. The Commission found that Japan's firms were dumping chips at prices 8.5 per cent to 206 per cent below production costs. In August 1989, Brussels finally followed Washington's lead and convinced Tokyo to agree to set semiconductor floor prices for 256K, 1, 4, and 16 megabit DRAMS. The price was based on the average production costs plus a 9.5 per cent profit.[97] The five-year agreement was signed by eleven Japanese producers in October 1989.

This Community agreement mirrored the flaws of Washington's 1986 agreement. VERs reward trade predators. By allowing Japan's producers to maintain floor prices, Brussels unwittingly allowed them to reap windfall profits and recoup the losses sustained by their earlier dumping campaign. In effect, the Brussels and Washington semiconductor agreements with Tokyo rewarded Japanese dumping and weakened their own industries. Washington and Brussels may have achieved some short-term relief for their besieged industries but at the cost of giving Japan's producers billions of dollars in windfall profits which were reinvested in production, research and development. Japan's semiconductor producers will strengthen steadily over the long-term while American and European producers just as steadily weaken.

The agreement encourages Japan's chipmakers to set up shop in Europe, a development which many deride as a 'Trojan horse'. George Grunberg, an executive at Bull SA, argued that 'the agreement might help the European semiconductor market in the short term, but in the medium-term it reinforces Japanese industry, allowing them to invest hundreds of millions of dollars in Europe. We will be faced with the Japanese on our own terrain'.[98] NEC, Hitachi, Mitsubishi, and Fujitsu have already established chip factories in Europe while other Japanese producers are planning to do so.

Tariffs, not quotas, are the only rational defense against Japanese dumping. Tariffs protect domestic producers, hurt Japanese producers, and go into government rather than Japanese bank accounts. If Brussels had imposed tariffs on Japanese semiconductors, Europe's weak industry would have been protected, the Community would have enjoyed the revenues, and the Japanese producers would have been correspondingly weakened. Meanwhile, direct subsidies to domestic producers would have allowed them to invest in the research and manufacturing facilities vital to remaining competitive. And, as in other industries, if Washington and Brussels had joined in a united front against Japan's semiconductor assault, American and European semiconductor industries would be all the stronger and Japan's all the weaker today.

Computers

America's computer makers still enjoy leadership in both Europe and the world, with a 65 per cent EC share and 70 per cent global share for minicomputers and mainframes, while the Japanese follow with 12 and 18 per cent shares respectively, and the Europeans with 28 and 12 per cent respectively. Like its semiconductor makers, Europe's computer makers are a distant third behind the United States and Japan. At number eight with $3.3 billion in manufacturing revenues, only Groupe Bull ranked in the world's top nine computer firms, compared to six American firms and two Japanese firms, NEC at number two with $6.4 billion and Fujitsu at number six with $3.6 billion.[97]

The EC computer market was $27.8 billion in sales in 1989, and it was dominated by Japanese and American producers. IBM has about one quarter (23.3 per cent) of Europe's market while the rest is divided up by dozens of large and small computer makers. Although the European producers have about one-third of the $60 billion Community computer market, most of them are suffering huge losses and are severely cutting back their production and workforce.[98]

Europe's producers are on the ropes. Japanese dumping, price wars, and a recent market downturn have battered Europe's computer makers. In the first half of 1990 Philips NV of the Netherlands announced $1 billion in losses, the layoff of 45,000 jobs, and closure of several plants; Groupe Bull SA a loss of $331 million and 3,000 jobs; and Olivetti a major restructuring and losses.[99] Europe's computer companies are increasingly becoming dependent on key Japanese components, and squeezed by both American and Japanese firms in finished goods. The Europeans are selling troubled divisions and even entire firms to the Japanese and Americans. In 1991, Philips sold off its computer division to Digital Equipment Corporation. The most alarming event was Fujitsu's buy out of Britain's International Computers and Sweden's Nokia Data.

Unable to catch up on their own, European companies are increasingly following an 'if you can't beat 'em, join 'em' strategy by either forming joint ventures or completely selling out to the Japanese. Like their American counterparts, Europe's computer makers have been marketing a range of Japanese products under their own labels and sometimes completely selling out to their Japanese rivals. Hitachi supplies mainframes to Italy's Olivetti and NEC to France's Groupe Bull. Fujitsu has produced semiconductors for Britain's largest and Europe's fifth largest hardware and software firm, International Computers Ltd (ICL), since 1981. In May 1991 Mitsubishi bought the personal computer maker Apricot.

The biggest shift in the balance of technology power between Europe and Japan, however, occurred in November 1991 when Fujitsu paid $1.29 billion for an 80 per cent shares in ICL. Canada's Northern Telecom owns the remaining 20 per cent. ICL had recently introduced a range of microprocessors developed by America's Sun Microsystems and had pretax profits of $192.4 million on revenues of $2.82 billion, and was a member of several EC high technology consortiums. Fujitsu already had a powerful base in Britain through a joint venture with its US affiliate, Amdahl Computer Company. Fujitsu's purchase allowed it to leapfrog Control Data to become the world's largest computer firm after IBM, and gave it important advanced technology, a dominant stake in Britain's market and a secure base from which to assault the rest of Europe and IBM. Fujitsu's ICL and Amdahl operations enjoy a 42 per cent market share in Britain compared to IBM's 36 per cent. Fujitsu's strategy continued. In May 1991 Fujitsu paid $402.3 via ICL for Sweden's Nokia Data, Europe's sixth largest computer firm. Nokia lost $192.4 million on $1.2 billion in sales, and owes creditors over $100 million.[100]

Japan's other computer makers have tried to follow Fujitsu's lead. In May 1991, NEC announced its intention to purchase five per cent of Groupe Bull, the state-owned French computer maker. The attempt posed a dilemma for the French government and its tough-talking Prime Minister Cresson. Groupe Bull has been struggling to avoid complete collapse for several years and was saved from extinction by a $1 billion government subsidy in 1990. It will probably not survive without Japanese technology, management, and financial aid. Yet selling out even part of one of France's industrial flagships to Japan would be virtually a treasonous act from the Prime Minister's perspective. If NEC is turned down it will undoubtedly follow Fujitsu's lead and gobble up smaller European computer makers – and compete even more fiercely against Groupe Bull in the long term.

How has Brussels responded to the virtual destruction of Europe's computer industry? It has yet to achieve a consensus on computer policy. The Community divisions reflect the widely differing national policies toward microelectronics. For example, while London responded to the loss of ICI with a *laissez-faire* shrug, Paris predictably tried desperately to shore up its own national champion, Groupe Bull, with a $1.1 billion capital infusion.

Groupe Bull lost $1.2 billion in 1990. Brussels did promote the European Strategic Program for Research in Information Technology (ESPRIT) which was intended to boost collaboration in semiconductors, software, and computers. ESPRIT has generally been considered unsuccessful. Brussels has also retaliated against Japanese dumping in key segments. In 1987, Brussels imposed its maximum duty (33.4 per cent) on seven Japanese computer printer makers – Brother, Citizen, Fujitsu, NEC, Seiko, Seikosha, and Tokyo Juki Industrial, and lesser amounts on a dozen other smaller offenders. Japan's market share had climbed from 49 per cent to 73 per cent between 1983 and 1986 through dumping at 4.8 per cent to 80 per cent below costs, while EC printers sold in Japan fell from 1,040 to zero in the same period. The Commission's investigation followed a petition by four EC producers – Honeywell, Mannesmann, Ing C. Olivetti, and Philips. But these band-aid approaches are unlikely to delay Japan's attack on Europe's computer market. But these efforts have failed to overcome decades of the computer industry's failure to invest or cooperate enough to match the Japanese and American efforts.

CONCLUSION

Forty years after its founding, the Community has still failed to forge and implement a common policy toward Japan. Other issues – dismantling internal trade barriers, assimiliating new members, negotiating GATT rounds, reassuring the Arab states and OPEC – always took precedence and left little time or energy for dealing with the ever-growing Japanese challenge. The Community remains divided between protectionist, tough-line states like France, Italy, and Spain, and free trade, soft-line states like Germany, Denmark, and Britain. Confronted with the range of member policies on any given issue, the Community is not inclined to formulate its own policies.

During the 1980s and into the 1990s, a number of trade disputes which had been simmering for years exploded. The Community's reaction to specific cases of Japanese neomercantilism varies greatly, with inaction the most common response. When the Commission is able to forge a consensus, protectionism is not a guaranteed response. Brussels, for example, condemned France's 'Poitiers defense' rather than using it as the basis for a tit-for-tat Community policy toward Japan. Even seemingly tough stands, such as the restrictions on Japanese automobile sales until 1999, fail to include the demand for genuine reciprocity. The Commission rejected a

French request that the automobile deal include the demand for an increased market share for European vehicles in Japan.

The Community has been entirely on the defensive in its economic conflicts with Japan. It has made no concerted attempt to remove Japan's concentric rings of import or investment barriers. Community policy becomes simply the sum of the widely differing and often outright contradictory policies of its members. It is a collection of *ad hoc* measures to counter particularly virulent Japanese export offensives.

While the Europeans have floundered over the past five decades, Tokyo has systematically pursued a policy geared toward steadily increasing its political economic power within Europe. Japan's strategy toward Europe has passed through two phases and is in the middle of a third. The normalization phase lasted almost two decades, from the war's end until the mid-1960s, as Tokyo tried to normalize its relations with Europe and expand the beacheads of its products. The trade phase lasted another two decades from the mid-1960s to the mid-1980s as trade expanded rapidly and Japan's deficit with the Community turned into a persistent surplus. Japan's third investment phase began in the mid-1980s as Japan's corporations began a massive investment drive in Europe to safeguard and expand gains made earlier by trade offensives and entangle Europe with investments that breach any new walls erected in 1992. Japan's lobby groups in Brussels and the national capitals have grown increasingly influential in shaping Community policy.

The Japanese take full advantage of the Community's divisions. The Community's failures have been Japan's successes. Adept Japanese diplomacy has exacerbated European disarray and divisions. Tokyo is as skilled at playing each of the twelve EC members against each other as it is playing off the fifty US states; the Europeans are just as bad at falling into bidding wars as the Americans. Rothacher writes that 'the persistence of European internal wrangles enabled the Japanese government to maintain a great deal of NTBs, which facing a more forceful and dynamic European representation, they might have had to abandon far earlier. European economic interests in Japan were the ones to suffer'.[103] The economic imbalance of power is thus shaped by the ability of Japan's corporations to circumvent a melange of both EC and bilateral quotas, tariffs, nontariff barriers, and OMAs to expand their market shares continually and to undermine their European rivals, while preventing the European firms from obtaining more than market slivers in Japan's market.

Another tactic Tokyo uses to dilute the Community's authority and cohesion is to insist on including the United States in trade talks, knowing that it can either play to Washington's obsession with geopolitics or play off Washington and Brussels against each other. Brussels attempts to counter this tactic by arguing that the Group of Seven already involves the United States and Canada, and that talks between Europe and Japan should remain bilateral and focused on the primary issue – Japanese neomercantilism.

The Community leadership and the Japanese Prime Minister meet annually, alternately in Tokyo and Brussels. In an attempt to divert European attention from Japanese neomercantilism, Tokyo continually tries to push geopolitical issues to the top of the summit agenda. The Europeans are just as determined to focus on Japan's import barriers and export offensives. They reject Tokyo's emphasis on such issues as nuclear missiles and Kurdish refugees, in part by arguing that those are beyond the Community's mandate, and in part by asserting that Japan's trade surplus and neomercantilism are the primary issue and must subside.

The biggest obstacle to a decisive European stand against Japan's neomercantilism is an ideological one. Although to a lesser extent than the United States, a decisive stand against Japanese neomercantilism is hobbled by the reliance on neoclassical economic theory as a policy basis. To base Community policies on a theory which bears no resemblance to the real world is self-defeating. For example, one assumption of neoclassical theory is that the faster a nation's economy grows, the more products it will import. During the late 1970s Washington and Brussels used this principle in urging Japan to boost growth, under the assumption that Japan would then buy more foreign goods. Japan's trade surplus, however, ultimately grew rather than sank as faster growth meant greater scale economies for Japanese industries and thus an even better comparative advantage with which to conquer global markets. If Japan was supposed to be the locomotive of economic growth, it uncoupled the United States and Europe and left them far behind.

The Community is edging toward a more realistic policy. In 1988, Brussels declared that its foreign economic relations must be based on 'reciprocity', which it defined as 'a balance of mutual advantage' or 'a guarantee of similar – or a least non-discriminatory – opportunities for firms from the Community to operate in foreign markets on the same basis as local firms'.[104] To this end, Brussels has been more willing than the United States to restrict markets by using tough dumping, local content, quotas, tariffs, and origin rules. But these defensive measures are not enough. Brussels finds itself in an even a worse position than the little Dutch boy at the dyke; the Community must plug countless leaks rather than just one.

One major failure was focusing on the safeguard clause as a basis on the bilateral relationships. Rothacher argues that the Community's insistence on a safeguard clause

did not strengthen the EC position, it just wrecked the negotiations. The safeguard clause itself was hardly any use. Without it the Italians could 'protect' their domestic market quite effectively. Britain which had a bilateral SC, never used it, and France and the Benelux employed theirs only once each during a decade and on marginal products (umbrellas and zip fasteners) . . . The Europeans wanted the SC, and the Japanese resented it, for reasons of pure psychology – wanting security and disliking discrimination.[105]

Rothacher goes on to remind us that 'bilateral trade expanded tremendously even without a trade agreement', hinting that Brussels' focus on achieving one may have been misplaced and precluded other agreements which could have better served the Community's interests.

In the Hague on 18 July 1991, the Japanese Prime Minister Kaifu, the EC Council Chairman Prime Minister Ruud Lubbers, and the Commission President Jacques Delors signed a six page declaration in which they pledged to work toward 'balanced and comprehensive relations' and to consult and coordinate policy on a range of international issues including security, human rights, and the global economy. The agreement capped six months of tough bargaining during which Tokyo struggled hard and largely succeeded in creating a document which stressed cooperation on common interests rather than trade differences. As usual, the French played hardball. Paris pressured Brussels to include a clause in which both sides pledged to work toward a balanced trade relationship. The Japanese refused, ironically claiming the French statement promoted managed rather than free trade. The result was an innocuous statement that identifies their 'resolve for equitable access to their respective markets and removing obstacles, whether structural or other, impeding the expansion of trade and investment on the basis of comparable opportunities.'[106]

Does Europe's failure to insist on a genuinely reciprocal relationship with Japan really matter? At most the failure systematically to confront Japanese neomercantilism means that the Community's economic growth will be slightly lower, while the direction of that development may be slightly different than if a level playing field had prevailed. The Community overall will be slightly less wealthy than it might have otherwise have been, with slightly less resources for ploughing back into the economy or dealing with social problems. Although trade between a neomercantilist and liberal economy is mostly zero sum with most benefits accruing to the former, the results may not be as catastrophic as is popularly believed. In the decades to come, although the Community will become increasingly dependent on Japanese capital, technology, and products, Europeans will retain their prosperity, culture, and political independence.

7 Europe and Japan into the 21st Century

It was no coincidence that the Commission chose the five hundredth anniversary of Columbus' landing in the Western hemisphere as the year for European unification.[1] For almost five hundred years, the world experienced an 'Age of Europe' in which the 'great powers' at one time or another either directly colonized or indirectly influenced virtually every region around the world. European hegemony finally collapsed with the devastation of World War Two. The 'Age of America' (or the 'American century' as some optimistically called it) took off in 1945 and lasted little more than a quarter-century. By the 1980s, the costs of rebuilding and serving the global political economy and containing communism had left the United States the world's greatest debtor nation.

Now Europeans are hoping that 1992 will represent the dawning of a new 'Age of Europe', characterized by the economic and political power of a unified continent of 345 million people rather than by the old Europe of eternally squabbling, conniving nation-states. Although dreams of unification are as old as Europe itself, Brussels will succeed in achieving what the Catholic Church and conquerers from Charlemange to Hitler failed to do. Soon Europeans will have the same passport, flag, and national anthem (Beethoven's 'Ode to Joy' from the Ninth Symphony) while nine languages will be official: Danish, Dutch, English, French, German, Greek, Italian, Portuguese, and Spanish. Meanwhile the line of nations waiting impatiently to join is growing. The 1991 agreement between the Community and European Free Trade Association created a 'Common Space' of 380 million consumers. The Community seems well on its way to fulfilling Jean Monnet's dream that: 'We don't combine states, we combine human beings!' (*Nous ne coalison pas d'etats, nous unissons des hommes!*).[2]

Yet some fear that after finally emerging from the shadow of America's political economic power and Soviet ideological and military power, the Community may simply be trampled underfoot by Japanese neomercantilism.

On 19 July 1991, the Community signed an agreement with Tokyo designed to strengthen cooperation on economic, cultural, and environmental issues, and to achieve 'equitable access to their respective markets and remove obstacles on the basis of comparable opportunities'.[3] The agreement will not lead to economic reciprocity and symmetry between the Community and Japan. Social Darwinist notions of international relations as a constant struggle in which superior 'races' triumph over the inferior, not liberal concepts of equality and cooperation, shape Japan's world view and policies. To triumph in this struggle, Japan has mastered an ever-expanding and dynamic virtuous cycle of economic development. Import barriers and export offensives simultaneously devastate foreign rivals and boost Japan's industries. Windfall profits are reinvested in the economy to fuel further expansion while rival nations sink into a vicious cycle of declining production, profits, investments, and wealth.

Nearly half a century of sustained neomercantilism has transformed Japan from a poverty-stricken inefficient nation into the world's most dynamic economic superpower. Japan is now the world's greatest banking, corporate, manufacturing, technological, and trade power. Throughout the 1980s alone, Japan's economy annually expanded at about 4.5 per cent compared to the Community's 2.7 per cent and America's 2.4 per cent. Japan's economic size will surpass that of both the European Community and the United States within a dozen years if current growth rates hold, thus making Japanese twice as wealthy as Americans on a per capita basis.

What can be done about the Japanese challenge? Some argue that 'if you can't beat 'em, join 'em'. Like their American counterparts, increasing numbers of Europe's most dynamic corporations, battered by Japanese dumping and import barriers, and the inability or unwillingness of their national government or Brussels systematically to promote them, are forming joint ventures and selling their technology to their Japanese rivals. Certainly that is how Tokyo wants foreign governments and corporations to respond to the Japanese onslaught.

Others plead that the Community must 'fight fire with fire'. As early as 1934, the British Federation of Industry (BFI) concluded after an extensive investigation in Japan that the only way to counter Japanese mercantilism was

> by a conscious directional control of exports; by means of a division of markets upon a percentage or some other quantitative basis; by some similar agreement on a territorial basis; by mutual action to develop in cooperation some of the more backward markets of the world; by agreements as to the level of export prices; by some rationalization of production according to type and quantity; or by joint manufacturing activities.[4]

Like many in the Community today, London rejected these recommendations as contrary to the spirit of free trade.

Whether Europe can rally and fend off the Japanese challenge is uncertain. The European Community faces many of the same crippling disadvantages *vis-a-vis* the Japanese as does the United States. Both the Community and United States are highly pluralistic political economies whose industries usually receive protection and promotion for political rather than strategic reasons. Despite the ever widening gap between Japan's rise into an economic superpower and Europe's economic stagnation and deepening trade and payments deficit with Japan, Brussels remained divided into the hardliners (like Italy and France) and softliners (like Denmark and Germany) with the others straddling the fence on all issues that do not directly affect them. The Union of Industries of the European Community (UNICE) attempts to speak for European industry, but like the US Business Round Table does not enjoy the close and extensive policy partnership that Japan's *Keidanren* shares with its national government.

Thus, the Community's response to the Japanese challenge has mostly been the sum total of its widely differing national policies. When the Commission does rule on an issue, it seems to follow no consistent guidelines. Brussels took a hands-off position on televisions and HDTV, yet negotiated a VER with Tokyo over VTRs. After taking two years to reach agreement on quotas for Japanese automobile imports and transplants, the Commission still does not have a clear ruling on domestic content. European efforts to cooperate on high technology research may well be too little too late to reverse Europe's rapid relative decline.

While the Community operates on liberal principles and will become even freer after 1992, Japan will remain neomercantilist in structure, policy, and outlook. After over a quarter-century of strenuous though unsystematic efforts, Washington failed to convert Tokyo to liberalism. There is no reason to believe that Brussels will succeed where Washington failed.

Unable to reform the Japanese, the Europeans can only reform themselves. Christian Sautter writes that the Community and its members face a choice: 'should governments remain passive and let "the invisible hand" organize or disorganize European-Japanese economic relations? Or should they take concrete action to support their national industrial "champions" in this world-wide "sumo" tournament?'[5] The choice may be even bleaker than Sautter acknowledges. If the Community and most of its members continue to rely largely on free market forces to shape their economies while Tokyo carefully manages Japan's industries and trade, then in reality Tokyo rather than markets will shape Europe's economy. Lehmann writes that for 'Europeans today, Japan is without a doubt, a menace on the economic front; there are many respects, however, in which she could also become a model'.[6]

Will Europe eventually adopt Tokyo-style industrial policies that develop the next wave of high technology industries while helping mature industries adjust to an increasingly frenzied global marketplace? Or will it continue to offer Washington-style ad hoc protectionism to threatened industries without any long-term goals and strategies?

Clearly Europeans must become one not only in markets but in outlook and policy as well. Many advocate combining the Commission's directorate-generals of industrial affairs and trade to form a Community equivalent of MITI. A European MITI could then rationally and systematically target Europe's strategic industries, technologies, and corporations for development through the same selective technology infusions, cartels, import barriers, and export promotion that Tokyo has mastered.

Yet even if they can cut free of the cement hobbles of division and tradition, the Europeans are unlikely to catch up to the Japanese or even with the Americans by any significant measurement. A 'Fortress Europe' response to Japan's challenge might hold the Japanese at bay in Europe but would do little to offset the steady loss by European firms of markets elsewhere around the globe. Any successful European policy must counter Japanese expansion in every significant foreign market. Europe's corporations must somehow design, manufacture, and sell products of comparable quality at a cheaper price than their Japanese rivals for several decades before they can even draw even. Meanwhile, the Japanese will not be standing still. Tokyo will continue to develop the economy into ever more sophisticated levels of technology, finance, and manufacturing, while Japan's corporations will expand their foreign conquests in one product and market after another.

Can the Europeans pull it off? 'I'd rather fight a coalition than be a member of one', Napoleon declared. Perhaps he was right.

An alternative solution would be to somehow get them involved in a large scale war in there own "backyard"

Notes

INTRODUCTION

1. Jean-Jacques Servan-Schreiber, *The American Challenge* (New York: Atheneum, 1968).
2. *Economist*, 1 and 8 September 1962.
3. *New York Times*, 16 May 1991.
4. Ibid., 17 May 1991.

1 EUROPEAN UNIFICATION, INSTITUTIONS AND LOYALTIES

1. Some argue that the major catalyst behind the ECSC was to contain Germany. Dick Leonard states bluntly that 'Adolf Hitler was the main catalyst of the European Community', *Pocket Guide to the European Community* (London: Basil Blackwell, 1988) p. 31.
2. See Ernst Hass, *The Uniting of Europe: Political, Social and Economic Forces* (Stanford, CA: Stanford University Press, 1958) p. 11. For other functionalist writers, see David Mitany, *A Working Peace System* (Chicago: Quadrangle Books, 1966).
3. Roy Ginsberg, *Foreign Policy Actions of the European Community: The Politics of Scale* (Boulder, CO: Lynne Rienner, 1989) pp. 29, 31.
4. For neofunctionalist works, see Philippe Schmitter, 'A Revised Theory of Regional Integration', *International Organization*, 24 (4), Autumn 1970; Ernst Haas and Edward Rowe, 'Regional Organizations in the United Nations: Is There Externalization?', *International Studies Quarterly*, 17 (1), March 1973; Ernst Haas, *The Obsolescence of Regional Integration Theory* (Berkeley, CA: University of California Press, 1975); Robert Keohane and Joseph Nye, *Power and Interdependence: World Politics and Transition* (Boston: Little, Brown, and Company, 1977); Ernst Hass, 'Turbulent Fields and the Theory of Regional Integration', *International Organization*, 30 (4), September 1976; Joseph Nye, *Peace in Parts: Integration and Conflict in Regional Organization* (Lanham, CT: University Press of America, 1987).
5. Robert Gogel and Jean-Claude Larreche, 'Pan European Marketing', in Spyros Makridakis (ed.), *Single Market Europe: Opportunities and Challenges for Business* (San Francisco: Jossey-Bass, 1991) p. 126.
6. Philippe Schmitter, 'Three Neofunctional Hypotheses About International Integration', *International Organization*, 23 (1), pp. 161–2.
7. Ibid.
8. Ernst Haas and Edward Rowe, 'Regional Organizations in the United Nations: Is There Externalization?', *International Studies Quarterly*, 17 (1), March 1973, p. 5.
9. Ginsberg, p. 152.
10. Ibid., p. 33.

11. Ibid., p. 34.
12. Ibid., p. 33.
13. Derek Unwin, *The Community of Europe* (London: Longman, 1991) p. 9. Although she is a great admirer of Churchill, Margaret Thatcher fiercely rejects his support of integration.
14. Alan S. Milward, *The Reconstruction of Western Europe, 1945–51* (London: Methuen, 1984) p. 96.
15. Unwin, op. cit., p. 32.
16. Ibid.
17. Ibid.
18. Ibid., p. 34.
19. Ibid., p. 44.
20. Quoted in Henry Paolucci, 'Europe After 1992: An End to Nationhood as Historically Defined', *The Washington Times*, 4 (12), December 1989, p. 499.
21. Unwin, op. cit., pp. 44, 45.
22. William Wallace, *The Transformation of Western Europe* (New York: Council on Foreign Relations Press, 1990) p. 74.
23. Unwin, op. cit., p. 31.
24. Ibid., p. 76.
25. The only exception was trade between East and West Germany. Bonn never recognized the legitimacy of the Berlin regime and thus treated all East German imports as if they were German. Other members would impose tariffs on either direct or transhippped East German imports.
26. Unwin, op. cit., p. 98.
27. Quoted in ibid., p. 98.
28. Christopher Tugendhat, 'Europe's Need for Self-Confidence', in *International Affairs*, 58 (1), Winter 1981–2, pp. 7–12. For pessimistic views of European unity, see Ulrich Everling, 'Possibilities and Limits of European Integration', *Journal of Common Market Studies*, 18 (3), 1980, pp. 217–28, and Paul Taylor, *The Limits of European Integration* (London: Croom Helm, 1983).
29. Stanley Hoffman, 'The European Community and 1992', *Foreign Affairs*, 68, Fall 1989, p. 29.
30. Quoted in Unwin, op. cit., p. 201.
31. For an excellent analysis of this question, see Wayne Sandholtz and John Zysman, '1992: Recasting the European Bargain', *World Politics*, 62 (1), October 1989.
32. For details of his vision, see Jacques Delors, 'Europe: Embarking on a New Course', in D. Bell and J. Gaffney (eds), *1992 and After* (Oxford: Pergamon Press, 1989) pp. 15–28.
33. Ibid., p. 96.
34. Giovanni Agnelli, 'The Europe of 1992', *Foreign Affairs*, 68, Fall 1986, p. 62.
35. Wayne Sandholtz and John Zysman, '1992: Recasting the European Bargain', *World Politics*, 62 (1), October 1989, p. 117.
36. Paolo Cecchini, *The European Challenge 1992: The Benefits of a Single Market* (Aldershot: Wildwood House for the EC Commission, 1988) p. 98. There have been several other studies of the economic effects of unification. Estimates of the benefits and costs of economic union vary wildly from one

economists and statistical method to the next. For an estimate below that of the Cecchini report see Merton Peck, 'Industrial Organization and the Gains from 1992', *Brookings Papers on Economic Activity*, 2, 1989, pp. 277–99, and Horst Siebert, 'The Single European Market – A Schumpeterian Event?', Kiel Discussion Paper 157 (Keil, FRG: Kiel Institute of World Economics, November 1989. For an estimate above that of the Cecchini Report see Richard Baldwin, 'The Growth Effects of 1992', *Economic Policy*, October 1989, pp. 248–81.

37. The Commission, *Europe 1992: Europe World Partner* (Brussels, October 1988) p. 2.
38. Ibid.
39. Quoted in Spyros G. Makridakis and Michelle Bainbridge, 'Evolution of the Single Market', in Spyros G. Makridakis (ed.), *Single Market Europe: Opportunities and Challenges for Business* (San Francisco: Jossey-Bass, 1991) p. 16.
40. Quoted in Unwin, op. cit., p. 240.
41. Ibid., pp. 164–5.
42. Sandholtz, Zysman, op. cit., p. 115.
43. Unwin, op. cit., p. 169.
44. Christopher Hill, 'European Foreign Policy: Power Bloc, Civilian Model, or Flop?' in Reinhardt Rummel (ed.), *The Evolution of an International Actor: Western Europe's New Assertiveness* (Boulder, CO: Westview Press, 1990) p. 52.
45. For an in-depth discussion of these and related questions, see William Wallace, *The Transformation of Western Europe* (New York: Concil on Foreign Relations, 1990).
46. Ibid., pp. 29–30.
47. Ibid., p. 19.
48. Ibid., p. 20.
49. Frances Condick, unpublished essay, 10 June 1992.
50. Wallace, op. cit., p. 29.
51. Pierre Hassner quoted in ibid., p. 94.

2   EUROPEAN UNIFICATION: POLICYMAKING AND POLICIES

1. Numerous studies have appeared analyzing Community policymaking: David Coombes, *Politics and Bureaucracy in the European Community* (London: Allen and Unwin, 1970); Helen Wallace, *National Governments and the European Communities* (London: Chatham House, PEP, 1973); Werner Feld and John K. Wildgen, 'National Administrative Elites and European Integration: Saboteurs at Work?', *Journal of Common Market Studies*, 13 (1), 1975; Jeff Bridgeford, 'European Political Co-operation and Its Impact on the Institutions of the European Community', *Studia Diplomatica*, 30 (2), 1977.
2. Spyros G. Makridakis and Michelle Bainbridge, 'Evolution of the Single Market', in Spyros Makridakis, et al., *Single Market Europe: Opportunities and Challenges for Business* (San Francisco: Jossey-Bass, 1991) p. 14.

3. For a good comparative study of industrial policy, see Peter Katzenstein (ed.), *Between Power and Plenty: Foreign Economic Policies of Advanced Industrial States* (Madison: University of Wisconsin Press, 1978).
4. Peter Montagnon, 'Introduction', in Peter Montagnon, *European Competition Policy* (New York: Council on Foreign Relations Press, 1990) p. 3.
5. Edward Nevin, *The Economics of Europe* (New York: St. Martin's Press, 1990), p. 130.
6. Joseph Gilchrist and David Deacon, 'Curbing Subsidies', in Montagnon, op. cit., pp. 36, 38.
7. Quoted in Montagnon, op. cit., p. 1.
8. Heinrich Holzler, 'Merger Control', in Montagnon, op. cit., p. 24.
9. Gilchrist and Deacon in Montagnon, op. cit., p. 39.
10. Willem Molle, *The Economics of European Integration* (Aldershot: Dartmouth, 1990), p. 267.
11. Ibid., pp. 255–9.
12. Ibid., p. 266.
13. Dick Leonard, *Pocket Guide to the European Community* (London: Basil Blackwell, 1988), p. 121.
14. Ibid., p. 137.
15. Molle, op. cit., p. 287.
16. Derek W. Unwin, *The Community of Europe: A History of European Integration since 1945* (London: Longman, 1991) p. 196.
17. Leonard, op. cit., p. 123.
18. Molle, op. cit., pp. 351–3.
19. Ibid., pp. 354–7.
20. Ibid., p. 291.
21. The automobile conflict between Europe and Japan will be addressed in Chapter 6.
22. Peter Montagnon, 'Regulating the Utilities', in Montagnon, op. cit., p. 53.
23. Peter Cowhey, 'Telecommunications', in Gary Hufbauer (ed.), *Europe 1992: An American Perspective* (Washington, DC: The Brookings Institute, 1990) p. 163.
24. Gary Hufbauer, 'An Overview', in ibid., p. 42.
25. Cowhey in ibid., op. cit., p. 220.
26. Hufbauer in ibid., p. 31.
27. For a concise overview of the Eureka project, see Knut Reintz, 'Eureka – Three Years Already! Result so far and Future Outlook', *European Affairs*, 3 (1), Spring 1989, pp. 112–14.
28. *New York Times*, 4 September 1990.
29. European Information Technology Industry Roundtable (EITIR), *White Paper on the European T.I. Industry and the Single Market* (Brussels: EITIR, 1989) p. 13
30. Ernst-Jurgen Horn, 'Germany: A Market-led Process', in Francois Duchene and Geoffrey Shepherd (eds), *Managing Industrial Change in Western Europe* (London: Frances Pinter, 1987) p. 50.
31. Ibid., p. 58.
32. Ibid., p. 50.
33. Quoted in Curzon Price, *Industrial Policies in the European Community* (New York: St. Martin's Press, 1981) p. 46.

34. Patrick Messerlin, 'France: The Ambitious State', in Duchene and Shepherd, op. cit., p. 107.
35. Ibid.
36. Ibid., p. 91.
37. Ibid., p. 102.
38. *New York Times*, 26 May, 1991.
39. Rippo Ranci, 'Italy: the Weak State', in Duchene and Shepherd, op. cit., p. 141.
40. Ibid., p. 135.
41. Ibid., p. 140.
42. Geoffrey Shepherd, 'United Kingdom: A Resistance to Change', in Duchene and Shepherd, op. cit., pp. 146–7.
43. Ibid., p. 152.
44. Peter Katzenstein, *Small States in World Markets: Industrial Policy In Europe* (Ithaca, NY: Cornell University Press, 1985).
45. Ibid., p. 47.
46. See Barington Moore, *The Social Origins of Dictatorship and Democracy: Land and Peasant in the Making of the Modern World* (Boston: Beacon, 1967).
47. Andrew Boyd, 'How the Storm Changed the Signs', *Economist*, 28, January 1978.
48. Ibid., p. 81.
49. For indepth accounts of Community foreign policy, see Roy Ginsberg, *Foreign Policy Actions of the European Community* (Boulder, CO: Lynne Rienner, 1989); Werner Feld, *The European Community in World Affairs: Economic Power and Political Influence* (New York: Alfred Publishing Co., 1977); William Wallace and William Patterson (eds), *Foreign Policy Making in Western Europe: A Comparative Approach* (New York: Praeger, 1978); Leon Lindber and Stuart Scheingold, *Europe's Would-Be Polity* (Englewood Cliffs, NJ: Prentice Hall, 1979); Helen Wallace, William Wallace, and Carole Webb (eds), *Policy-Making in the European Communities* (New York: Wiley, 1983); Christopher Hill, *National Foreign Policies and European Political Cooperation* (London: George Allen and Unwin, 1983); Panayiotis Ifestos, *European Political Cooperation: Towards a Framework of Supranational Diplomacy?* (Brookfield, CT: Avebury, 1987); Werner Feld, *The European Common Market and the World* (Englewood Cliffs, NJ: Prentice Hall, 1967); Ralf Dahrendorf, 'Possibilities and Limits of the European Community's Foreign Policy', *The World Today*, 27 (3), 1971; Robert McGeehan and Steven J. Warnecke, 'Europe's Foreign Policies: Economics, Politics or Both?' *Orbis*, 17 (4), 1974; Roger P. Morgan, 'Introduction: European Integration and the European Community's External Relations', *International Journal of Politics*, 5 (2), 1975; Ralf Dahrendorf, 'The Foreign Policy of the EEC', *The World Today*, 29 (3), 1973; Panayotis Soldatis, 'La Theorie de la politique etrangere et sa pertinance pour l'etude des relations exterieures des Communautes Europenne', *Etudes International*, 9 (1), 1978; Glenda G. Rosenthal, *The Men Behind the Decisions* (Lexington, Mass.: Lexington Books, 1975); Maurice Torrelli, 'L'elaboration des relations exterieure de la C.E.E.', *Revue du Marche Commun*, 167, 1973; Roger Morgan, *High Politics, Low Politics: Towards a Foreign*

Policy of Western Europe (London: Sage Publications, 1973); Sjostedt Gunnar, *The External Role of the European Community* (Farnborough: Saxon House, 1988); Ralf Dahrendorf, 'It is not easy for a Community to have a Foreign Policy', *International Journal of Politics*, 5 (4), 1975; Charles Pentland, 'Linkage Politics: Canada's Contract and the Development of the European Communities External Relations', *International Journal*, 32 (1), 1977; Geoffrey Goodwin, 'The External Relations of the European Community – Shadow and Substance', *British Journal of International Studies*, 3 (2), 1977; Roger Rieber, 'The Future of the European Community in International Affairs', *Canadian Journal of Political Science*, 32 (1), 1977; David Allen, 'Foreign Policy at the European Level: Beyond the Nation-state', in William Wallace and W. E. Patterson (eds), *Foreign Policy-Making in Western Europe* (Farnborough: Saxon House, 1978).

50. Unwin, op. cit., p. 149.
51. Albrecht Rothacher, *Economic Diplomacy Between the European Community and Japan, 1959–1981* (London: Gower Publishers, 1983) p. 41.
52. Ginsberg, *Foreign Policy . . .*, op. cit., p. 13.
53. Ibid., p. 86.
54. Ibid., p. 62.
55. Ibid., p. 166.
56. The Commission, *Europe 1992: Europe World Partner*, Brussels, October 1988, p. 2.
57. Ibid.
58. Case 6/64 Costa v. ENEL (1964) E.C.R. 1141, 15 July 1964; Case 22/70 (AETR) Commission v. Council (1971 E.C.R. 263, 31 March 1971. Case 1/75 (1975) E.C.R. 1353, 11 November 1975; Case 1/78 (1978) E.C.R. 2151, 14 November 1978.
59. Martin Wolf, '1992 Global Implications of the European Community's Programme for Completing the Internal Market' (New York: Lehrman Institute Policy Paper, (1), 1989) pp. 223–42
60. Kenjiro Ishikawa, *Japan and the Challenge of Europe 1992* (London: Pinter Publishers, 1990) p. 82.
61. *Financial Times*, 18 November 1988.
62. *Bulletin of the European Communities*, September 1986, p. 15.
63. Quoted in Michael Calingaert, *The 1992 Challenge from Europe: Development of the European Community's Internal Market* (Washington: National Planning Association, 1988) p. 120.
64. Roy Ginsberg, 'European Trade Policy at Mid-Decade: Coping with the Internal Menace and the External Challenge', in Reinhardt Rummel (ed.), *The Evolution of an International Actor: Western Europe's New Assertiveness* (Boulder, Co.: Westview Press, 1990) p. 75.
65. Ginsberg, *Foreign Policy . . .*, op. cit., p. 33.
66. Raymond Barre, '1987 Alastair Buchan Memorial Lecture: Foundations for European Security and Cooperation', *Survival*, 29 (4), July/August 1987, p. 298.
67. *New York Times*, 5 November 1991.
68. Christopher Hill, 'European Foreign Policy: Power Bloc, Civilian Model, or Flop?' in Rummel, op. cit., p. 48.
69. Ibid., pp. 53–4.

3 JAPAN AT HOME: THE CORPORATIST STATE

1. *Businessweek*, 26 August 1991.
2. T. J. Pempel, 'Corporatism without Labor', in Philippe Schmitter and Gerhard Lembruch (eds), *Trends toward Corporate Intervention* (London: Sage, 1979).
3. J. A. A. Stockwin, *Dynamic and Immobilist Politics in Japan* (London: Macmillan, 1988) p. 10.
4. *Nikkei Weekly*, 14 September 1991, p. 1. The law requires that civil servants must wait two years after retirement before accepting employment in a profitmaking industry which they formerly regulated. The National Personnel Administration (NPA), however, rubber stamps as exceptions virtually any applications from ex-bureaucrats for employment in such industries.
5. J. L. Bower, *When Markets Quake* (Boston: Harvard Business School Press, 1986) pp. 220–1.
6. Chalmers Johnson, *MITI and the Japanese Miracle: The Growth of Industrial Policy, 1925–1975* (Palo Alto, CA: Stanford University Press, 1982) pp. 20–1. See also Takashi Inoguchi, *Gendai Nihon Seiji Keizai no Kozu: Seifu to Shijo (The Structure of Contemporary Japanese Politics and Economics)* (Tokyo: Toyo Keizai Shinposha, 1983).
7. Seizaburo Sato and Tetsuhisa Matsuzaki, *Jiminto Seiken (The Liberal Democratic Party)* (Tokyo: Chuo Koronsha, 1986); Takashi Inoguchi and Tomoaki Iwai, *"Zokugiin" no Kenkyu: Jiminto Seiken o Gyujiru Shuyaku-Tachi (A Study of "Zoku" Representatives: Main Actors Controlling Japanese Politics)* (Tokyo: Nihon Keizai Shimbunsha, 1987).
8. Karl van Wolferen, *The Enigma of Japanese Power: People and Politics in a Stateless Nation* (New York: Alfred Knopf, 1989).
9. William Nester, *The Foundations of Japanese Power: Continuities, Changes, Challenges* (Armonk, NY: 1990).
10. See Kent Calder, *Crisis and Compensation: Public Policy and Political Stability in Japan* (Princeton, NJ: Princeton University Press, 1988).
11. Ezra Vogel, *Japan as Number One: Lessons for America* (Cambridge, Mass.: Harvard University Press, 1979) p. 94.
12. Stephen Wilks and Maurice Wright, 'The Japanese Bureaucracy in the Industrial Policy Process', in Stephen Wilks and Maurice Wright (eds), *The Promotion and Regulation of Industry in Japan* (New York: St. Martin's Press, 1991) p. 32.
13. *Nikkei Weekly*, 14 September 1991, p. 3.
14. *New York Times*, 7 March 1991.
15. Daiichi Ito, 'Government-Business Relations', in Wilks and Wright, op. cit., p. 67.
16. Statistics culled from Yukio Noguchi, 'Budget Policymaking in Japan', in Samuel Kernell (ed.), *Parallel Politics: Economic Policymaking in Japan and the United States* (Washington, DC: Brookings Institution, 1991) pp. 120–1.
17. *1991 Japan*, Keizai Koho Center, Japan Institute for Social and Economic Affairs, 1990. Among the most important studies of MITI are: Johnson, op. cit; Richard Samuels, *The Business of the Japanese State: Energy Markets in Comparative and Historical Perspective* (Ithaca, NY: Cornell University Press, 1987); and Daniel Okimoto, *Between MITI and the Marketplace:*

Japanese Industrial Policy for High Technology (Stanford, CA: Stanford University Press, 1989).

18. *Far Eastern Economic Review*, 20 June 1991.

19. Albrecht Rothacher, *Economic Diplomacy between the European Community and Japan, 1959–1981* (London: Gower, 1983), p. 58.

20. Quoted in ibid., p. 58.

21. Haruhiro Fukui and Shigeko Fukai, 'Elite Recruitment and Political Leadership', *Political Science and Politics*, 25 (1), March 1992, p. 34.

22. Ibid., p. 31.

23. Louise do Rosario, 'A Strong Case for Reform', *Far Eastern Economic Review*, 20 June 1991, p. 47.

24. Ellis Krauss, 'Politics and the Policymaking Process', in Takeshi Ishida and Ellis Krauss (eds), *Democracy in Japan* (Pittsburgh, PA: University of Pittsburgh Press, 1989).

25. See William Bryant, *Japanese Private Economic Diplomacy: An Analysis of Business-Government Linkages* (New York: Praeger Publishers, 1975).

26. *Nikkei Weekly*, 14 September, 1991, p. 2.

27. Nester, op. cit., p. 234.

28. Ibid., p. 267.

29. *Nikkei Weekly*, 14 September 1991, p. 2. In 1988, the JSP changed its English name to the Social Democratic Party of Japan (SDPJ) although its Japanese name (*Nihonshakaito*) remained the same. The action was clearly designed as a public relations gesture toward foreigners, although what the JSP hoped to accomplish remains unclear.

30. James Abegglen, 'Industrial Policy', in Loukas Tsoukalis and Maureen White (eds), *Japan and Western Europe* (New York: St. Martin's Press, 1982) p. 54. For other works on Japanese industrial policy see: Chalmers Johnson (ed.), *The Industrial Policy Debate* (San Francisco: San Francisco Press, 1984); Carol Gluck, *Japan's Modern Myths: Ideology in the Late Meiji Period* (Princeton, NJ: Princeton University Press, 1985); Hugh Patrick (ed.), *Japan's High Technology Industries* (Seattle: University of Washington Press, 1986); Stephen Wilks and Maurice Wright (eds), *Comparative Government-Industry Relations: Western Europe, the United States, and Japan* (Oxford: Clarendon Press, 1987); Samuels, op. cit.; T. J. Pempel, 'The Unbundling of "Japan Inc."', *Journal of Japanese Studies*, 13 (2), 1987, pp. 271–306; K. Yamamura and Y. Yasuba (eds), *The Political Economy of Japan: The Domestic Context* (Stanford, CA: Stanford University Press, 1987); Haruhiro Fukui, 'The Policy Research Council of Japan's Liberal Democratic Party', *Asian Thought and Society*, 34 (12), 1987; Takashi Inoguchi and Daniel Okimoto (eds), *The Political Economy of Japan: The International Context* (Stanford, CA: Stanford University Press, 1988); Calder, op. cit.; Gavin McCormack and Yoshi Sugimoto (eds), *The Japanese Trajectory: Modernization and Beyond* (Cambridge: Cambridge University Press, 1988); John Fulcher, 'The Bureaucratization of the State and the Rise of Japan', *The British Journal of Sociology*, 39 (3), 1988, pp. 228–54; R. Komiya, M. Okuno, and K. Suzumura (eds), *Industrial Policy of Japan* (Tokyo: Academic Press, 1988); Chalmers Johnson, 'The Japanese Political Economy: A Crisis in Theory', *Ethics and International Affairs*, 27 (2), 1988; J. Shoven (ed.), *Government Policy Towards Industry*

in the United States and Japan (Cambridge: Cambridge University Press, 1988); Gregory Noble, 'The Japanese Industrial Policy Debate', in Stephen Haggard and Chung-in Moon (eds), *Pacific Dynamics: The International Politics of Industrial Change* (Boulder, CO: Westview Press, 1989); Okimoto, op. cit.; Chalmers Johnson, Laura Tyson, and John Zysman, *Politics and Productivity: How Japan's Development Strategy Works* (New York: Ballinger, 1989); Wilks and Wright, op. cit.

31. Johnson, op. cit. p. 20.
32. Ibid., p. 114.
33. Ellis Krauss, 'Political Economy: Policymaking and Industrial Policy in Japan', *Political Science and Politics*, 25 (1), March 1992, pp. 53–4.
34. Y. Murakami, 'Towards a Socioinstitutional Explanation', in K. Yamamura (ed.), *Policy and Trade Issues of the Japanese Economy* (Tokyo: Tokyo University Press, 1982) p. 104.
35. Ibid., p. 105.
36. *Nikkei Weekly*, 22 June 1991, p. 3.
37. Dan Okimoto, 'Regime Characteristics of Japanese Industrial Policy', in Patrick, op. cit., p. 53.
38. See Jeremy Howell and Ian Neary, 'Science and Technology Policy in Japan: The Pharmaceutical Industry and New Technology' (pp. 81–109); Masami Tanaka, 'Government Policy and Biotechnology in Japan: The Pattern and Impact of Rivalry Between Ministries' (pp. 110–34); both in Wilks and Wright, op. cit.
39. Howell and Neary, p. 87.
40. Boyd and Nagamori argue that these laws were no more than a 'legislative afterthought' to processes of adjustment which had been occurring in years leading up to the 1978 law, which simply codified and legalized existing practices. Richard Boyd and Seiichi Nagamori, 'Industrial Policy Making: Electoral, Diplomatic and Other Adjustments to Crisis in the Japanese Shipbuilding Industry', in Wilks and Wright, op. cit., p. 168.
41. See Michael Young, 'Structural Adjustment of Mature Industries in Japan: Legal Institutions, Industry Associations, and Bargaining' (pp. 135–66); Boyd and Nagamori, op. cit. (pp. 167–206); both in Wilks and Wright, op. cit.
42. Young, op. cit., p. 144.
43. Boyd and Nagamori, op. cit., p. 182.
44. D. Friedman, op. cit., p. 33.

4 JAPAN ABROAD: THE MERCANTILIST STATE

1. *New York Times*, 16 May 1991.
2. *New York Times*, 17 May 1991.
3. For the best analysis of Japanese history, see John Hall, *Japan: From Prehistory to Modern Times* (New York: Delcorte Press, 1970).
4. Hall Chamberlain, *Things Japanese* (London: Murray, 1905) p. 83.
5. Quoted in John Welfield, *An Empire in Eclipse: Japan in the Postwar*

American Alliance System (Atlantic Highlands, NJ: the Athlone Press, 1988).

6. Quoted in ibid., p. 7.
7. Quoted in Richard Storry, *Japan and the Decline of the West in Asia, 1894–1943* (London: Macmillan, 1979) p. 30.
8. See my books: *Japan's Growing Power over East Asia and the World Economy: Ends and Means* (London: Macmillan, 1990); *The Foundations of Japanese Power: Continuities, Changes, Challenges* (London: Macmillan, 1990); *Japan's Industrial Targeting: The Neomercantilist Path to Economic Superpower* (London: Macmillan, 1991); and *Japan and the Third World: Patterns, Power, Prospects* (London: Macmillan, 1991).
9. Masayoshi Hotta, quoted in Steven Schossenstein, *Trade War: Greed, Power, and Industrial Policy on Opposite Sides of the Pacific* (New York: Gongdon Weed, 1984) p. 105.
10. Quoted in John Dower, *Empire and Aftermath: Yoshida Shigeru and the Japanese Experience, 1874–1954* (Cambridge, MA: Harvard University Press, p. 307).
11. Quoted in ibid., p. 91.
12. Saburo Okita, 'Japan's Quiet Strength', *Foreign Affairs*, 56 (2), Summer 1989, p. 131.
13. Office of the US Trade Representatives, *1985 National Trade Estimate Report on Foreign Trade Barriers* (Washington DC: General Printing Office, 1986) p. 12.
14. Robert Lawrence, 'Imports in Japan: Closed Markets or Closed Minds?', *Brookings Occasional Papers on Economic Activity*, 2, 1987, pp. 537–8.
15. Office of the US Trade Representative, *1989 National Trade Estimate Report on Foreign Trade Barriers*, pp. 97–114.
16. For an analysis of these anomolies see Bela Balassa and Marcus Noland, *Japan in the World Economy* (Washington: Institute for International Economics, 1988), and Edward Lincoln, *Japan's Unequal Trade* (Washington: Brookings Institute, 1990).
17. Quoted in Lincoln, op. cit., p. 118.
18. See ibid., chapter 3.
19. Lawrence, op. cit., p. 520.
20. Lincoln, op. cit., p. 47.
21. Ibid., pp. 76, 78.
22. Mordechai Kreinin, 'How Closed Is Japan's Market?', *World Economy*, 7 (4), December 1988, pp. 529–41.
23. Kester, pp. 8–10.
24. Ibid., p. 83.
25. Ibid., p. 95.
26. See ibid., chapter 4 for case studies of the Nippon Steel merger.
27. See Walter L. Ames and Michael K. Young, 'Foreign Acquisitions in Japan: Hurdling the Ultimate Barrier', *The Journal of the American Chamber of Commerce in Japan*, January 1986, pp. 10–29.
28. Kester, op. cit., p. 137; see also Kelly Charles Crabb, 'The Reality of Extralegal Barriers to Mergers and Acquisitions in Japan', *The International Lawyer*, Winter 1987, pp. 97–128.
29. Kester, op. cit., p. 268.

30. *Far Eastern Economic Review*, 20 June 1991.
31. Lincoln, op. cit., p. 64.
32. Ibid., pp. 100–1.
33. Ibid., p. 61.
34. Ibid., p. 18.
35. Michael Blaker, *Japan's International Negotiating Style* (New York: Columbia University Press, 1977).
36. Ibid., p. 40.
37. Rothacher, op. cit., p. 67.
38. For the leading Japanese apologists for Tokyo's neomercantilism, see Ryutaro Komiya, 'Nichibei Keizai Masatsu to Kokusai Kyocho' (US-Japan Economic Friction and International Cooperation), *Toyo Keizai*, no. 4653, 26 April 1986; Reijiro Hashiyama, 'Nichibei Masatsu to Nihon no Taiosaku: Naiju Kakudai dewa Mondai wa Kaiketsu Shinai' (US-Japan Friction and Japan's Policy Response: Demand Expansion Will Not Solve the Problem), *Toyo Keizai*, no. 4738, 25 July 1987; Yutaka Kosai, 'Beikoku Hogoshugi Boshi e Isso no Shijo Kaiho o!' (Open the Market Much More to Hold Off American Protectionism), *Toyo Keizai*, no. 4729, 6 June 1987; Takashi Eguchi and Manabu Matsuda, *Boeki Masatsu: Mienai Senso – Nihon to Taio to Kaiketsu no Michi (Trade Friction: The Invisible War – The Road for Japan's Response and Solution)* (Tokyo: TBS Britannica, 1987); Hajime Karatsu, *Tough Words for American Industry* (Cambridge, Mass.: Productivity Press, 1987). Gary Saxonhouse is probably the most prolific and systematic foreign Japanese apologist. He is a consultant for MITI and the Japanese government.
39. See Pat Choate, *Agents of Influence* (New York: Basic Books, 1991).
40. Ishikawa, pp. 40, 43.
41. Kazuo Sato, 'Increasing Returns and International Trade: The Case of Japan'. Quoted in Lincoln, op. cit., p. 75.
42. Masamichi Hanabusa, 'The Trade Dispute: A Japanese View', in Loukas Tsoukalis and Maureen White (eds), *Japan and Western Europe* (New York: St. Martin's Press, 1982) p. 124.
43. *Japan 1991: An Comparison*, Keizai Koho Center (Japan Institute for Social and Economic Affairs), Tokyo, 1992.
44. For an expanded argument, see Lincoln, op. cit., chapter 4.
45. Ibid., p. 90.
46. Unless otherwise indicated, all aid statistics were taken from the OECD's annual ODA publication.
47. For an indepth study, see Nester, *Japan and the Third World*, op. cit.
48. *Economist*, 1 September 1990.
49. Robert Scalapino, 'Asia and the United States: The Challenge Ahead', *Foreign Affairs*, 69(1), 1990, p. 114.

5 THE IMBALANCE OF POWER

1. Kenneth Twitchell (ed.), *Europe and the World* (London: Europa Publications, 1976) p. 8.

2. John Pinder, 'Adjustment Without Tears: Can Europe Learn a Japanese Lesson?', in Loukas Tsoukalis and Maureen White (eds), *Japan and West Europe* (New York: St. Martin's Press, 1982) p. 154.

3. Curzon Price, *Industrial Policies of the European Community* (New York: St. Martin's Press, 1981) p. 19.

4. Quoted in William Wallace, *The Transformation of Western Europe* (New York: Council on Foreign Relations Press, 1990) p. 89.

5. Francois Duchene and Geoffrey Shepherd, 'Sources of Industrial Policy' in Duchene and Shepherd, op. cit., p. 12.

6. Alexander Hamilton, 'Report on Manufacture' (5 December 1791), in Jacob E. Cooke (ed.), *The Reports of Alexander Hamilton* (New York: Harper Torchbooks, 1964) p. 147.

7. Quoted in John Spanier, *Games Nations Play* (New York: Holt, Rinehart and Winston, 1984) p. 354.

8. See Paul Krugman, 'Strategic Sectors and International Competition', in Stern, ed. *U.S. Trade Policy*; Paul K. Krugman and Richard E. Baldwin, *The Persistence of the U.S. Trade Deficit* (Washington, DC: Brookings Papers on Economic Activity, no. 1, 1987); Rudiger Dornbusch, Paul Krugman, and Yung Chul Park, *Meeting World Challenges: U.S. Manufacturing in the 1990s* (Rochester, NY: Eastman Kodak, 1989); Rudiger Dornbusch, 'Is There a Case for Aggressive Bilateralism and How Best to Practice it?' (Brookings Institute Conference on Alternative Trade Strategies for the United States, Washington, DC, 12 September 1989); J. David Richardson, 'Empirical Research on Trade Liberalization with Imperfect Competition', *OECD Economic Studies*, no. 12, 1989.

9. Peter Katzenstein (ed.), *Between Power and Plenty: Foreign Economic Policies of Advanced Industrial States* (Madison: University of Wisconsin Press, 1978) p. 129.

10. Pinder, op. cit., p. 154.

11. Ibid., p. 156.

12. Chalmers Johnson (ed.), *The Industrial Policy Debate* (San Francisco: San Francisco Press, 1984).

13. Aurelia George, 'Japanese Interest Group Behavior', in J. A. A. Stockwin, *Dyanamic and Immobilist Politics in Japan* (London: Macmillan, 1988) pp. 122–3, 131; see also Arend Lijphart, 'Consociational Democracy', *World Politics*, 21 (3), October 1968; Kenneth D. McRae, *Consociational Democracy: Political Accommodation in Segmented Societies* (Toronto: McClelland and Stewart, 1974); Hans Daalder, 'The Consociational Democracy Theme', *World Politics*, 26 (2), July 1974; Jeffry Obler, Jurg Steiner, and Guido Diericx, *Decision-Making in Smaller Democracies: The Consociational Burden* (Beverly Hills, CA: Sage Publications, 1977); Philippe C. Schmitter and Gerhard Lehmbruch (eds), *Trends Towards Corporatist Intermediation* (Beverly Hills, CA: Sage Publications, 1979); Suzanne D. Berger (ed.), *Organizing Interests in Western Europe* (Cambridge: Cambridge University Press, 1981); Philippe C. Schmitter and Gerhard Lehmbruch (eds), *Patterns of Corporatist Policymaking* (Beverly Hills, CA: Sage Publications, 1982).

14. Michael Shalev, 'Class Politics and the Western Welfare State', in Shimon E. Spiro and Ephraim Yuchtman-Yaar (eds), *Evaluating the Welfare State: Social and Political Perspectives* (New York: Academic Press, 1983) p. 46.

15. Alexander Gerschenkron, *Economic Backwardness in Historical Perspective: A Book of Essays* (Cambridge, MA: Harvard University Press and Belnap Press, 1962); Alexander Gerschenkron, *Continuity in History and Other Essays* (Cambridge, MA: Harvard University Press and Belnap Press, 1968).

16. William Nester, *The Foundation of Japanese Power: Continuities, Changes, Challenges* (London: Macmillan, 1990). See also William Nester, *Japan's Growing Power over East Asia and the World Economy: Ends and Means* (London: Macmillan, 1990); William Nester, *Japanese Industrial Targeting: The Neomercantilist Path to Economic Superpower* (London: Macmillan, 1991); William Nester, *Japan and the Third World: Patterns, Power, Prospects* (London: Macmillan, 1992); T. J. Pempel and Keiichi Tsunekawa, 'Corporatism without Labor?: The Japanese Anomoly', in Schmitter and Lehmbruch, op. cit., pp. 231–70; Chalmers Johnson, *MITI and the Japanese Miracle* (Stanford, CA: Stanford University Press, 1984).

17. Unless otherwise indicated, all statistics have been culled from various issues of *Japan: An International Comparison* (Keizai Koho Center); *Nippon: Jetro Business Facts and Figures; IMF Direction of Trade.*

18. *New York Times*, 9 December 1991.

19. Ibid., 6 December 1991.

20. Ibid., 27 January 1992.

21. Ibid.

22. Spyros Makridakis, 'Competition and Competition', in Spyros Makridakis et. al. (eds), *Single Market Europe* (San Francisco: Jossey-Bass, 1991) pp. 47, 50.

23. Ibid.

24. *Businessweek*, 15 July 1991.

25. Makridakis, p. 59.

26. Gary Hufbauer, 'An Overview', in Gary Hufbauer (ed.), *Europe 1992: An American Perspective* (Washington, DC: The Brooking Institute, 1990), p. 47.

27. *Moody's Bank and Finance Manual*, 1991; *New York Times*, 2 June 1992.

28. Carter H. Golembe and David Holland, 'Banking and Securities', in Hufbauer, op. cit., pp. 83–5.

29. *New York Times*, 20 March 1991.

30. National Academy of Engineering, *Strengthening U.S. Engineering Through International Cooperation: Some Reconsiderations for Action* (Washington, DC: National Academy Press, 1987); Clyde Prestowitz, *Trading Places: How We Lost to the Japanese* (New York: Basic Books, 1988) p. 37.

31. *New York Times*, 28 May 1991.

32. Robert Reich, 'The Quiet Path to Technological Preeminence', *Scientific America*, October 1989, p. 43.

33. *New York Times*, 28 April 1991.

34. Francois Duchene and Geoffrey Shepherd. 'Western Europe: A Family of Contrasts', in Duchene and Shepherd, op. cit., p. 24.

35. Ibid., p. 36.

36. Hufbauer, op. cit., pp. 24–5.

37. Douglas Rosenthal, 'Competition Policy', in Hufbauer, op. cit., p. 315.

38. *Far Eastern Economic Review*, 27 June 1991.

39. *New York Times*, 10 May 1991.

40. *Economist*, 20 April 1991.
41. Quoted in Ishikawa, op. cit., p. 103.
42. *Financial Times*, 11 September 1986.
43. *New York Times*, 3 March 1992.
44. Makridakis, op. cit., p. 48.
45. Duchene and Shepherd, op. cit., p. 32.
46. *Far Eastern Economic Review*, 20 July, 1991.
47. 'Special Message to the Congress on Foreign Trade', *Public Affairs of the Presidents: John F. Kennedy, 1962* (Government Printing Office, 1962) pp. 68–77.

6 EUROPEAN COMMUNITY-JAPANESE RELATIONS

1. For an analysis of the relationship between Japan's foreign relations and internal power struggles see William Nester, *The Foundation of Japanese Power* (London: Macmillan, 1990).
2. For excellent indepth analysis see Michael Montgomery, *Imperial Japan* (New York: St. Martin's Press, 1988).
3. Ibid., p. 87
4. See Nester, op. cit., chapters 13 and 14.
5. See Robert Jervis, *Perception and Misperception in International Relations* (Princeton, NJ: Princeton University Press, 1976).
6. For the most indepth study of this subject, see Endymion Wilkinson, *Japan versus Europe: A History of Misunderstanding* (London: Penguin, 1983).
7. See Edward Said, *Orientalism* (London: Routledge and Kegan Paul, 1968).
8. Jean Pierre Lehmann, 'Mutual Images', in Loukas Tsoukalis and Maureen White (eds), *Japan and Western Europe* (New York: St. Martin's Press, 1982) p. 19.
9. Quoted in Wilkinson, op. cit., p. 64.
10. B. H. Chamberlain, *Things Japanese* (London, 1890) p. 261.
11. Quoted in Wilkinson, op. cit., p. 57.
12. Ibid., p. 60.
13. See Wilkinson, notes, p. 269.
14. Spyros Makridakis, 'Future Challenges for Single Market Europe', in Makridakis, op. cit., pp. 344–59.
15. Lehmann, op. cit., p. 22.
16. Ibid.
17. Ibid., p. 24.
18. Quoted in Wilkinson, op. cit., p. 133.
19. Fritz Stern, 'The Giant from Afar – Visions of Europe from Algiers to Tokyo', *Foreign Affairs*, 55 (3), 1977.
20. Wilkinson, op. cit., p. 154
21. Ibid., p. 17.
22. Lehman, op. cit., p. 23.
23. Wilkinson, op. cit., p. 257.
24. Ibid., p. 155.
25. Rothacher, op. cit., p. 86.

26. Ibid., p. 88.
27. Ibid., p. 105.
28. Ibid., p. 110.
29. Unless otherwise noted all trade statistics come from annual issues of the International Monetary Fund's *Direction of Trade*.
30. Quoted in Rothacher, op. cit., p. 134.
31. Quoted in Wilkinson, op. cit., p. 133.
32. Ironically, one of the first books warning of a looming Japanese challenge came out of free-trade oriented West Germany: Hakan Hedberg, *Die Japanische Herausforderung* (Hambury: Hoffman and Campe, 1970).
33. Rothacher, op. cit., p. 159.
34. Quoted in Ishikawa, op. cit., p. 17.
35. Rothacher, op. cit., p. 163.
36. Ibid., p. 166.
37. Ibid., p. 172.
38. Unless otherwise indicated all economic statistics come from annual editions of the *World Bank Yearbook*.
39. Rothacher, op. cit., p. 222.
40. Quoted in ibid., p. 253.
41. Quoted in ibid., p. 259.
42. Quoted in ibid., p. 263.
43. Quoted from Benedict Meynell, 'Relations with Japan', in Loukas Tsoukalis and Maureen White (eds), *Japan and Western Europe* (New York: St. Martin's Press, 1982) p. 116.
44. *Newsweek*, 16 April 1979.
45. Rothacher, op. cit., p. 176.
46. Quoted in Meynell, op. cit., p. 102.
47. Masamichi Hanabusa, 'The Trade Dispute: A Japanese View', in Loukas Tsoukalis and Maureen White (eds), *Japan and Western Europe* (New York: St. Martin's Press, 1982) p. 119.
48. Quoted in Rothacher, op. cit., p. 234.
49. Shigeru Yoshida, *The Yoshida Memoirs* (Boston: Houghton Mifflin, 1962) pp. 119–20.
50. Ibid., p. 115.
51. Ishikawa, op. cit., p. 93.
52. *New York Times*, 30 September 1991.
53. Ishikawa, pp. 66–7.
54. *Far Eastern Economic Review*, 11 July 1991.
55. *Bulletin of the European Communities*, September 1986, p. 15.
56. *The Times*, 24 September 1986.
57. Declaration of the European Council in Rhodes, The European Commission, *Europe 1992: Europe World Partner* (Brussels: October 1988) p. 2.
58. Quoted in Ishikawa, pp. 111, 122.
59. *Financial Times* 12 October 1988.
60. Sueo Sekiguchi, 'Japanese Direct Investment in Europe', in Loukas Tsoukalis and Maureen White (eds), *Japan and Western Europe* (New York: St. Martin's Press, 1982) p. 167.
61. *New York Times*, 20 May 1991.
62. Quoted in Ishikawa, p. 103.

63. *Financial Times*, 11 September 1986.
64. Ishikawa, op. cit., p. 82.
65. Ibid., pp. 85–91.
66. *Financial Times*, 9 March 1988.
67. Ibid., 18 November 1988.
68. *Economist*, 18 February 1989.
69. Ibid.
70. Ishikawa, op. cit., pp. 66–7.
71. Brian Hindley, 'EC Imports of VCRs from Japan: A Costly Precedent', *Journal of World Trade Law*, 20 (2), March–April 1986, p. 177.
72. Alasdair Smith and Anthony Venables, 'Automobiles', in Hufbauer, op. cit., p. 127.
73. *Financial Times*, 9 February 1981.
74. *New York Times*, 7 February 1991.
75. Ibid.
76. Smith and Venables, op. cit., p. 126.
77. Quoted in Ishikawa, op. cit., p. 26.
78. *Independent*, 27 January 1989.
79. *Japan Economic Journal*, 16 March 1991.
80. Ibid.
81. *New York Times*, 20 May 1991.
82. Ibid., 8 October 1990.
83. Ibid., 27 July 1991.
84. Ibid., 30 April 1989.
85. Quoted in Smith and Venables, op. cit., p. 138.
86. Quoted in Sylvia Ostry, *Governments and Corporations in a Shrinking World: Trade and Innovation Policies in the United States, Europe, and Japan* (New York: Council on Foreign Relations Press, 1990), p. 74.
87. Geoffrey Shepherd, 'The Japanese Challenge to Western Europe's New Crisis Industries', *World Economy*, 4 (4), December 1981.
88. *Independent*, 27 September 1988.
89. *Financial Times*, 19 November 1982.
90. Ibid., 5 December 1982.
91. Ibid., pp. 173–5.
92. Ibid., pp. 180–2.
93. Quoted in Kenneth Flamm, in Hufbauer, op. cit., p. 288.
94. *New York Times*, 4 September 1991; *Japan Economic Journal*, 30 March 1991.
95. *Economist*, 18 February 1989.
96. Flamm, op. cit., p. 271.
97. *Electronic Business*, 25 June 1990.
98. Ibid.
99. *New York Times*, 4 September 1991.
100. Ibid.
101. *Washington Post National Weekly*, 5–11 November 1990.
102. *New York Times*, 30 May 1991.
103. Rothacher, op. cit., p. 200.
104. *Europe World Partner*, op. cit., p. 2.
105. Rothacher, op. cit., p. 210.
106. *Far Eastern Economic Review*, 1 August 1991.

7 EUROPE AND JAPAN INTO THE TWENTY-FIRST CENTURY

1. For a highly thought-provoking, erudite discourse on this theme, see Henry Paolucci, 'Europe After 1991: An End to Nationhood as Historically Defined', *The World and I*, Washington, DC: The Washington Times Inc., vol. 4, no. 12, December 1989.
2. Quoted in ibid., p. 499.
3. *New York Times*, 19 July 1991.
4. Quoted in Endymion Wilkinson, *Japan versus Europe* (New York: Penguin, 1990) p. 167.
5. Christian Sautter, 'A European Policy of Competitive Co-operation', in Loukas Tsoukalis and Maureen White (eds), *Japan and Western Europe* (New York: St. Martin's Press, 1982) p. 198.
6. Jean Pierre Lehmann, 'Mutual Images', in Loukas Tsoukalis and Maureen White (eds), *Japan and Western Europe* (New York: St. Martin's Press, 1982).

Bibliography

GENERAL

Berger, Suzanne D. (ed.), *Organizing Interests in Western Europe* (Cambridge: Cambridge University Press, 1981).

Bower, J.L, *When Markets Quake* (Boston: Harvard Business School Press, 1986).

Daalder, Hans, 'The Consociational Democracy Theme', *World Politics*, 26 (2), July 1974.

Deutsch, Karl, *Nationalism and Social Communication* (New York: Wiley, 1953).

Dornbusch, Rudiger, Paul Krugman, and Yung Chul Park, *Meeting World Challenges: U.S. Manufacturing in the 1990s* (Rochester, NY: Eastman Kodak, 1989).

Dornbusch, Rudiger, 'Is There a Case for Aggressive Bilateralism and How Best to Practice it?', Brookings Institute Conference on Alternative Trade Strategies for the United States, Washington, DC, 12 September 1989.

Freedman, Lawrence, 'Logic, Politics, and Foreign Policy Processes: A Critique of the Bureaucratic Politics Model', *International Affairs*, 52 (3), 1976.

Gerschenkron, Alexander, *Economic Backwardness in Historical Perspective: A Book of Essays* (Cambridge, MA: Harvard University Press/Belnap Press, 1962).

Gerschenkron, Alexander, *Continuity in History and Other Essays* (Cambridge, MA: Harvard University Press/Belnap Press, 1968).

Haas, Ernst, *Beyond the Nation State* (Palo Alto, CA: Stanford University Press, 1964).

Haas, Ernst, *The Obsolescence of Regional Integration Theory* (Berkeley, CA: University of California Press, 1975).

Haas, Ernst, 'Turbulent Fields and the Theory of Regional Integration', *International Organization*, 30 (4), September 1976.

Haas, Ernst, and Edward Rowe, 'Regional Organizations in the United Nations: Is There Externalization?', *International Studies Quarterly*, 17 (1), March 1973.

Hamilton, Alexander, 'Report on Manufacture', (5 December 1791), in Jacob E. Cooke (ed.), *The Reports of Alexander Hamilton* (New York: Harper Torchbooks, 1964).

Halperin, Morton, *Bureaucratic Politics and Foreign Policy* (Washington, DC: The Brookings Institute, 1974).

Jervis, Robert, *Perception and Misperception in International Relations* (Princeton, NJ: Princeton University Press, 1976).

Johnson, Chalmers (ed.), *The Industrial Policy Debate* (San Francisco: San Francisco Press, 1984).

Katzenstein, Peter (ed.), *Between Power and Plenty: Foreign Economic Policies of Advanced Industrial States* (Madison: University of Wisconsin Press, 1978).

Katzenstein, Peter, *Small States in World Markets: Industrial Policy in Europe* (Ithaca, NY: Cornell University Press, 1985).

Keohane, Robert, and Joseph Nye, *Power and Interdependence: World Politics and Transition* (Boston: Little, Brown, and Company, 1977).

Krugman, Paul, and Richard E. Baldwin, *The Persistence of the U.S. Trade Deficit* (Washington, DC) Brookings Papers on Economic Activity, 1, 1987.

Lijphart, Arend, 'Consociational Democracy', *World Politics*, 21 (3), October 1968.

McRae, Kenneth D., *Consociational Democracy: Political Accommodation in Segmented Societies* (Toronto: McClelland and Stewart, 1974).

Mitany, David, *A Working Peace System* (Chicago: Quadrangle Books, 1966).

Moore, Barington, *The Social Origins of Dictatorship and Democracy: Land and Peasant in the Making of the Modern World* (Boston: Beacon, 1967).

Nye, Joseph, *Peace in Parts: Integration and Conflict in Regional Organization* (Lanham, CT: University Press of America, 1987).

Obler, Jeffry, Jurg Steiner, and Guido Diericx, *Decision-Making in Smaller Democracies: The Consociational Burden* (Beverly Hills: Sage Publications, 1977).

Reich, Robert, 'The Quiet Path to Technological Preeminence', *Scientific American*, October 1989.

Richardson, J. David, 'Empirical Research on Trade Liberalization with Imperfect Competition', *OECD Economic Studies*, 12, 1989.

Said, Edward, *Orientalism* (London: Routledge and Kegan Paul, 1968).

Saunders, C. (ed.), *The Political Economy of New and Old Industrial Countries* (London: Butterworths, 1981).

Schmitter, Philippe, 'A Revised Theory of Regional Integration', *International Organization*, 24 (4), Autumn 1970.

Schmitter, Philippe C., and Gerhard Lehmbruch (eds), *Trends Toward Corporatist Intermediation* (Beverly Hills: Sage, 1979).

Schmitter, Philippe C., and Gerhard Lehmbruch (eds), *Patterns of Corporatist Policymaking* (Beverly Hills: Sage, 1982).

Shalev, Michael, 'Class Politics and the Western Welfare State', in Shimon E. Spiro and Ephraim Yuchtman-Yaar (eds), *Evaluating the Welfare State: Social and Political Perspectives* (New York: Academic Press, 1983).

Spanier, John, *Games Nations Play* (New York: Holt, Rinehart, and Winston, 1984).

EUROPEAN INTEGRATION, FOREIGN, AND INDUSTRIAL POLICIES

Adams, W.J., and C. Stoffas, *French Industrial Policy* (Washington, DC: Brookings Institution, 1986).

Allen, David, 'Foreign Policy at the European Level: Beyond the Nation-state', in William Wallace and W.E. Patterson (eds), *Foreign Policy Making in Western Europe* (Farnborough, Hants: Saxon House, 1978).

Agnelli, Giovanni, 'The Europe of 1992', *Foreign Affairs*, 68, Fall 1986.

Baldwin, Richard, 'The Growth Effects of 1992', *Economic Policy*, October 1989.

Barre, Raymond, 'Foundations for European Security and Cooperation', 1987 Alastair Buchan Memorial Lecture: *Survival*, 29 (4), July/August 1987.

Berger, Suzanne, *Organizing Interests in Western Europe: Pluralism, Corporatism, and the Transformation of Politics* (New York: Cambridge University Press, 1981).

Bridgeford, Jeff, 'European Political Co-operation and Its Impact on the Institutions of the European Community', *Studia Diplomatica*, 30 (2), 1977.

Calingaert, Michael, *The 1992 Challenge from Europe: Development of the European Community's Internal Market* (Washington: National Planning Association, 1988).

Cechinni, Paolo, Michael Catinat, and Alexis Jacquemin, *The European Challenge 1992: The Benefits of a Single Market* (Aldershot: Wildwood House, 1988).

Coombes, David, *Politics and Bureaucracy in the European Community* (London: Allen and Unwin, 1970).

Cowhey, Peter, 'Telecommunications', in Hufbauer, op. cit.

Dahrendorf, Ralf, 'Possibilities and Limits of the European Community's Foreign Policy', *The World Today*, 27 (3), 1971.

Dahrendorf, Ralf, 'The Foreign Policy of the EEC', *The World Today*, 29 (3), 1973.

Dahrendorf, Ralf, 'It is not easy for a Community to have a Foreign Policy', *International Journal of Politics*, 5 (4), 1975.

Delors, Jacques, 'Europe: Embarking on a New Course', in D. Bell and J. Gaffney (eds), *1992 and After* (Oxford: Pergamon Press, 1989).

Deutsch, Karl (ed.), *Political Community and the North Atlantic Area* (Princeton, NJ: Princeton University Press, 1957).

Duchene, Francois, and Geoffrey Shepard (eds), *Managing Industrial Change in Western Europe* (London: Frances Pinter, 1987).

Duchene, Francois, and Geoffrey Shepherd, 'Sources of Industrial Policy', in Duchene and Shepherd, op. cit.

Duchene, Francois, and Geoffrey Shepherd, 'Western Europe: A Family of Contrasts', in Duchene and Shepherd, op. cit.

European Commission, *Completing the Internal Market*: White Paper from the Commission to the European Council (Brussels: Commission of the European Communities, June 1985).

European Commission, *Europe 1992: Europe World Partner* (Brussels, October 1988).

Everling, Ulrich, 'Possibilities and Limits of European Integration', *Journal of Common Market Studies*, 18 (3), 1980, pp. 217–28.

Feld, Werner, *The European Common Market and the World* (Englewood Cliffs, NJ: Prentice Hall, 1967).

Feld, Werner, *The European Community in World Affairs* (Port Washington, NY: Aldred Publishing Company, 1976).

Feld, Werner, *The European Community in World Affairs: Economic Power and Political Influence* (New York: Alfred Publishing Co., 1977).

Feld, Werner, and John K. Wildgen, 'National Administrative Elites and European Integration: Saboteurs at Work?', *Journal of Common Market Studies*, 13 (1), 1975.

Gilchrist, Joseph, and David Deacon, 'Curbing Subsidies', in Montagnon, op. cit.

Ginsberg, Roy H., *Foreign Policy Actions of the European Community: The Politics of Scale* (Boulder, Co.: Lynne Rienner, 1989).

Ginsberg, Roy, 'European Trade Policy at Mid-Decade: Coping with the Internal Menace and the External Challenge', in Rummel, op. cit.

Gogel, Robert, and Jean-Claude Larreche, 'Pan European Marketing', in Makridakis, op. cit.

Golembe, Carter H., and David Holland, 'Banking and Securities', in Hufbauer, op. cit.

Goodwin, Geoffrey L., 'The External Relations of the European Community – Shadow and Substance', *British Journal of International Studies*, 3 (2), 1977.

Gunnar, Sjostedt, *The External Role of the European Community* (Farnborough, Hants: Saxon House, 1988).

Haas, Ernest B., *The Uniting of Europe* (Palo Alto, CA: Stanford University Press, 1958).
Hall, G. (ed.), *European Industrial Policy* (London: Croom Helm, 1986).
Hill, Christopher, *National Foreign Policies and European Political Cooperation* (London: George Allen and Unwin, 1983).
Hill, Christopher, 'European Foreign Policy: Power Bloc, Civilian Model, or Flop?' in Rummel, op. cit.
Hiritus, T., *European Community Economics* (New York: St. Martin's Press, 1991).
Hoffman, Stanley, 'The European Community and 1992', *Foreign Affairs*, 68, Fall 1989.
Holzler, Heinrich, 'Merger Control', in Montagnon, op. cit.
Horn, Ernst-Jurgen, 'Germany: A Market-led Process', in Duchene and Shepherd, op. cit.
Hufbauer, Gary Clyde (ed.), *Europe 1992: An American Perspective* (Washington, DC: The Brookings Institute, 1990).
Hufbauer, Gary, 'An Overview', in Hufbauer, op. cit.
Jacquemin, Alexis, et al., *Merger and Competition Policy in the European Community* (London: Basil Blackwell, 1990).
Katzenstein, Peter J. (ed.), *Between Power and Plenty: Foreign Economic Policies of Advanced Industrial States* (Madison: University of Wisconsin Press, 1978).
Katzenstein, Peter J., *Small States in World Markets: Industrial Policy in Europe* (Ithaca, NY: Cornell University Press, 1985).
Kreile, Michael, 'West Germany: The Dynamics of Expansion', in Katzenstein, *Power and Plenty*, op. cit.
Lindberg, Leon N., *The Political Dynamics of European Integration* (Palo Alto, CA: Stanford University Press, 1963).
Lindberg, Leon, and Stuart Scheingold, *Europe's Would-Be Polity* (Englewood Cliffs, NJ: Prentice Hall, 1979).
Makridakis, Spyros, et al. (eds), *Single Market Europe: Opportunities and Challenges for Business* (San Francisco: Jossey-Bass Publishers, 1991).
Makridakis, Spyros, 'Competition and Competition', in Makridakis, op. cit.
Makridakis, Spyros, and Michelle Bainbridge, 'Evolution of the Single Market', in Makridakis, op. cit.
McGeehan, Robert, and Steven J. Warnecke, 'Europe's Foreign Policies: Economics, Politics or Both?', *Orbis*, 17 (4), 1974.
Messerlin, Patrick, 'France: The Ambitious State', in Duchene and Shepherd, op. cit.
Milward, Alan S., *The Reconstruction of Europe, 1945–51* (London: Methuen, 1984).
Mitrany, David, *A Working Peace System* (London: Royal Institute of International Affairs, 1943).
Montagnon, Peter (ed.), *European Competition Policy* (New York: Council on Foreign Relations Press, 1990).
Montagnon, Peter, 'Regulating the Utilities', in Montagnon, op. cit.
Morgan, Roger P., *High Politics, Low Politics: Towards a Foreign Policy of Western Europe* (London: Sage Publications, 1973).
Morgan, Roger P., 'Introduction: European Integration and the European Community's External Relations', *International Journal of Politics*, 5 (2), 1975.
Nevin, Edward, *The Economics of Europe* (New York: St. Martin's Press, 1990).

Olson, Mancur, *The Rise and Decline of Nations: Economic Growth, Stagflation, and Social Rigidities* (New Haven: Yale University Press, 1982).

Ostry, Sylvia, *Governments and Corporations in a Shrinking World* (New York: Council on Foreign Relations Press, 1990).

Paolucci, Henry, 'Europe After 1992: An End to Nationhood as Historically Defined', *The Washington Times*, 4 (12), December 1989.

Panayiotis, Ifestos, *European Political Cooperation: Towards a Framework of Supranational Diplomacy?* (Brookfield, CT: Avebury, 1987).

Peck, Merton, 'Industrial Organization and the Gains from 1992', *Brookings Papers on Economic Activity*, 2 1989, pp. 277–99.

Pentland, Charles, 'Linkage Politics: Canada's Contract and the Development of the European Communities External Relations', *International Journal*, 32 (1), 1977.

Pinder, John, *European Community* (Oxford: Oxford University Press, 1991).

Pinder, John, 'Adjustment Without Tears: Can Europe Learn a Japanese Lesson?', in Loukas Tsoukalis and Maureen White (eds), *Japan and West Europe* (New York: St. Martin's Press, 1982).

Pollard, S., *Peaceful Conquest: The Industrialization of Europe 1760–1970* (Oxford: Oxford University Press, 1981).

Posner, Alan R., 'Italy: Dependence and Political Fragmentation', in Katzenstein, *Between Power and Plenty*, op. cit.

Price, Victoria C., *Industrial Policies in the European Community* (New York: St. Martin's Press, 1981).

Rieber, Roger A., 'The Future of the European Community in International Affairs', *Canadian Journal of Political Science*, 32 (1), 1977.

Ranci, Rippo, 'Italy: the Weak State', in Duchene and Shepherd, op. cit.

Reintz, Knut, 'Eureka – Three Years Already! Result so far and Future Outlook', *European Affairs*, 3 (1), Spring 1989.

Rosenthal, Glenda G., *The Men behind the Decisions* (Lexington, Mass.: Lexington Books, 1975).

Rummel, Reinhardt, *The Evolution of an International Actor: Western Europe's New Assertiveness* (Boulder, Co.: Westview, 1990).

Sandholtz, Wayne, and John Zysman, '1992: Recasting the European Bargain', *World Politics*, 62 (1), October 1989.

Shepherd, Geoffrey, 'United Kingdom: A Resistance to Change', in Duchene and Shepherd, op. cit.

Shepherd, Geoffrey, Francois Duchene, and Christopher Saunders, (eds), *Europe's Industries: Public and Private Strategies for Changes* (London: Frances Pinter, 1983).

Siebert, Horst, 'The Single European Market – A Schumpeterian Event?', Kiel Discussion Paper 157 (FRG: Kiel Institute of World Economics, November 1989).

Soldatis, Panayotis, 'La Theorie de la politique etrangere et sa pertinance pour l'etude des relations exterieures des Communautes Europenne', *Etudes International*, 9 (1), 1978.

Swann, Dennis, *Competition and Industrial Policy in the European Community* (London, Methuen, 1983).

Taylor, Paul, *The Limits of European Integration* (London: Croom Helm, 1983).

Torrelli, Maurice, 'L'elaboration des relations exterieure de la C.E.E.', *Revue du Marche Commun*, 167, 1973.

Tugendhat, Christopher, 'Europe's Need for Self-Confidence', *International Affairs*, 58 (1), Winter 1981–2.

Twitchell, Kenneth (ed.), *Europe and the World* (London: Europa Publications, 1976).

Ullman, Richard, *Securing Europe* (Princeton, NJ: Princeton University Press, 1991).

Unwin, Derek W., *The Community of Europe: A History of European Integration since 1945* (London: Longman, 1991).

Unwin, Derek W. and W.E. Paterson, *Politics in Western Europe Today: Perspectives, Policies, and Problems since 1980* (London: Longman, 1990).

Wallace, Helen, *National Governments and the European Communities* (London: Chatham House PEP, 1973).

Wallace, Helen, William Wallace, and Carole Webb (eds), *Policy-Making in the European Communities* (New York: Wiley, 1983).

Wallace, William, *The Transformation of Western Europe* (New York: Council on Foreign Relations Press, 1990).

Wallace, William, and William Patterson (eds), *Foreign Policy-Making in Western Europe: A Comparative Approach* (New York: Praeger, 1978).

Wells, Samuel F., 'A New Transatlantic Bargain', *Washington Quarterly*, 12 (4), Autumn 1989.

Wolf, Martin, '1992 Global Implications of the European Community's Programme for Completing the Internal Market', New York: Lehrman Institute Policy Paper, 1, 1989.

Zysman, John, 'The French State in the International Economy', in Katzenstein, *Between Power and Plenty* op. cit.

JAPAN POLICYMAKING AND POLICIES

Abegglen, James, 'Industrial Policy', in Tsoukalis and White, op. cit.

Ames, Walter L., and Michael K. Young, 'Foreign Acquisitions in Japan: Hurdling the Ultimate Barrier', *Journal of the American Chamber of Commerce in Japan*, January 1986.

Balassa, Bela, and Marcus Noland, *Japan in the World Economy* (Washington: Institute for International Economics, 1988).

Blaker, Michael, *Japan's International Negotiating Style* (New York: Columbia University Press, 1977).

Boyd, Richard, and Seiichi Nagamori, 'Industrial Policy Making: Electoral, Diplomatic and Other Adjustments to Crisis in the Japanese Shipbuilding Industry', in Wilks and Wright, op. cit.

Bryant, William, *Japanese Private Economic Diplomacy: An Analysis of Business-Government Linkages* (New York: Praeger, 1975).

Calder, Kent, *Crisis and Compensation: Public Policy and Political Stability in Japan* (Princeton, NJ: Princeton University Press, 1988).

Chamberlain, B.H., *Things Japanese* (London, 1890).

Choate, Pat, *Agents of Influence* (New York: Basic Books, 1991).

Crabb, Kelly Charles, 'The Reality of Extralegal Barriers to Mergers and Acquisitions in Japan', *The International Lawyer*, Winter 1987.

Dower, John, *Empire and Aftermath: Yoshida Shigeru and the Japanese Experience, 1874–1954* (Cambridge, MA: Harvard University Press).

Drifte, Reinhard, *Japan's Foreign Policy* (London: Royal Institute of International Affairs, 1990).

Fukui, Haruhiro, 'The Policy Research Council of Japan's Liberal Democratic Party', *Asian Thought and Society*, 34 (12), 1987.

Fukui, Haruhiro, and Shigeko Fukai, 'Elite Recruitment and Political Leadership', *Political Science and Politics*, 25 (1), March 1992.

Fulcher, John, 'The Bureaucratization of the State and the Rise of Japan', *The British Journal of Sociology*, 39 (3), 1988.

George, Aurelia, 'Japanese Interest Group Behavior', in Stockwin, op. cit.

Gluck, Carol, *Japan's Modern Myths: Ideology in the Late Meiji Period* (Princeton, NJ: Princeton University Press, 1985).

Hall, John, *Japan: From Prehistory to Modern Times* (New York: Delcorte Press, 1970).

Hanabusa, Masamichi, 'The Trade Dispute: A Japanese View', in Tsoukalis and White, op. cit.

Howell, Jeremy, and Ian Neary, 'Science and Technology Policy in Japan: The Pharmaceutical Industry and New Technology', in Wilks and Wright, op. cit.

Inoguchi, Takashi, *Gendai Nihon Seiji Keizai no Kozu: Seifu to Shijo (The Structure of Contemporary Japanese Politics and Economics)* (Tokyo: Toyo Keizai Shinposha, 1983).

Inoguchi, Takashi, and Tomoaki Iwai, *'Zokugiin' no Kenkyu: Jiminto Seiken o Gyujiru Shuyaku-Tachi (A Study of 'Zoku' Representatives: Main Actors Controlling Japanese Politics)* (Tokyo: Nihon Keizai Shimbunsha, 1987).

Inoguchi, Takashi, and Dan Okimoto (eds), *The Political Economy of Japan: The International Context* (Stanford, CA: Stanford University Press, 1988).

Ishida, Takeshi, and Ellis S. Krauss (eds), *Democracy in Japan* (Pittsburgh: University of Pittsburgh Press, 1989).

Ito, Daiichi, 'Government-Business Relations', in Wilks and Wright, op. cit.

Johnson, Chalmers, *MITI and the Japanese Miracle* (Stanford, CA: Stanford University Press, 1984).

Johnson, Chalmers, 'The Japanese Political Economy: A Crisis in Theory', *Ethics and International Affairs*, 1988.

Johnson, Chalmers, Laura Tyson, and John Zysman, *Politics and Productivity: How Japan's Development Strategy Works* (New York: 1990).

Kernell, Samuel (ed.), *Parallel Politics: Economic Policymaking in Japan and the United States* (Washington, DC: Brookings Institution, 1991).

Komiya, R., M. Okuno, and K. Suzumura (eds), *Industrial Policy of Japan* (Tokyo: Academic Press, 1988).

Krauss, Ellis, 'Politics and the Policymaking Process', in Ishida and Krauss, op. cit.

Krauss, Ellis, 'Political Economy: Policymaking and Industrial Policy in Japan', *Political Science and Politics*, 25 (1), March 1992.

Kreinin, Mordechai, 'How Closed Is Japan's Market?', *World Economy*, 7 (4), December 1988.

Lawrence, Robert, 'Imports in Japan: Closed Markets or Closed Minds?', *Brookings Occasional Papers on Economic Activity*, (2), 1987.

Lincoln, Edward J., *Japan's Unequal Trade* (Washington, DC: Brookings Institute, 1990).

Lockwood, William Wirt, *The Economic Development of Japan: Growth and Structural Change, 1968–1938* (Princeton, NJ: Princeton University Press, 1954).

McCormack, Gavin and Yoshi Sugimoto (eds), *The Japanese Trajectory: Modernization and Beyond* (Cambridge: Cambridge University Press, 1988).

Montgomery, Michael, *Imperial Japan* (New York: St. Martin's Press, 1990).

Murakami, Y., 'Towards a Socioinstitutional Explanation', in K. Yamamura (ed.), *Policy and Trade Issues of the Japanese Economy* (Tokyo: Tokyo University Press, 1982).

Nester, William, *Japan's Growing Power over East Asia and the World Economy: Ends and Means* (London: Macmillan Press, 1990; New York: St. Martin's Press, 1990).

Nester, William, *The Foundation of Japanese Power: Continuities, Changes, Challenge* (London: Macmillan Press, 1990; Armonk, NY: M.E. Sharpe, 1990).

Nester, William, *Japanese Industrial Targeting: The Neomercantilist Path to Economic Superpower* (London: Macmillan Press, 1991; New York: St. Martin's Press, 1991).

Nester, William, *Japan and the Third World: Patterns, Power, Prospects* (London: Macmillan Press, 1992; New York: St. Martin's Press, 1992).

Nester, William, *American Power, the New World Order, and the Japanese Challenge* (London: Macmillan Press, 1993).

Noble, Gregory, 'The Japanese Industrial Policy Debate', in Stephen Haggard and Chung-in Moon (eds), *Pacific Dynamics: The International Politics of Industrial Change* (Boulder, CO: Westview Press, 1989).

Noguchi, Yukio, 'Budget Policymaking in Japan', in Samuel Kernell (ed.), *Parallel Politics: Economic Policymaking in Japan and the United States* (Washington, DC: Brookings Institution, 1991).

Norman, H., *The Real Japan* (New York: Scribner, 1892).

Okimoto, Dan, 'Regime Characteristics of Japanese Industrial Policy', in Patrick, op. cit.

Okimoto, Daniel, *Between MITI and the Marketplace* (Stanford, CA: Stanford University Press, 1989).

Okita, Saburo, 'Japan's Quiet Strength', *Foreign Affairs*, 56 (2), Summer 1989.

Patrick, Hugh (ed.), *Japan's High Technology Industries* (Seattle: University of Washington Press, 1986).

Pempel, T.J., 'The Unbundling of "Japan Inc."', *Journal of Japanese Studies*, 13 (2), 1987.

Pempel, T.J. Pempel and Keiichi Tsunekawa, 'Corporatism without Labor?: The Japanese Anamoly', in Philippe Schmitter and Gerhard Lehmbruch (eds), *Trends Toward Corporatist Intermediation* (Beverly Hills: Sage, 1979).

Prestowitz, Clyde, *Trading Places: How We Lost to the Japanese* (New York: Basic Books, 1987).

Samuels, Richard, *The Business of the Japanese State: Energy Markets in Comparative and Historical Perspective* (Ithaca, NY: Cornell University Press, 1987).

Sato, Seizaburo, and Tetsuhisa Matsuzaki, *Jiminto Seiken (The Liberal Democratic Party)* (Tokyo: Chuo Koronsha, 1986).

Schossenstein, Steven, *Trade War: Greed, Power, and Industrial Policy on Opposite Sides of the Pacific* (New York: Gongdon Weed, 1984).

Shoven, John (ed.), *Government Policy towards Industry in the United States and Japan* (Cambridge: Cambridge University Press, 1988).

Stockwin, J.A.A., *Dynamic and Immobilist Politics in Japan* (London: Macmillan, 1989).

Storry, Richard, *Japan and the Decline of the West in Asia, 1894–1943* (London: Macmillan, 1979).

Tanaka, Masami, 'Government Policy and Biotechnology in Japan: The Pattern and Impact of Rivalry Between Ministries', in Wilks and Wright, op. cit., pp. 110–34.

Tsoukalis, Loukas, and Maureen White (eds), *Japan and Western Europe* (New York: St. Martin's Press, 1982).

Vogel, Ezra, *Japan as Number One: Lessons for America* (Cambridge, Mass.: Harvard University Press, 1979).

Welfield, John, *An Empire in Eclipse: Japan in the Postwar American Alliance System* (Atlantic Highlands, NJ: the Athone Press, 1988).

Wilks, Stephen, and Maurice Wright, *The Promotion and Regulation of Industry in Japan* (New York: St. Martin's Press, 1991).

Wilks, Stephen, and Maurice Wright, 'The Japanese Bureaucracy in the Industrial Policy Process', in Wilks and Wright, op. cit.

Wolferen, Karl van, *The Enigma of Japanese Power: People and Politics in a Stateless Nation* (New York: Alfred Knopf, 1989).

Yamamura, K., and Y. Yasuba (eds), *The Political Economy of Japan: The Domestic Context* (Stanford, CA: Stanford University Press, 1987).

Yoshida, Shigeru, *The Yoshida Memoirs: the Story of Japan in Crisis* (Westport, CT: Greenwood Press, 1962).

EUROPE-JAPAN RELATIONS

Curzon, Gerard, and Victoria Curzon, 'Follies in European Trade Relations with Japan', *World Economy*, 10 (2), June 1987.

European Commission, *The Trade Policy of the Community and Japan: A Reexamination* (Brussels, 15 July 1980).

European Commission, *EC-Japan Relations, Arguments, and Counterarguments* (Brussels, April 1982).

European Commission, *Analysis of the Relations Between the Community and Japan* (Brussels, 15 October 1985).

Hanabusa, Masamichi, *Trade Problems between Japan and Western Europe* (Westmead, CT: Saxon House, 1979).

Hanabusa, Masamichi, 'The Trade Dispute: A Japanese View', in Tsoukalis and White, op. cit.

Hedberg, Hakan, *Die Japanische Herausforderung* (Hamburg: Hoffman and Campe, 1970).

Hindley, Brian, 'EC Imports of VCRs from Japan', *Journal of World Trade Law*, 20 (2), March–April 1986.

Hufbauer, Gary Clyde (ed.), *Europe 1992: An American Perspective* (Washington, DC: Brookings Institute, 1990).

Ishikawa, Kenjiro, *Japan and the Challenge of Europe 1992* (London: Pinter, 1990).

Lehmann, Jean Pierre, 'Mutual Images', in Tsoukalis and White, op. cit.

Lehmann, Jean-Pierre, 'Agenda for Action on Issues in Euro-Japanese Relations', *World Economy*, 7 (3), September 1984.

Mendl, Wolf, *Western Europe and Japan: Between the Superpowers* (Beckenham: Croom Helm, 1984).

Meynell, Benedict, 'Relations with Japan', in Tsoukalis and White, op. cit.

Murata, Ryohei, 'Political Relations between the United States and Western Europe: their Implications for Japan', *International Affairs*, 64 (1), 1988.

Ostry, Sylvia, *Governments and Corporations in a Shrinking World: Trade and Innovation Policies in the United States, Europe, and Japan* (New York: Council on Foreign Relations Press, 1990).

Pinder, John, 'Adjustment Without Tears: Can Europe Learn a Japanese Lesson?', in Tsoukalis and White, op. cit.

Rothacher, Albrecht, *Economic Diplomacy Between the European Community and Japan, 1959–1981* (London: Gower, 1983).

Sekiguchi, Sueo, 'Japanese Direct Investment in Europe', in Tsoukalis and White, op. cit.

Shepard, Geoffrey, 'The Japanese Challenge to Western Europe's New Crisis Industries', *World Economy*, 4 (4), December 1981.

Smith, Alasdair and Anthony Venables, 'Automobiles', in Hufbauer, op. cit.

Stern, Fritz,'The Giant from Afar – Visions of Europe from Algiers to Tokyo', *Foreign Affairs*, 55 (3), 1977.

Taylor, Robert, *China, Japan, and the European Community* (London: Athlone Press, 1990).

Tsoukalis, Loukas, and Maureen White (eds), *Japan and Western Europe: Conflict and Cooperation* (New York: St. Martin's Press, 1982).

Venn, Pieter Van, F.H. Saelens, and Th. van Bergen, 'Japan's Trade and Investments with the European Economic Community', in Philip West (ed.), *The Pacific Rim and the Western World* (Boulder, CO: Westview Press, 1987).

Wilkinson, Endymion, *Japan versus Europe: A History of Misunderstanding* (London: Penguin 1983).

Wilks, Stephen and Maurice Wright (eds), *Comparative Government-Industry Relations: Western Europe, the United States, and Japan* (Oxford: Clarendon Press, 1987).

Index